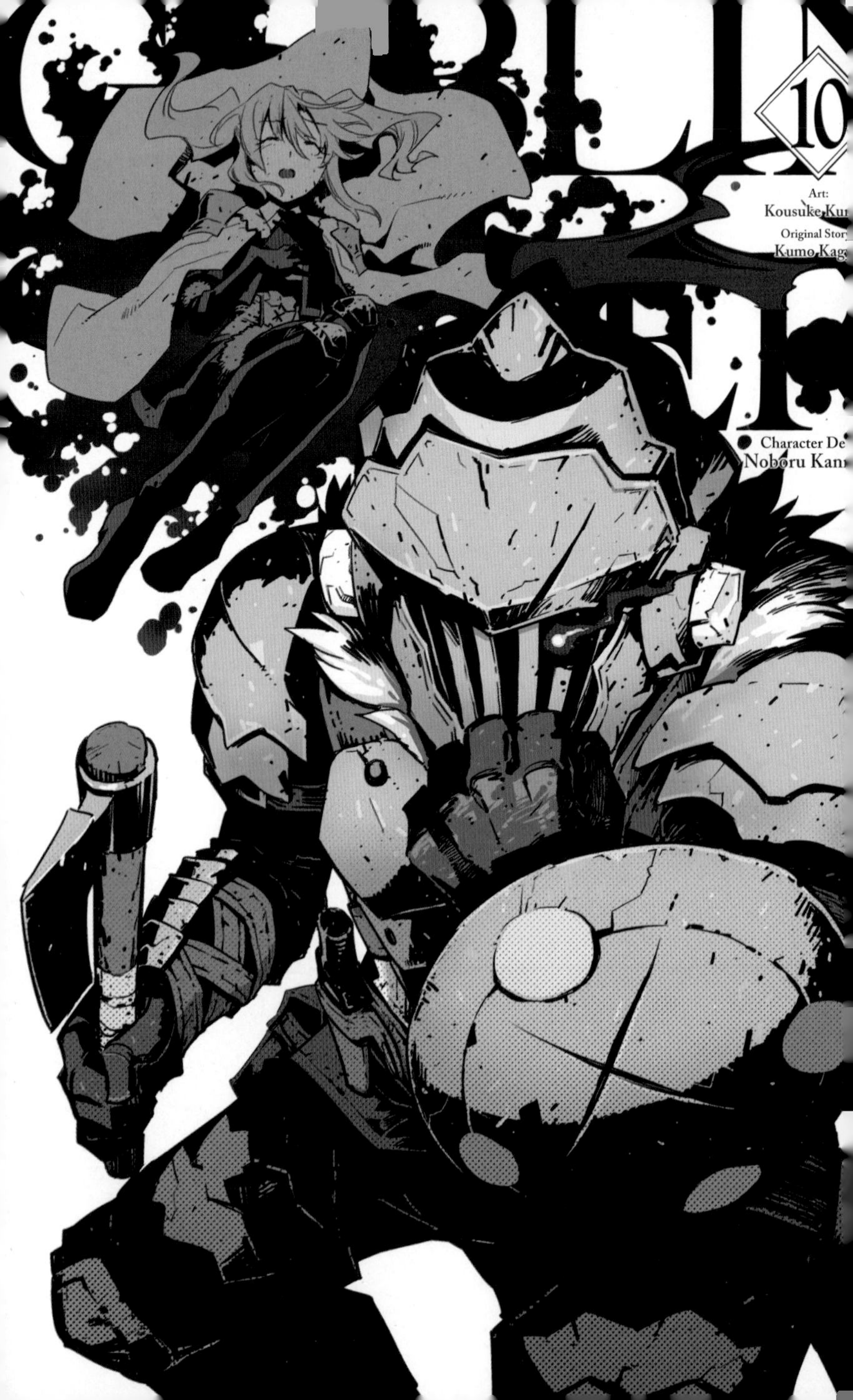
10
Art:
Kousuke Ku
Original Story
Kumo Kag
Character De
Noboru Kan

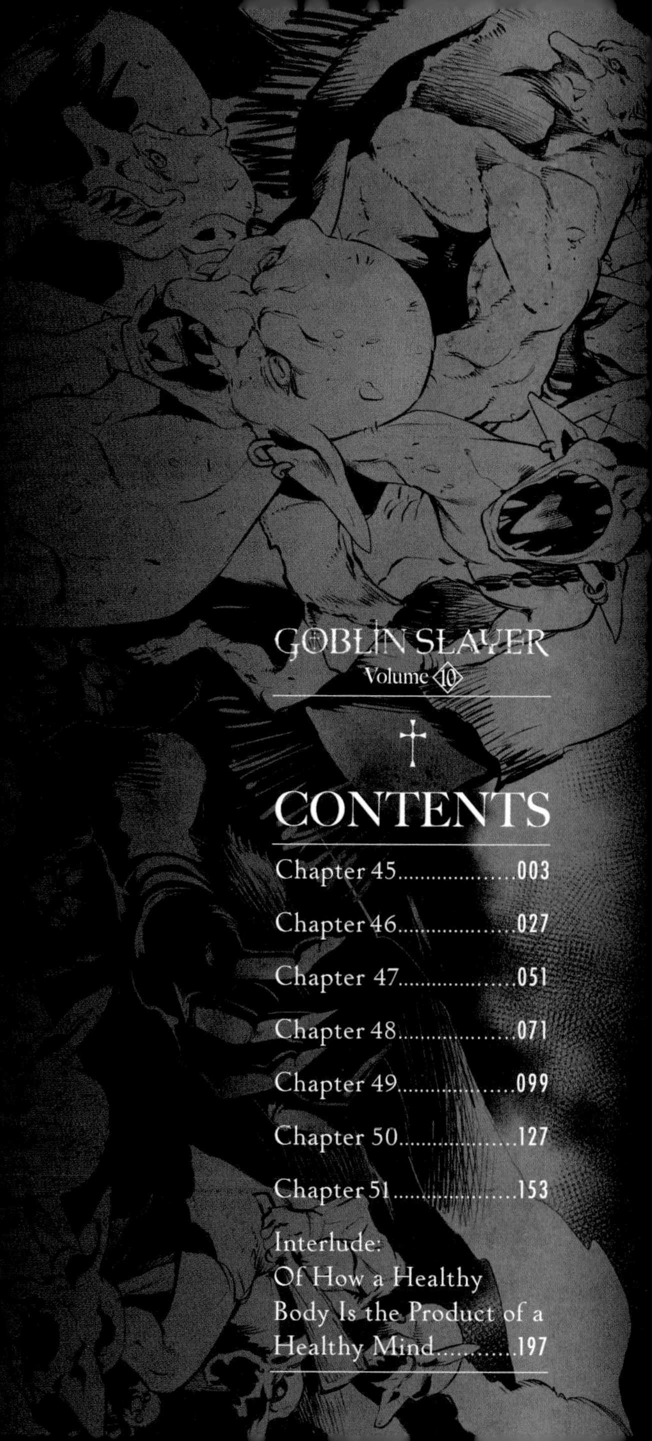

He does not let anyone roll dice

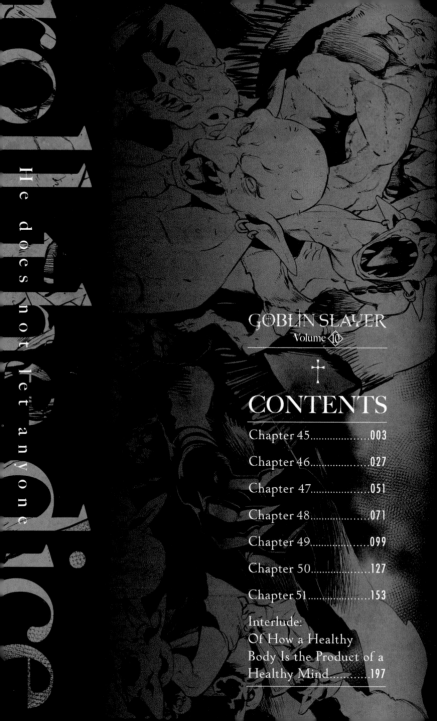

GOBLIN SLAYER
Volume 10

CONTENTS

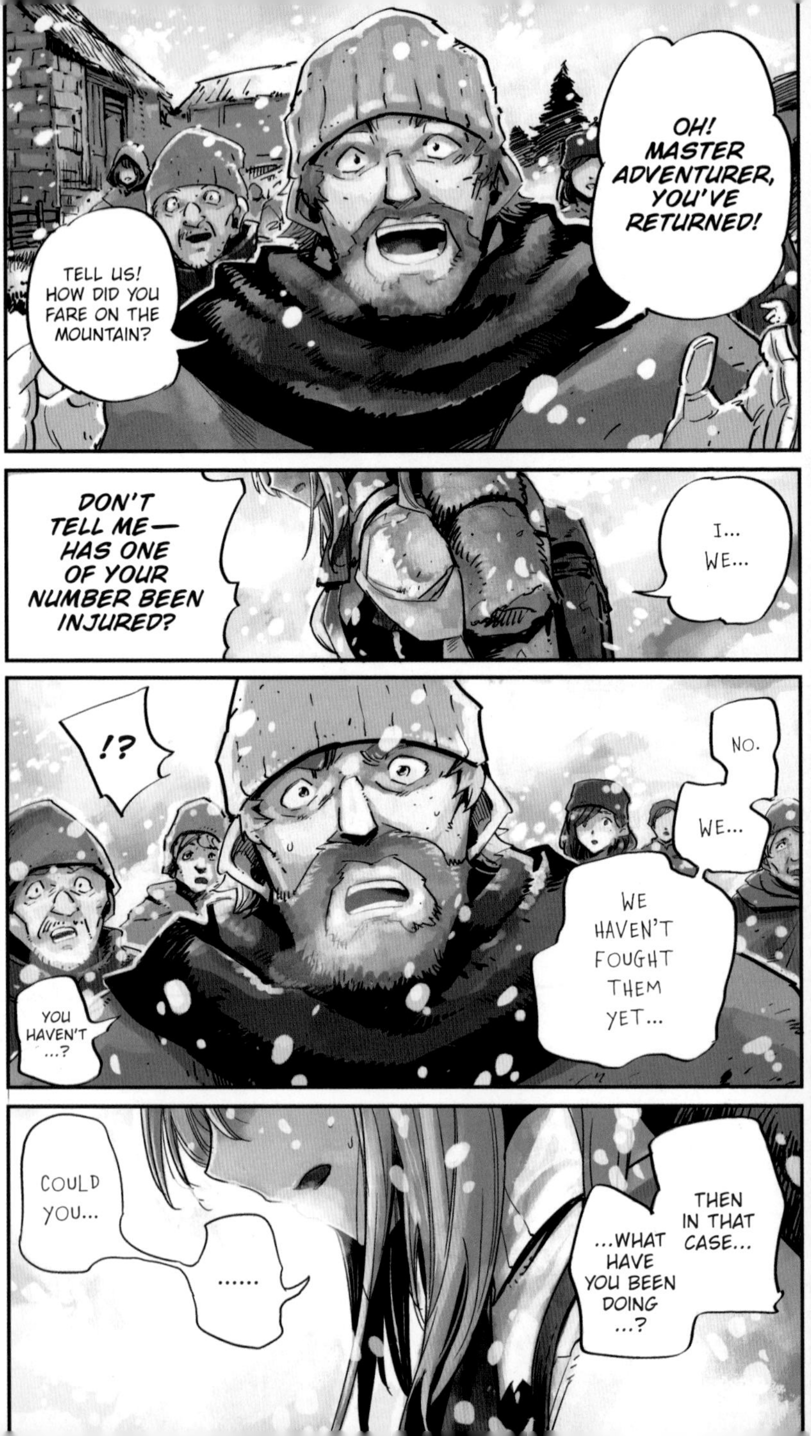
OH! MASTER ADVENTURER, YOU'VE RETURNED!
TELL US! HOW DID YOU FARE ON THE MOUNTAIN?
I... WE...
DON'T TELL ME— HAS ONE OF YOUR NUMBER BEEN INJURED?
NO.
WE...
WE HAVEN'T FOUGHT THEM YET...
!?
YOU HAVEN'T ...?
THEN IN THAT CASE...
...WHAT HAVE YOU BEEN DOING ...?
COULD YOU...
......

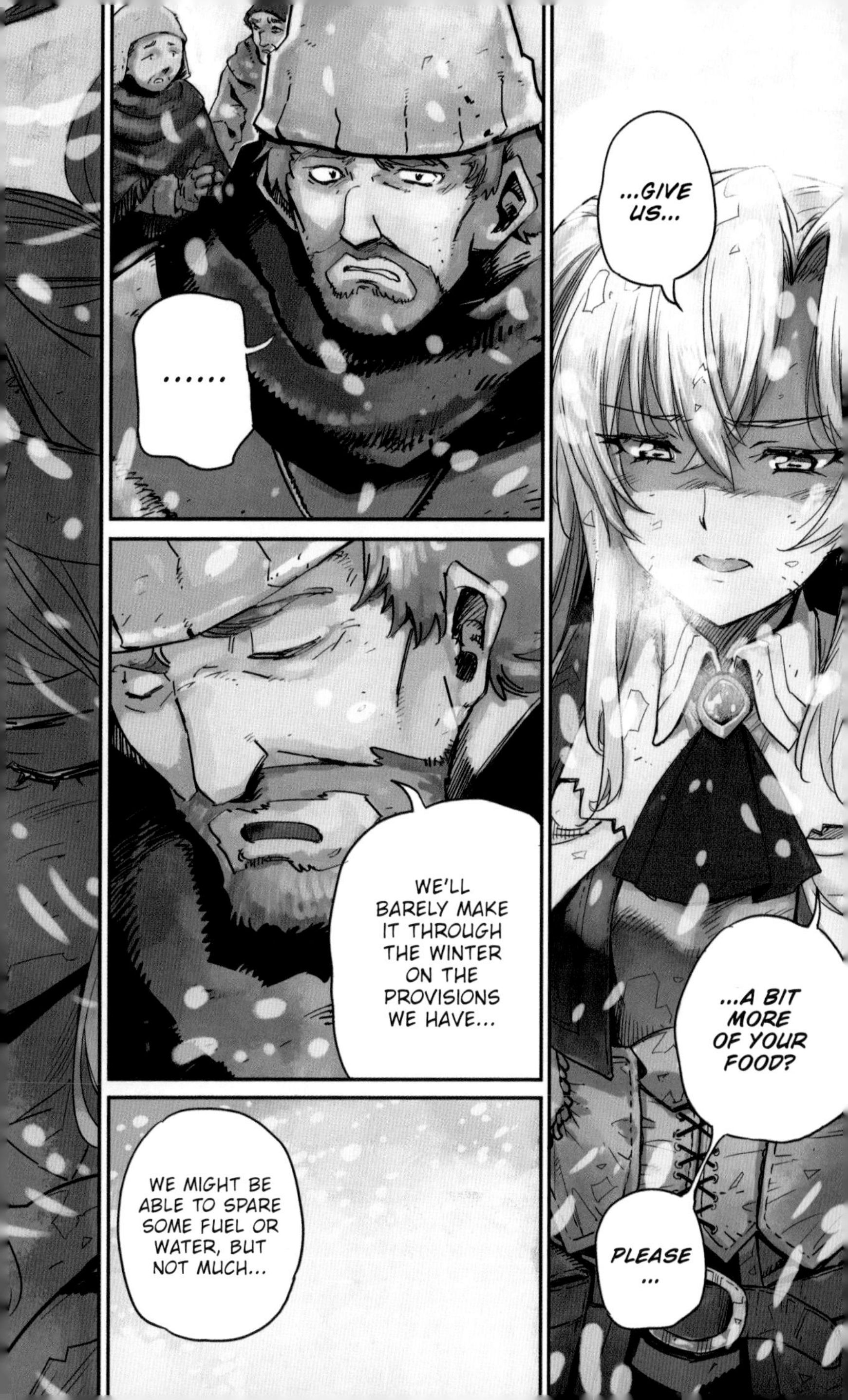
...GIVE US...
...A BIT MORE OF YOUR FOOD?
PLEASE ...
......
WE'LL BARELY MAKE IT THROUGH THE WINTER ON THE PROVISIONS WE HAVE...
WE MIGHT BE ABLE TO SPARE SOME FUEL OR WATER, BUT NOT MUCH...

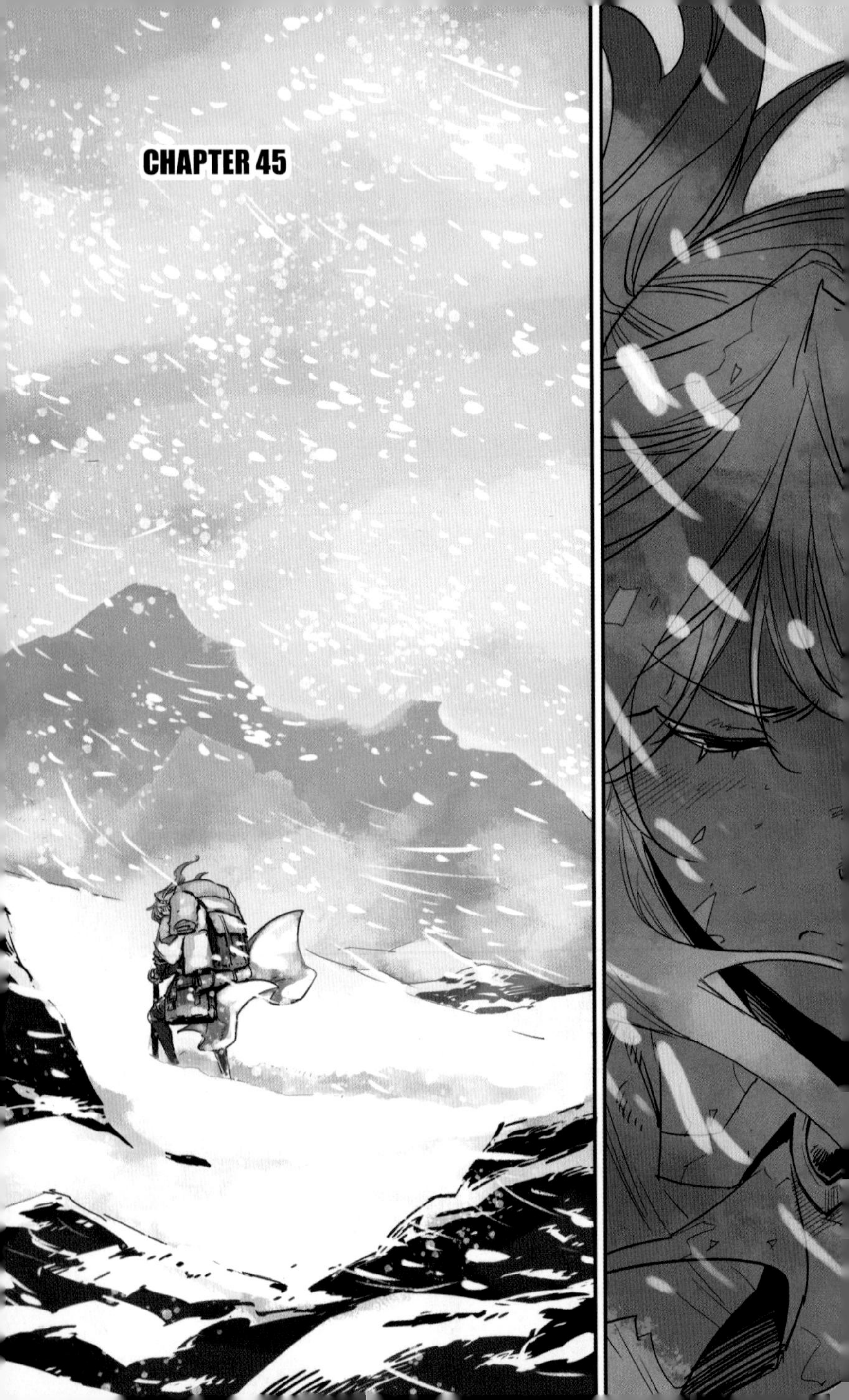
CHAPTER 45

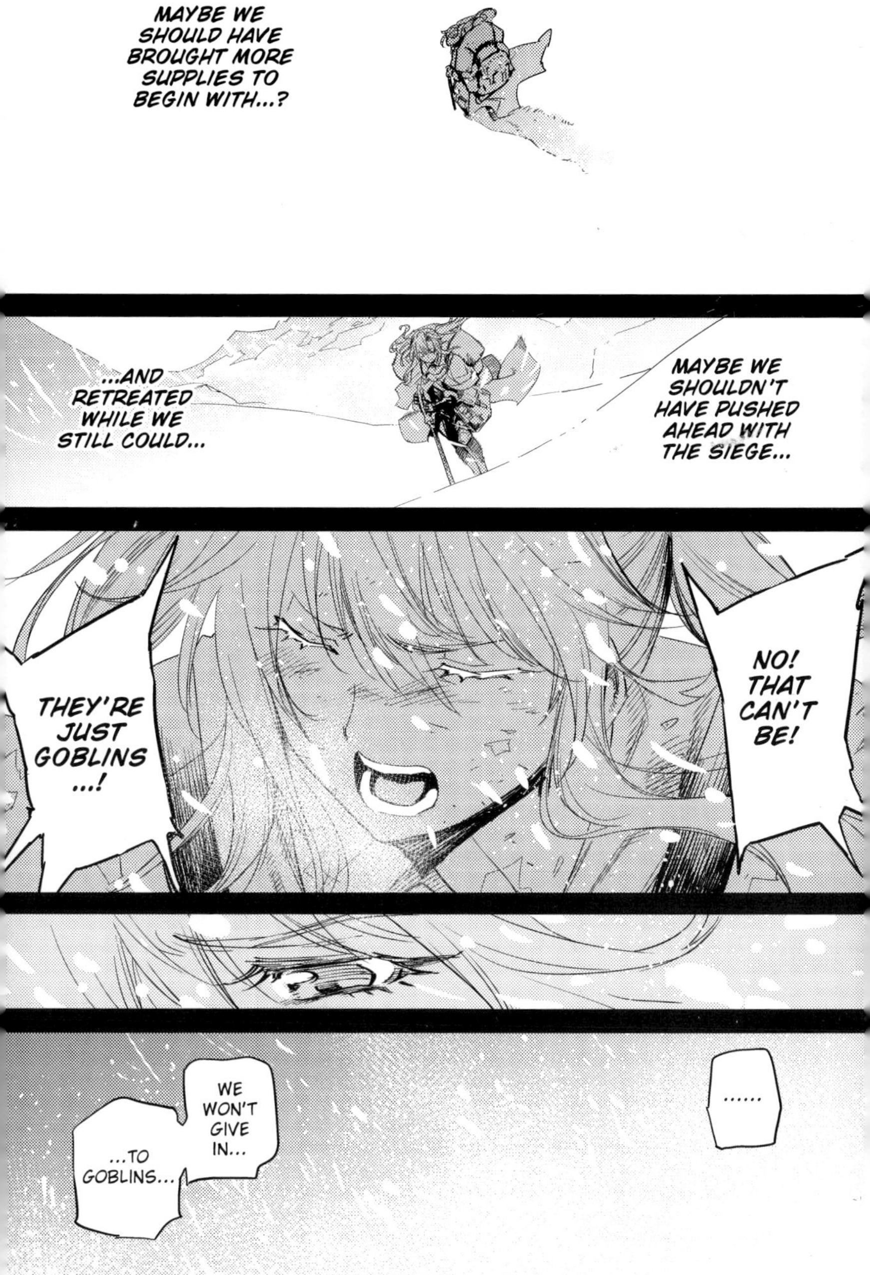
MAYBE WE SHOULD HAVE BROUGHT MORE SUPPLIES TO BEGIN WITH...?
MAYBE WE SHOULDN'T HAVE PUSHED AHEAD WITH THE SIEGE...
...AND RETREATED WHILE WE STILL COULD...
NO! THAT CAN'T BE!
THEY'RE JUST GOBLINS ...!
......
WE WON'T GIVE IN...
...TO GOBLINS...

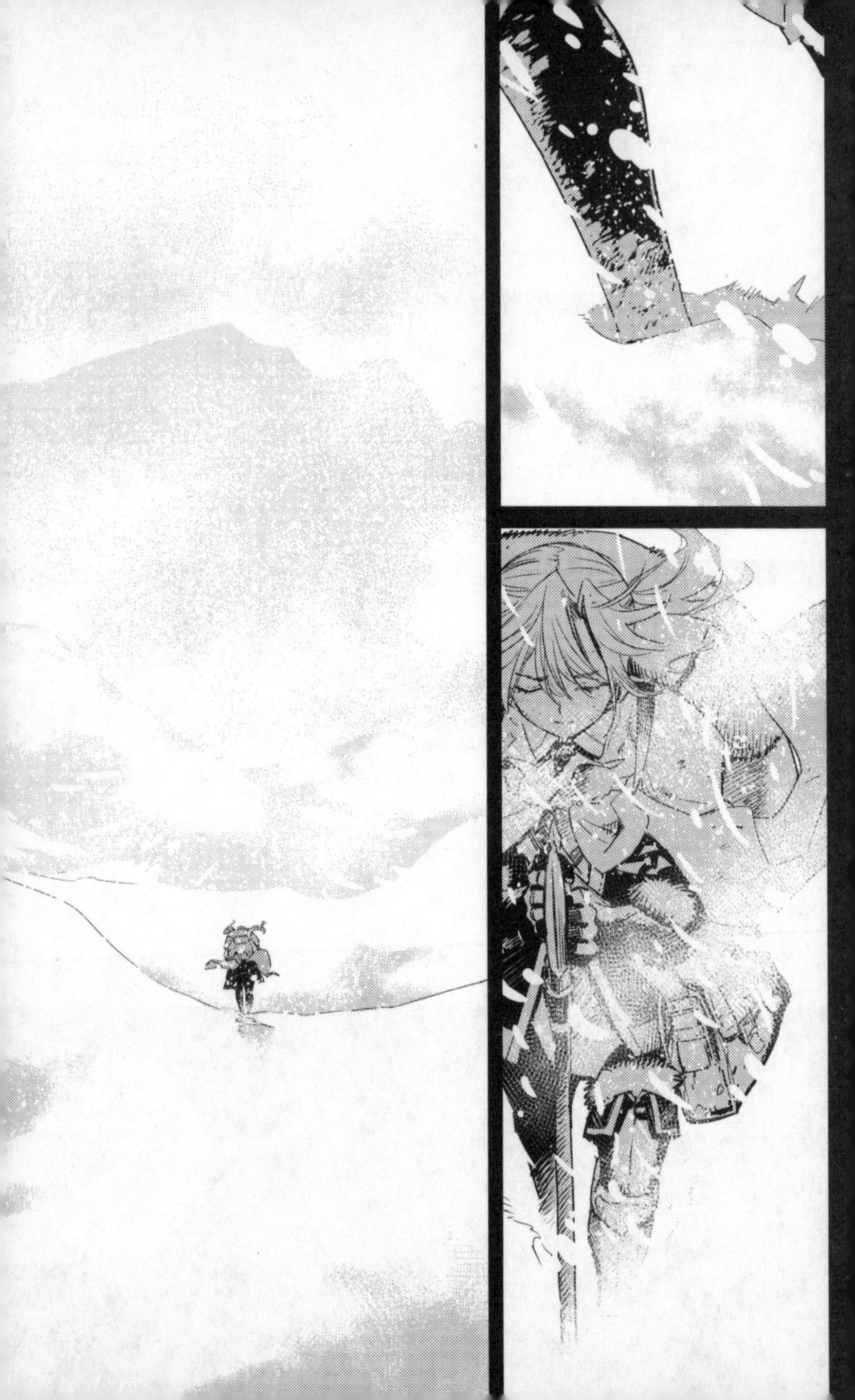

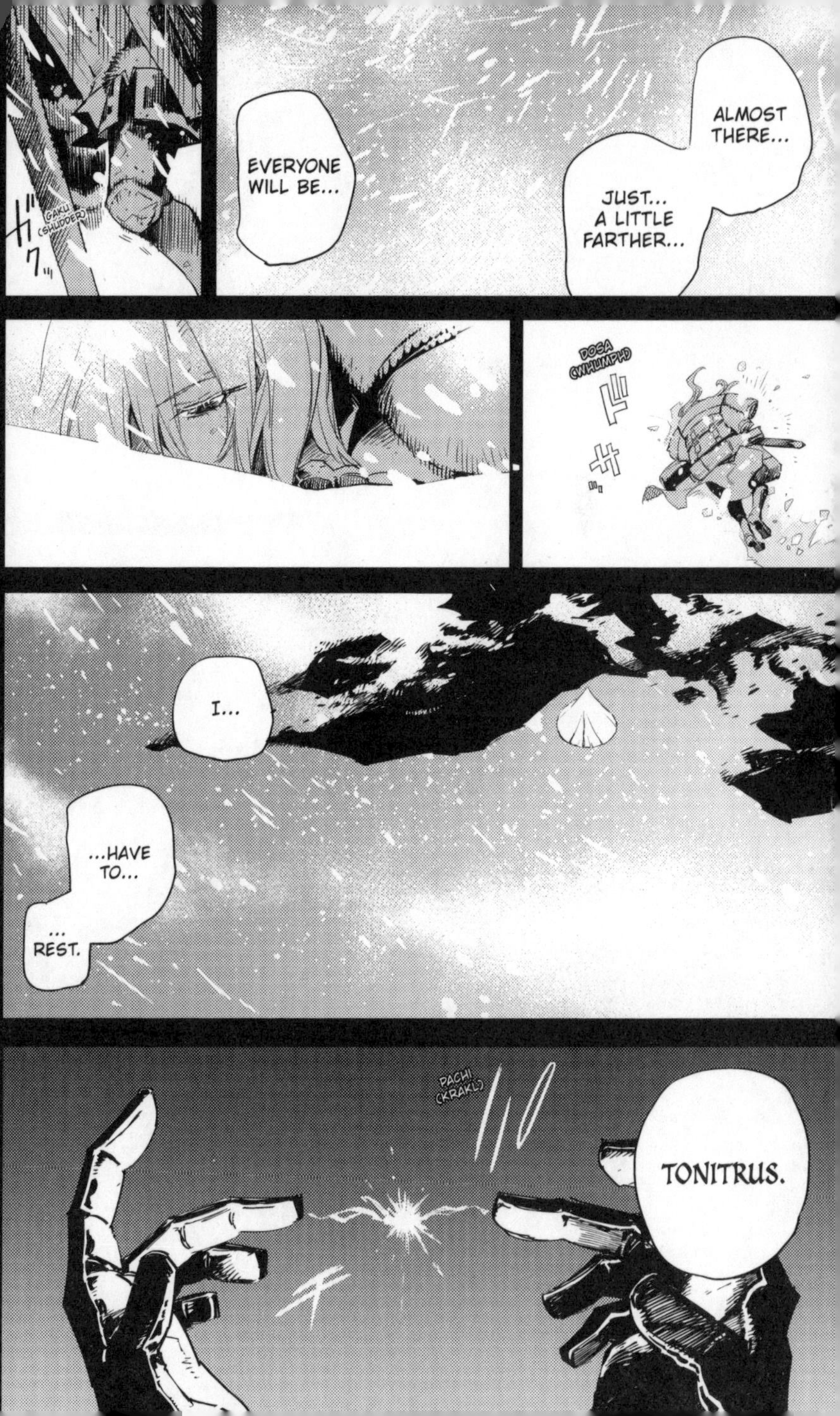
ALMOST THERE...
JUST... A LITTLE FARTHER...
EVERYONE WILL BE...
GAKU (SHUDDER)
DOSA (WHUMPH)
I...
...HAVE TO...
... REST.
PACHI (KRAKL)
TONITRUS.

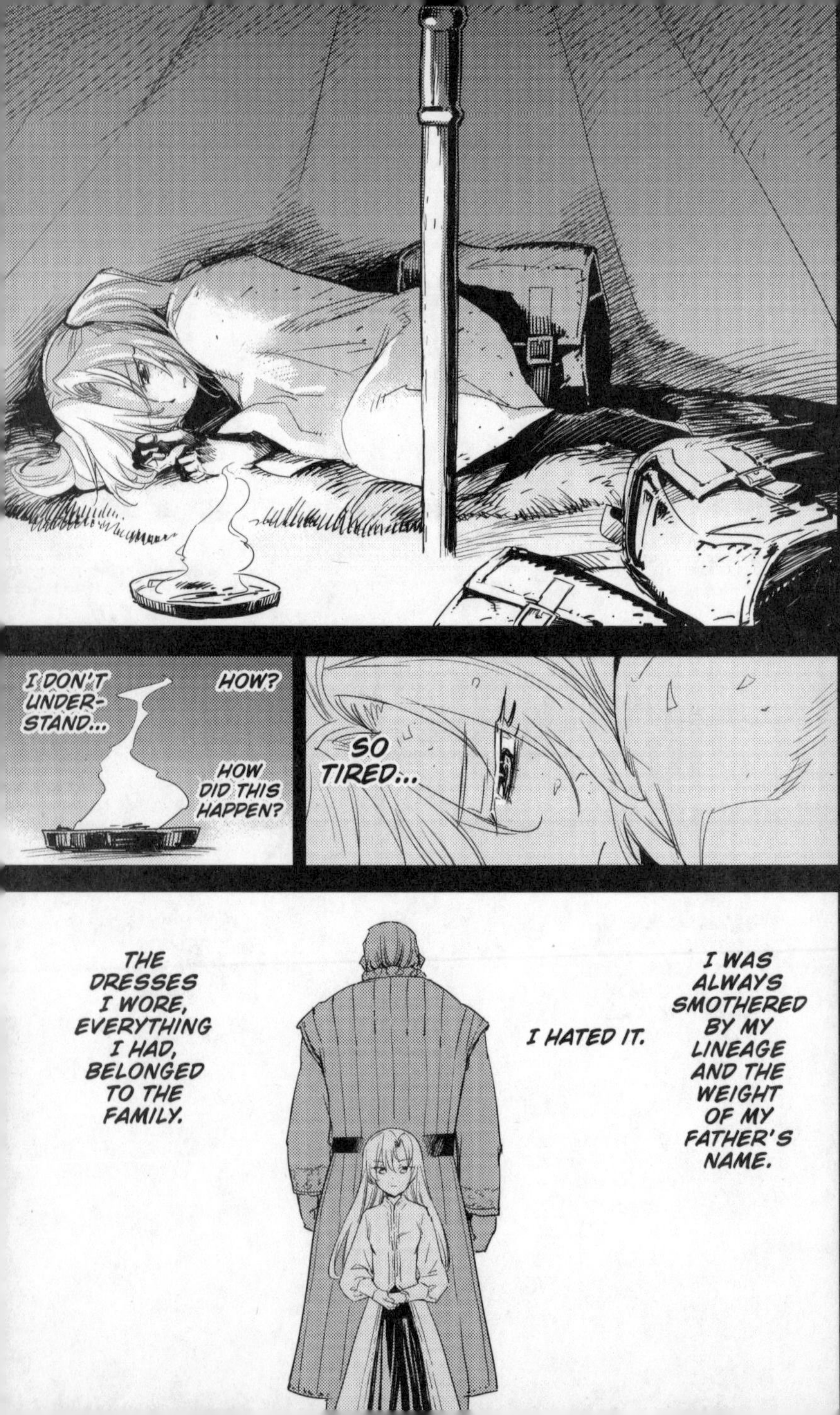
SO TIRED...
HOW?
I DON'T UNDER-STAND...
HOW DID THIS HAPPEN?
I WAS ALWAYS SMOTHERED BY MY LINEAGE AND THE WEIGHT OF MY FATHER'S NAME.
I HATED IT.
THE DRESSES I WORE, EVERYTHING I HAD, BELONGED TO THE FAMILY.

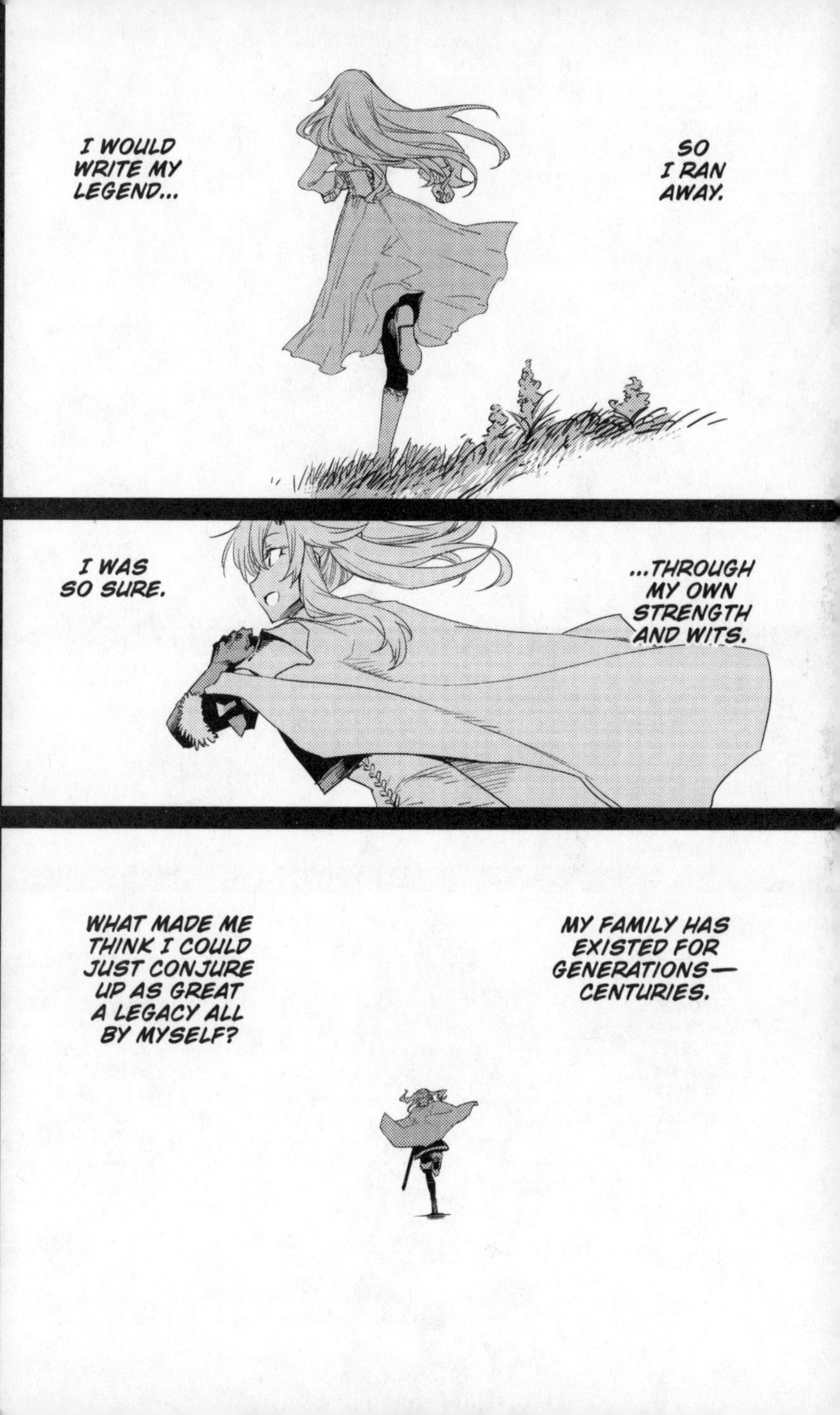
SO I RAN AWAY.
I WOULD WRITE MY LEGEND...
...THROUGH MY OWN STRENGTH AND WITS.
I WAS SO SURE.
MY FAMILY HAS EXISTED FOR GENERATIONS—CENTURIES.
WHAT MADE ME THINK I COULD JUST CONJURE UP AS GREAT A LEGACY ALL BY MYSELF?

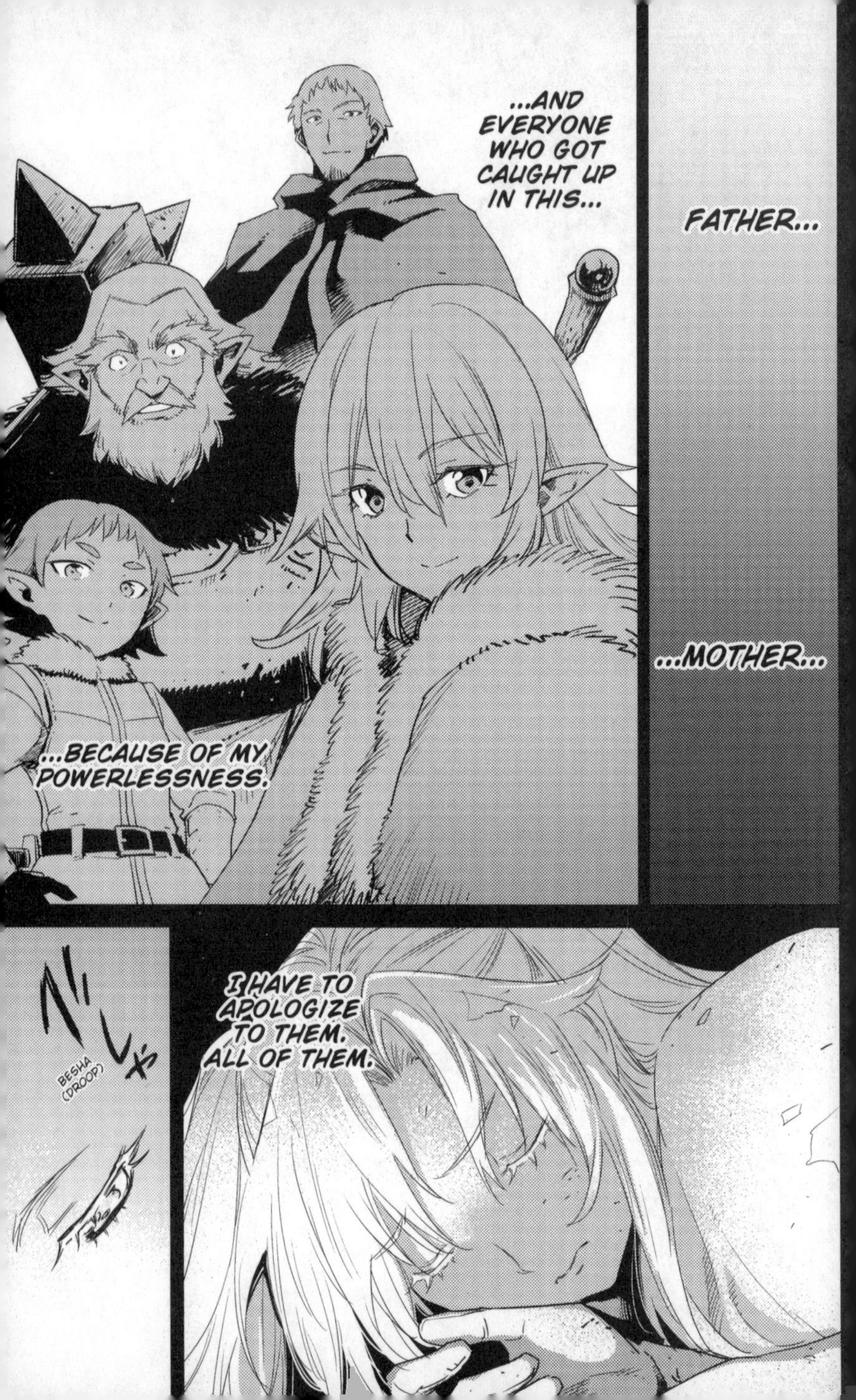
FATHER...
...MOTHER...
...AND EVERYONE WHO GOT CAUGHT UP IN THIS...
...BECAUSE OF MY POWERLESSNESS.
I HAVE TO APOLOGIZE TO THEM. ALL OF THEM.
BESHA (DROOP)

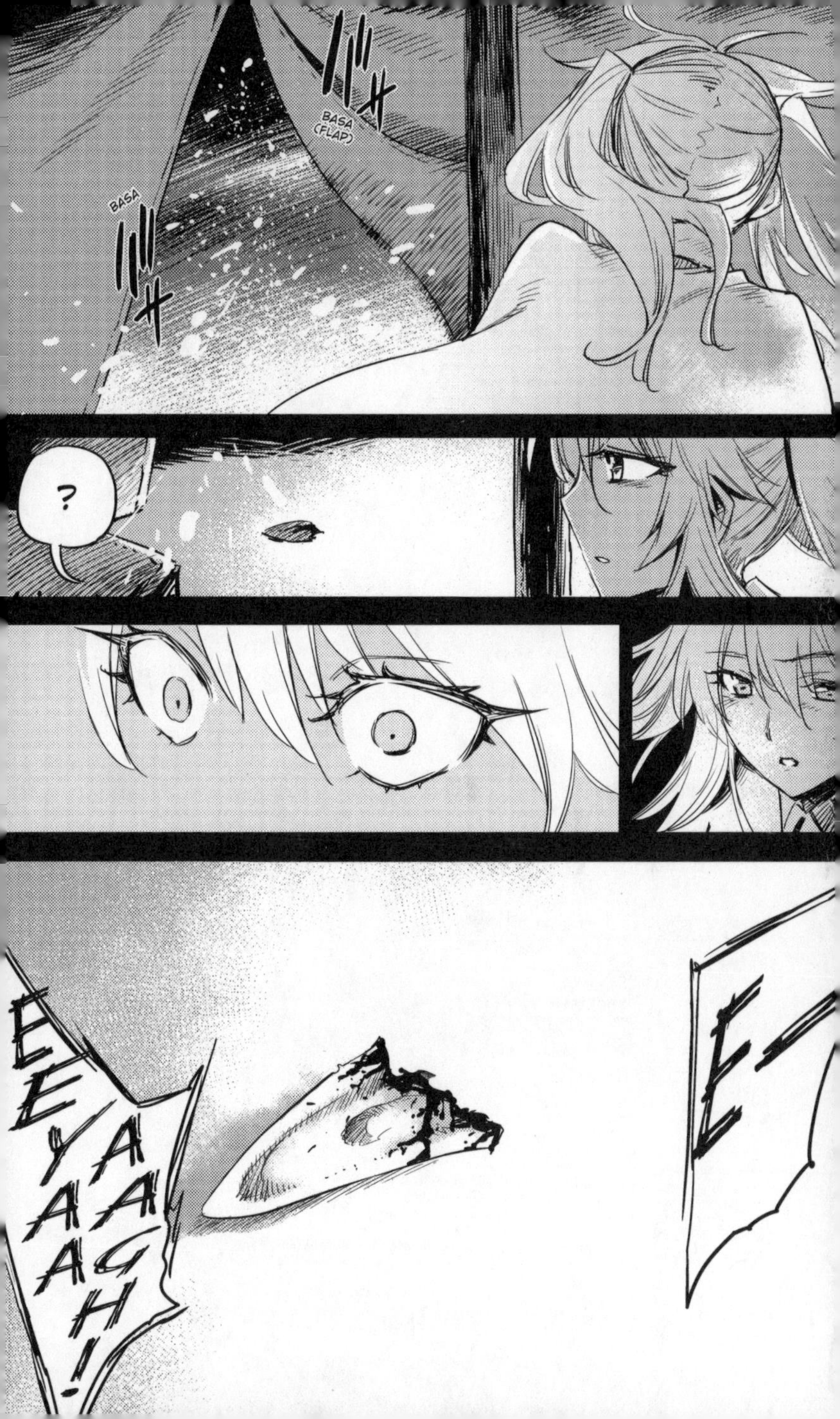

BASA (FLAP)
BASA
?
E-
EEYAAAAAGH!-

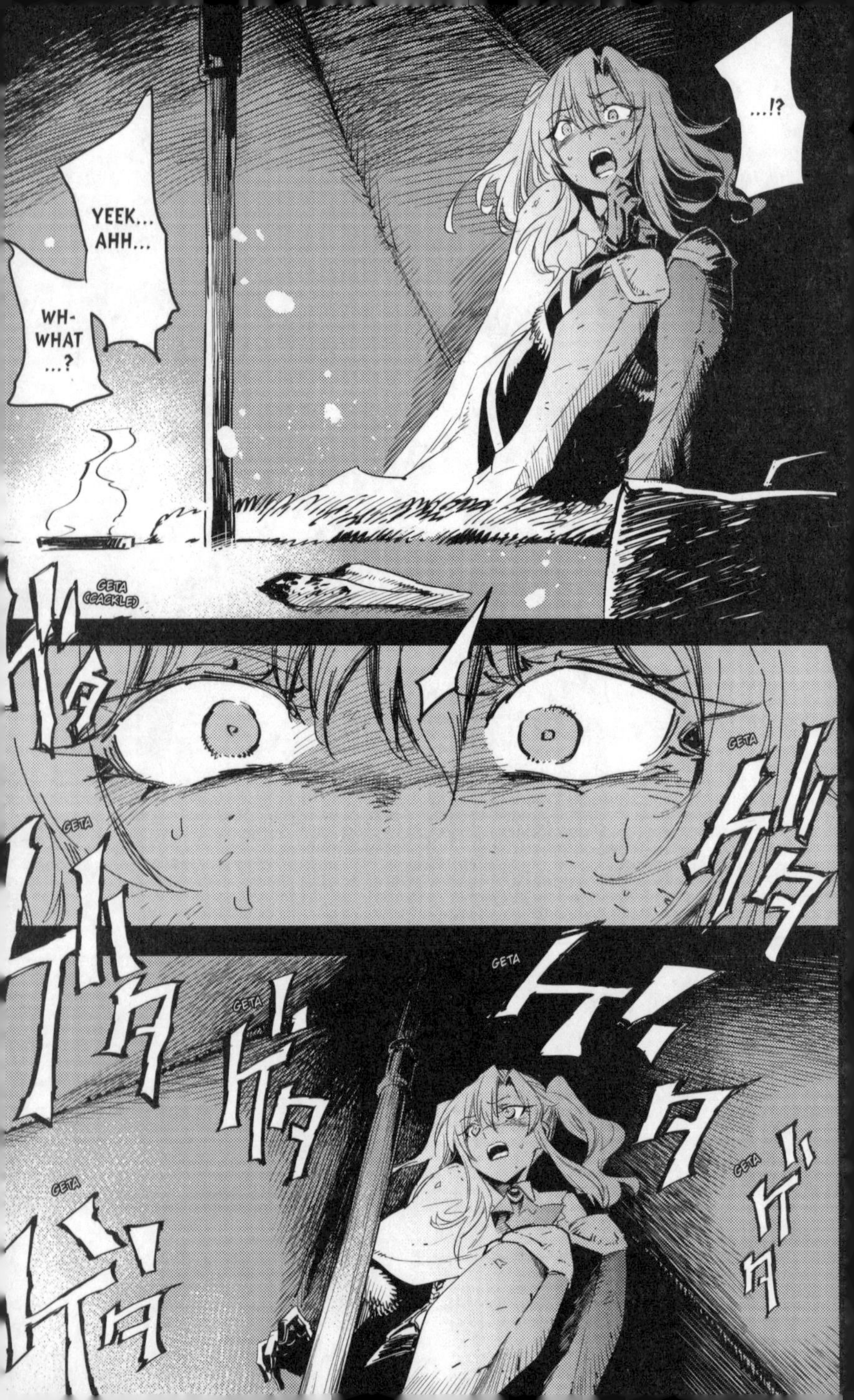
...!?
YEEK... AHH...
WH-WHAT ...?
GETA (CACKLED)
GETA
GETA
GETA
GETA
GETA
GETA

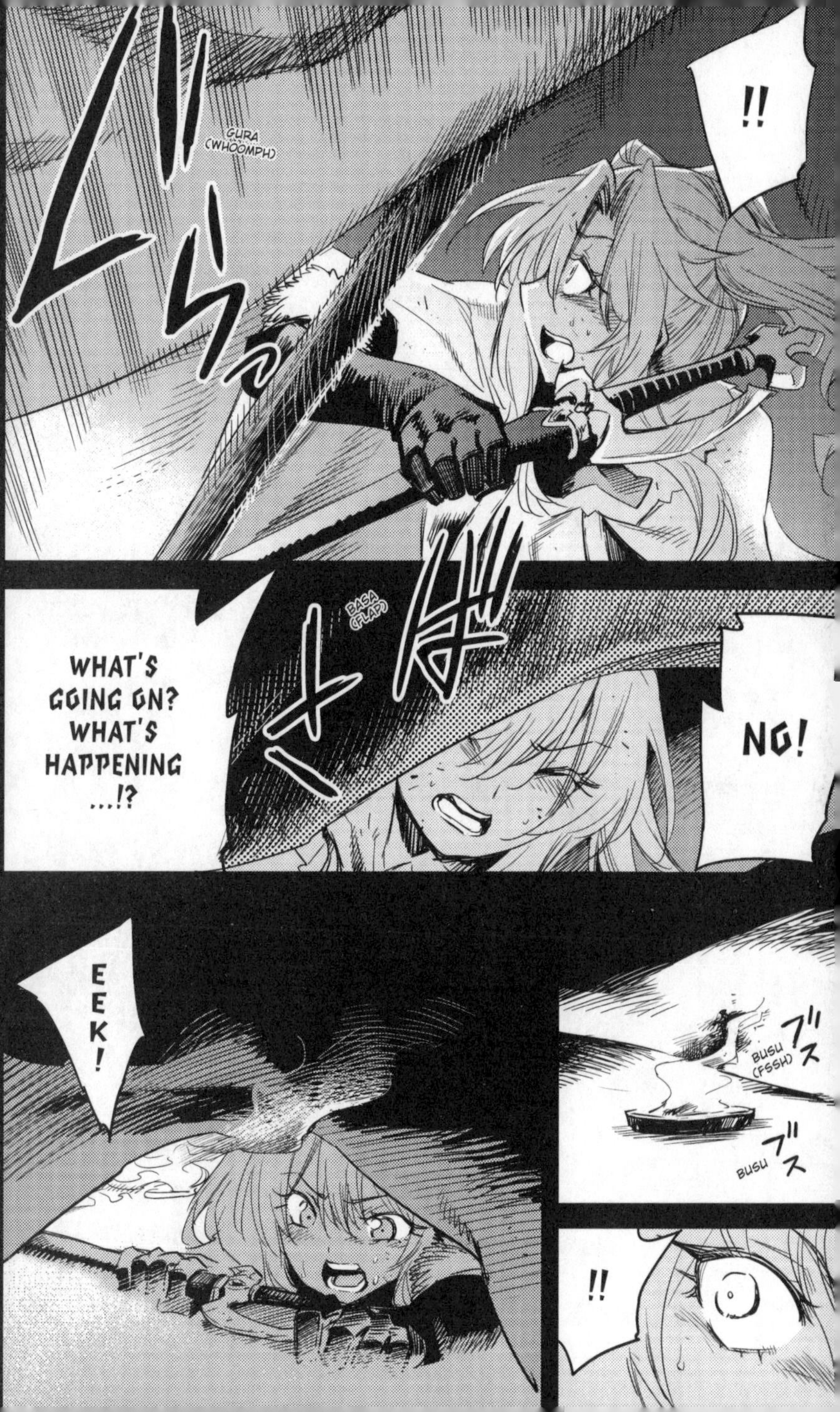
!!
GURA (WHOOMPH)
NG!
BASA (FLAP)
WHAT'S GOING ON? WHAT'S HAPPENING ...!?
ブス
BUSU (FSSH)
ブス
BUSU
!!
EEK!

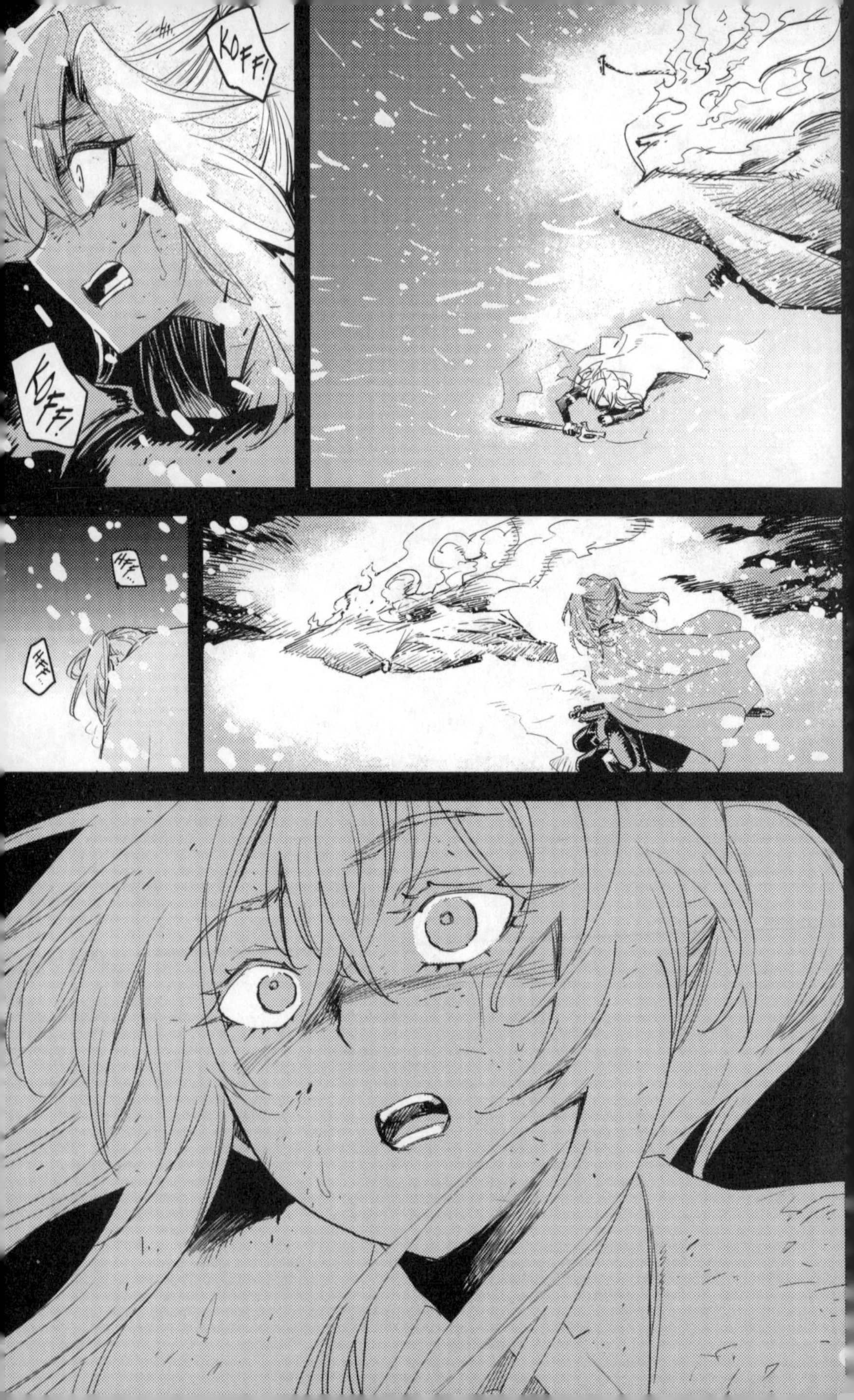
KOFF!
KOFF!
HFF...
HFF...

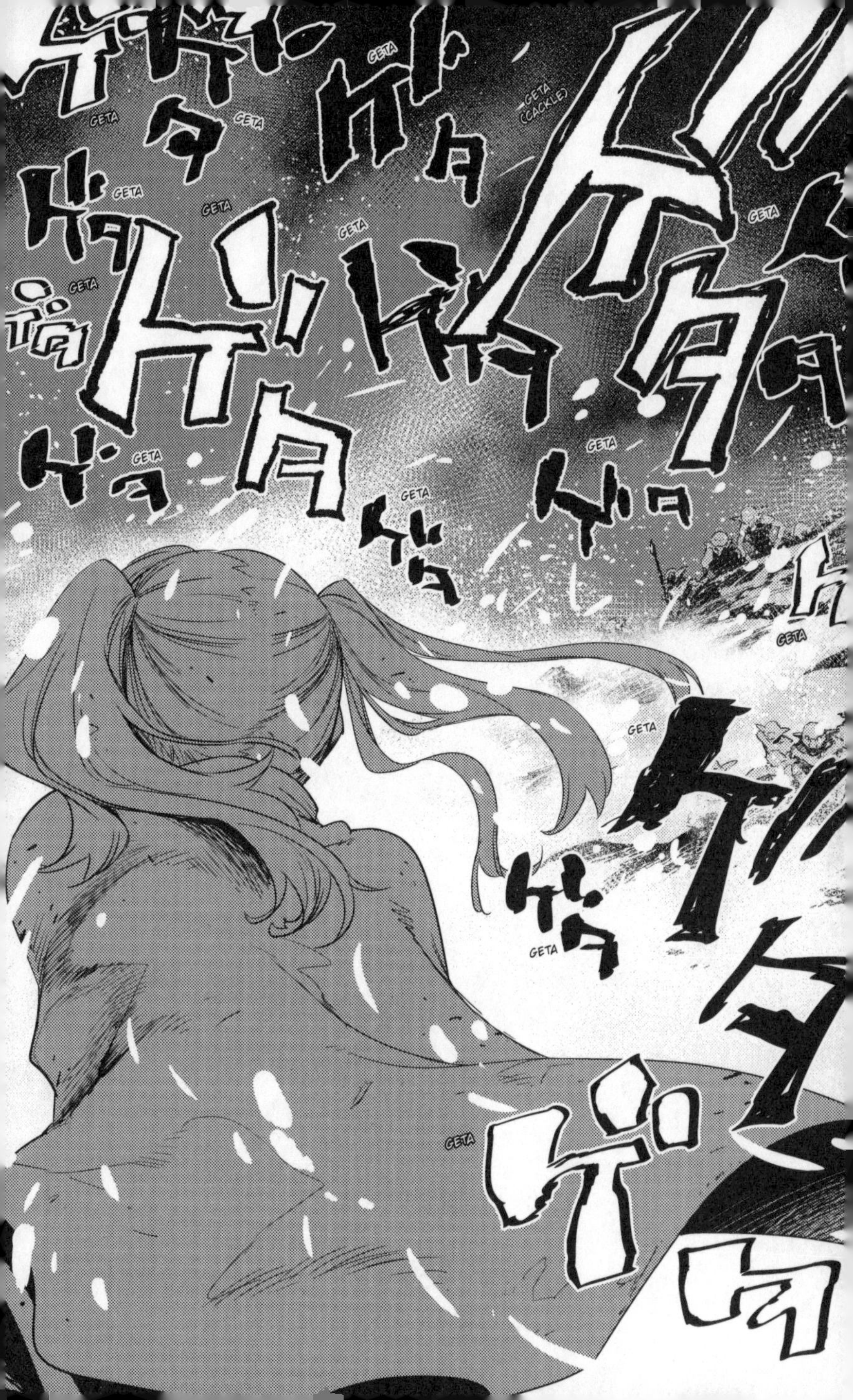
GETA
GETA (CACKLE)
GETA
GETA
GETA
GETA
GETA
GETA
GETA
GETA
GETA
GETA
GETA
GETA
GETA
GETA

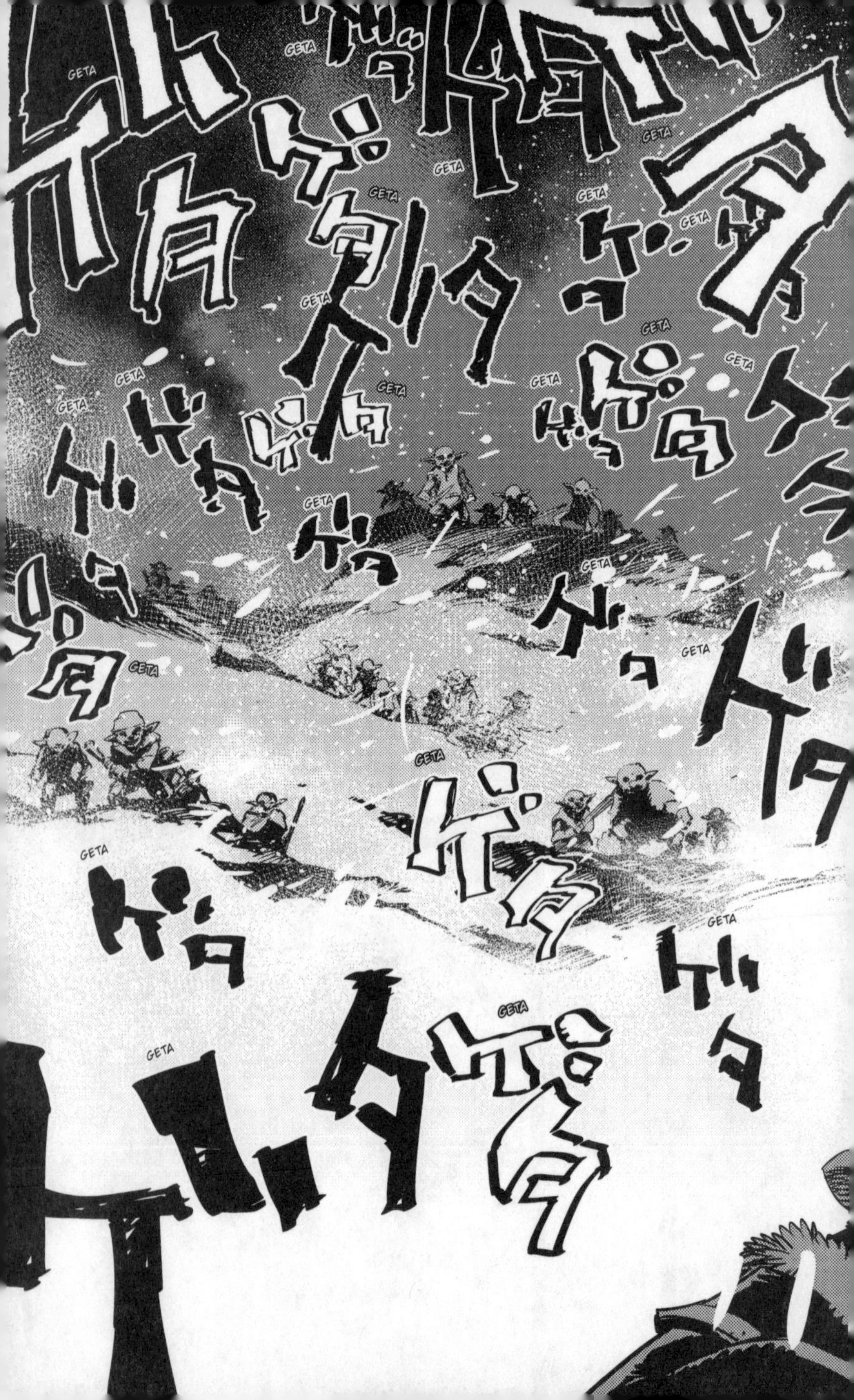
GETA
GETA
GETA
GETA
GETA
GETA
GETA
GETA
GETA
GETA
GETA
GETA
GETA
GETA
GETA
GETA
GETA
GETA
GETA
GETA
GETA
GETA
GETA

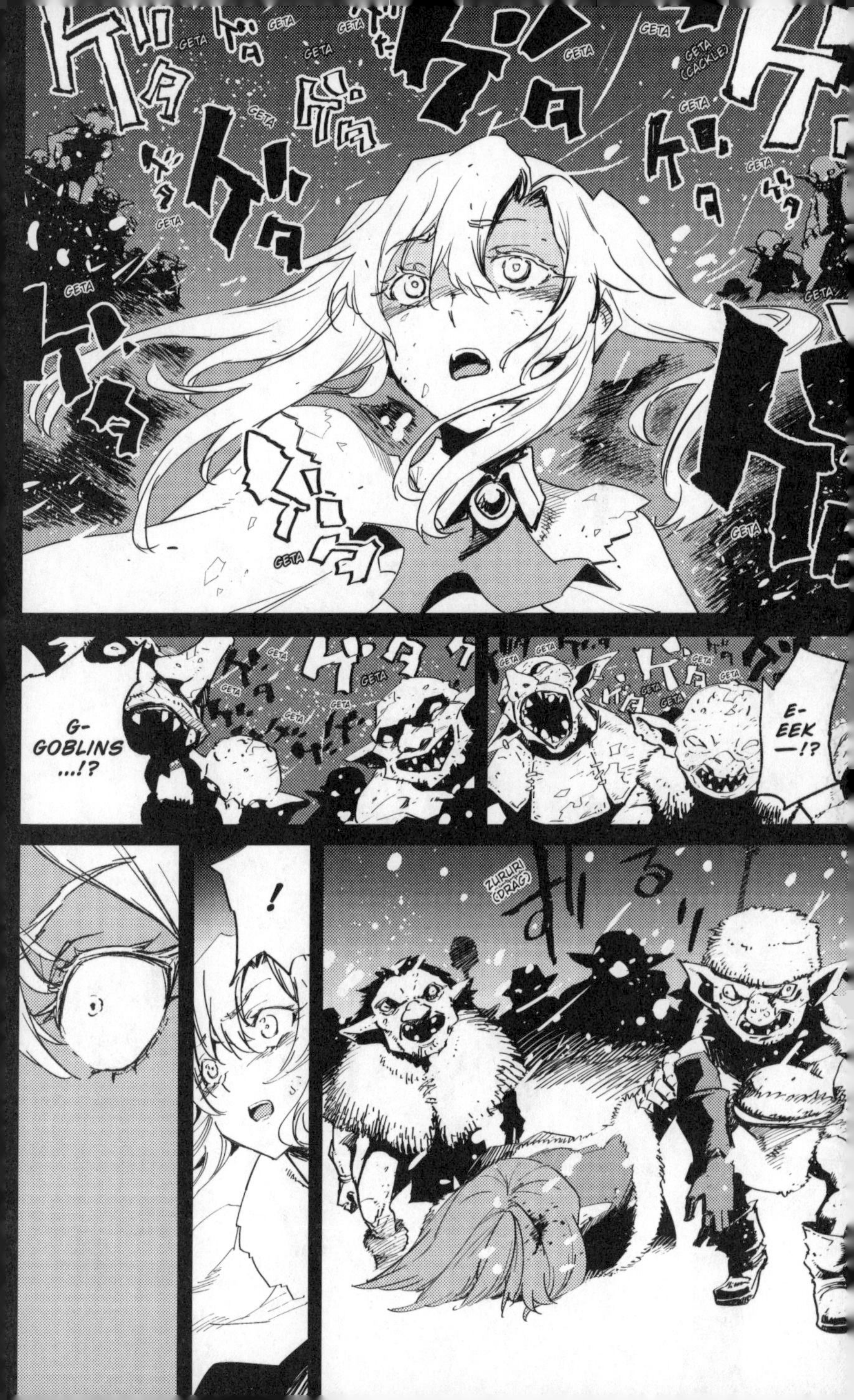
GETA (CACKLE)
GETA
GETA
GETA
GETA
GETA
GETA
GETA
GETA
GETA
GETA
GETA
GETA
GETA
GETA
E-EEK—!?
GETA
GETA
GETA
GETA
GETA
GETA
G-GOBLINS ...!?
ZURURI (DRAG)
!

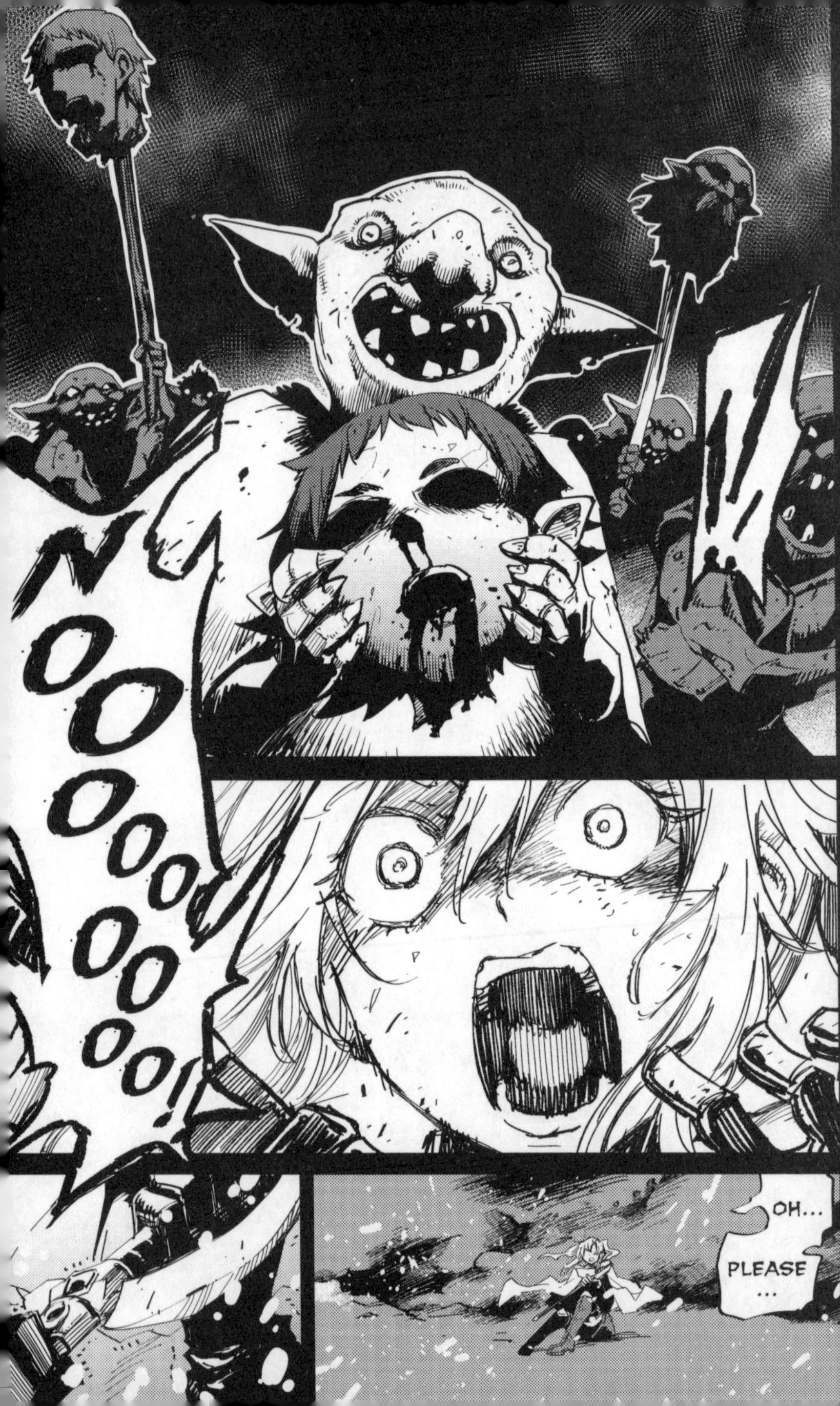
NOOOOOOOOOOOOO!
OH...
PLEASE
...

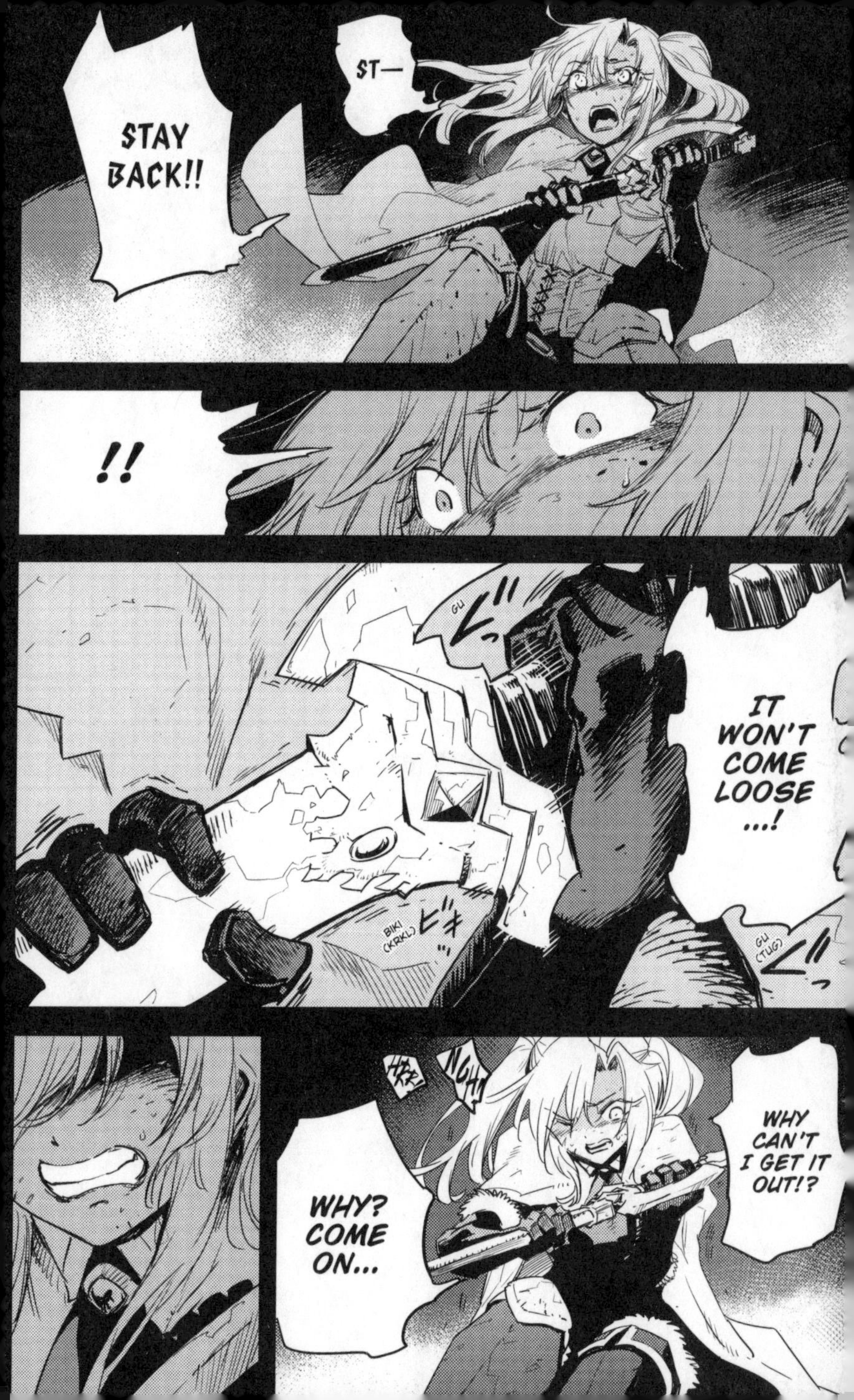
ST—
STAY BACK!!
!!
IT WON'T COME LOOSE...!
GU (TUG)
GU
BIKI (KRKL)
WHY CAN'T I GET IT OUT!?
NGH!
HRR!
WHY? COME ON...

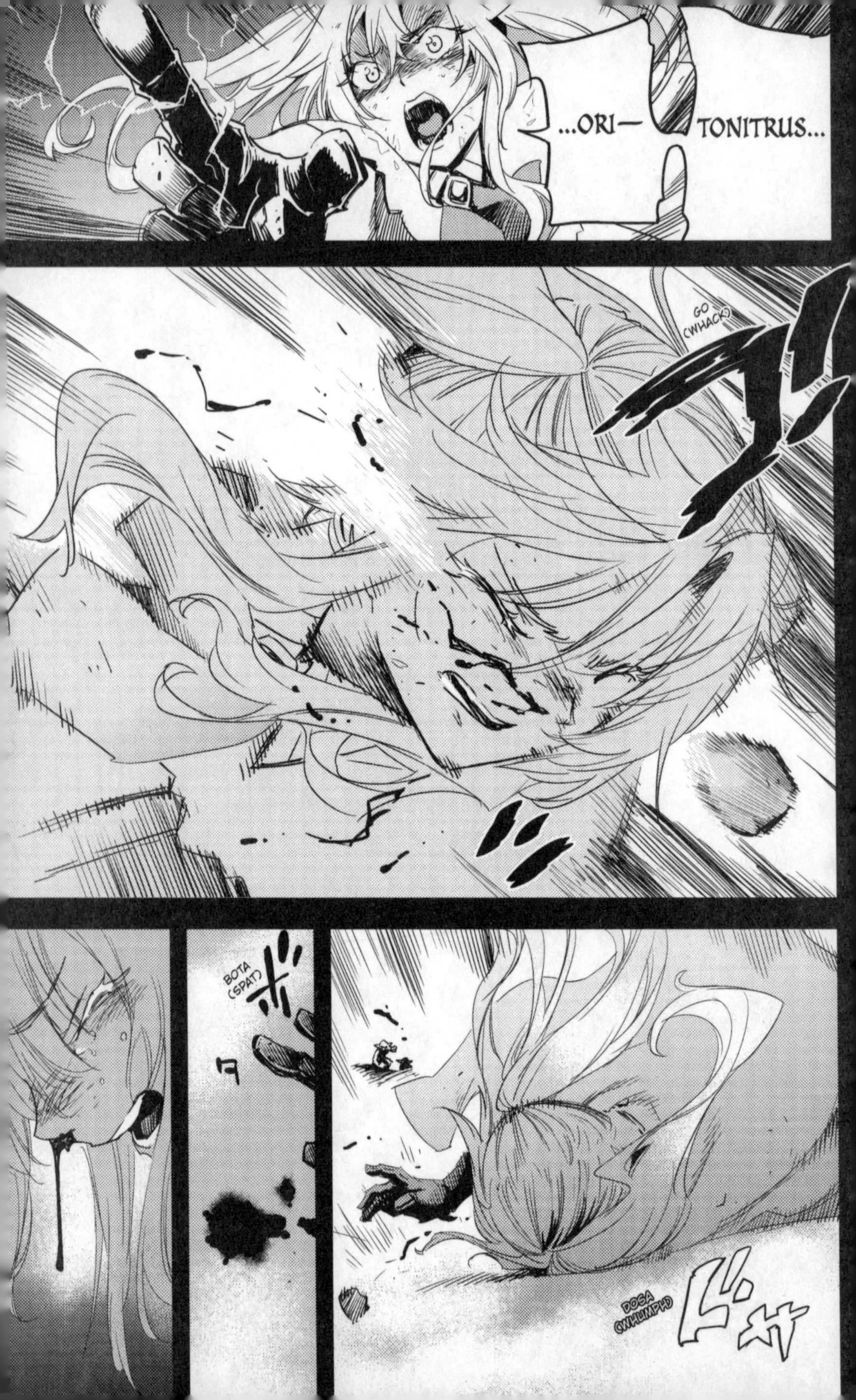
TONITRUS...
...ORI—
GO (WHACK)
DOSA (WHUMPH)
BOTA (SPAT)

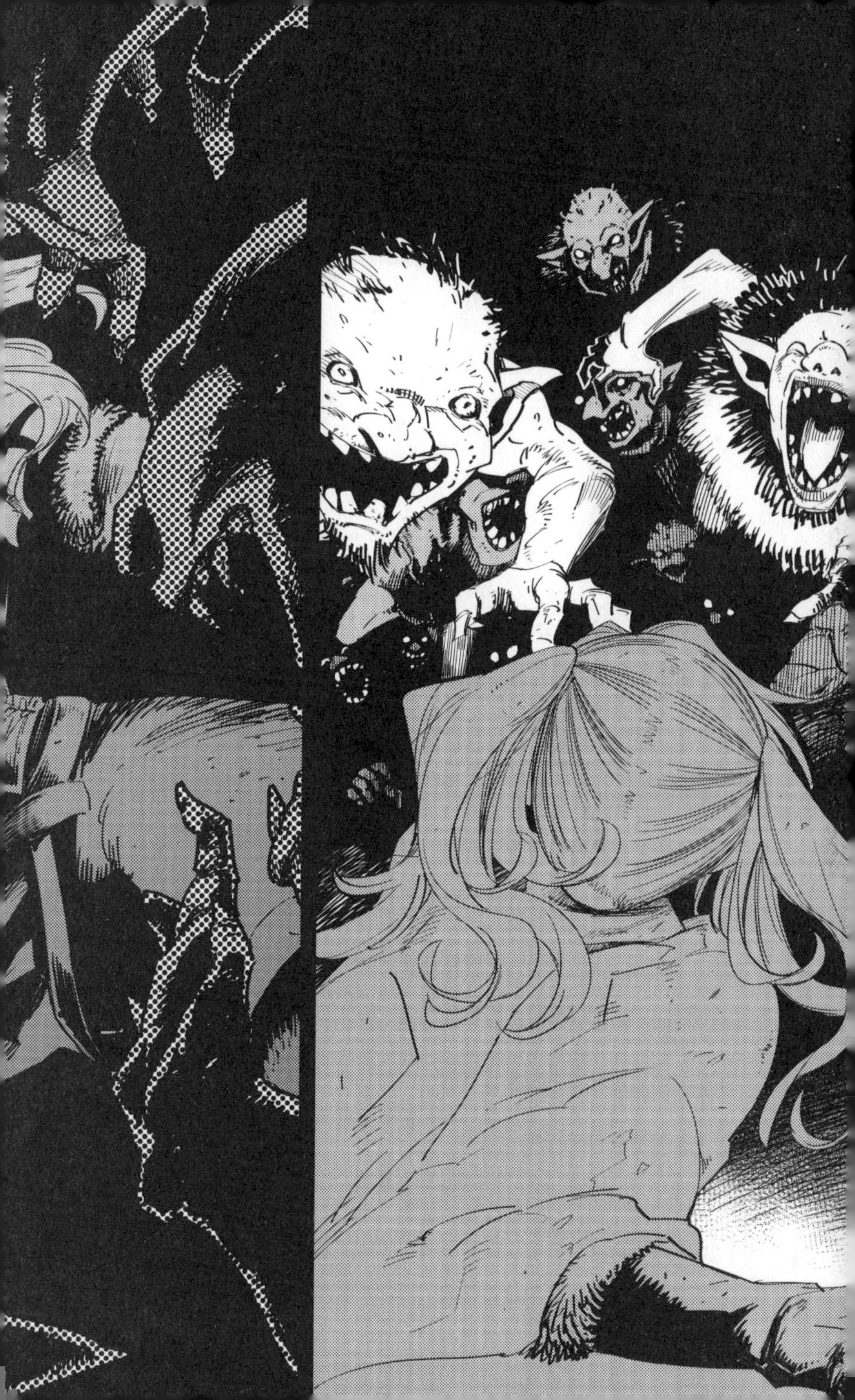

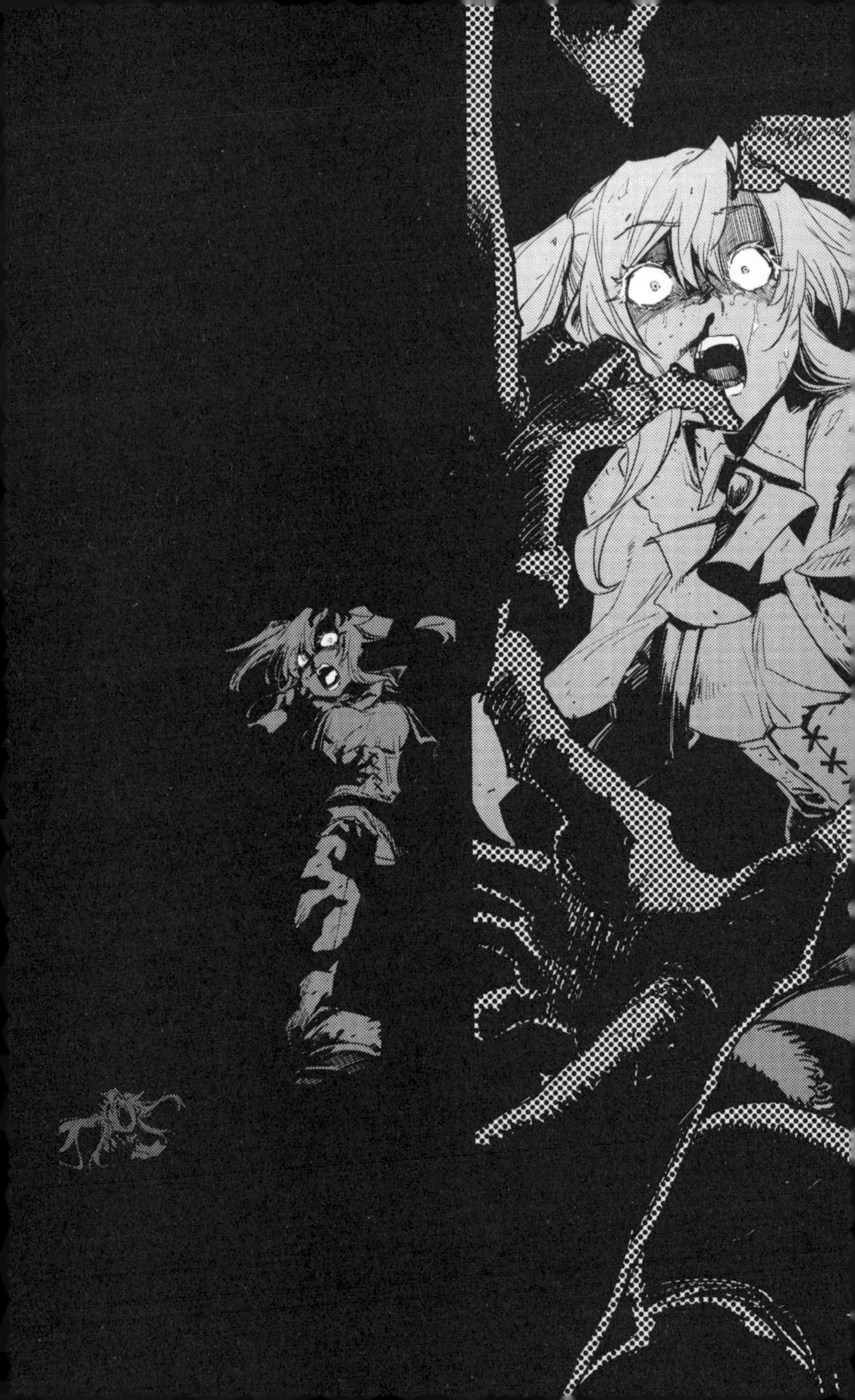

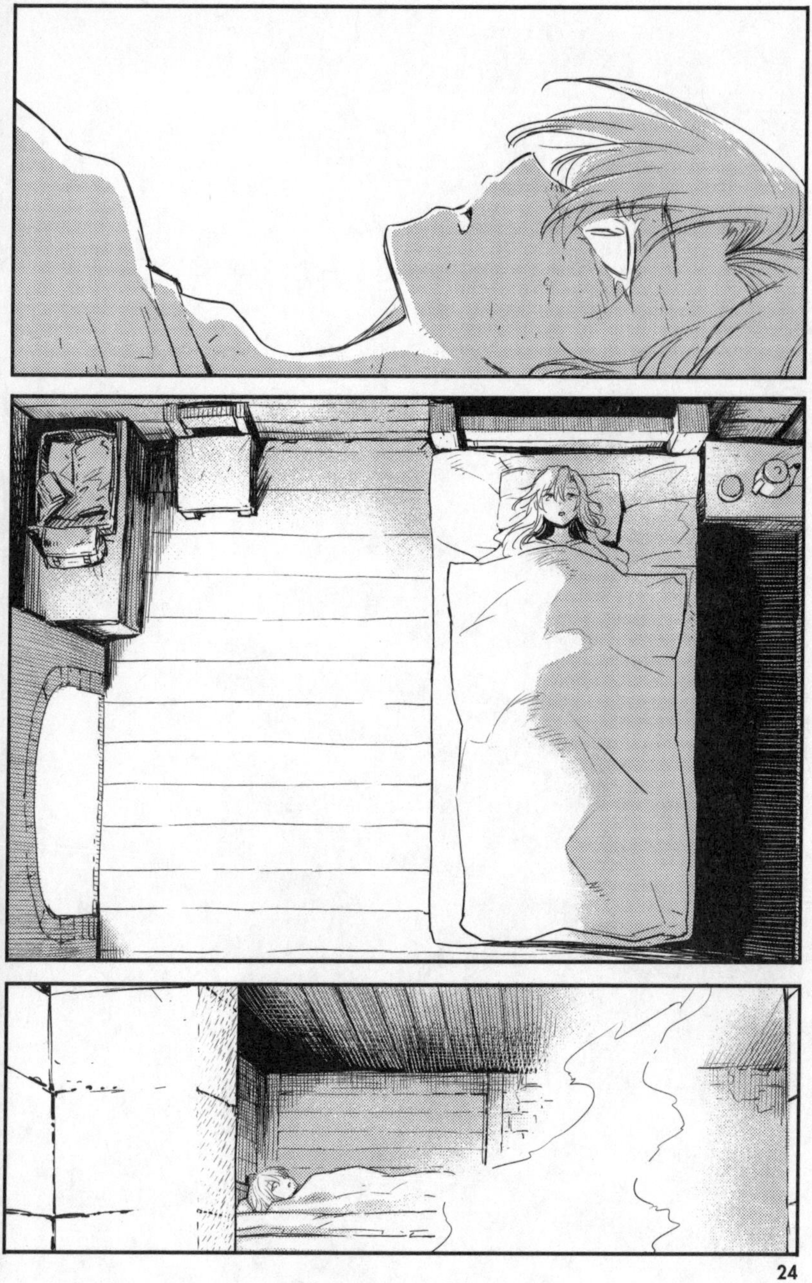

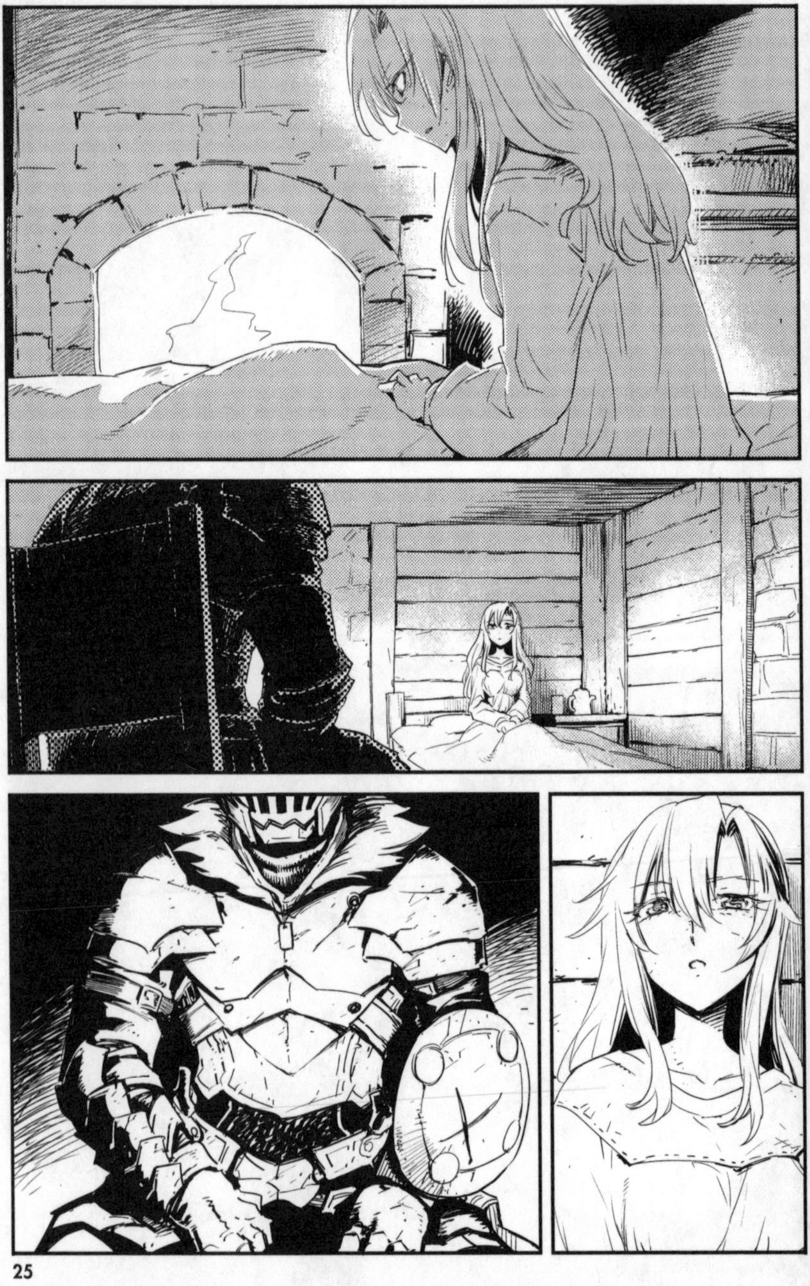

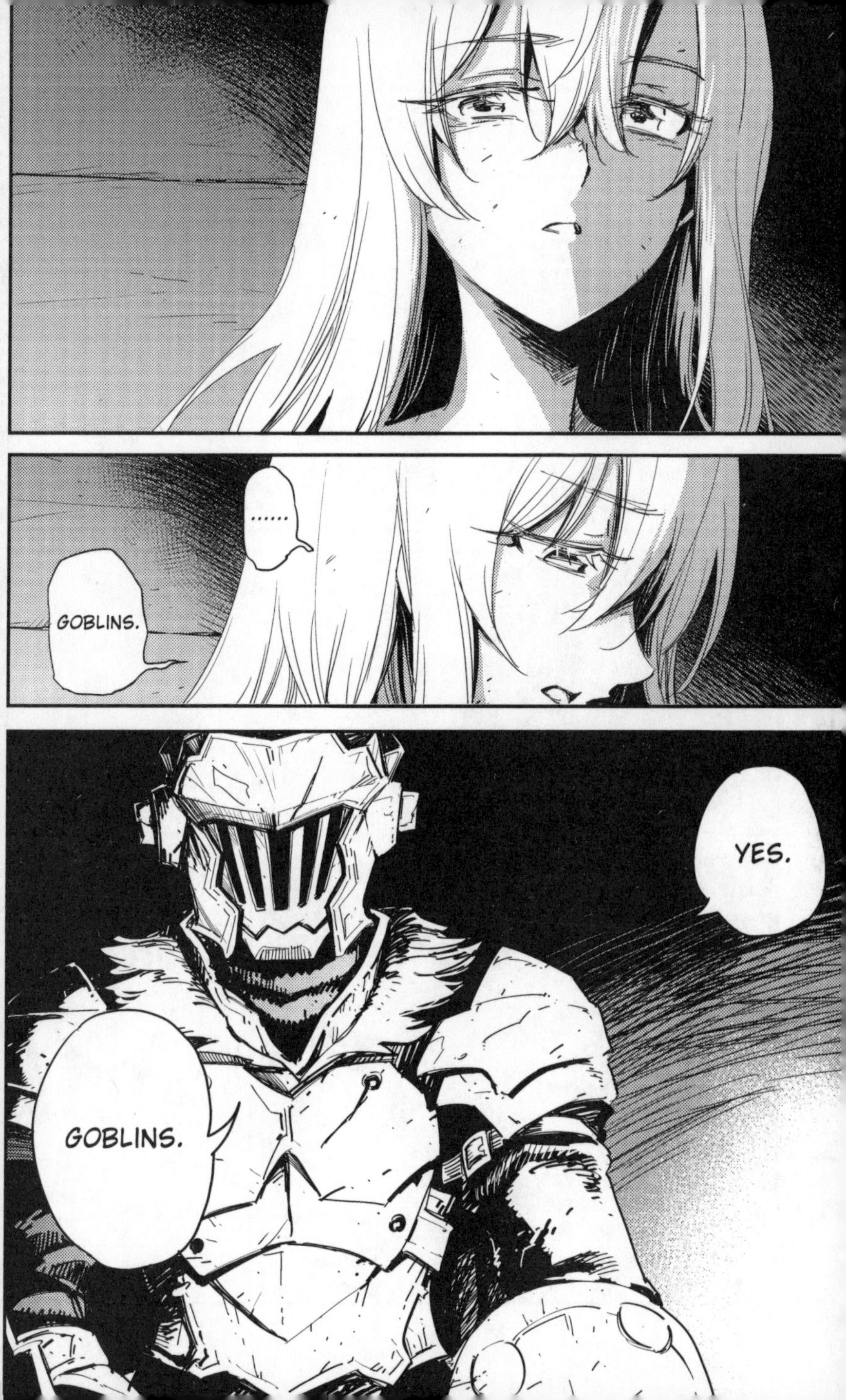
......
GOBLINS.
YES.
GOBLINS.

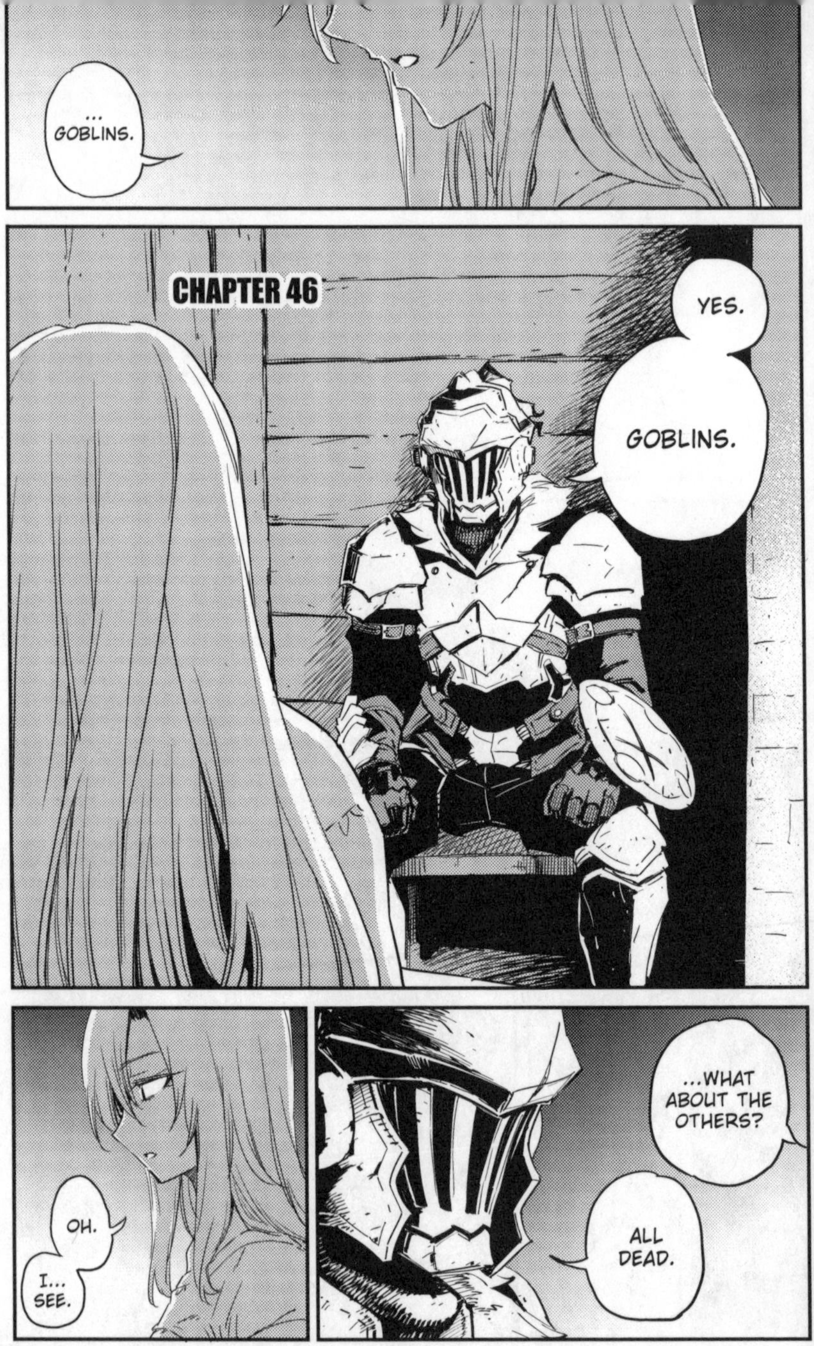
... GOBLINS.
CHAPTER 46
YES.
GOBLINS.
...WHAT ABOUT THE OTHERS?
ALL DEAD.
OH.
I... SEE.

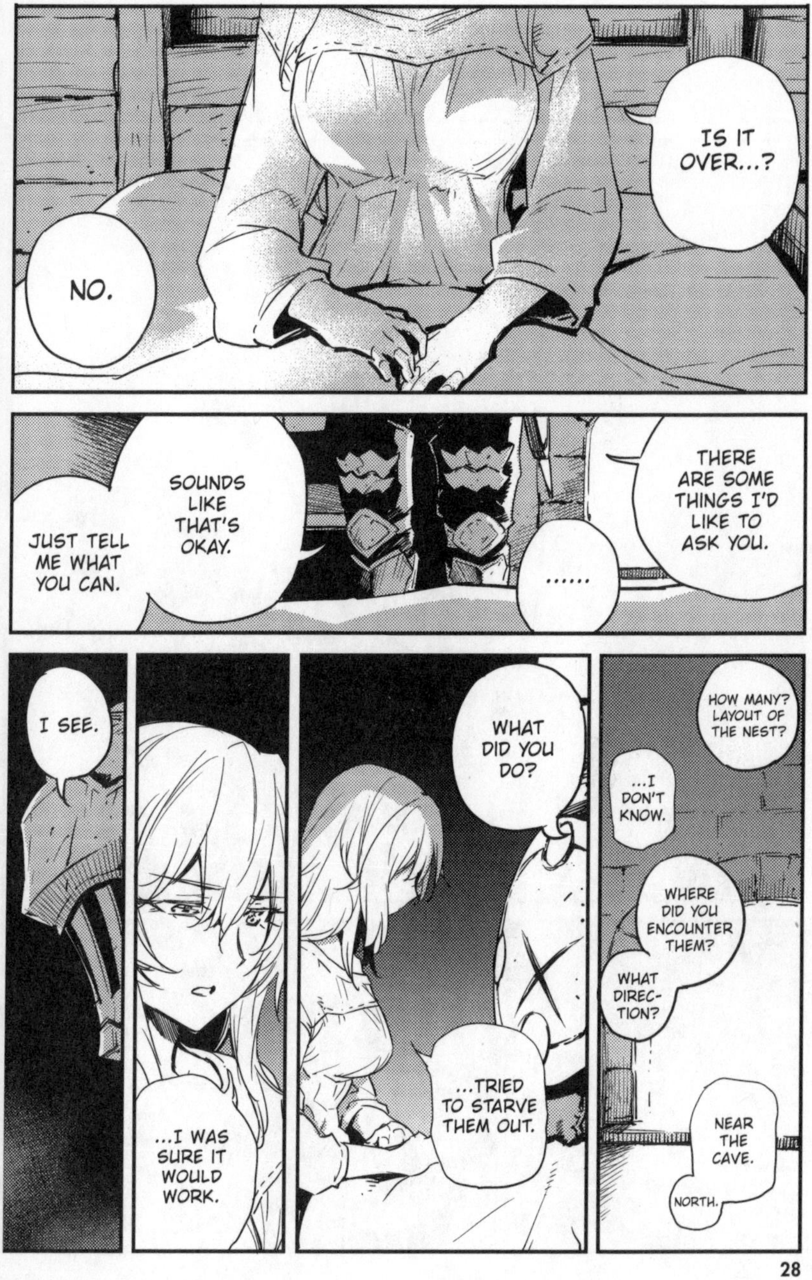
IS IT OVER...?
NO.
THERE ARE SOME THINGS I'D LIKE TO ASK YOU.
......
SOUNDS LIKE THAT'S OKAY.
JUST TELL ME WHAT YOU CAN.
HOW MANY? LAYOUT OF THE NEST?
...I DON'T KNOW.
WHERE DID YOU ENCOUNTER THEM?
WHAT DIREC-TION?
NEAR THE CAVE.
NORTH.
WHAT DID YOU DO?
...TRIED TO STARVE THEM OUT.
...I WAS SURE IT WOULD WORK.
I SEE.

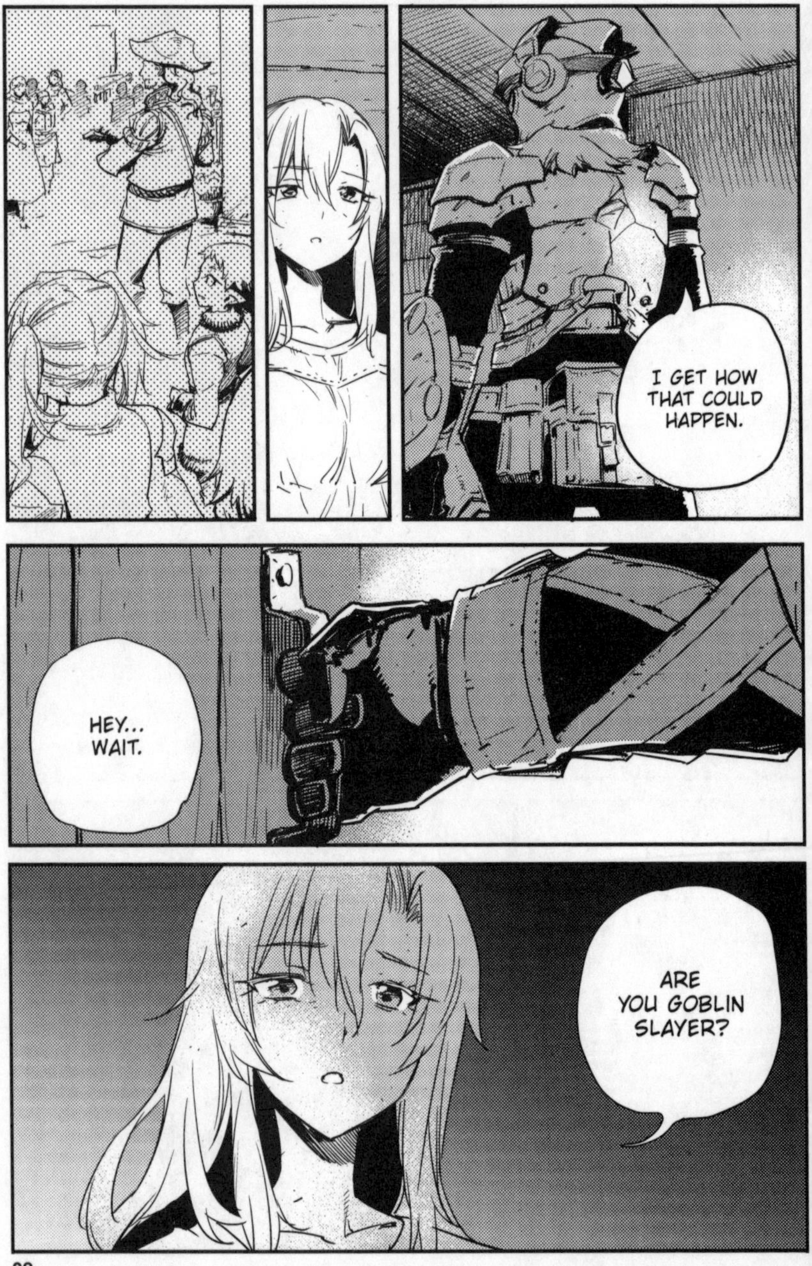
I GET HOW THAT COULD HAPPEN.
HEY... WAIT.
ARE YOU GOBLIN SLAYER?

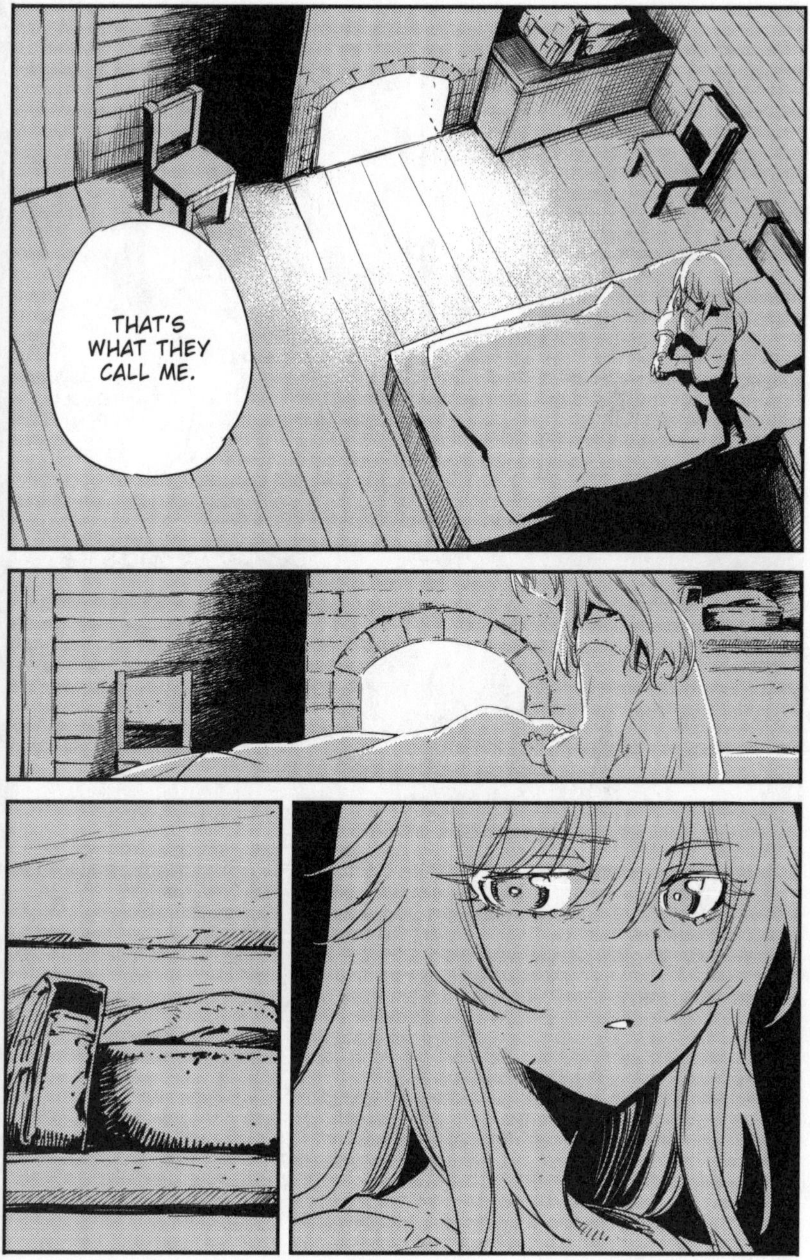
THAT'S WHAT THEY CALL ME.

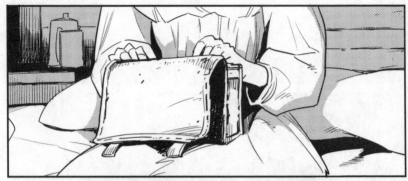

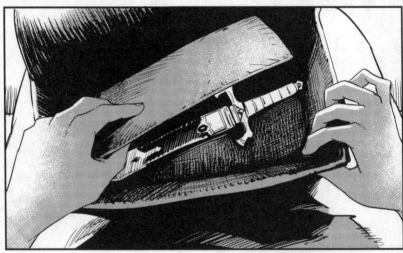

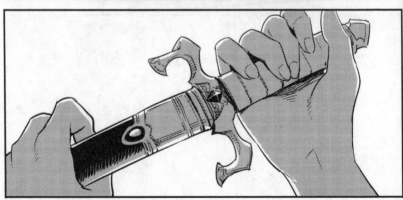

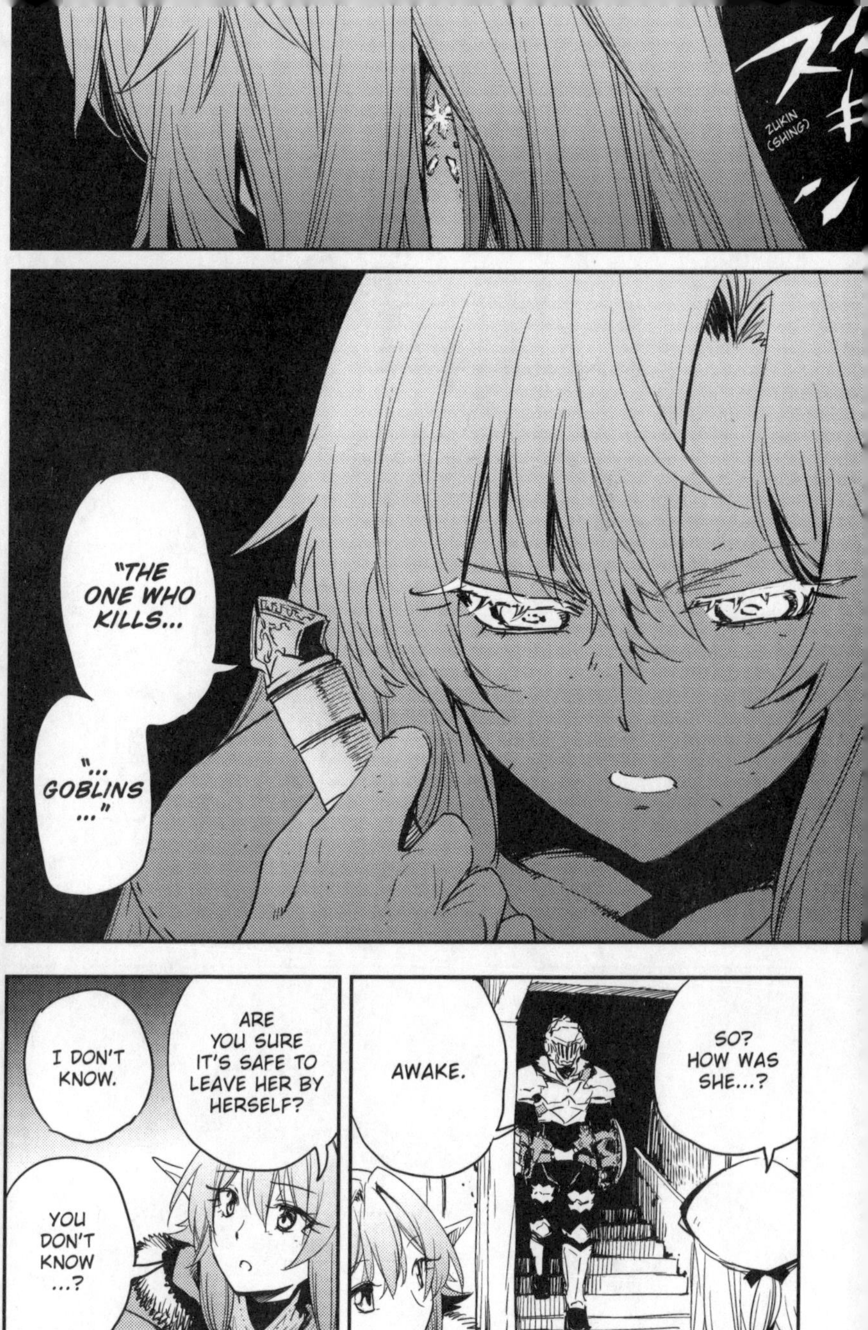
ZUKIN (SHING)
"THE ONE WHO KILLS...
"... GOBLINS ..."
SO? HOW WAS SHE...?
AWAKE.
ARE YOU SURE IT'S SAFE TO LEAVE HER BY HERSELF?
I DON'T KNOW.
YOU DON'T KNOW ...?

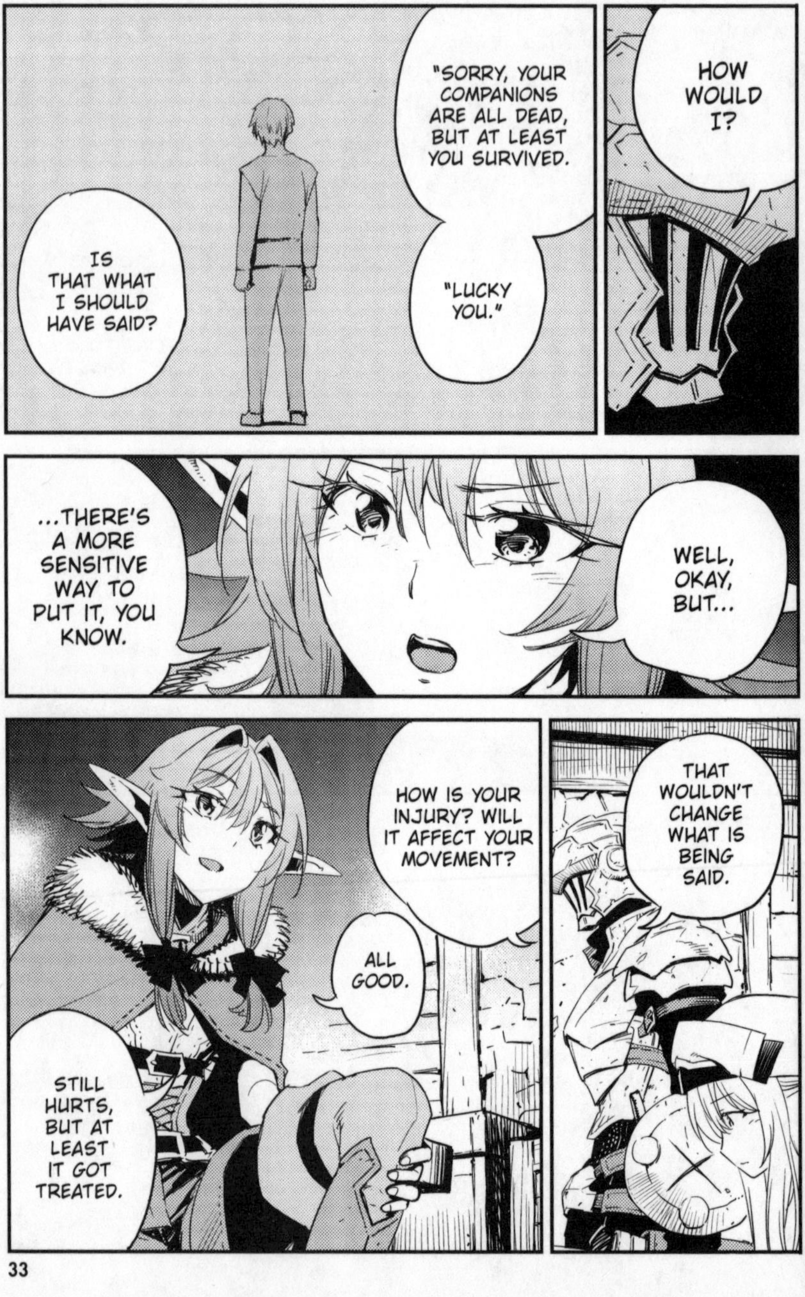
HOW WOULD I?
"SORRY, YOUR COMPANIONS ARE ALL DEAD, BUT AT LEAST YOU SURVIVED.
"LUCKY YOU."
IS THAT WHAT I SHOULD HAVE SAID?
WELL, OKAY, BUT...
...THERE'S A MORE SENSITIVE WAY TO PUT IT, YOU KNOW.
THAT WOULDN'T CHANGE WHAT IS BEING SAID.
HOW IS YOUR INJURY? WILL IT AFFECT YOUR MOVEMENT?
ALL GOOD.
STILL HURTS, BUT AT LEAST IT GOT TREATED.

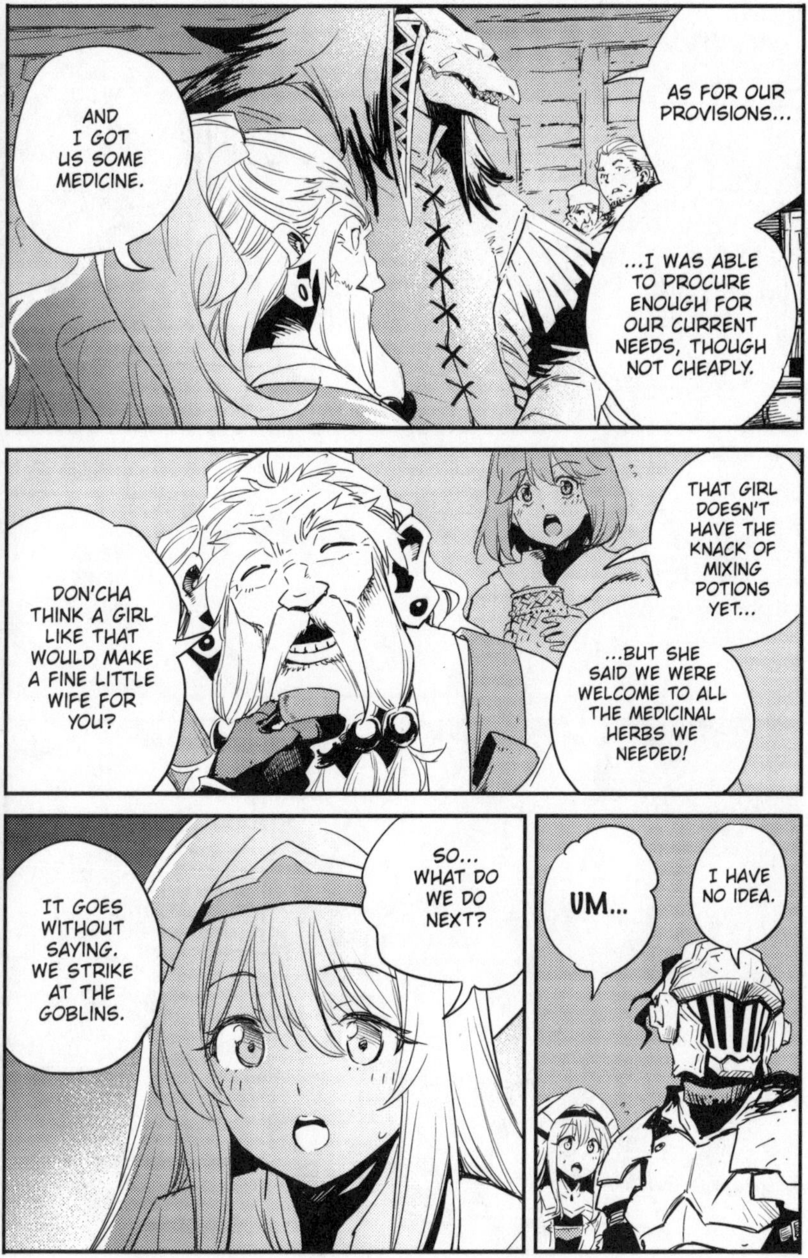
AS FOR OUR PROVISIONS...
...I WAS ABLE TO PROCURE ENOUGH FOR OUR CURRENT NEEDS, THOUGH NOT CHEAPLY.
AND I GOT US SOME MEDICINE.
THAT GIRL DOESN'T HAVE THE KNACK OF MIXING POTIONS YET...
...BUT SHE SAID WE WERE WELCOME TO ALL THE MEDICINAL HERBS WE NEEDED!
DON'CHA THINK A GIRL LIKE THAT WOULD MAKE A FINE LITTLE WIFE FOR YOU?
I HAVE NO IDEA.
UM...
SO... WHAT DO WE DO NEXT?
IT GOES WITHOUT SAYING. WE STRIKE AT THE GOBLINS.

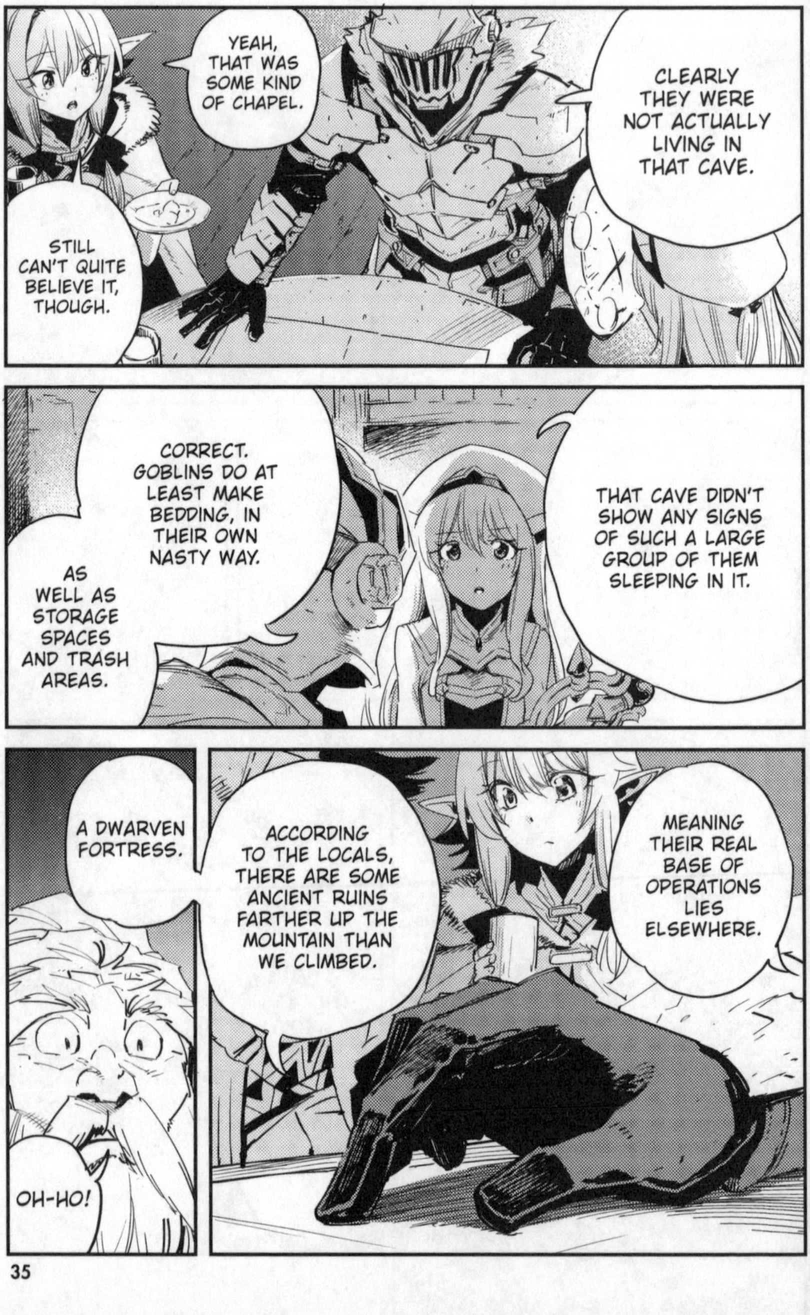
CLEARLY THEY WERE NOT ACTUALLY LIVING IN THAT CAVE.
YEAH, THAT WAS SOME KIND OF CHAPEL.
STILL CAN'T QUITE BELIEVE IT, THOUGH.
THAT CAVE DIDN'T SHOW ANY SIGNS OF SUCH A LARGE GROUP OF THEM SLEEPING IN IT.
CORRECT. GOBLINS DO AT LEAST MAKE BEDDING, IN THEIR OWN NASTY WAY.
AS WELL AS STORAGE SPACES AND TRASH AREAS.
MEANING THEIR REAL BASE OF OPERATIONS LIES ELSEWHERE.
ACCORDING TO THE LOCALS, THERE ARE SOME ANCIENT RUINS FARTHER UP THE MOUNTAIN THAN WE CLIMBED.
A DWARVEN FORTRESS.
OH-HO!

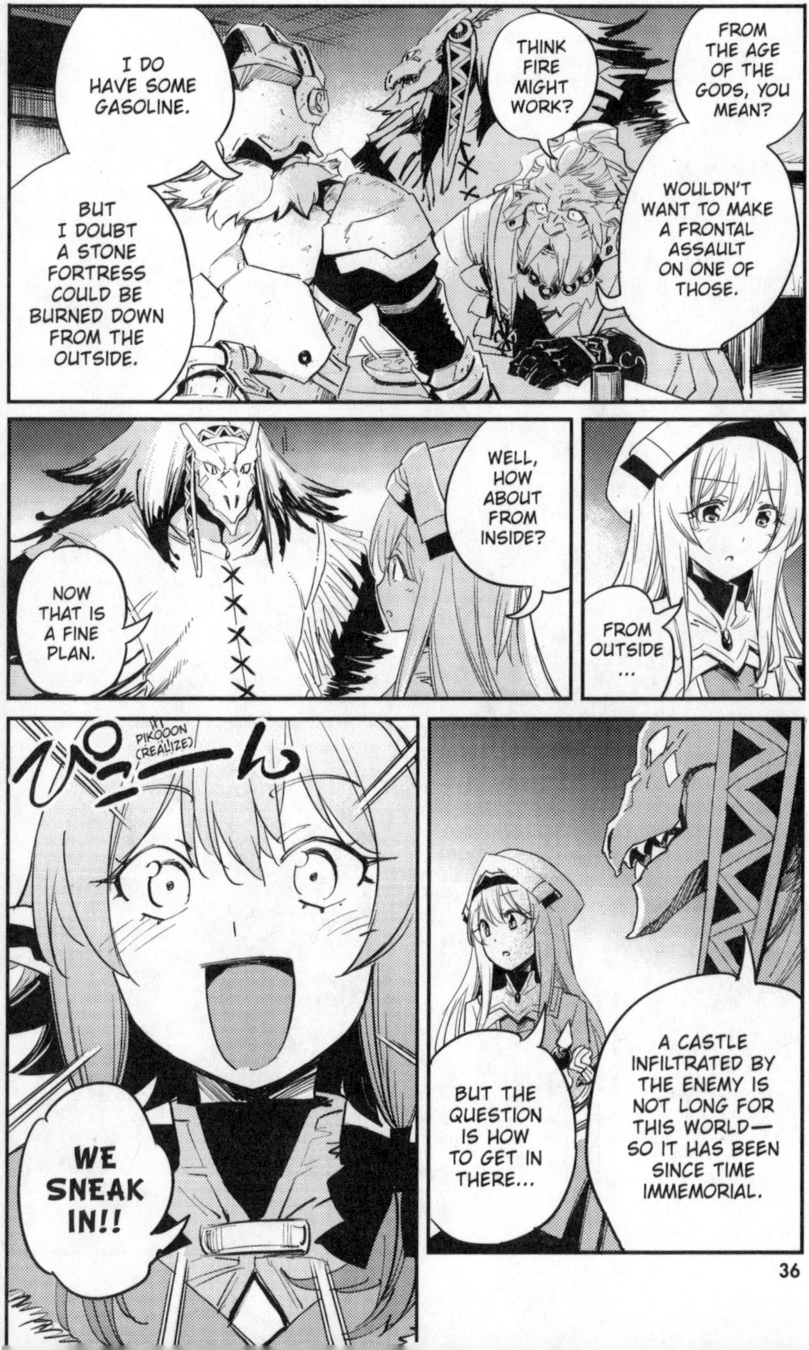
FROM THE AGE OF THE GODS, YOU MEAN?
THINK FIRE MIGHT WORK?
WOULDN'T WANT TO MAKE A FRONTAL ASSAULT ON ONE OF THOSE.
I DO HAVE SOME GASOLINE.
BUT I DOUBT A STONE FORTRESS COULD BE BURNED DOWN FROM THE OUTSIDE.
FROM OUTSIDE...
WELL, HOW ABOUT FROM INSIDE?
NOW THAT IS A FINE PLAN.
A CASTLE INFILTRATED BY THE ENEMY IS NOT LONG FOR THIS WORLD— SO IT HAS BEEN SINCE TIME IMMEMORIAL.
BUT THE QUESTION IS HOW TO GET IN THERE...
PIKOOON (REALIZE)
ぴこーん
WE SNEAK IN!!

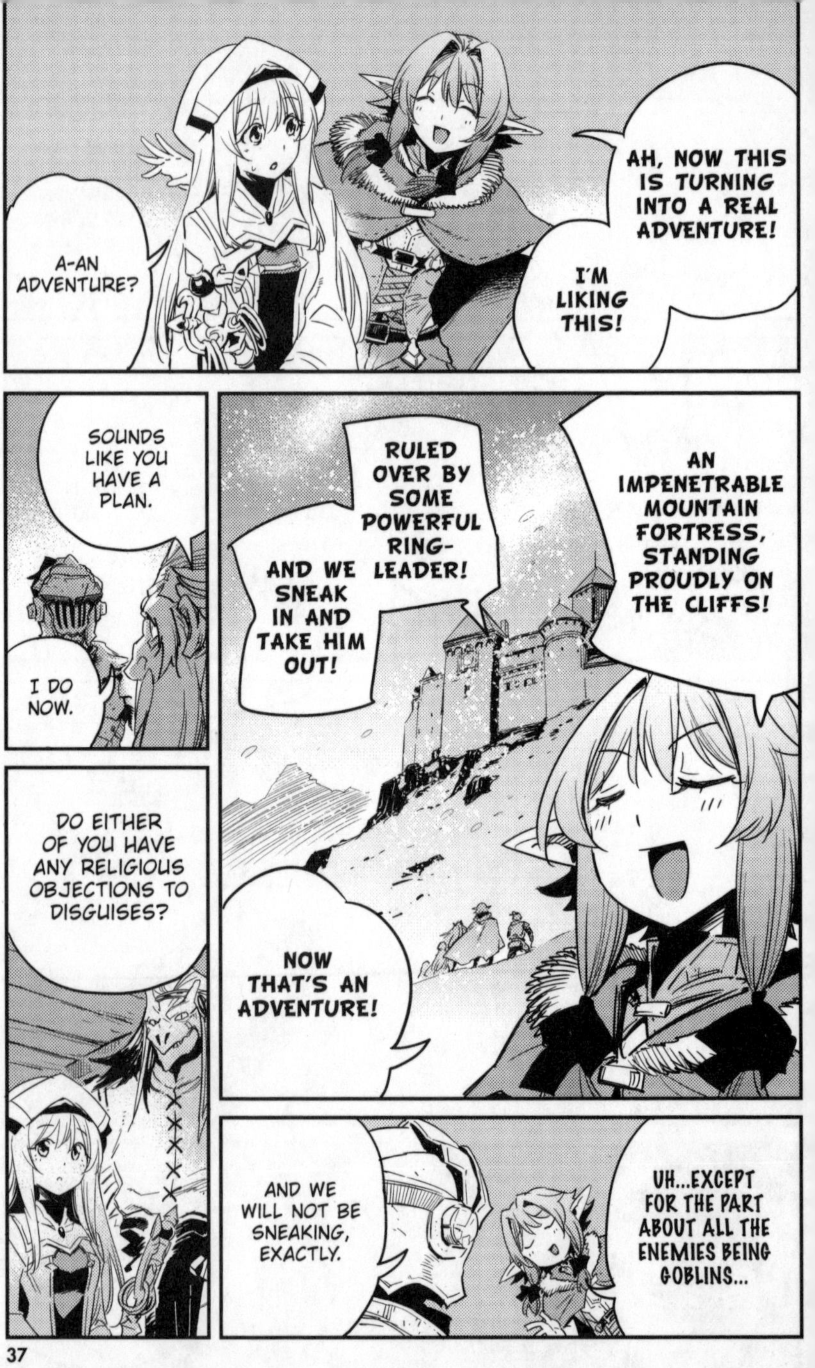
AH, NOW THIS IS TURNING INTO A REAL ADVENTURE!
I'M LIKING THIS!
A-AN ADVENTURE?
AN IMPENETRABLE MOUNTAIN FORTRESS, STANDING PROUDLY ON THE CLIFFS!
RULED OVER BY SOME POWERFUL RING-LEADER!
AND WE SNEAK IN AND TAKE HIM OUT!
NOW THAT'S AN ADVENTURE!
UH...EXCEPT FOR THE PART ABOUT ALL THE ENEMIES BEING GOBLINS...
AND WE WILL NOT BE SNEAKING, EXACTLY.
SOUNDS LIKE YOU HAVE A PLAN.
I DO NOW.
DO EITHER OF YOU HAVE ANY RELIGIOUS OBJECTIONS TO DISGUISES?

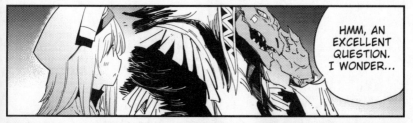

HMM, AN EXCELLENT QUESTION. I WONDER...

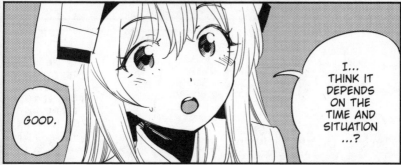

GOOD.

I... THINK IT DEPENDS ON THE TIME AND SITUATION ...?

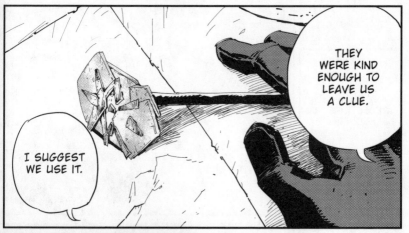

THEY WERE KIND ENOUGH TO LEAVE US A CLUE.

I SUGGEST WE USE IT.

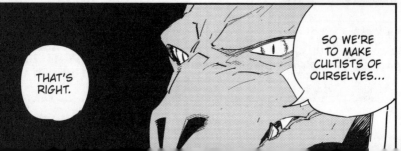

THAT'S RIGHT.

SO WE'RE TO MAKE CULTISTS OF OURSELVES...

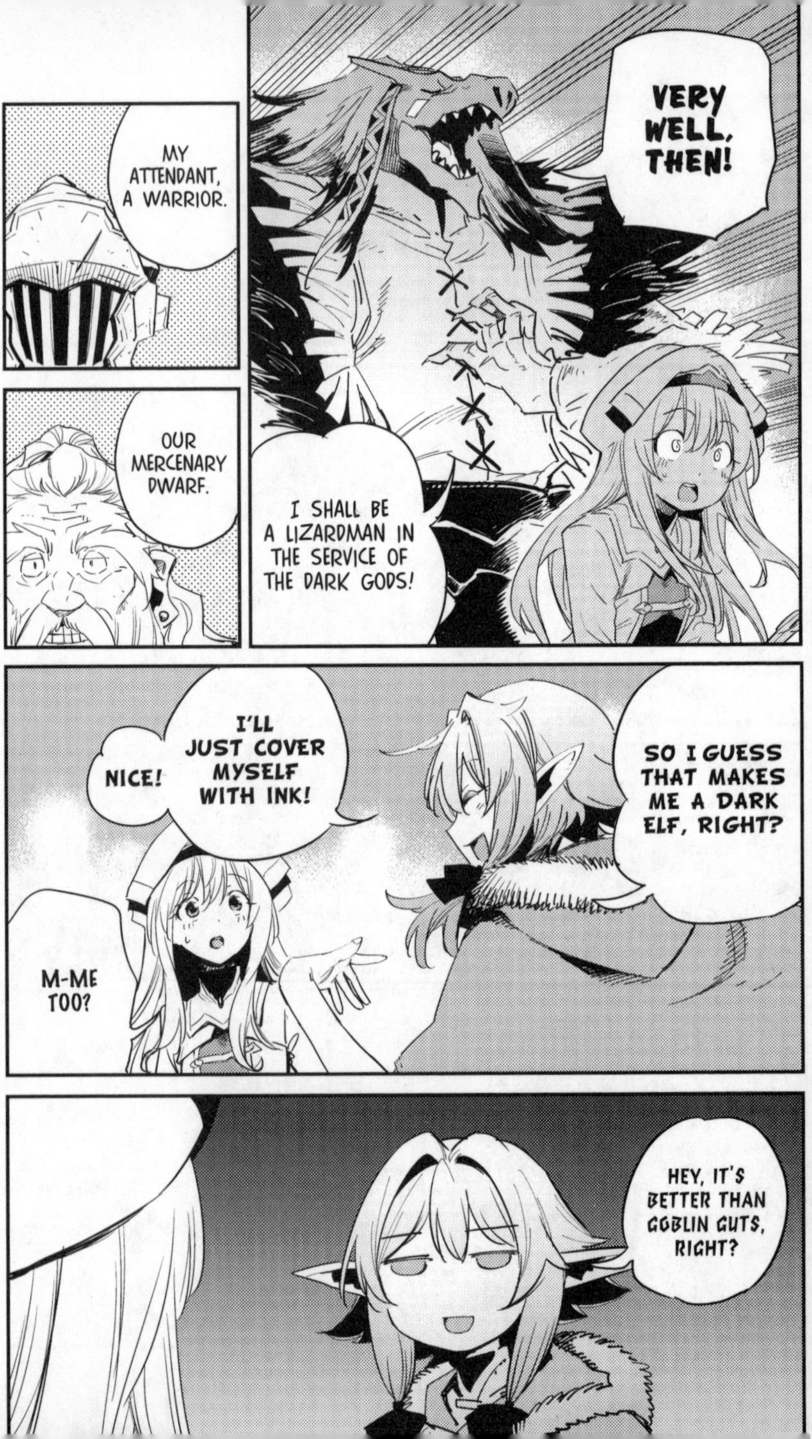
VERY WELL, THEN!
I SHALL BE A LIZARDMAN IN THE SERVICE OF THE DARK GODS!
MY ATTENDANT, A WARRIOR.
OUR MERCENARY DWARF.
SO I GUESS THAT MAKES ME A DARK ELF, RIGHT?
I'LL JUST COVER MYSELF WITH INK!
NICE!
M-ME TOO?
HEY, IT'S BETTER THAN GOBLIN GUTS, RIGHT?

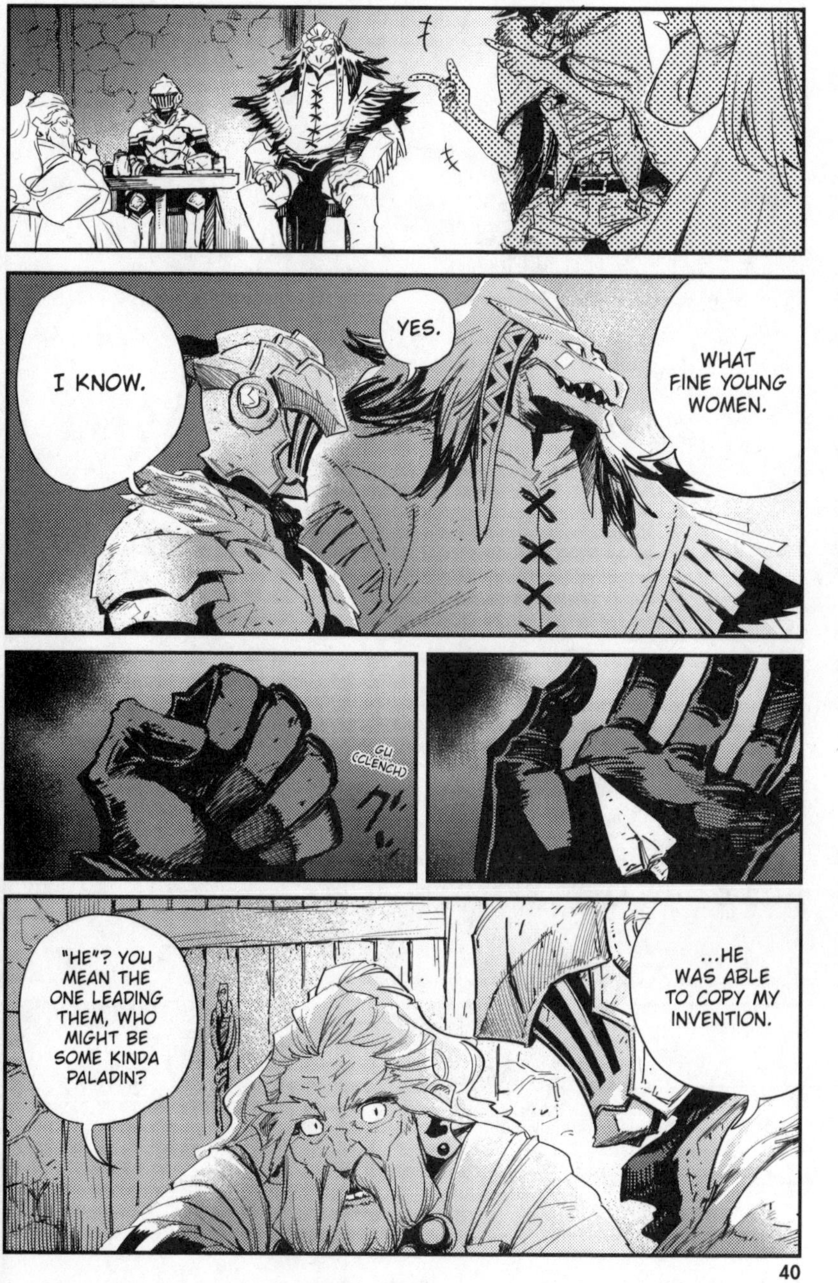
WHAT FINE YOUNG WOMEN.
YES.
I KNOW.
GU (CLENCH)
...HE WAS ABLE TO COPY MY INVENTION.
"HE"? YOU MEAN THE ONE LEADING THEM, WHO MIGHT BE SOME KINDA PALADIN?

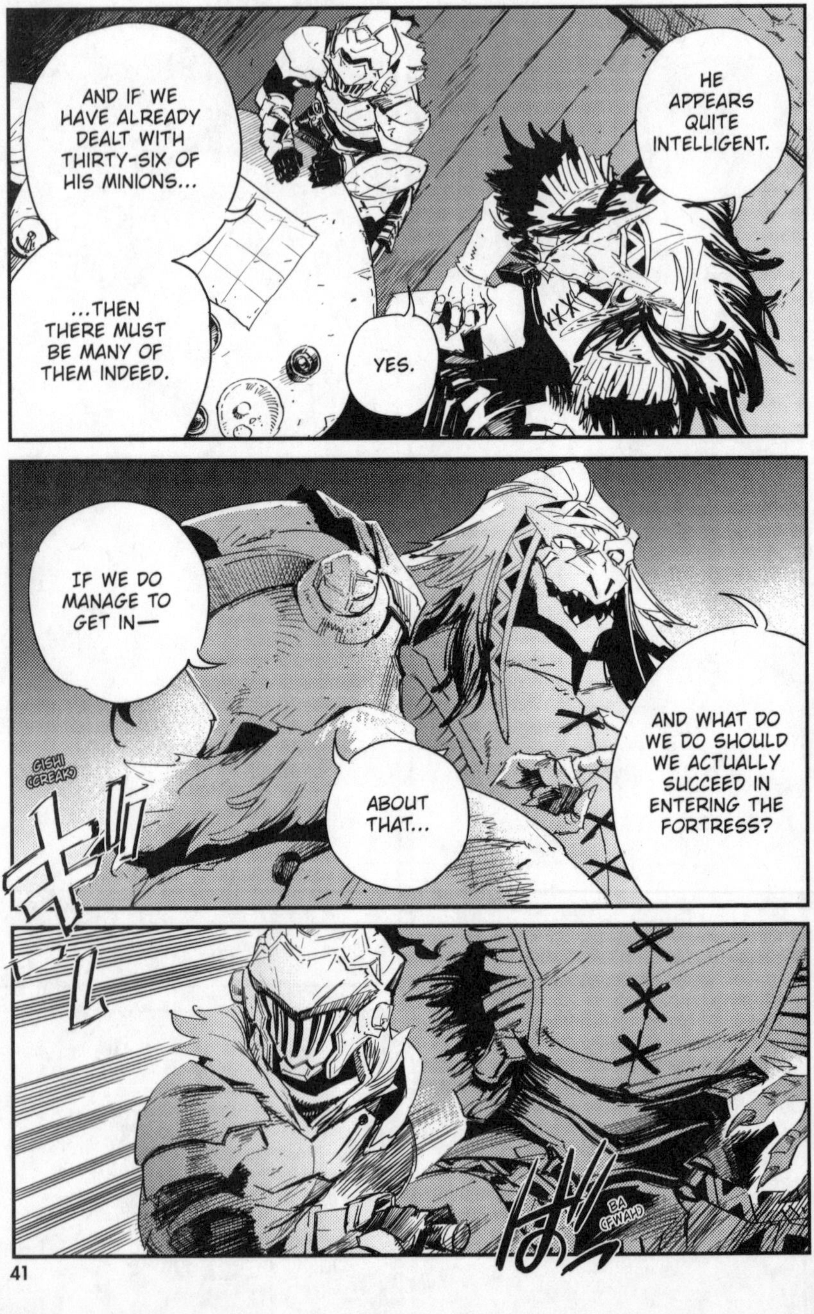
HE APPEARS QUITE INTELLIGENT.
AND IF WE HAVE ALREADY DEALT WITH THIRTY-SIX OF HIS MINIONS...
YES.
...THEN THERE MUST BE MANY OF THEM INDEED.
IF WE DO MANAGE TO GET IN—
AND WHAT DO WE DO SHOULD WE ACTUALLY SUCCEED IN ENTERING THE FORTRESS?
ABOUT THAT...
GISHI (CREAK)
BA (FWAH)

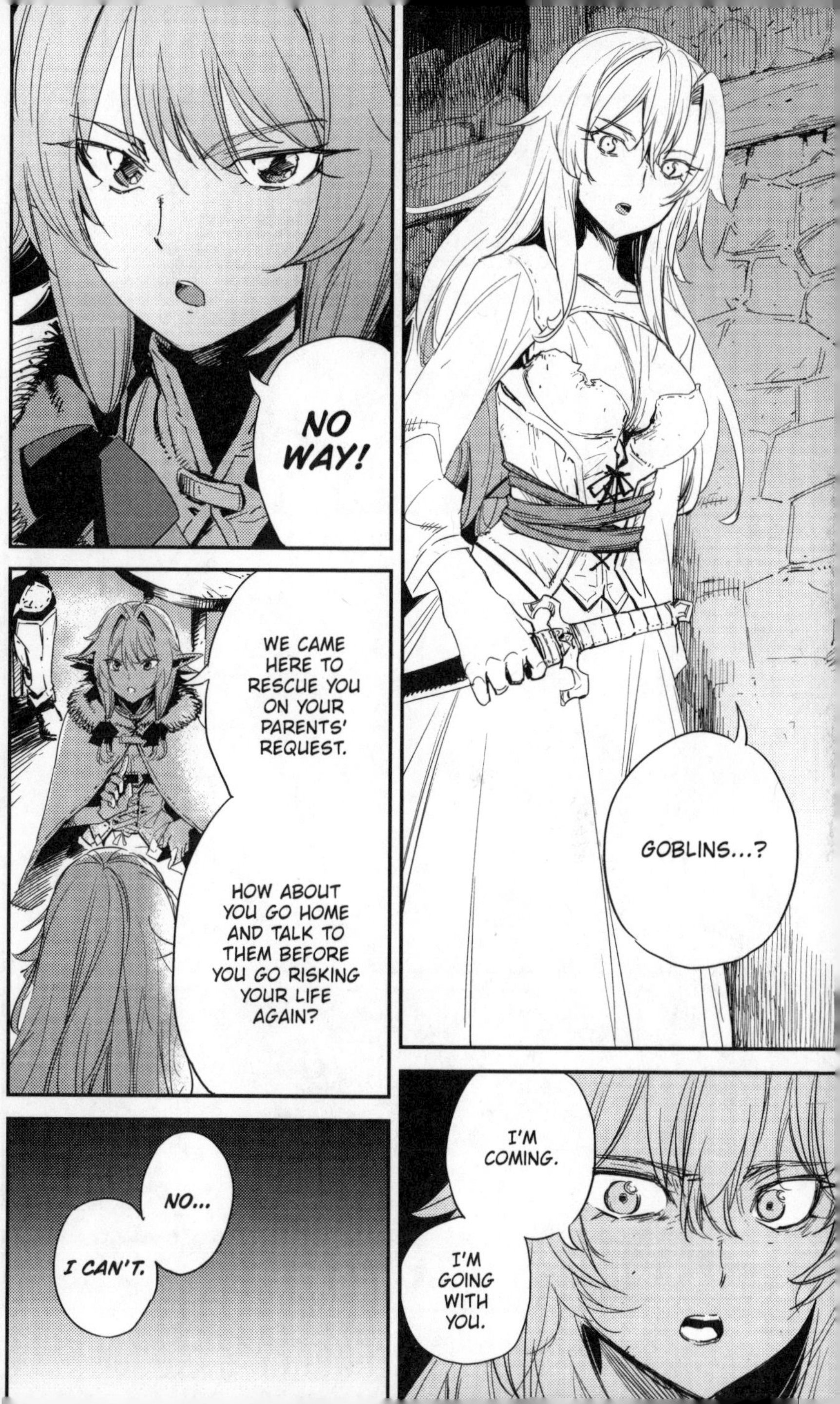
GOBLINS...?
NO WAY!
WE CAME HERE TO RESCUE YOU ON YOUR PARENTS' REQUEST.
HOW ABOUT YOU GO HOME AND TALK TO THEM BEFORE YOU GO RISKING YOUR LIFE AGAIN?
I'M COMING.
I'M GOING WITH YOU.
NO...
I CAN'T.

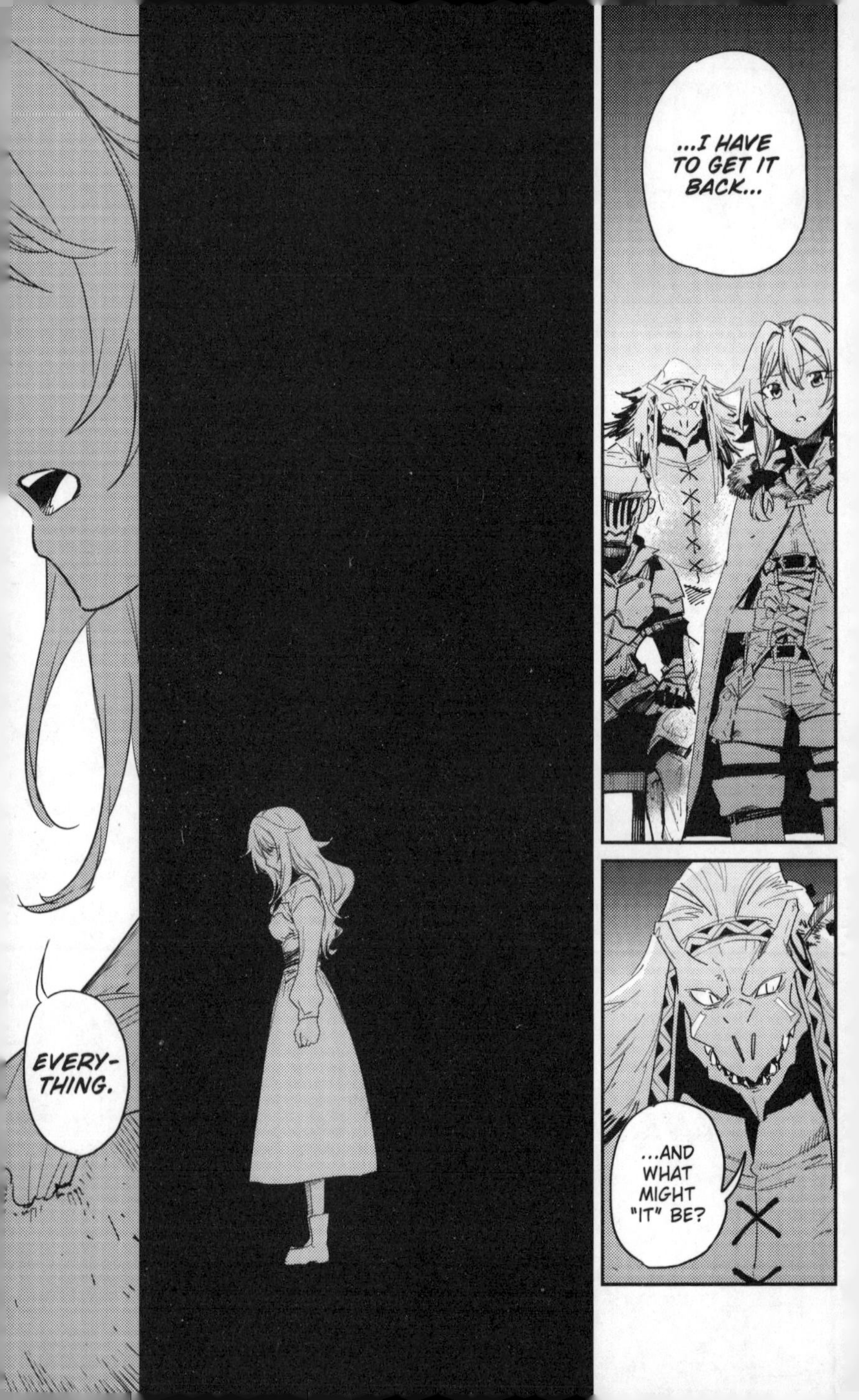
...I HAVE TO GET IT BACK...
...AND WHAT MIGHT "IT" BE?
EVERY-THING.

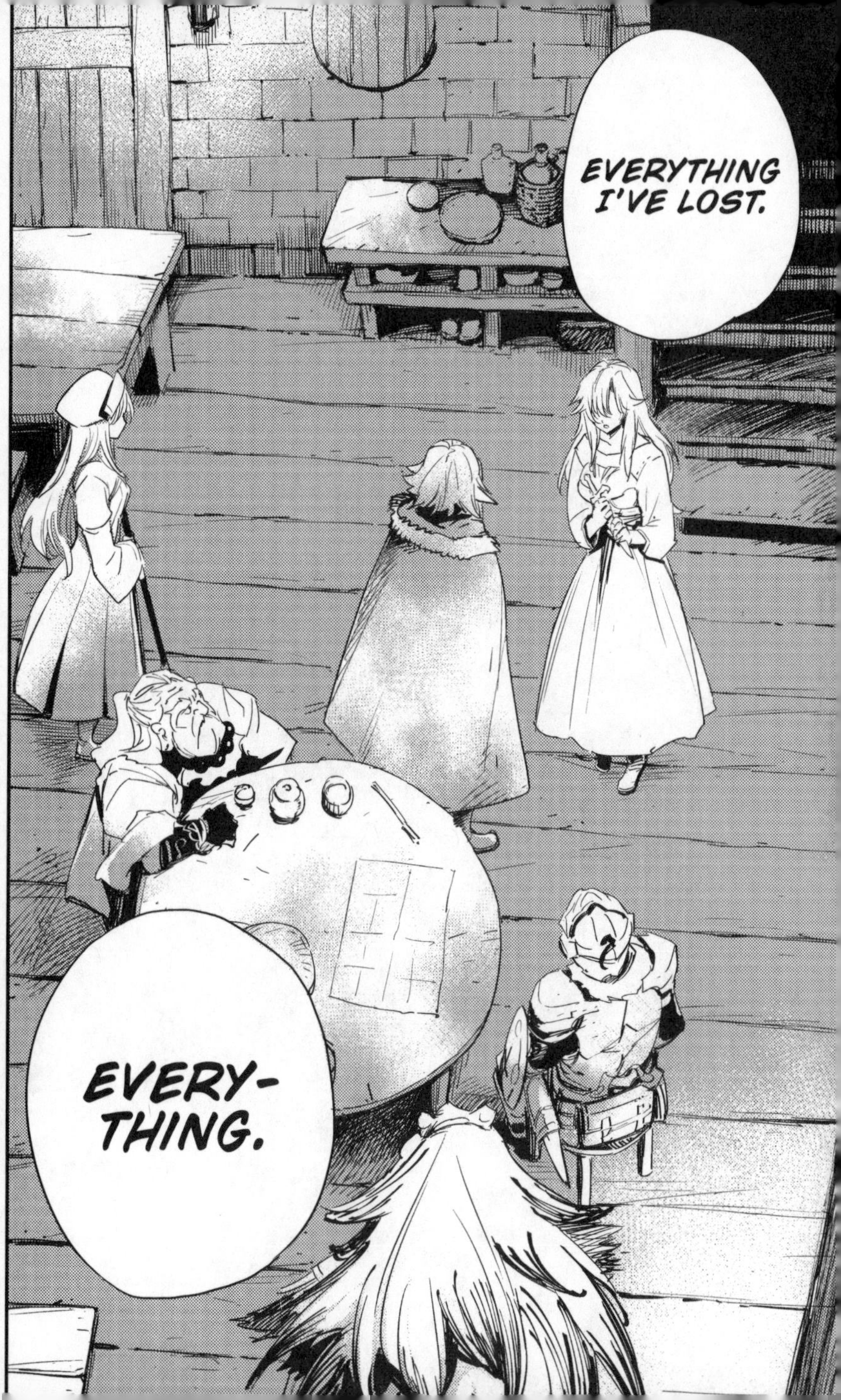
EVERYTHING I'VE LOST.
EVERY-THING.

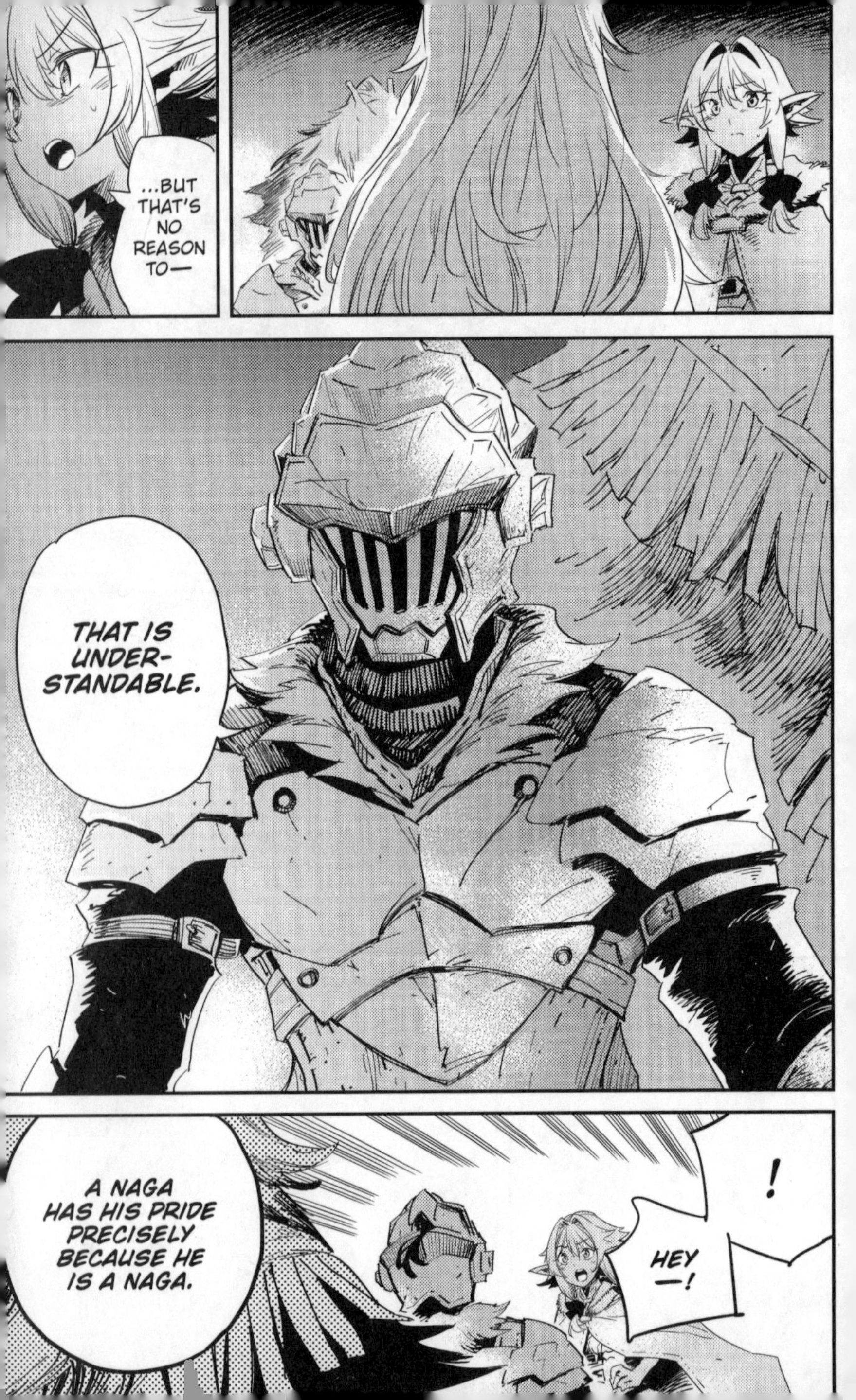
...BUT THAT'S NO REASON TO—
THAT IS UNDER-STANDABLE.
!
HEY—!
A NAGA HAS HIS PRIDE PRECISELY BECAUSE HE IS A NAGA.

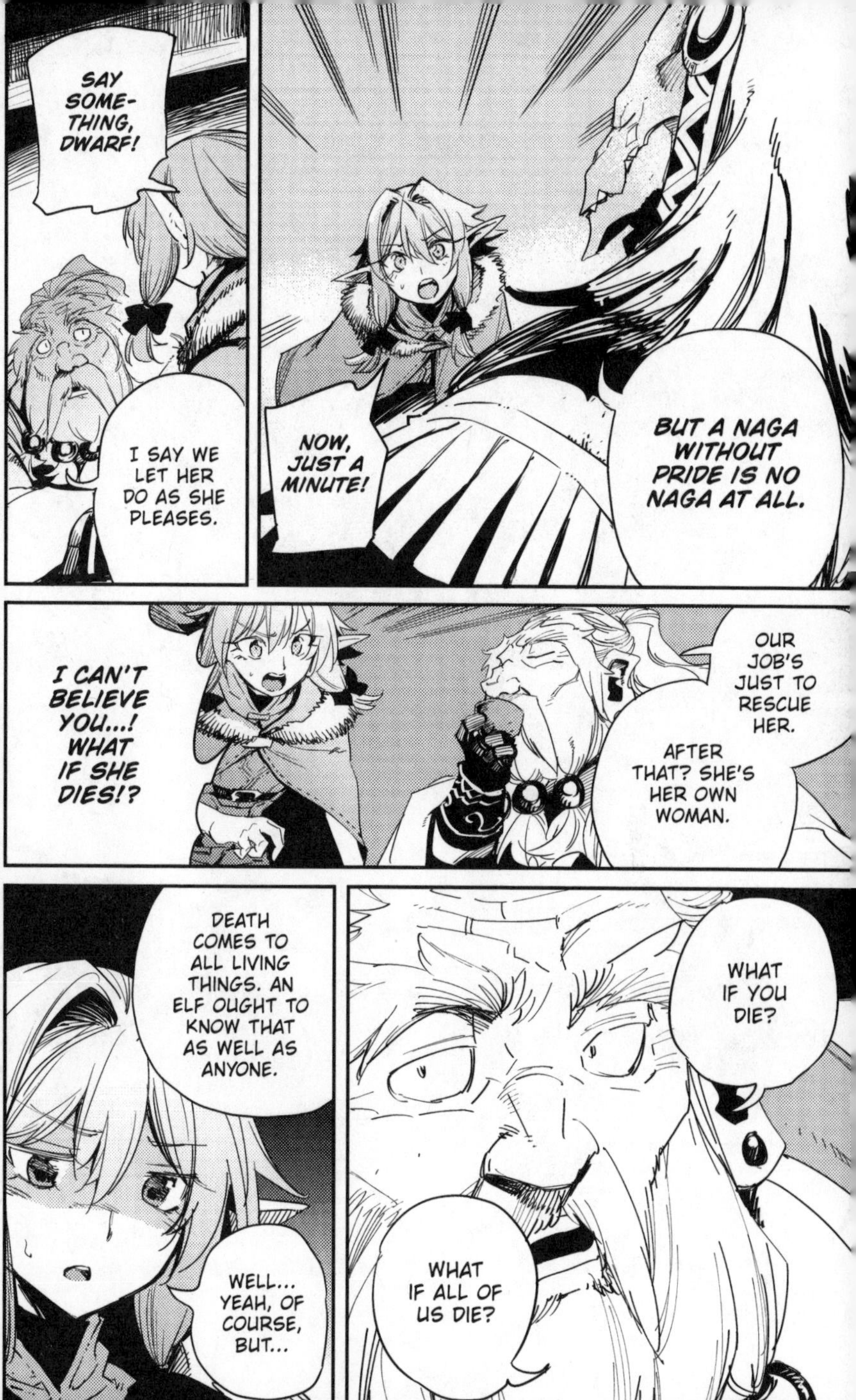
BUT A NAGA WITHOUT PRIDE IS NO NAGA AT ALL.
NOW, JUST A MINUTE!
SAY SOMETHING, DWARF!
I SAY WE LET HER DO AS SHE PLEASES.
OUR JOB'S JUST TO RESCUE HER.
AFTER THAT? SHE'S HER OWN WOMAN.
I CAN'T BELIEVE YOU...! WHAT IF SHE DIES!?
WHAT IF YOU DIE?
WHAT IF ALL OF US DIE?
DEATH COMES TO ALL LIVING THINGS. AN ELF OUGHT TO KNOW THAT AS WELL AS ANYONE.
WELL... YEAH, OF COURSE, BUT...

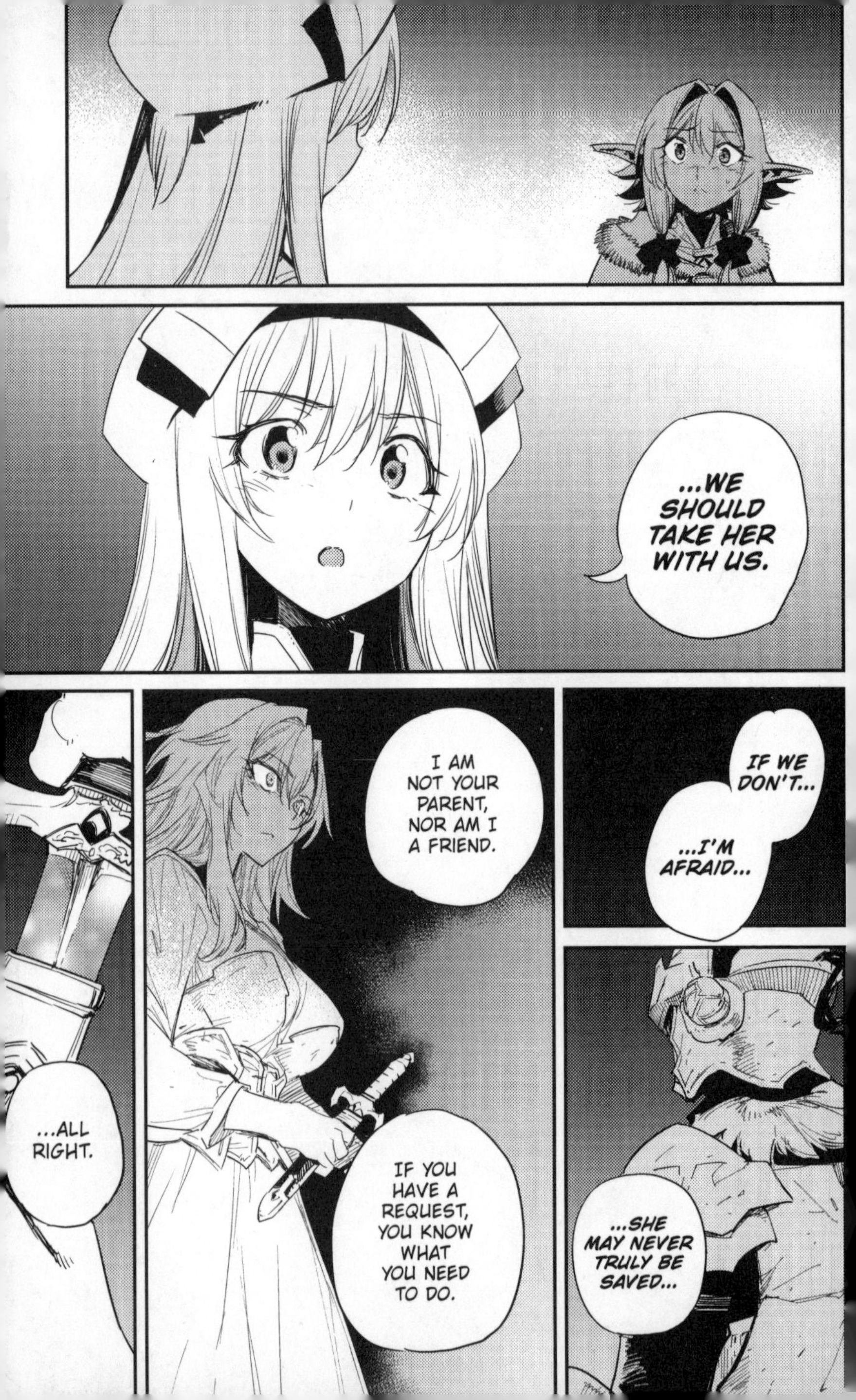
...WE SHOULD TAKE HER WITH US.
IF WE DON'T...
...I'M AFRAID...
...SHE MAY NEVER TRULY BE SAVED...
I AM NOT YOUR PARENT, NOR AM I A FRIEND.
IF YOU HAVE A REQUEST, YOU KNOW WHAT YOU NEED TO DO.
...ALL RIGHT.

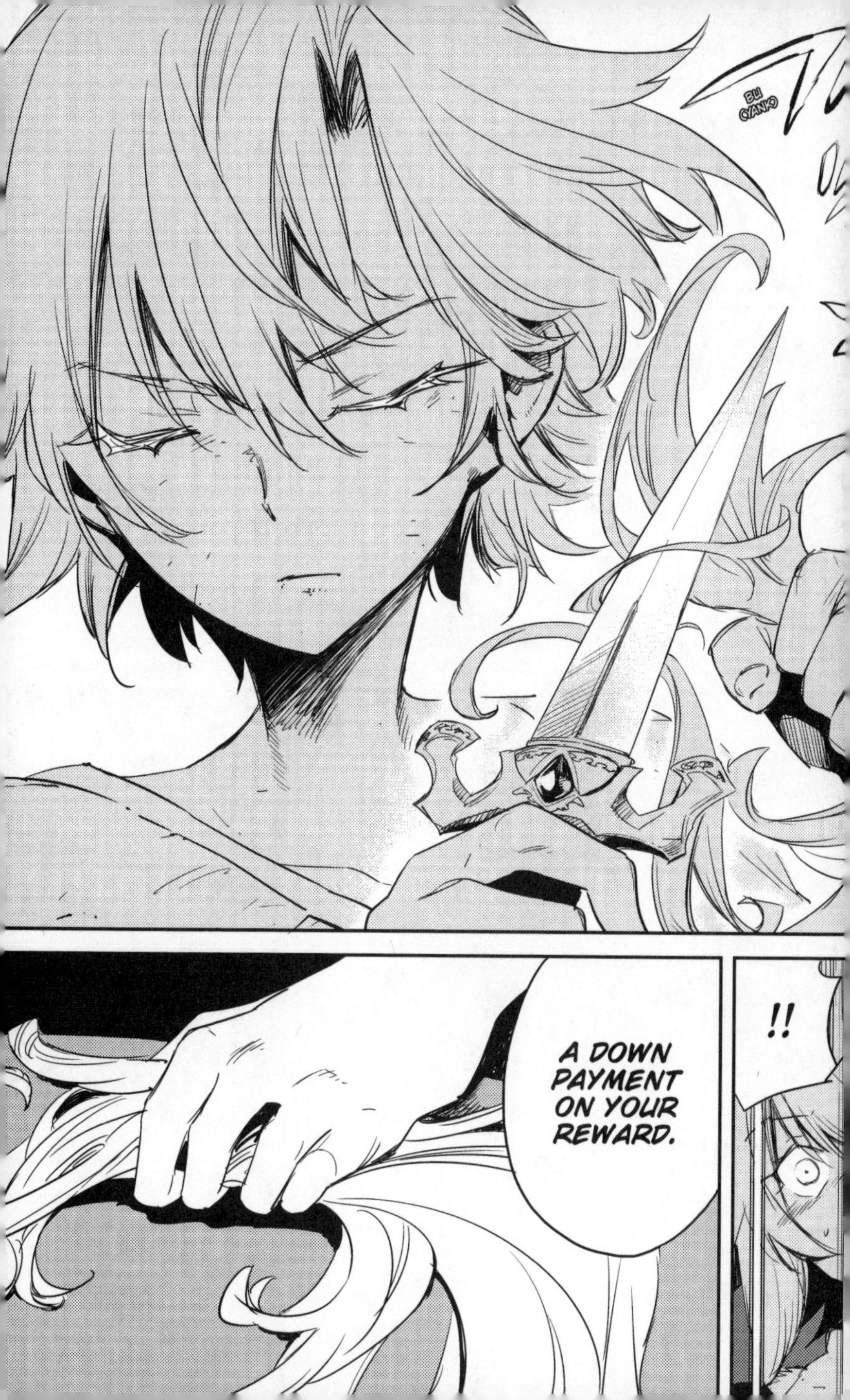
BU (YANK)
!!
A DOWN PAYMENT ON YOUR REWARD.

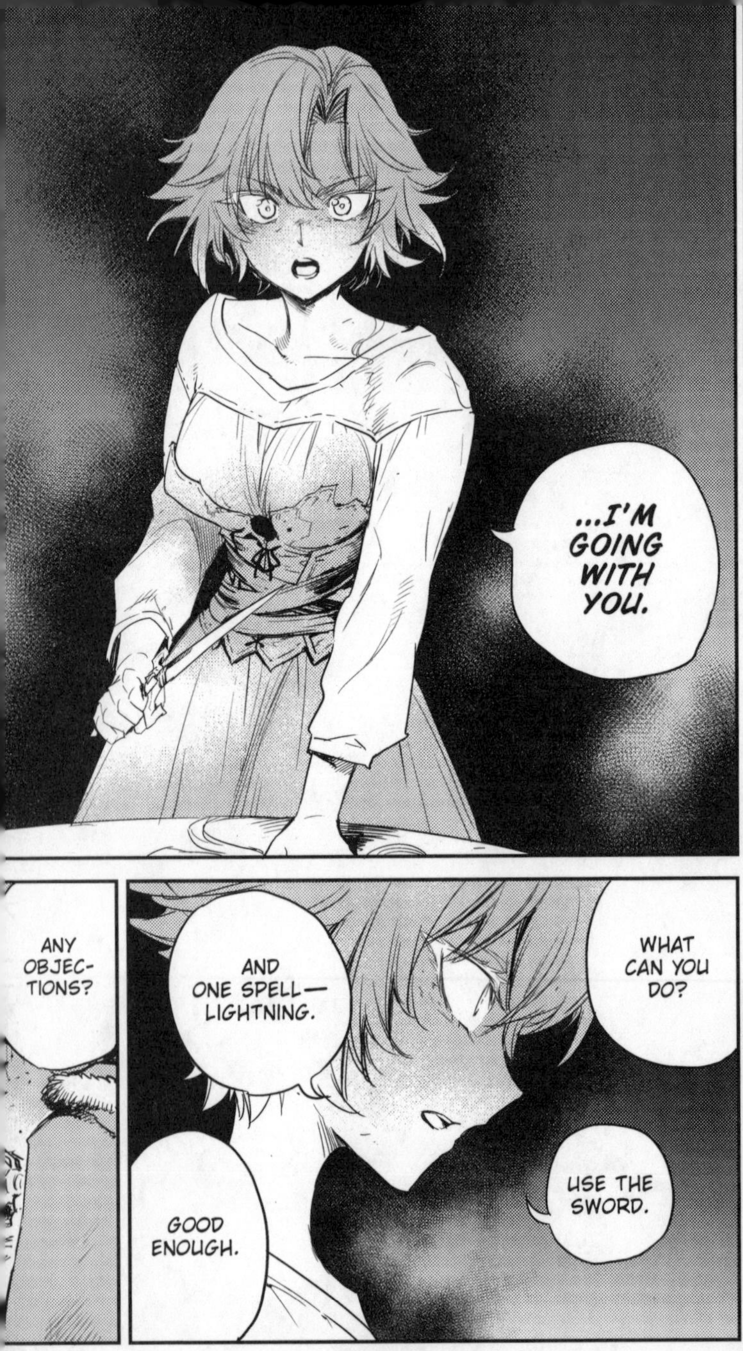
...I'M GOING WITH YOU.
WHAT CAN YOU DO?
USE THE SWORD.
AND ONE SPELL—LIGHTNING.
GOOD ENOUGH.
ANY OBJECTIONS?

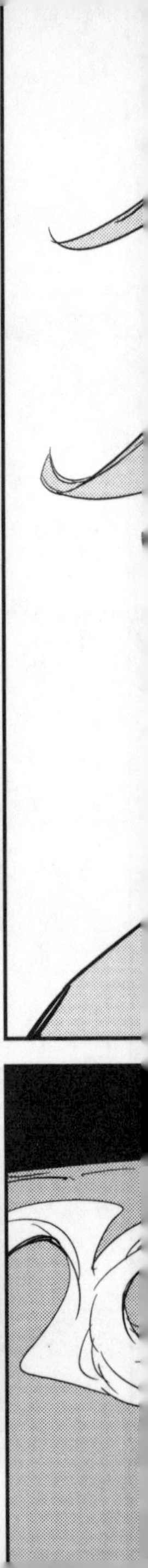

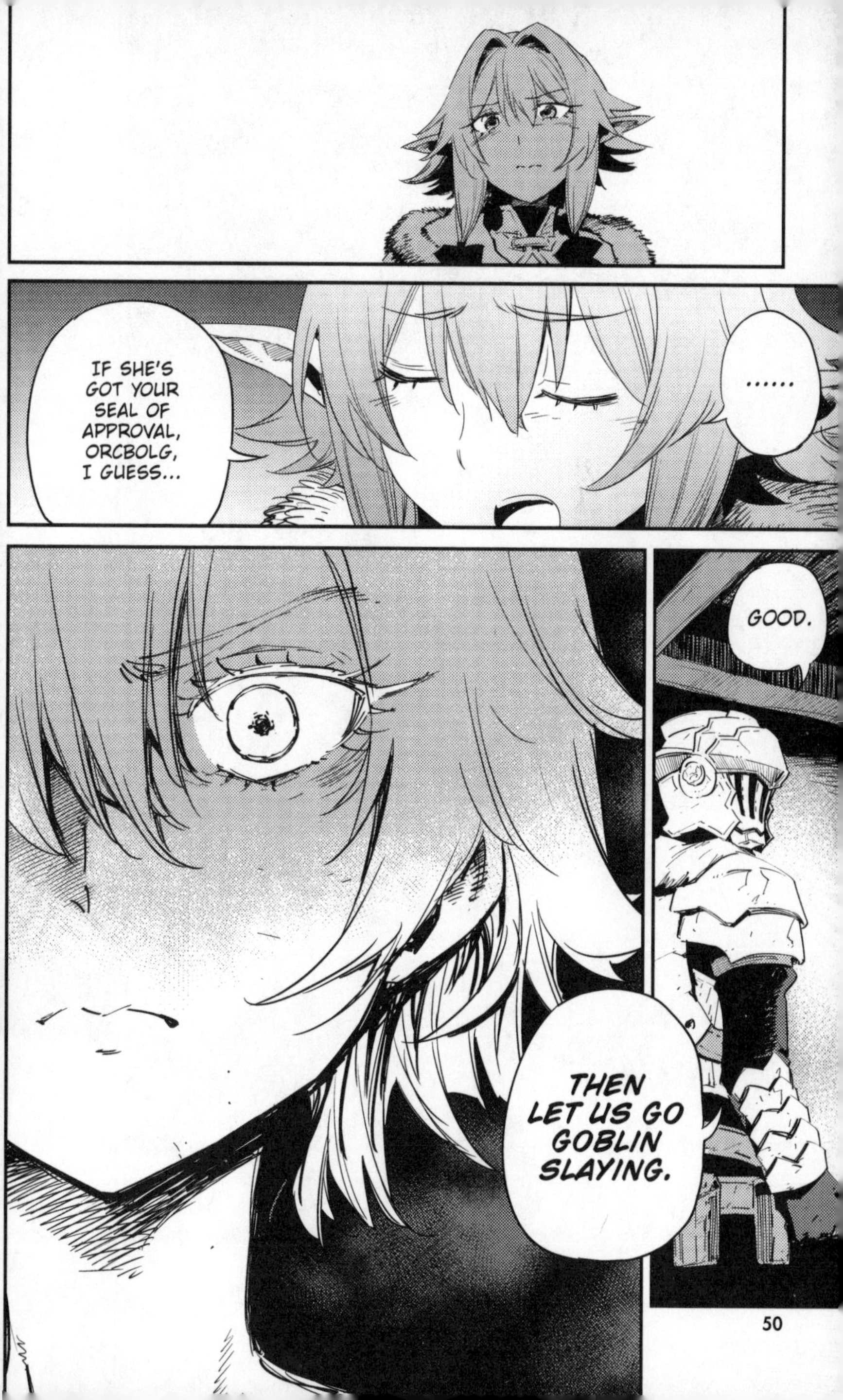
......
IF SHE'S GOT YOUR SEAL OF APPROVAL, ORCBOLG, I GUESS...
GOOD.
THEN LET US GO GOBLIN SLAYING.

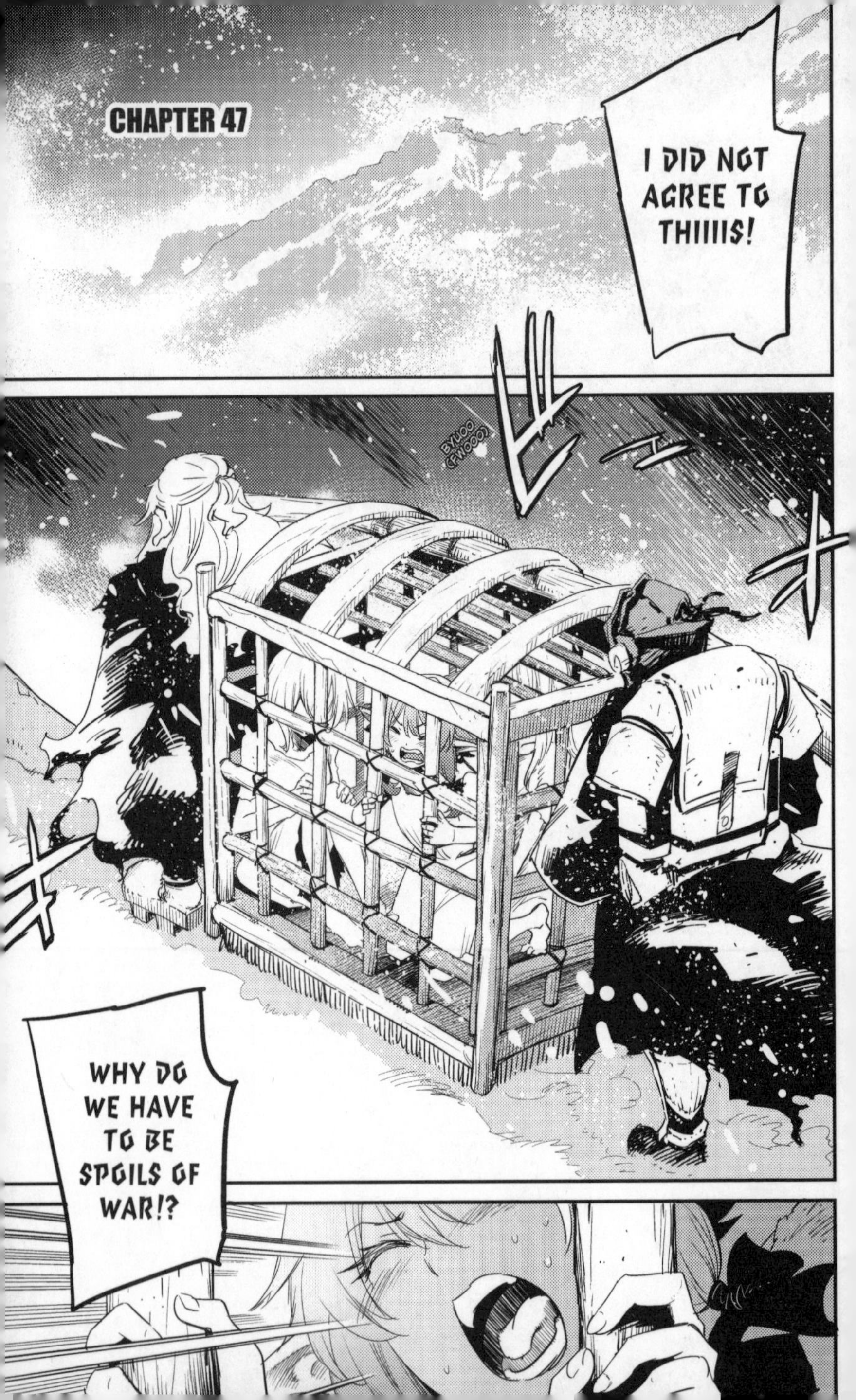
CHAPTER 47
I DID NOT AGREE TO THIIIIS!
BYUOO (FWOOO)
WHY DO WE HAVE TO BE SPOILS OF WAR!?

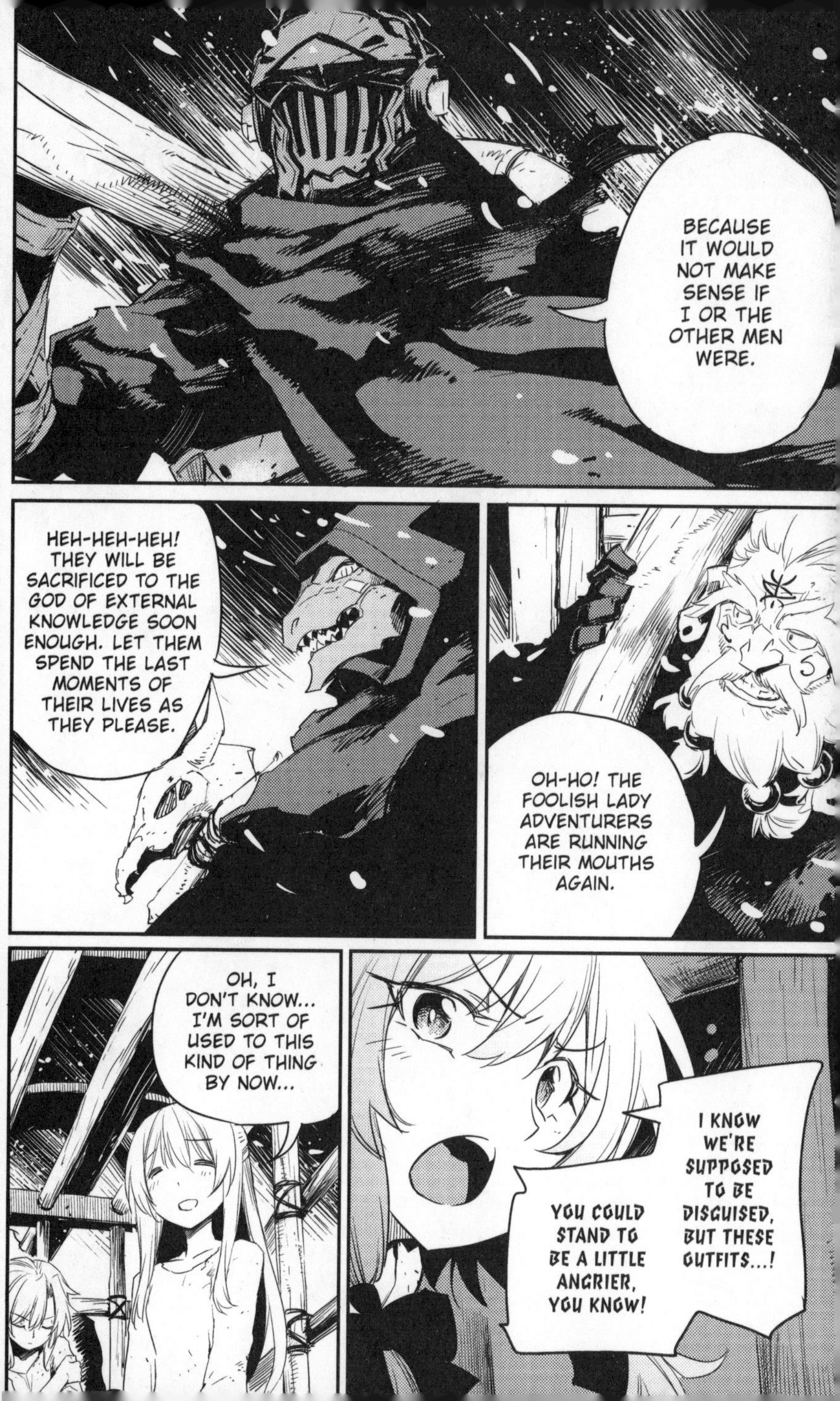
BECAUSE IT WOULD NOT MAKE SENSE IF I OR THE OTHER MEN WERE.
OH-HO! THE FOOLISH LADY ADVENTURERS ARE RUNNING THEIR MOUTHS AGAIN.
HEH-HEH-HEH! THEY WILL BE SACRIFICED TO THE GOD OF EXTERNAL KNOWLEDGE SOON ENOUGH. LET THEM SPEND THE LAST MOMENTS OF THEIR LIVES AS THEY PLEASE.
I KNOW WE'RE SUPPOSED TO BE DISGUISED, BUT THESE OUTFITS...!
YOU COULD STAND TO BE A LITTLE ANGRIER, YOU KNOW!
OH, I DON'T KNOW... I'M SORT OF USED TO THIS KIND OF THING BY NOW...

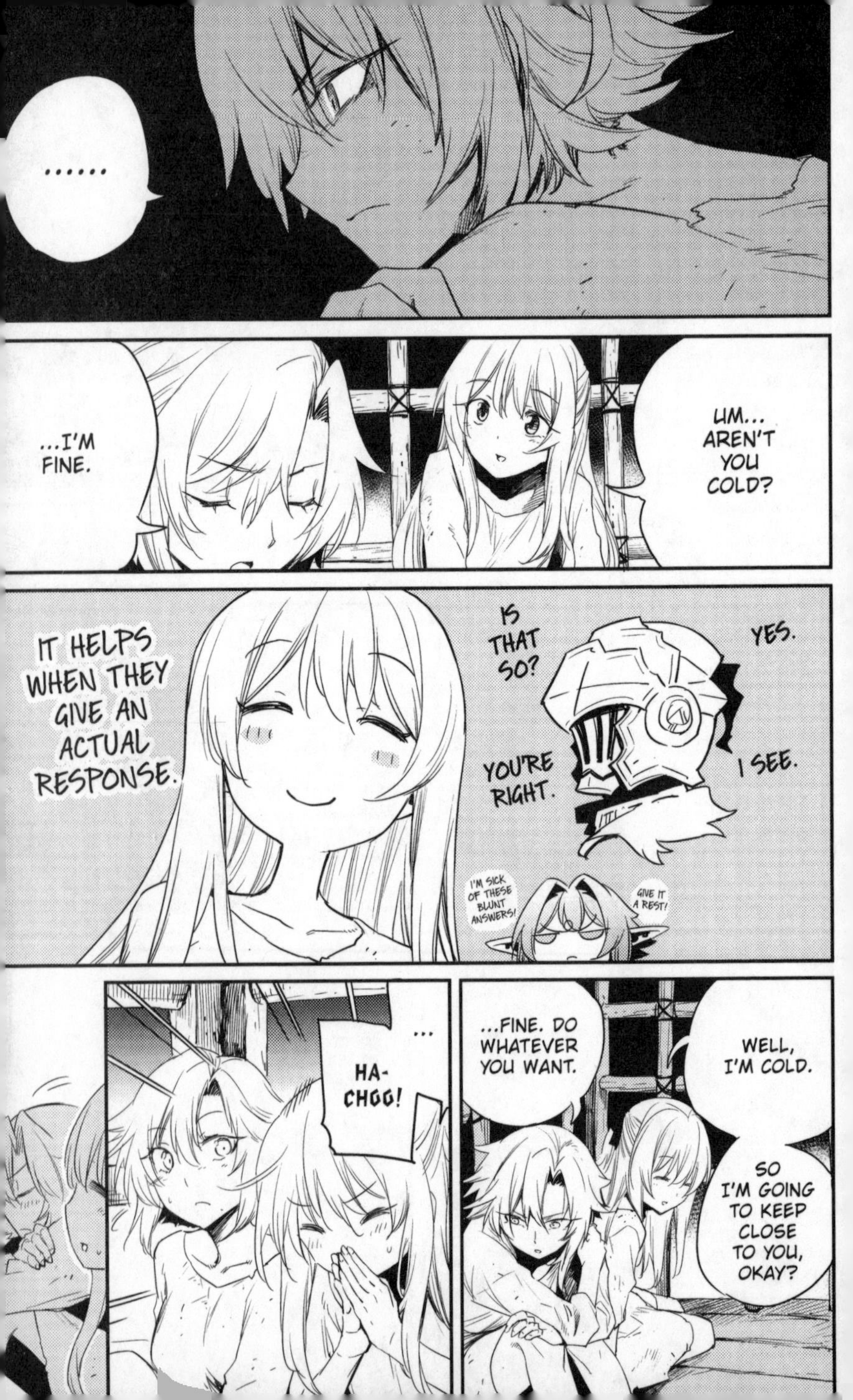
......
UM... AREN'T YOU COLD?
...I'M FINE.
YES.
IS THAT SO?
I SEE.
YOU'RE RIGHT.
IT HELPS WHEN THEY GIVE AN ACTUAL RESPONSE.
GIVE IT A REST!
I'M SICK OF THESE BLUNT ANSWERS!
WELL, I'M COLD.
SO I'M GOING TO KEEP CLOSE TO YOU, OKAY?
...FINE. DO WHATEVER YOU WANT.
...
HA-CHOO!

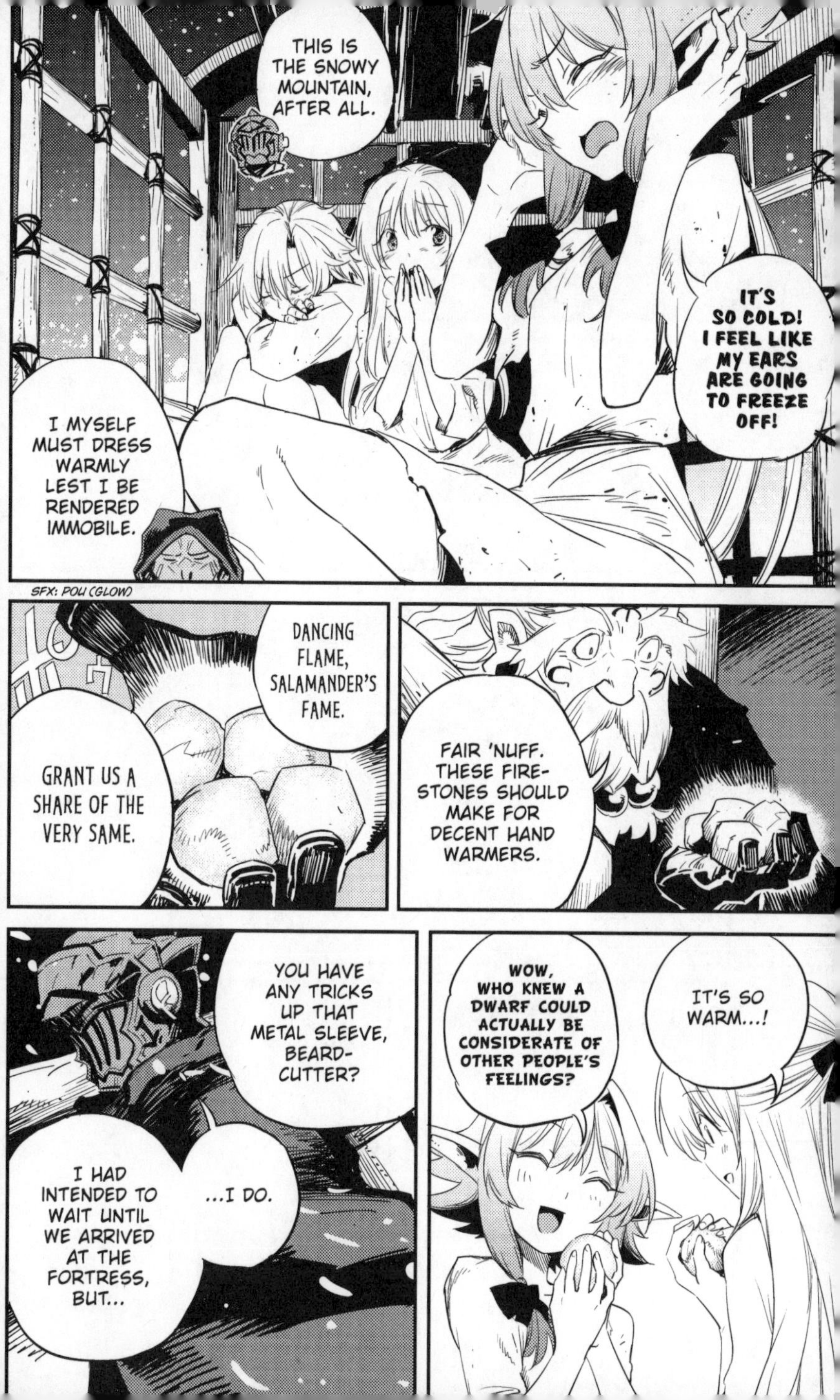
IT'S SO COLD! I FEEL LIKE MY EARS ARE GOING TO FREEZE OFF!
THIS IS THE SNOWY MOUNTAIN, AFTER ALL.
I MYSELF MUST DRESS WARMLY LEST I BE RENDERED IMMOBILE.
SFX: POU (GLOW)
FAIR 'NUFF. THESE FIRE-STONES SHOULD MAKE FOR DECENT HAND WARMERS.
DANCING FLAME, SALAMANDER'S FAME.
GRANT US A SHARE OF THE VERY SAME.
IT'S SO WARM...!
WOW, WHO KNEW A DWARF COULD ACTUALLY BE CONSIDERATE OF OTHER PEOPLE'S FEELINGS?
YOU HAVE ANY TRICKS UP THAT METAL SLEEVE, BEARD-CUTTER?
...I DO.
I HAD INTENDED TO WAIT UNTIL WE ARRIVED AT THE FORTRESS, BUT...

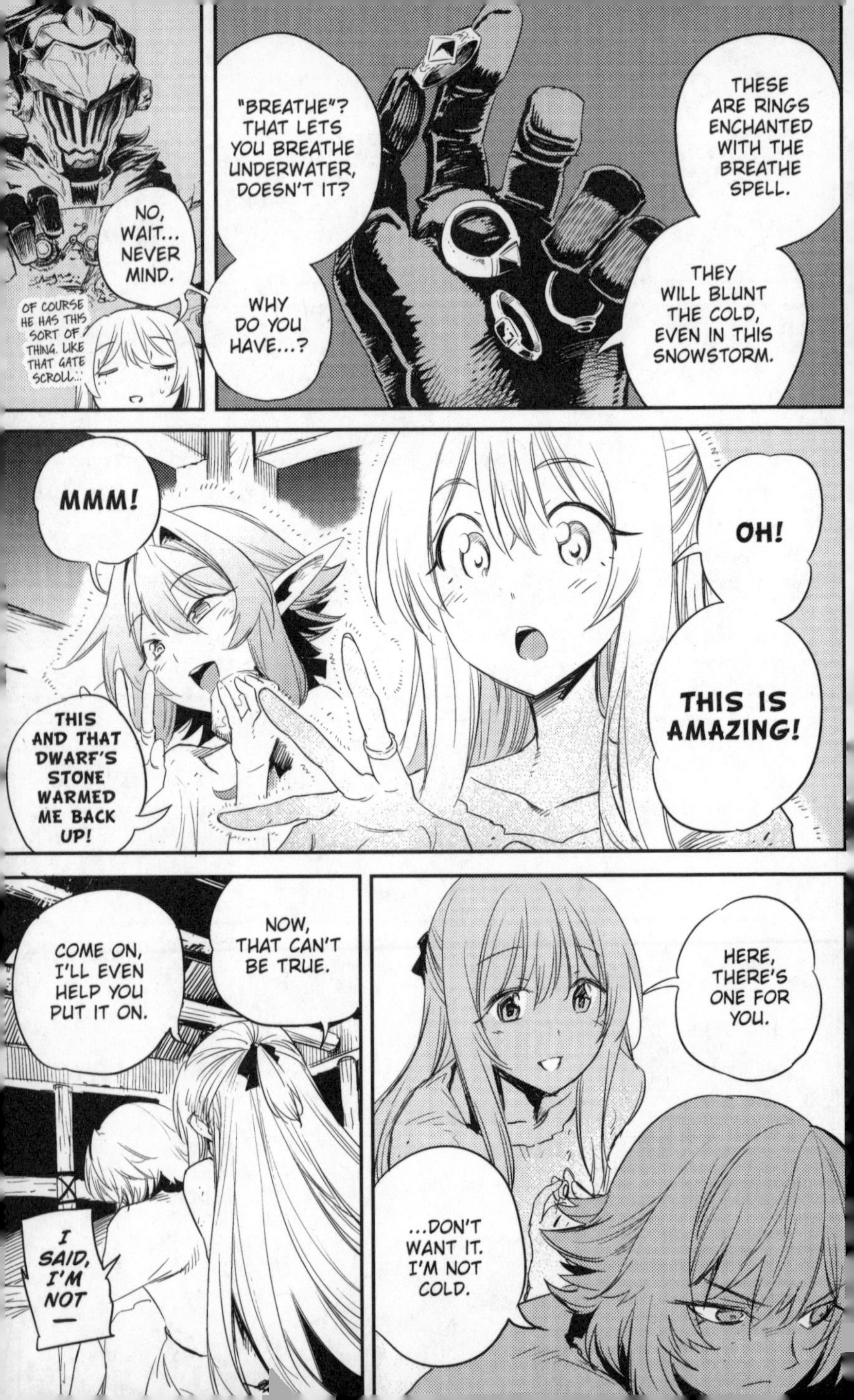

THESE ARE RINGS ENCHANTED WITH THE BREATHE SPELL.
THEY WILL BLUNT THE COLD, EVEN IN THIS SNOWSTORM.
"BREATHE"? THAT LETS YOU BREATHE UNDERWATER, DOESN'T IT?
WHY DO YOU HAVE...?
NO, WAIT... NEVER MIND.
OF COURSE HE HAS THIS SORT OF THING. LIKE THAT GATE SCROLL...
OH!
THIS IS AMAZING!
MMM!
THIS AND THAT DWARF'S STONE WARMED ME BACK UP!
HERE, THERE'S ONE FOR YOU.
...DON'T WANT IT. I'M NOT COLD.
NOW, THAT CAN'T BE TRUE.
COME ON, I'LL EVEN HELP YOU PUT IT ON.
I SAID, I'M NOT—

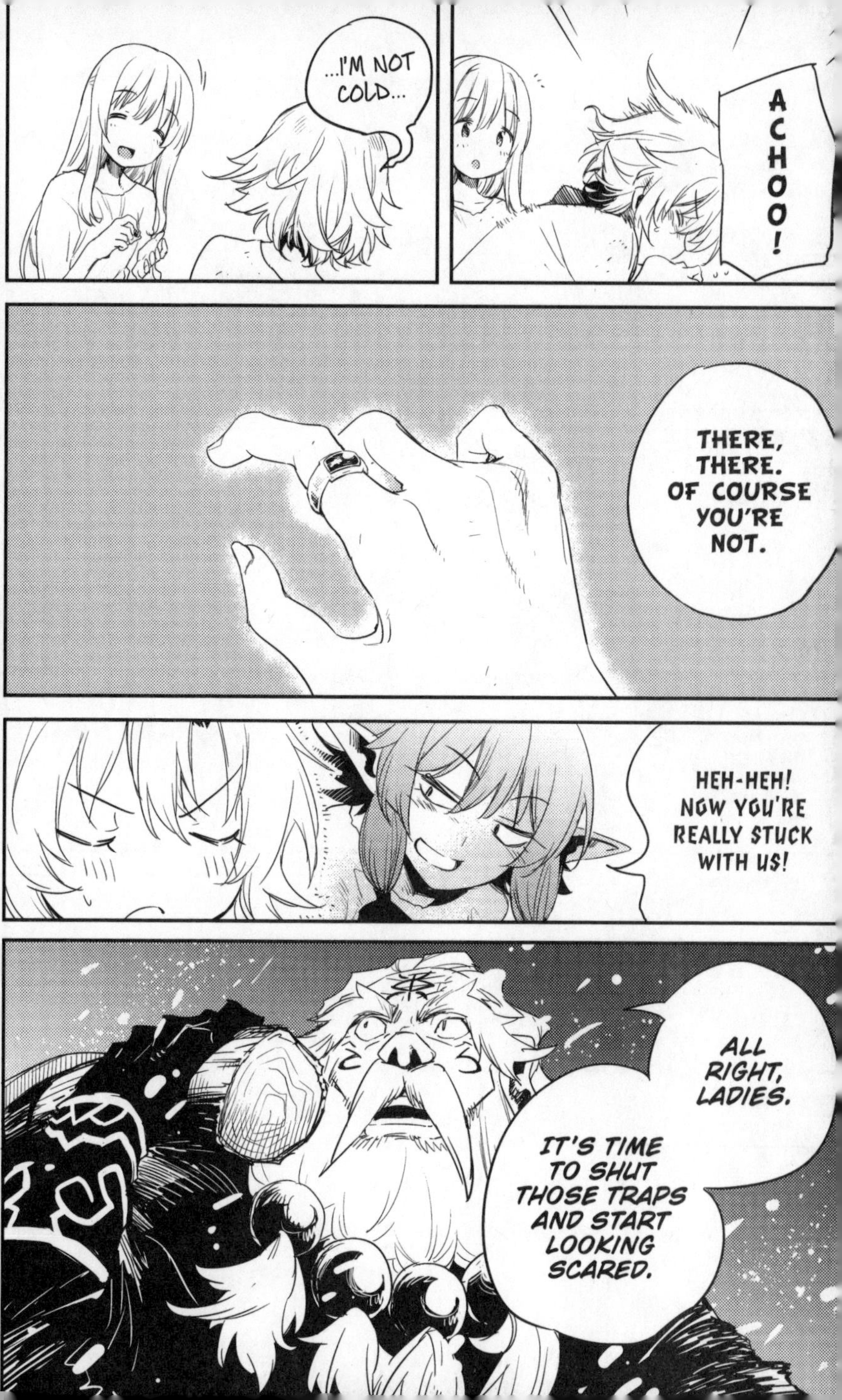
ACHOO!
...I'M NOT COLD...
THERE, THERE. OF COURSE YOU'RE NOT.
HEH-HEH! NOW YOU'RE REALLY STUCK WITH US!
ALL RIGHT, LADIES.
IT'S TIME TO SHUT THOSE TRAPS AND START LOOKING SCARED.

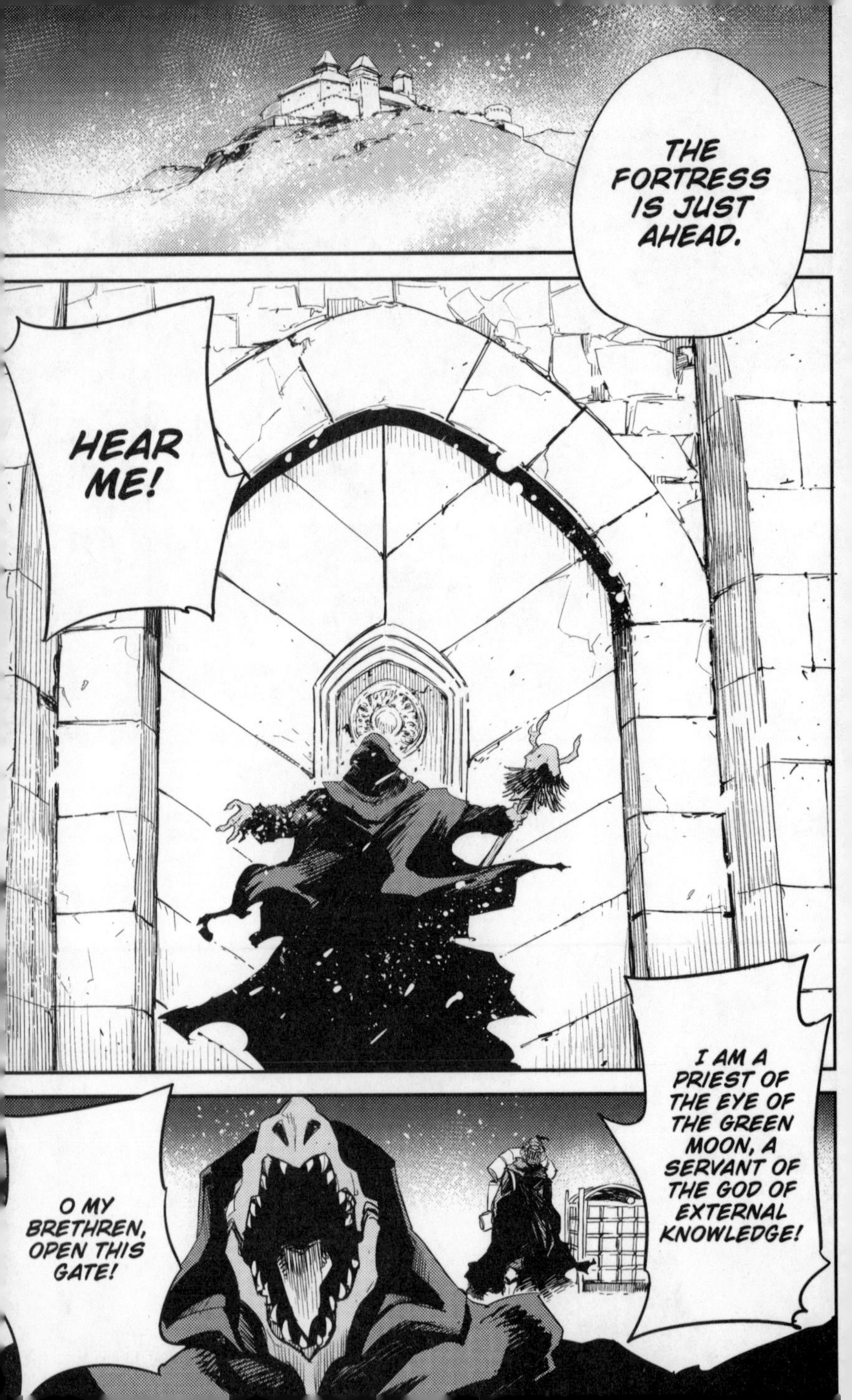
THE FORTRESS IS JUST AHEAD.
HEAR ME!
I AM A PRIEST OF THE EYE OF THE GREEN MOON, A SERVANT OF THE GOD OF EXTERNAL KNOWLEDGE!
O MY BRETHREN, OPEN THIS GATE!

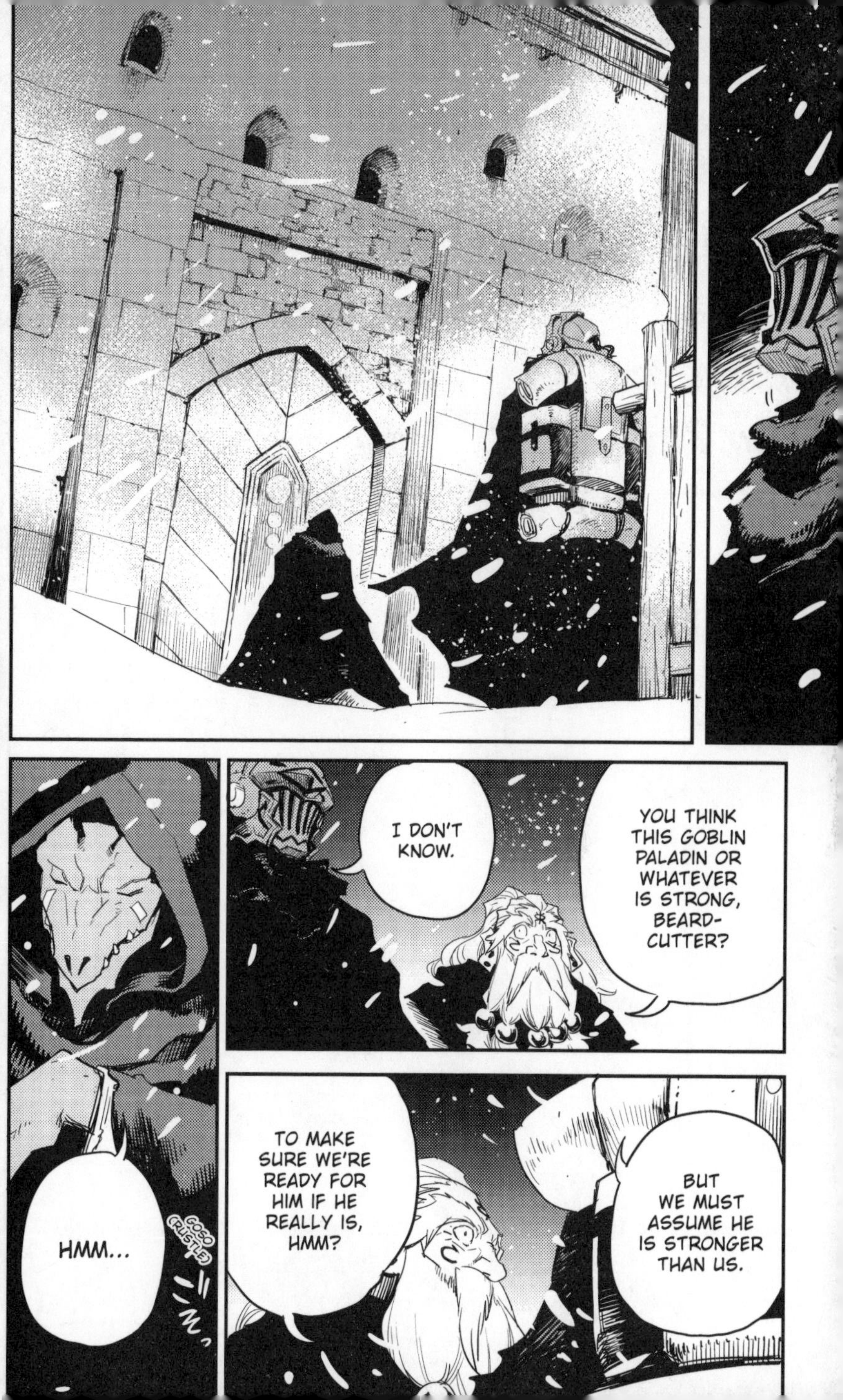
YOU THINK THIS GOBLIN PALADIN OR WHATEVER IS STRONG, BEARD-CUTTER?
I DON'T KNOW.
BUT WE MUST ASSUME HE IS STRONGER THAN US.
TO MAKE SURE WE'RE READY FOR HIM IF HE REALLY IS, HMM?
GOSO (RUSTLE)
HMM...

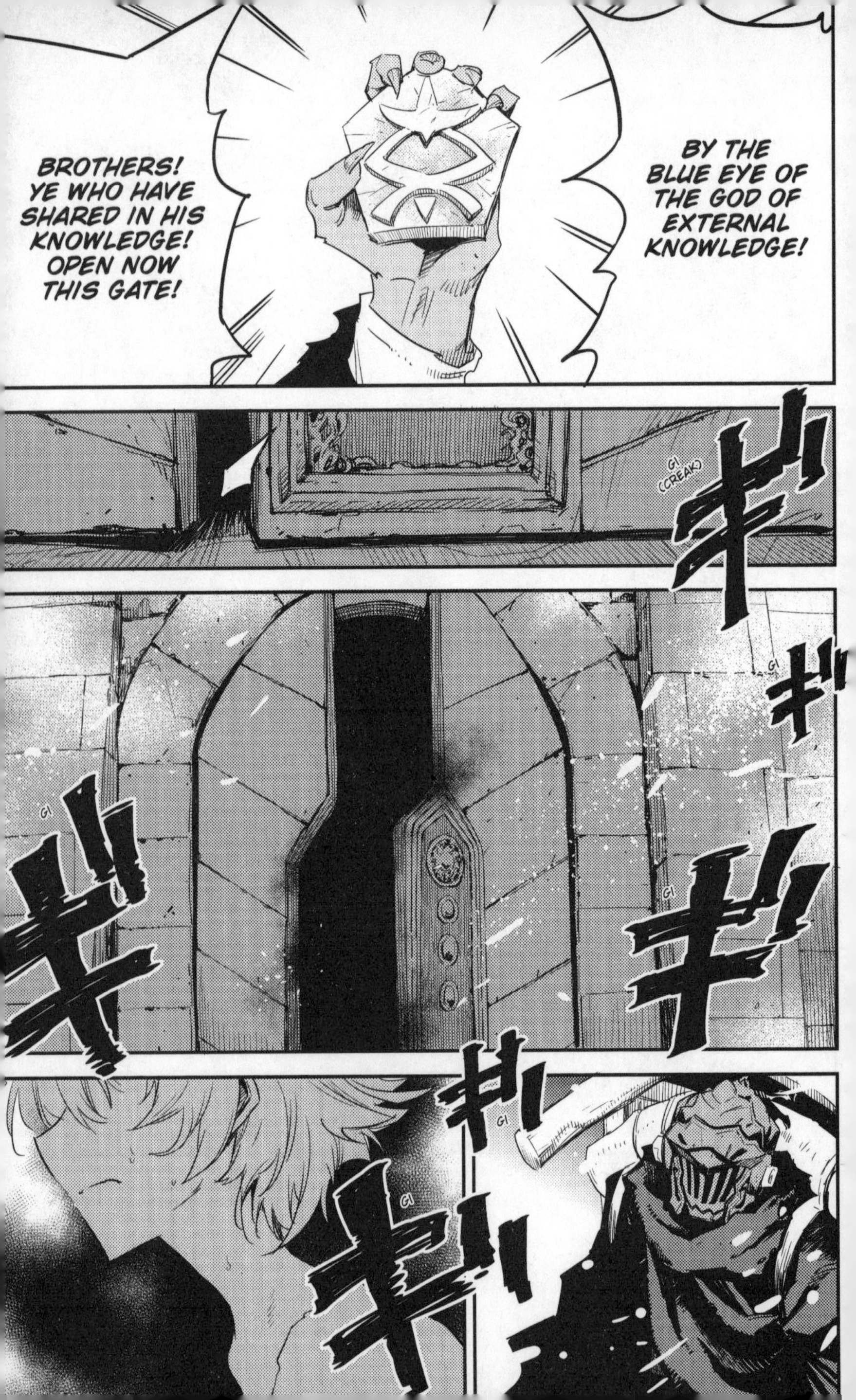
BY THE BLUE EYE OF THE GOD OF EXTERNAL KNOWLEDGE!
BROTHERS! YE WHO HAVE SHARED IN HIS KNOWLEDGE! OPEN NOW THIS GATE!
GI (CREAK)
GI
GI
GI
GI
GI

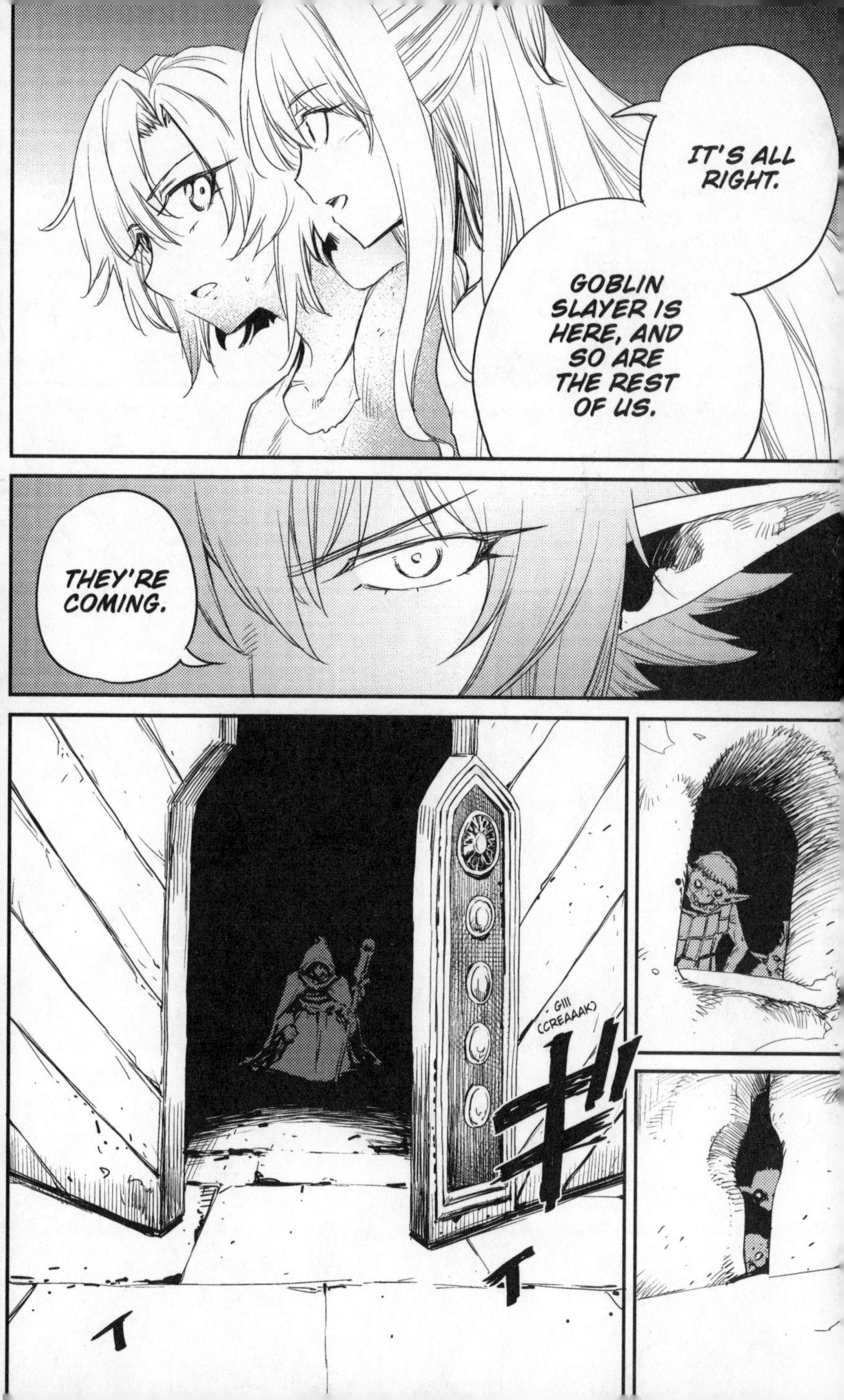
IT'S ALL RIGHT.
GOBLIN SLAYER IS HERE, AND SO ARE THE REST OF US.
THEY'RE COMING.
GIII (CREAAAK)

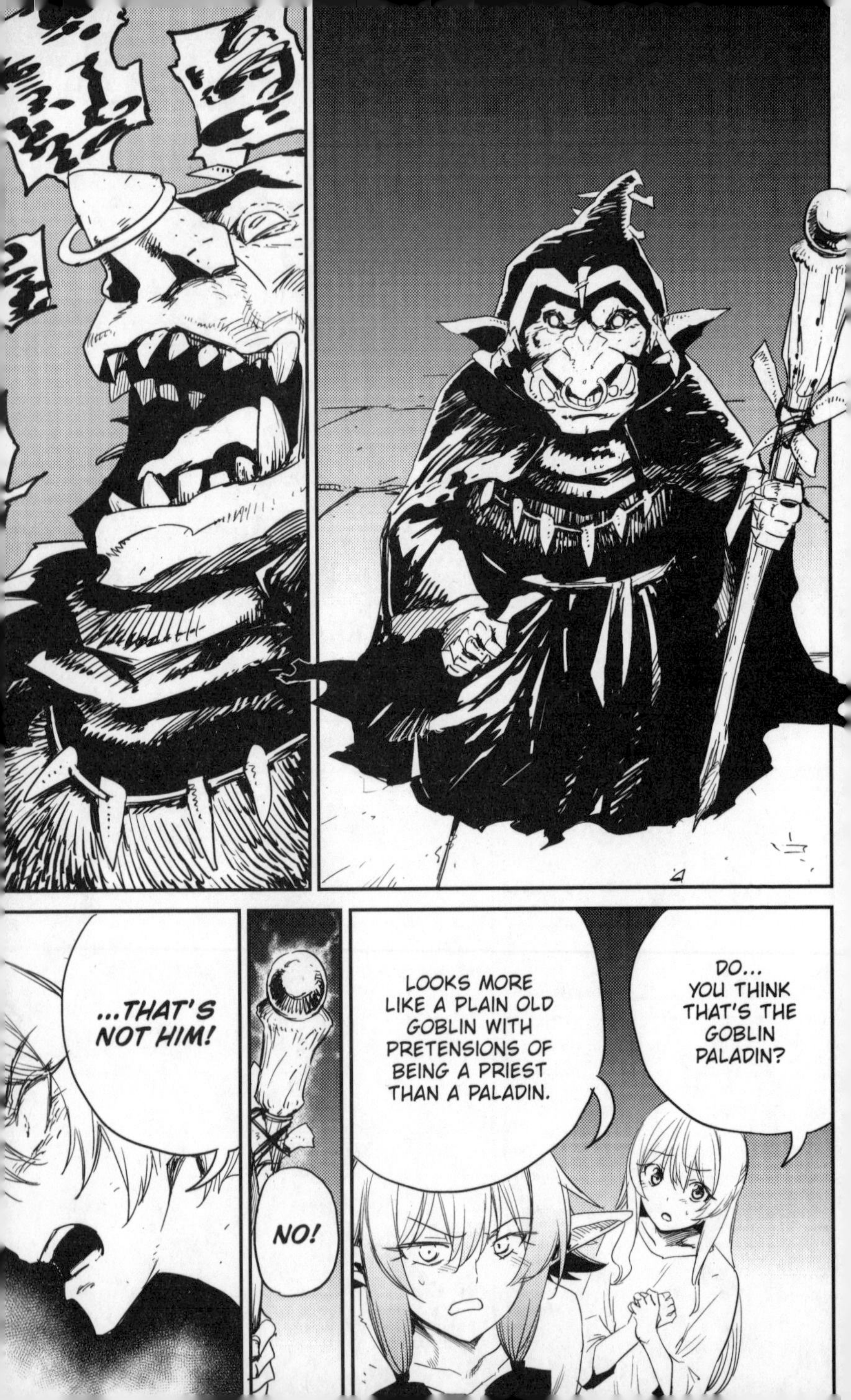
DO... YOU THINK THAT'S THE GOBLIN PALADIN?
LOOKS MORE LIKE A PLAIN OLD GOBLIN WITH PRETENSIONS OF BEING A PRIEST THAN A PALADIN.
NO!
...THAT'S NOT HIM!

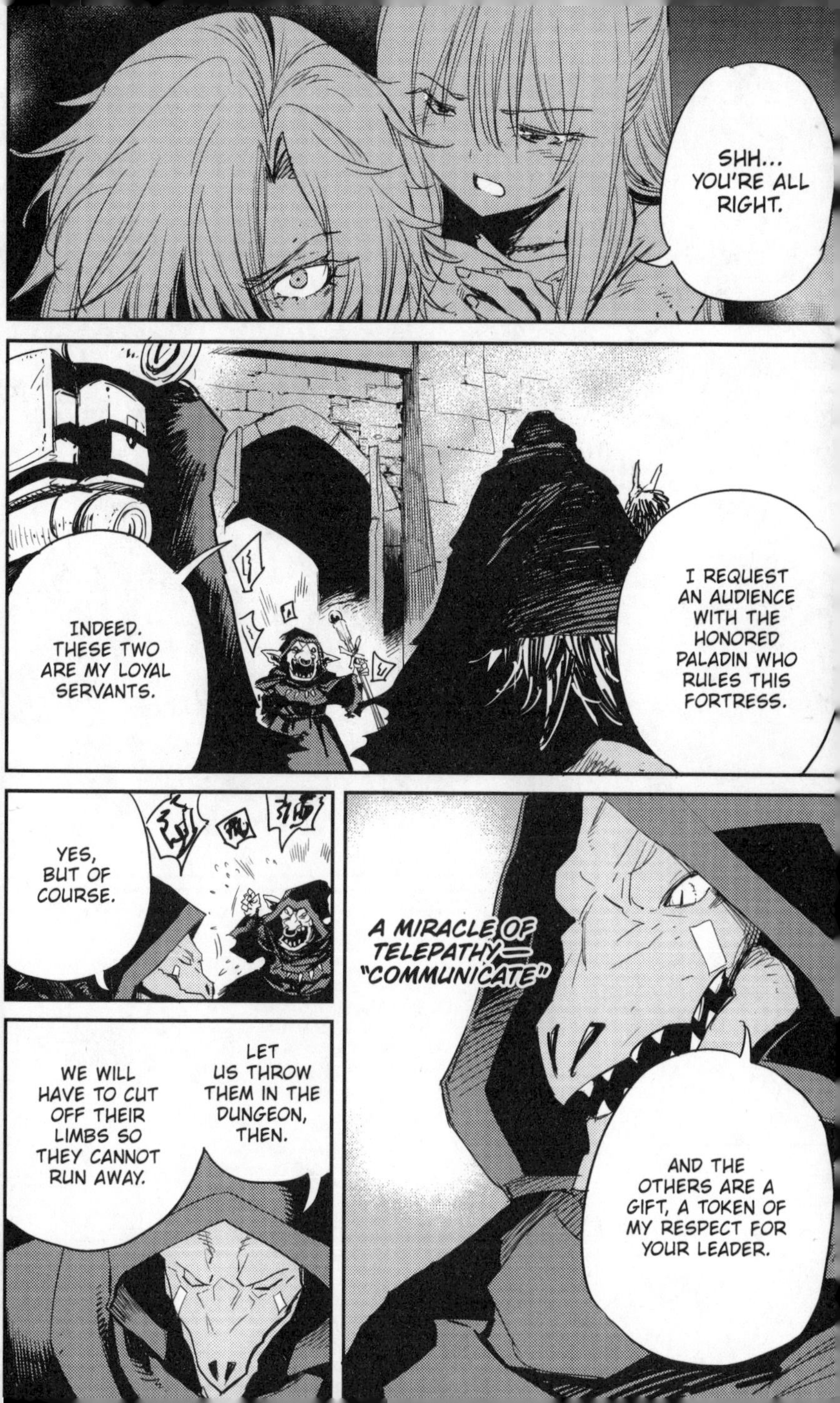
SHH... YOU'RE ALL RIGHT.
I REQUEST AN AUDIENCE WITH THE HONORED PALADIN WHO RULES THIS FORTRESS.
INDEED. THESE TWO ARE MY LOYAL SERVANTS.
A MIRACLE OF TELEPATHY— "COMMUNICATE"
AND THE OTHERS ARE A GIFT, A TOKEN OF MY RESPECT FOR YOUR LEADER.
YES, BUT OF COURSE.
LET US THROW THEM IN THE DUNGEON, THEN.
WE WILL HAVE TO CUT OFF THEIR LIMBS SO THEY CANNOT RUN AWAY.

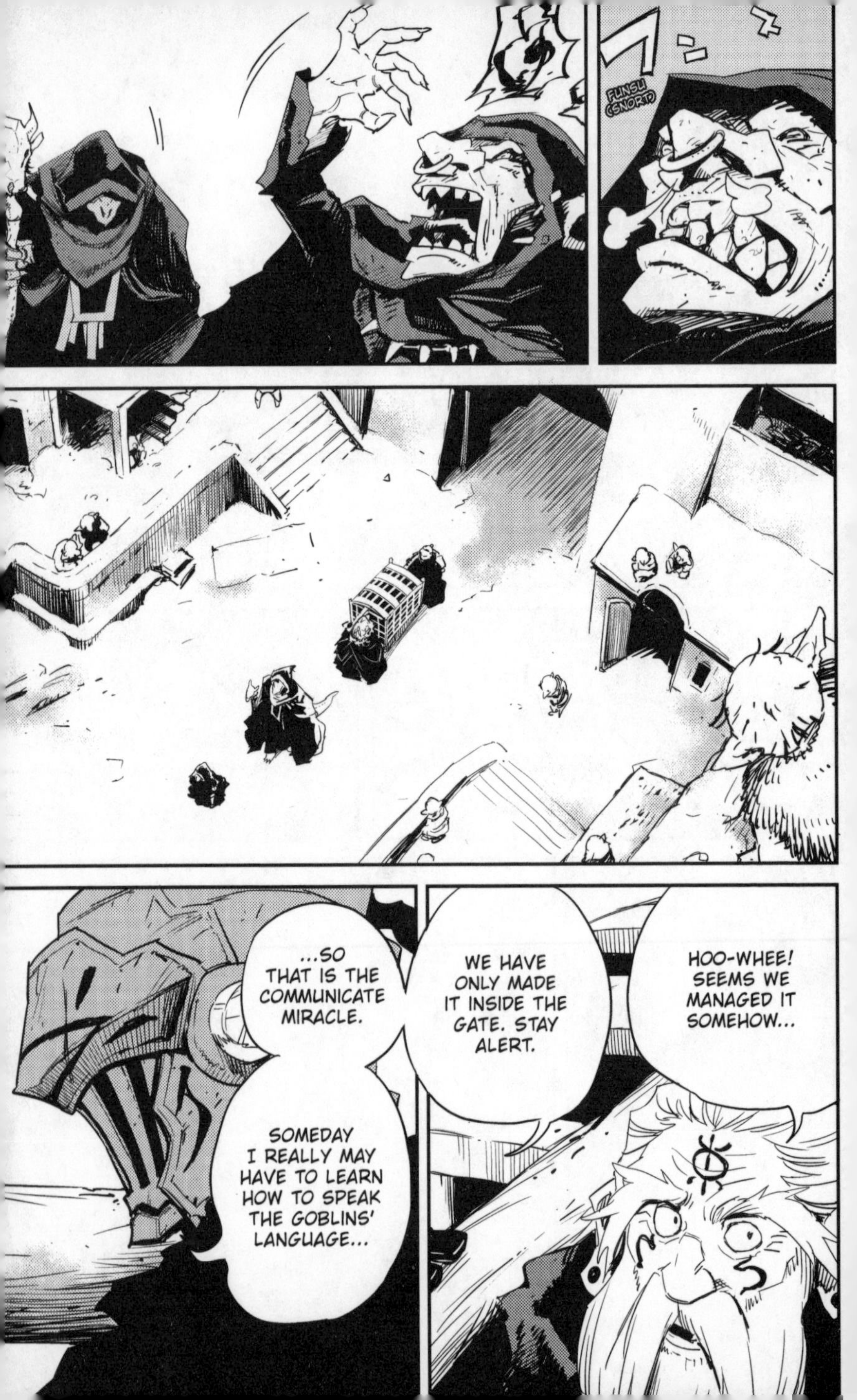
FUNSU (SNORT)
HOO-WHEE! SEEMS WE MANAGED IT SOMEHOW...
WE HAVE ONLY MADE IT INSIDE THE GATE. STAY ALERT.
...SO THAT IS THE COMMUNICATE MIRACLE.
SOMEDAY I REALLY MAY HAVE TO LEARN HOW TO SPEAK THE GOBLINS' LANGUAGE...

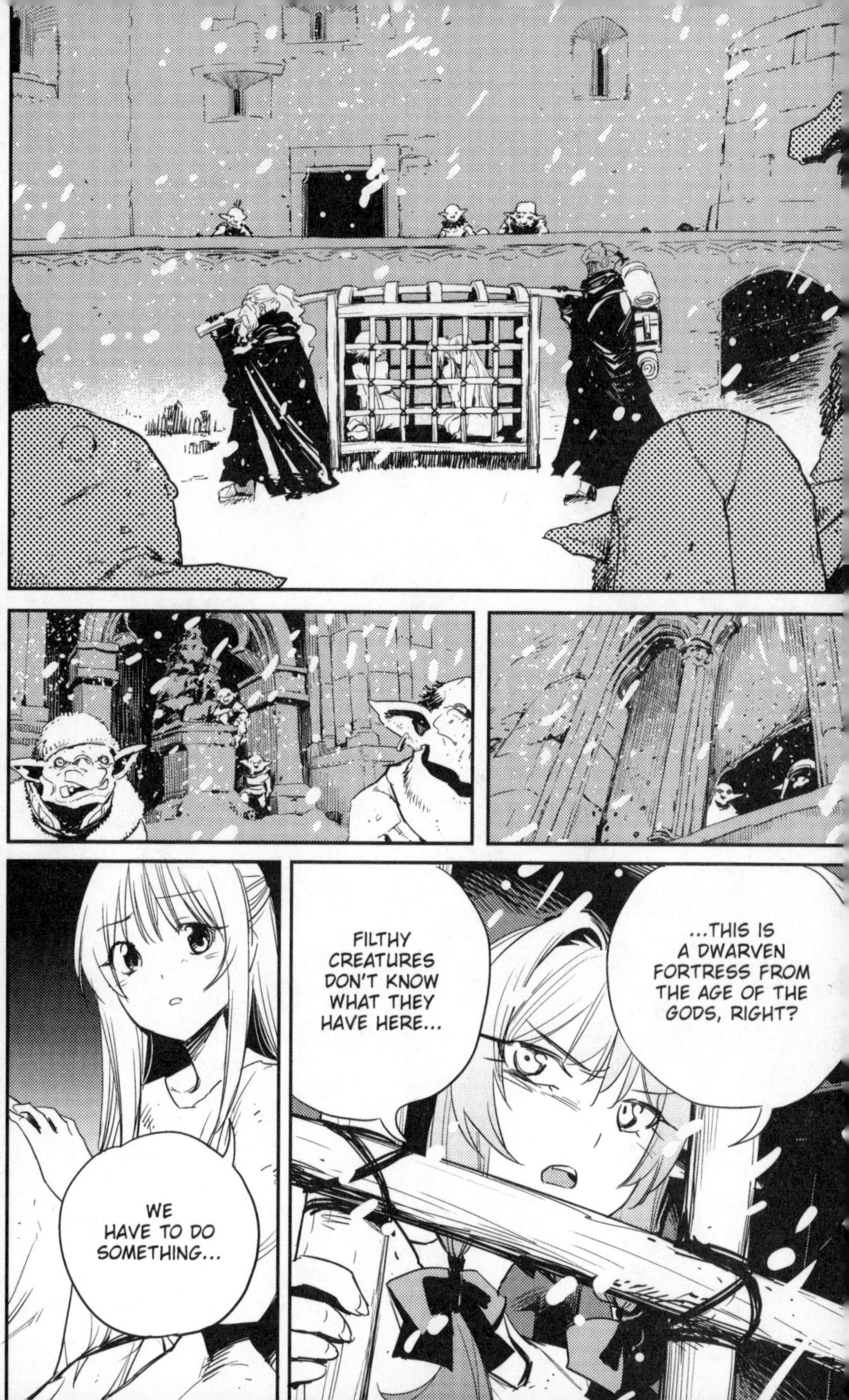
...THIS IS A DWARVEN FORTRESS FROM THE AGE OF THE GODS, RIGHT?
FILTHY CREATURES DON'T KNOW WHAT THEY HAVE HERE...
WE HAVE TO DO SOMETHING...

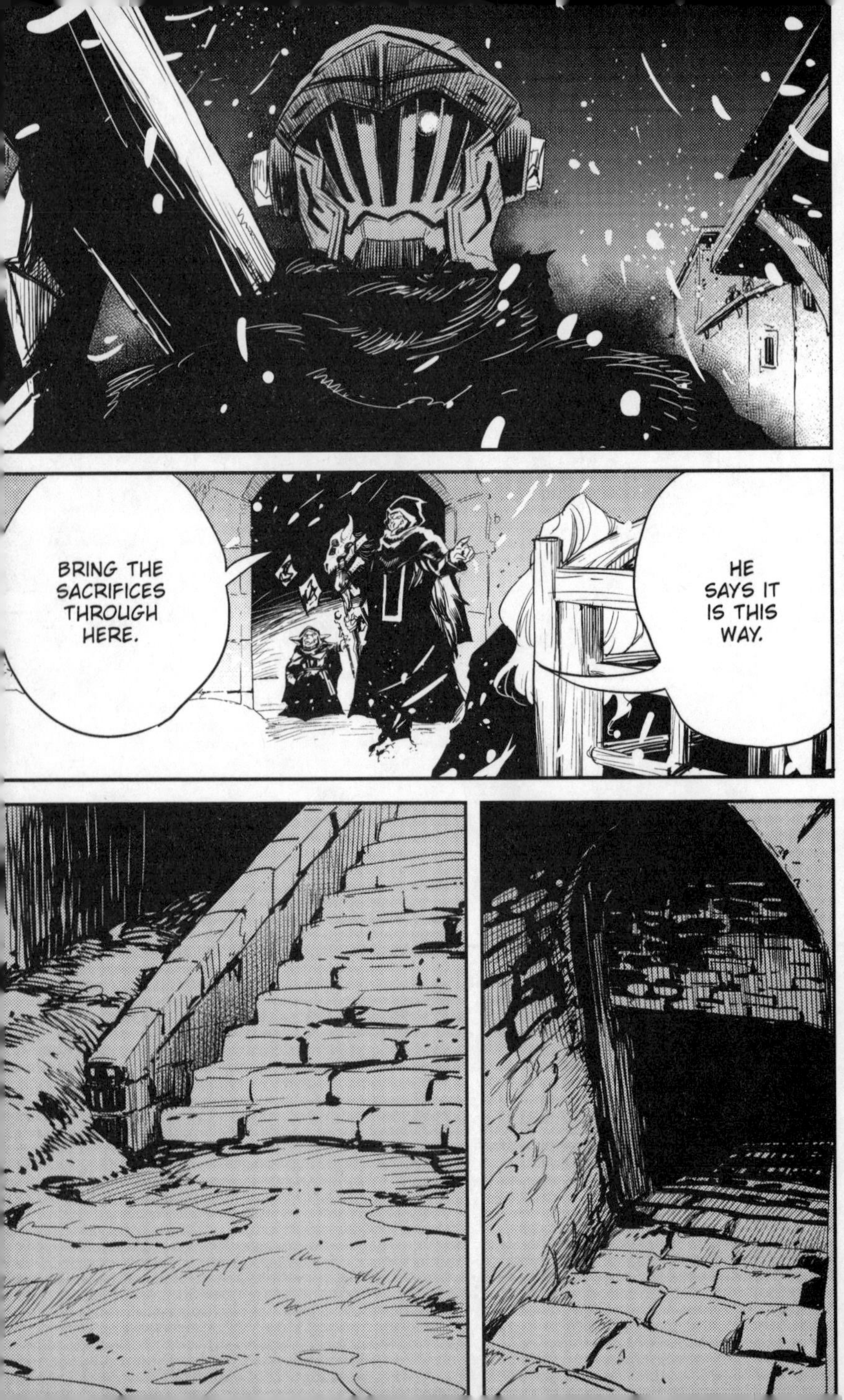
HE SAYS IT IS THIS WAY.
BRING THE SACRIFICES THROUGH HERE.

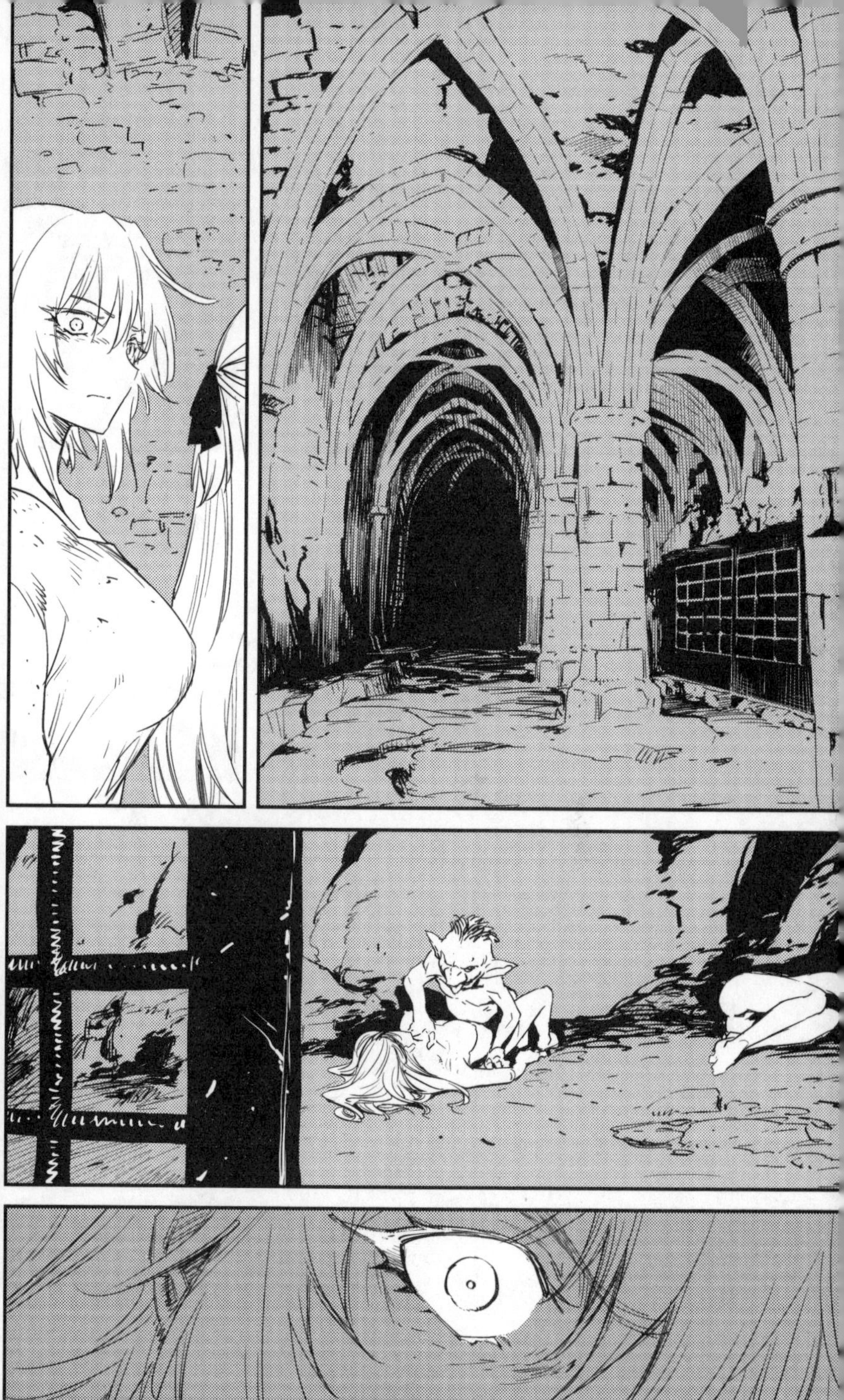

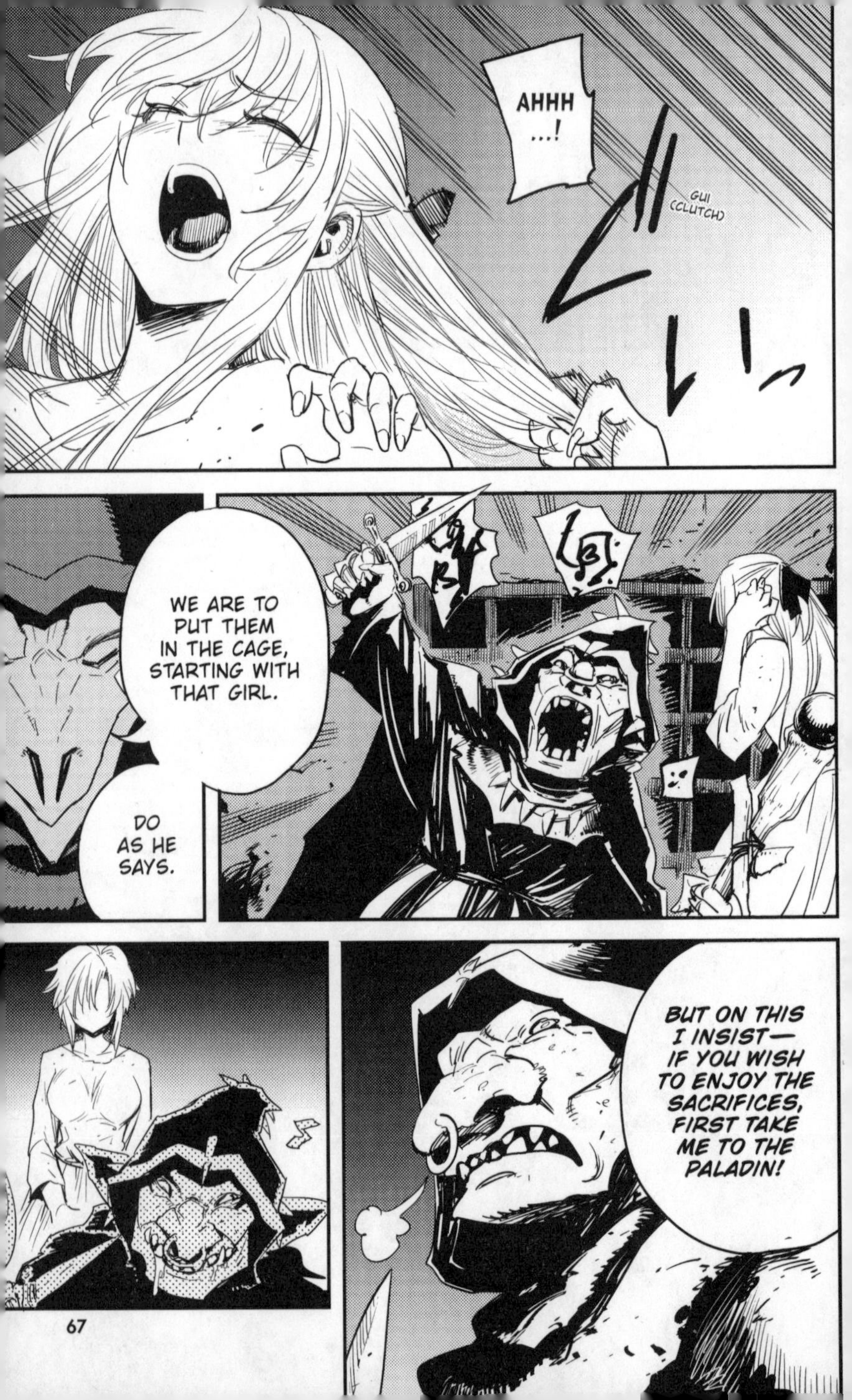
AHHH ...!
GUI (CLUTCH)
WE ARE TO PUT THEM IN THE CAGE, STARTING WITH THAT GIRL.
DO AS HE SAYS.
BUT ON THIS I INSIST— IF YOU WISH TO ENJOY THE SACRIFICES, FIRST TAKE ME TO THE PALADIN!

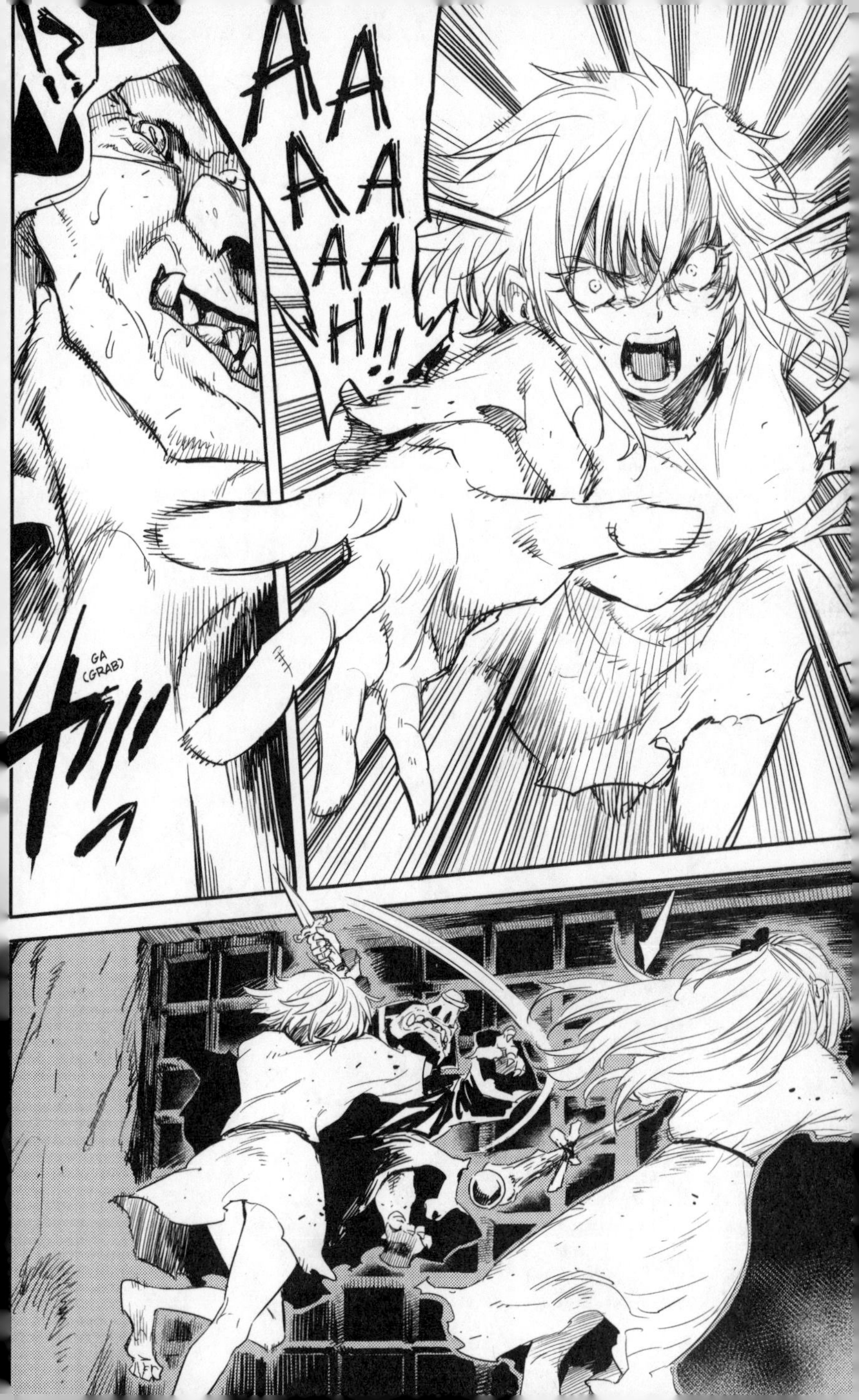
AAAAAAAH!!
YAA
!?
GA (GRAB)

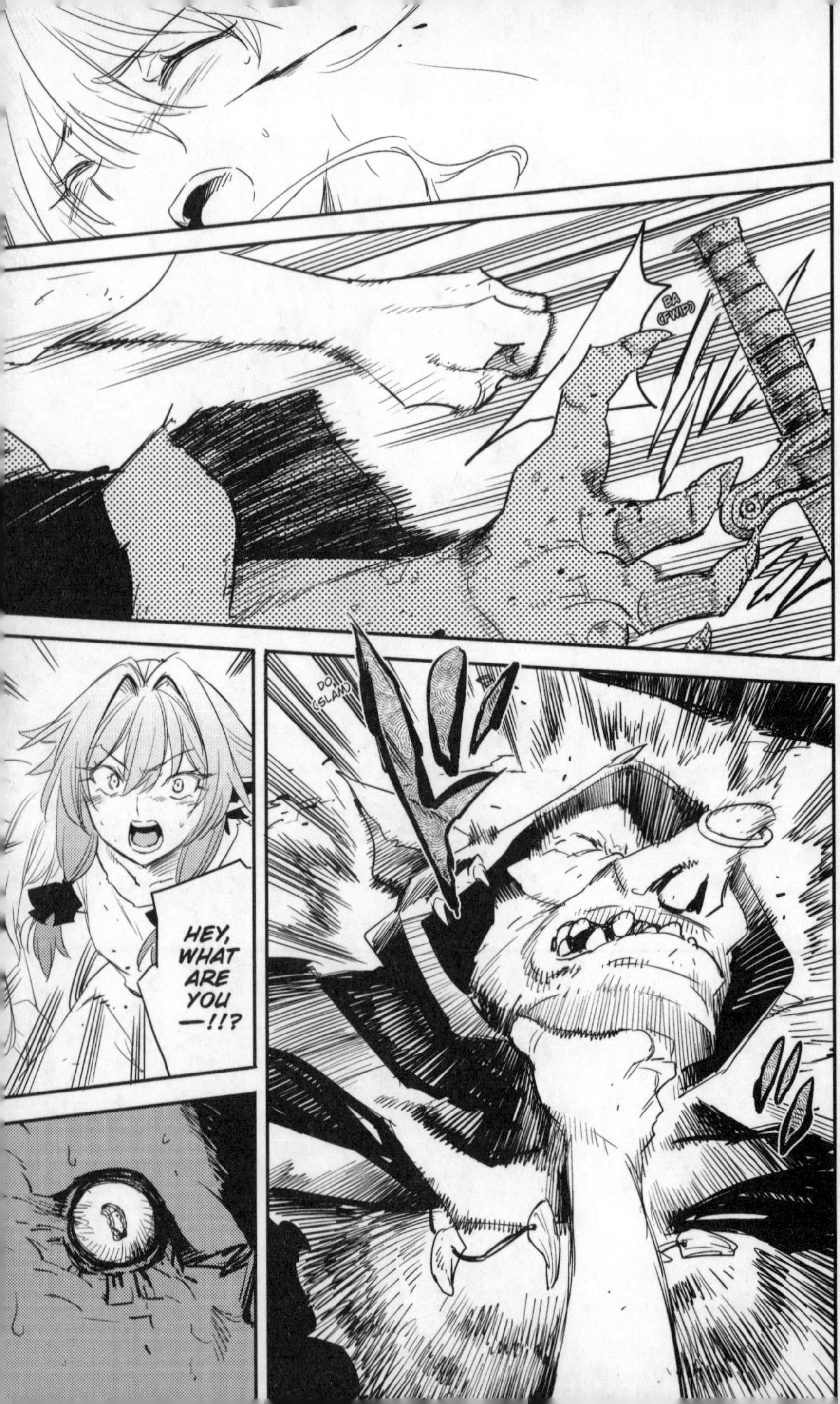
BA
(FWIP)
DO
(SLAM)
HEY, WHAT ARE YOU—!!?

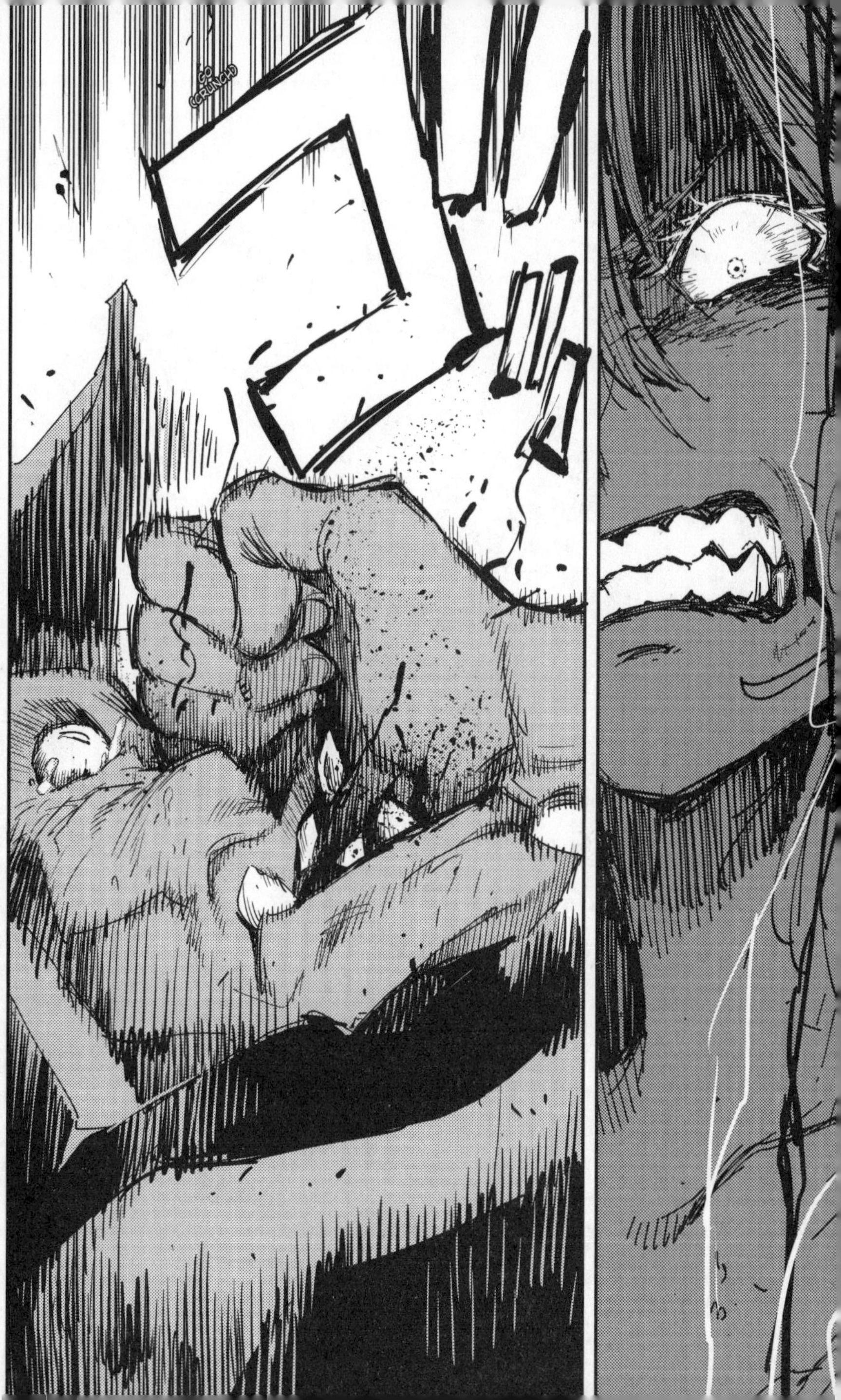
GO
(CRUNCH)

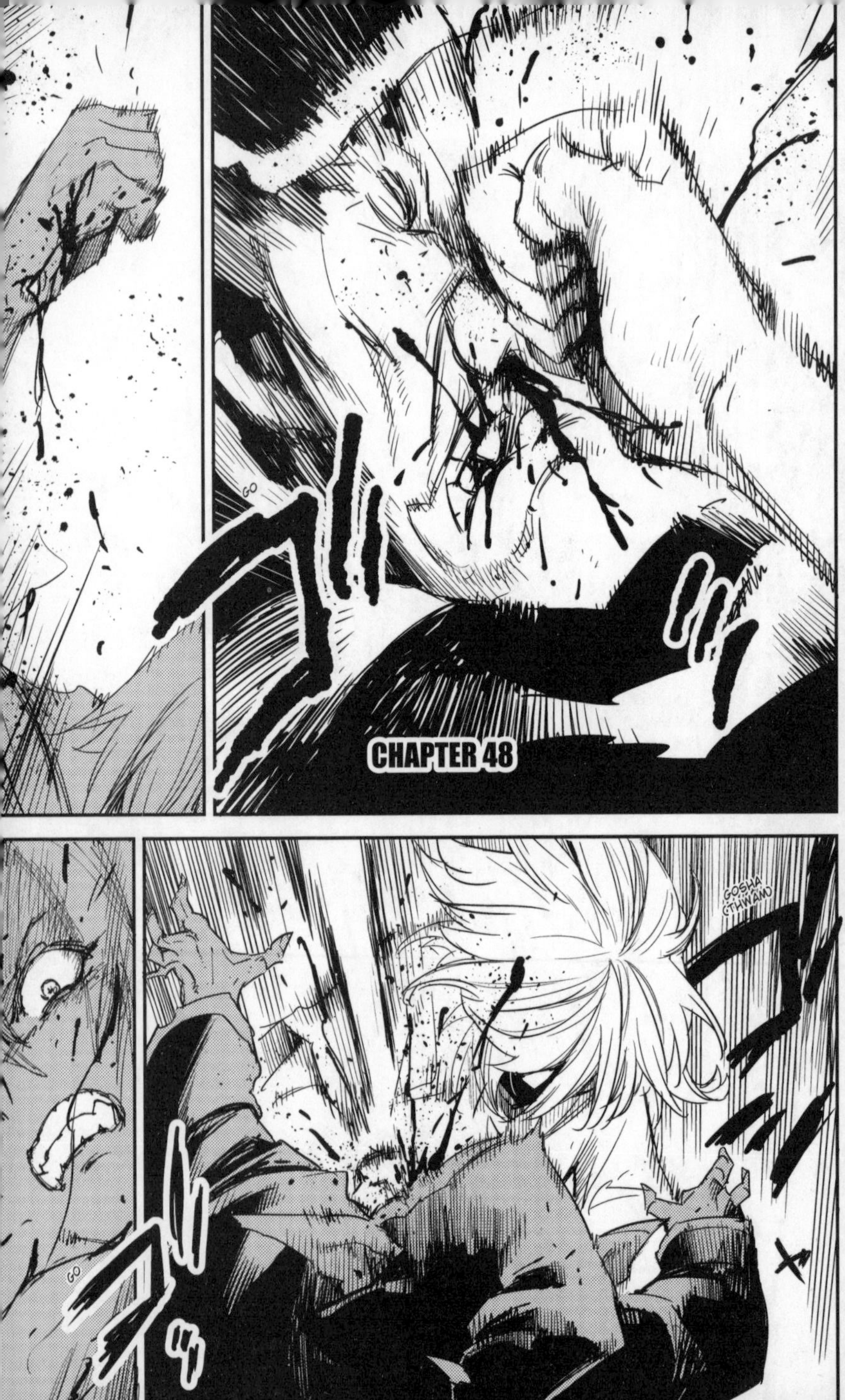
GO
CHAPTER 48
GOSHA (THWAM)
GO

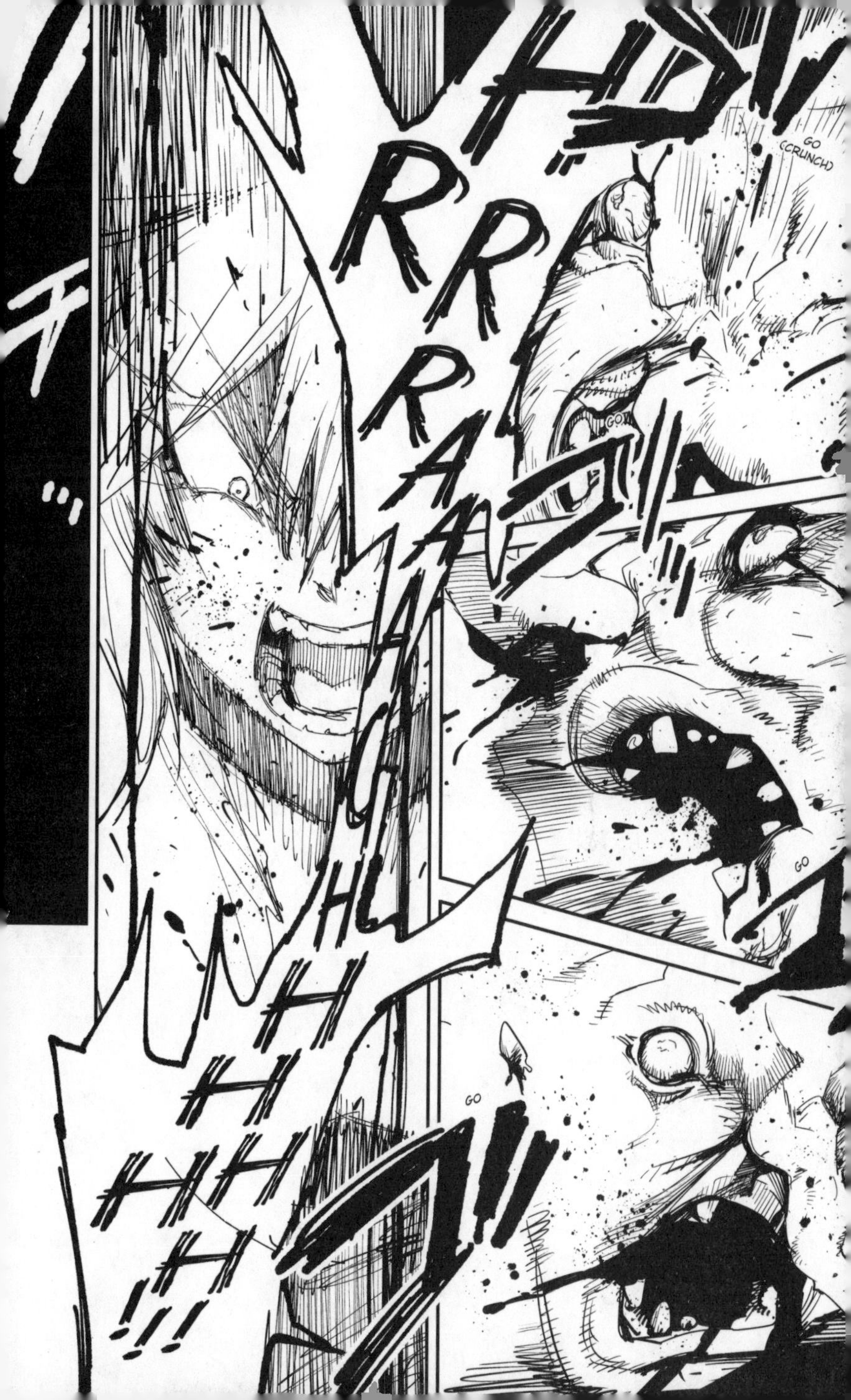
GO
(CRUNCH)
GO
GO
GO

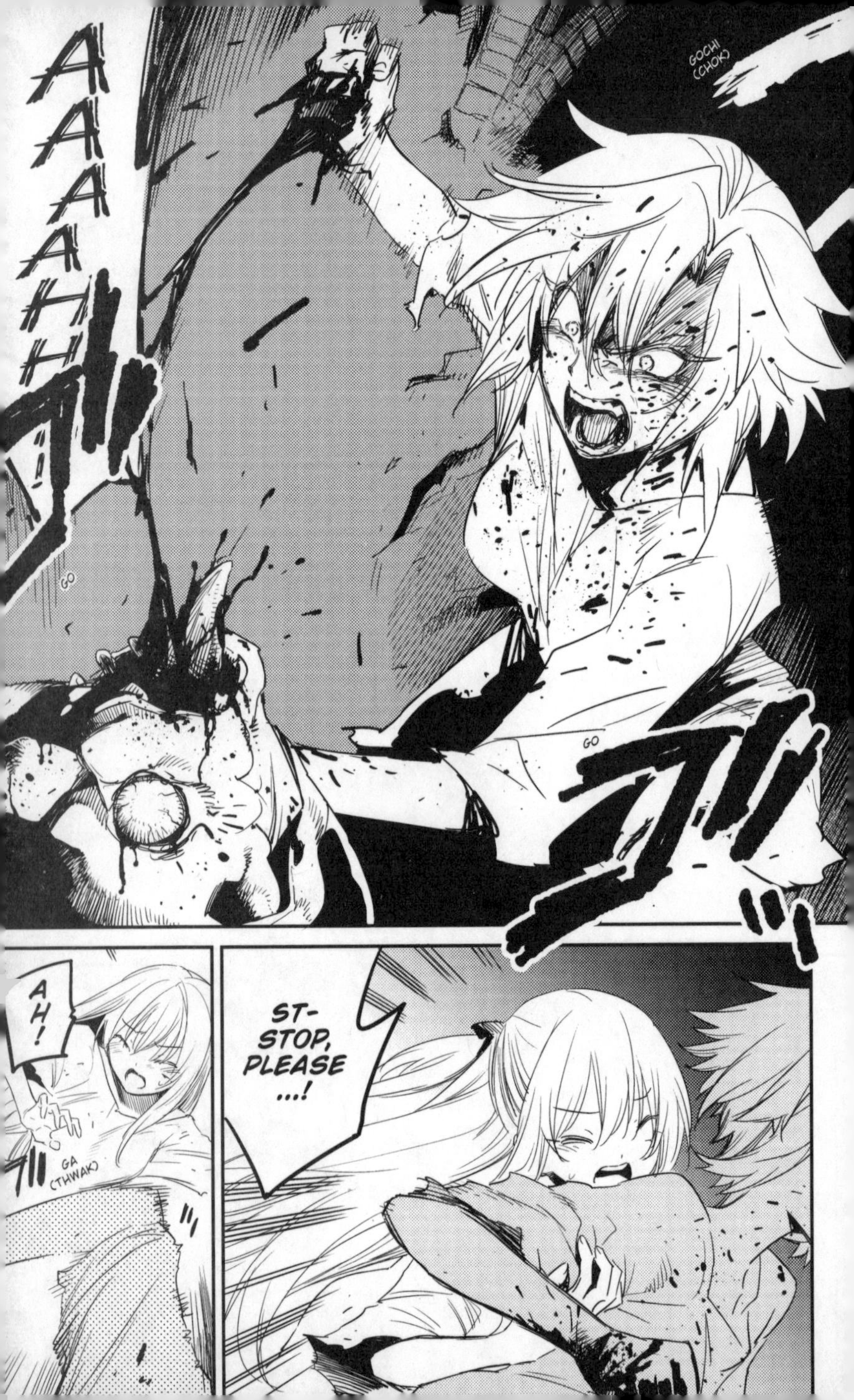
GOCHI (CHOK)
AAAAAHH
GO
GO
ST-STOP, PLEASE...!
AH!
GA (THWAK)

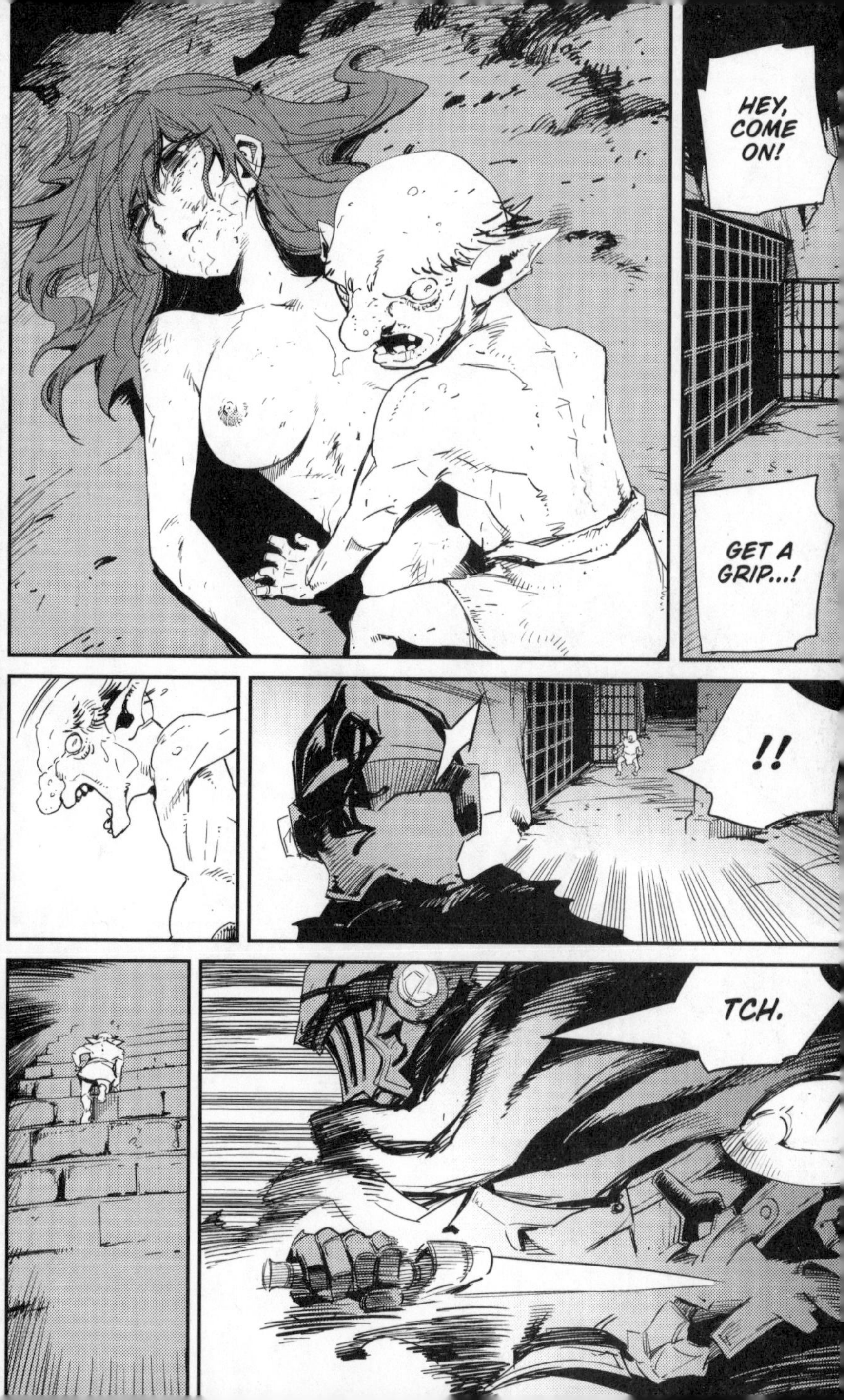
HEY, COME ON!
GET A GRIP...!
!!
TCH.

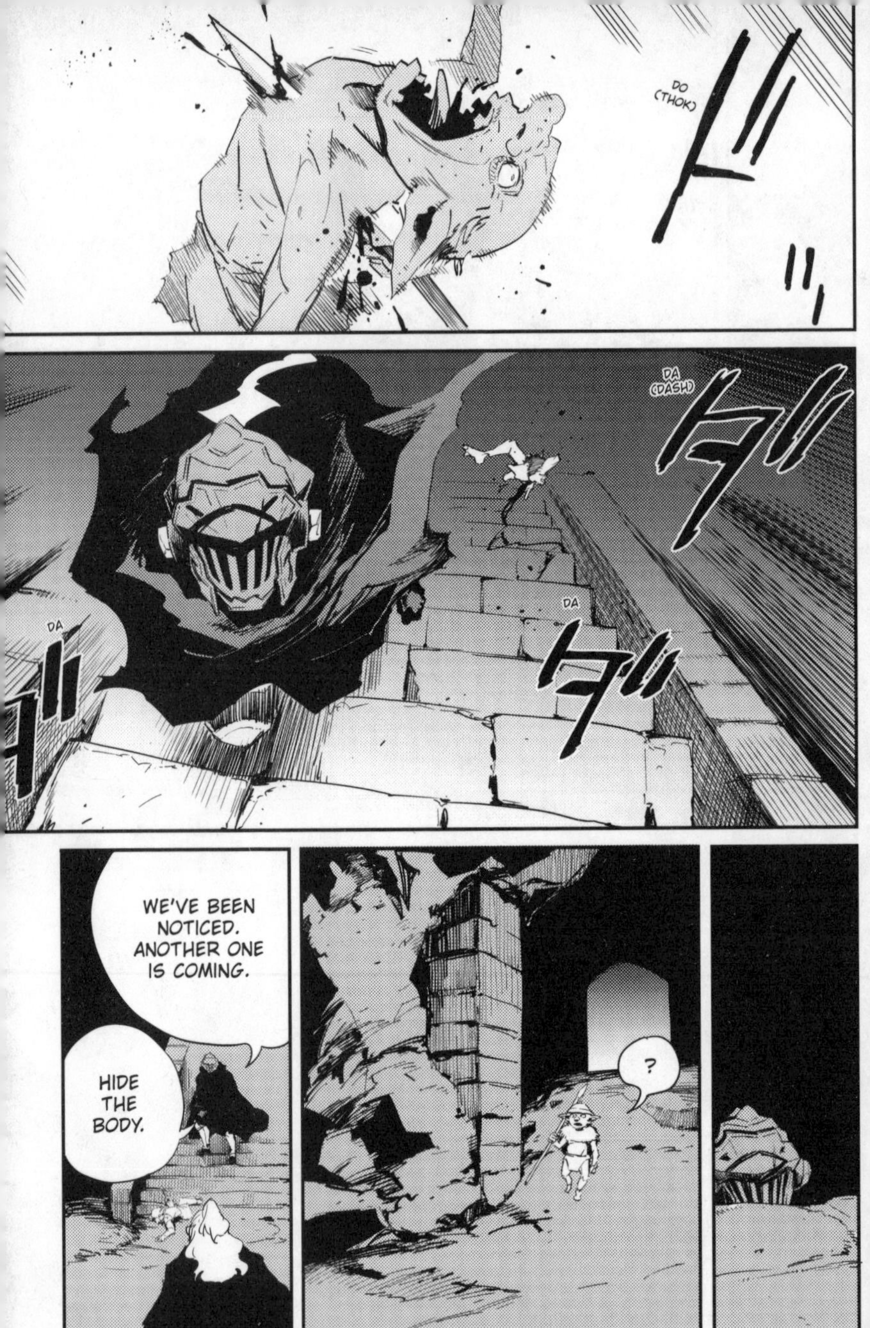
DO (THOK)
DA (DASH)
DA
DA
?
WE'VE BEEN NOTICED. ANOTHER ONE IS COMING.
HIDE THE BODY.

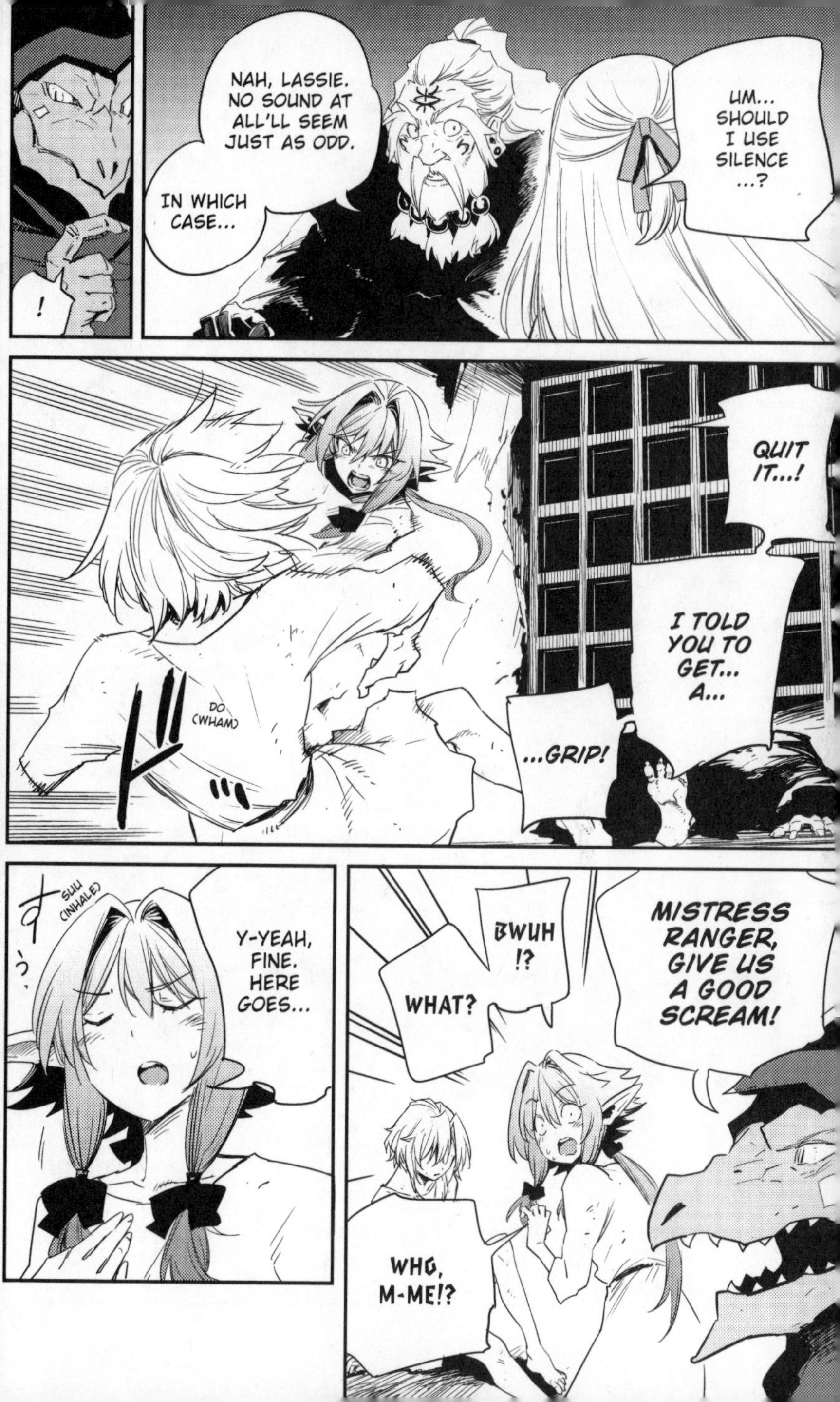
UM... SHOULD I USE SILENCE...?
NAH, LASSIE. NO SOUND AT ALL'LL SEEM JUST AS ODD.
IN WHICH CASE...
!
QUIT IT...!
I TOLD YOU TO GET... A...
...GRIP!
DO (WHAM)
MISTRESS RANGER, GIVE US A GOOD SCREAM!
BWUH!?
WHAT?
WHO, M-ME!?
SUU (INHALE)
Y-YEAH, FINE. HERE GOES...

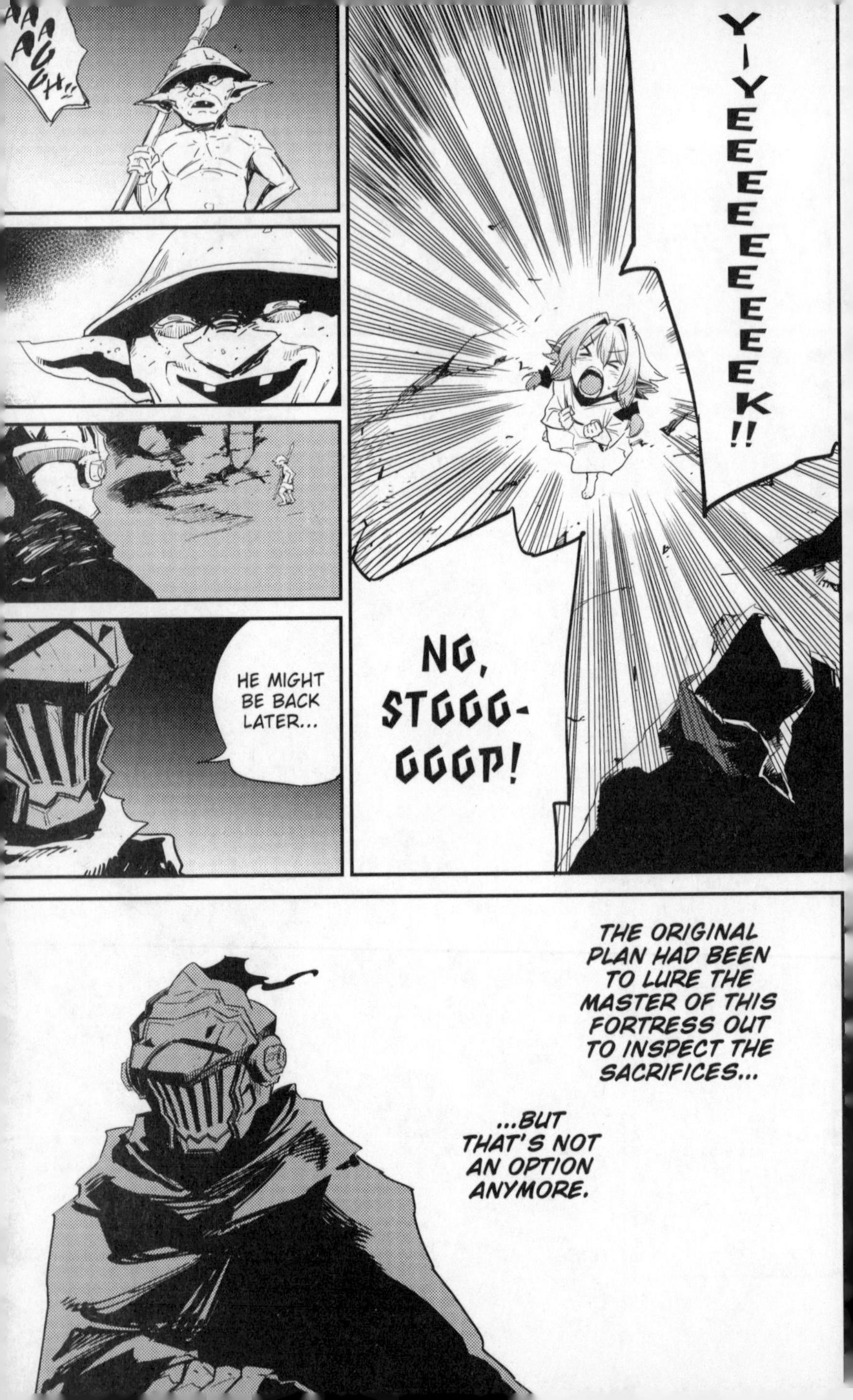
Y-YEEEEEEEEK!!
NO, STOOO-OOOP!
AAAAAUUH!!
HE MIGHT BE BACK LATER...
THE ORIGINAL PLAN HAD BEEN TO LURE THE MASTER OF THIS FORTRESS OUT TO INSPECT THE SACRIFICES...
...BUT THAT'S NOT AN OPTION ANYMORE.

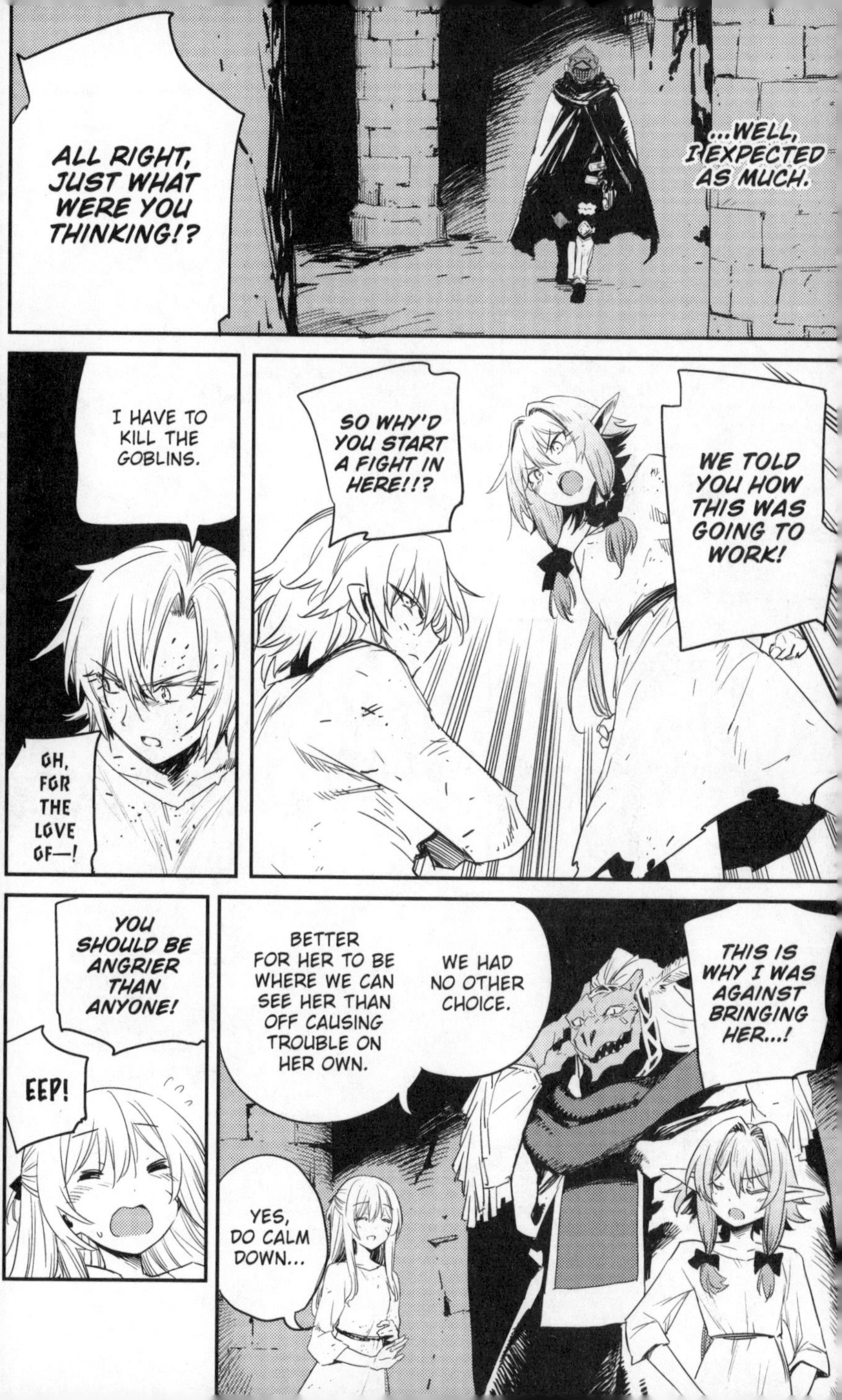
...WELL, I EXPECTED AS MUCH.
ALL RIGHT, JUST WHAT WERE YOU THINKING!?
WE TOLD YOU HOW THIS WAS GOING TO WORK!
SO WHY'D YOU START A FIGHT IN HERE!!?
I HAVE TO KILL THE GOBLINS.
OH, FOR THE LOVE OF—!
THIS IS WHY I WAS AGAINST BRINGING HER...!
WE HAD NO OTHER CHOICE.
BETTER FOR HER TO BE WHERE WE CAN SEE HER THAN OFF CAUSING TROUBLE ON HER OWN.
YES, DO CALM DOWN...
YOU SHOULD BE ANGRIER THAN ANYONE!
EEP!

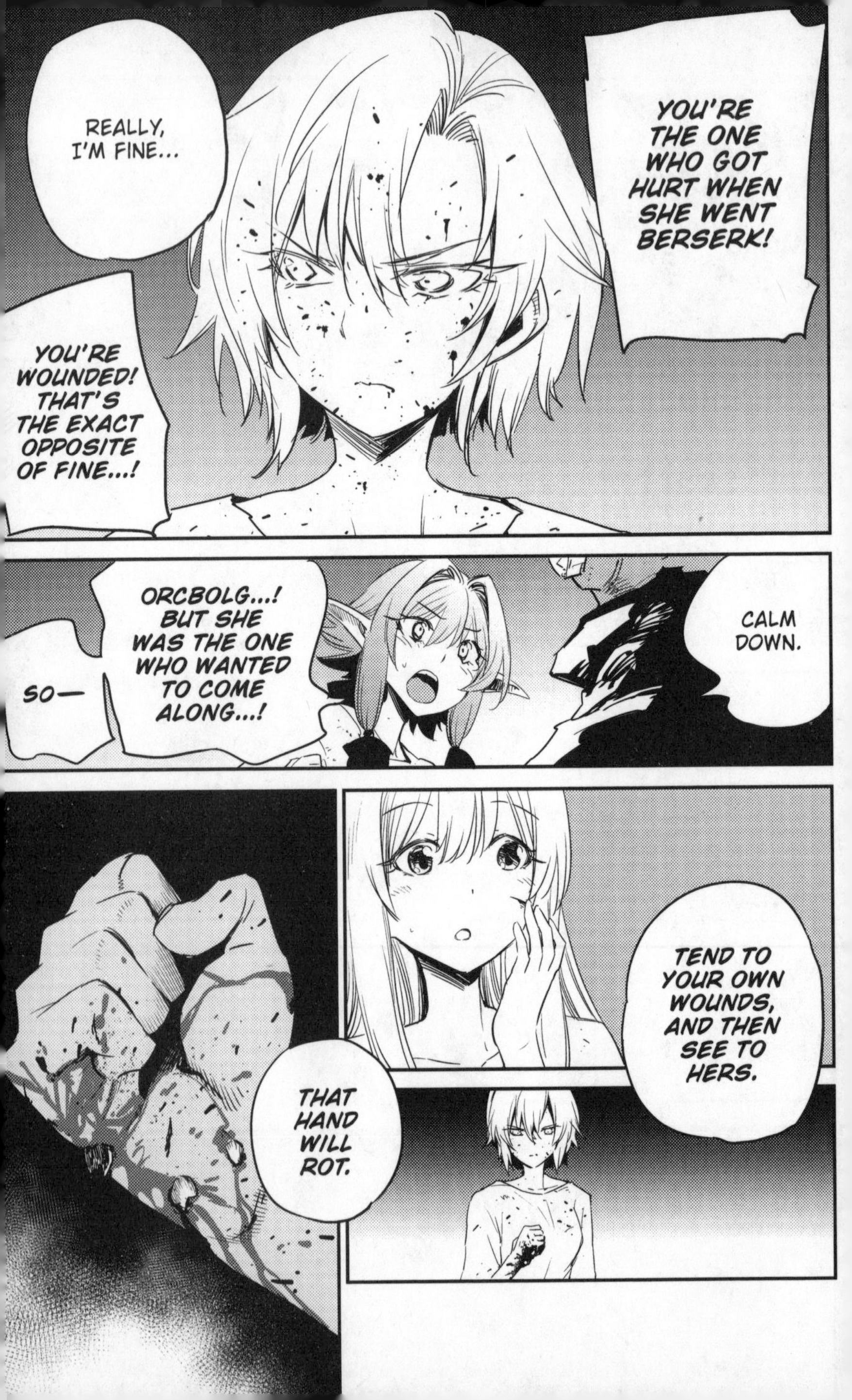
YOU'RE THE ONE WHO GOT HURT WHEN SHE WENT BERSERK!
REALLY, I'M FINE...
YOU'RE WOUNDED! THAT'S THE EXACT OPPOSITE OF FINE...!
CALM DOWN.
ORCBOLG...! BUT SHE WAS THE ONE WHO WANTED TO COME ALONG...!
SO—
TEND TO YOUR OWN WOUNDS, AND THEN SEE TO HERS.
THAT HAND WILL ROT.

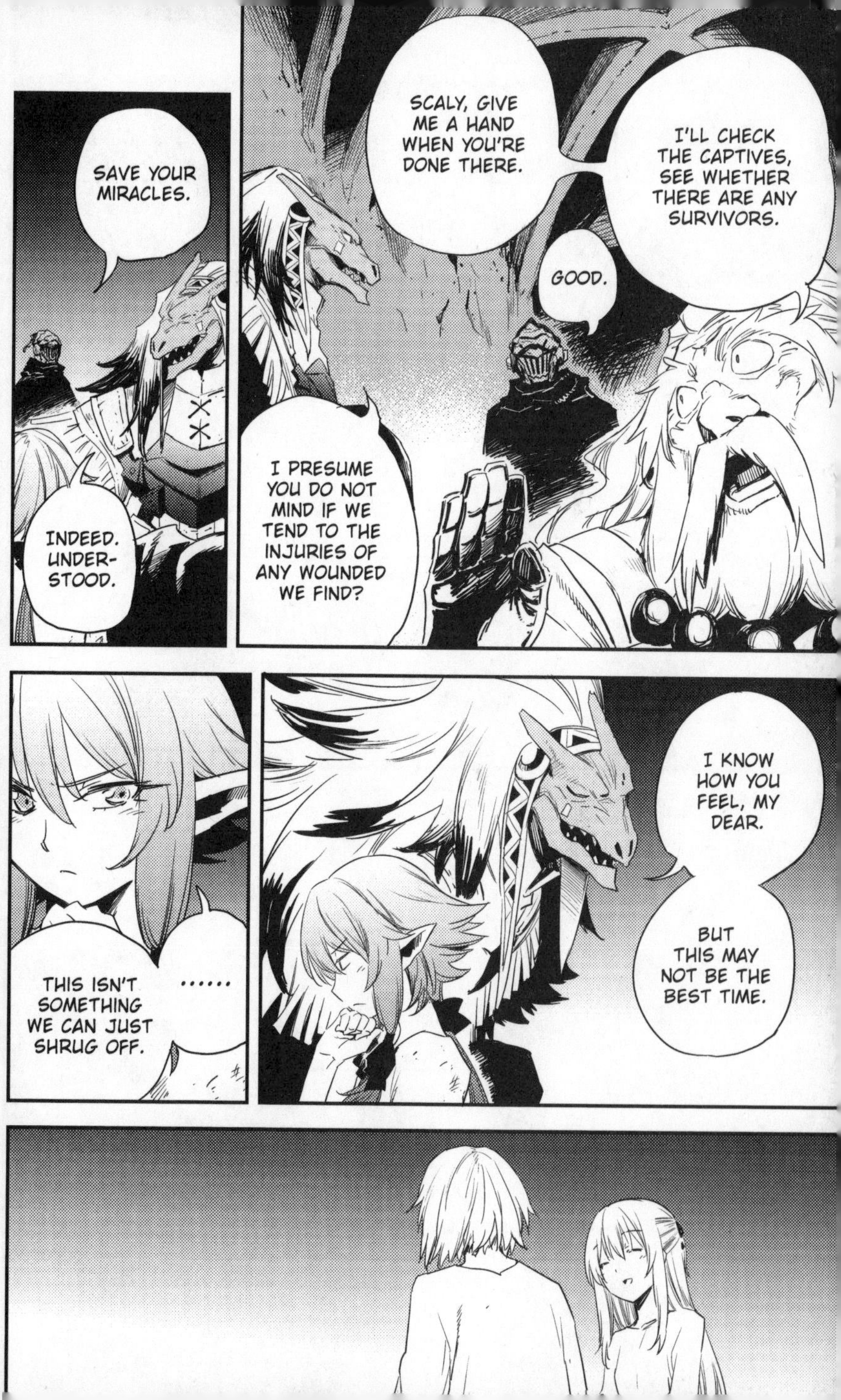
I'LL CHECK THE CAPTIVES, SEE WHETHER THERE ARE ANY SURVIVORS.
SCALY, GIVE ME A HAND WHEN YOU'RE DONE THERE.
GOOD.
I PRESUME YOU DO NOT MIND IF WE TEND TO THE INJURIES OF ANY WOUNDED WE FIND?
SAVE YOUR MIRACLES.
INDEED. UNDER-STOOD.
I KNOW HOW YOU FEEL, MY DEAR.
BUT THIS MAY NOT BE THE BEST TIME.
......
THIS ISN'T SOMETHING WE CAN JUST SHRUG OFF.

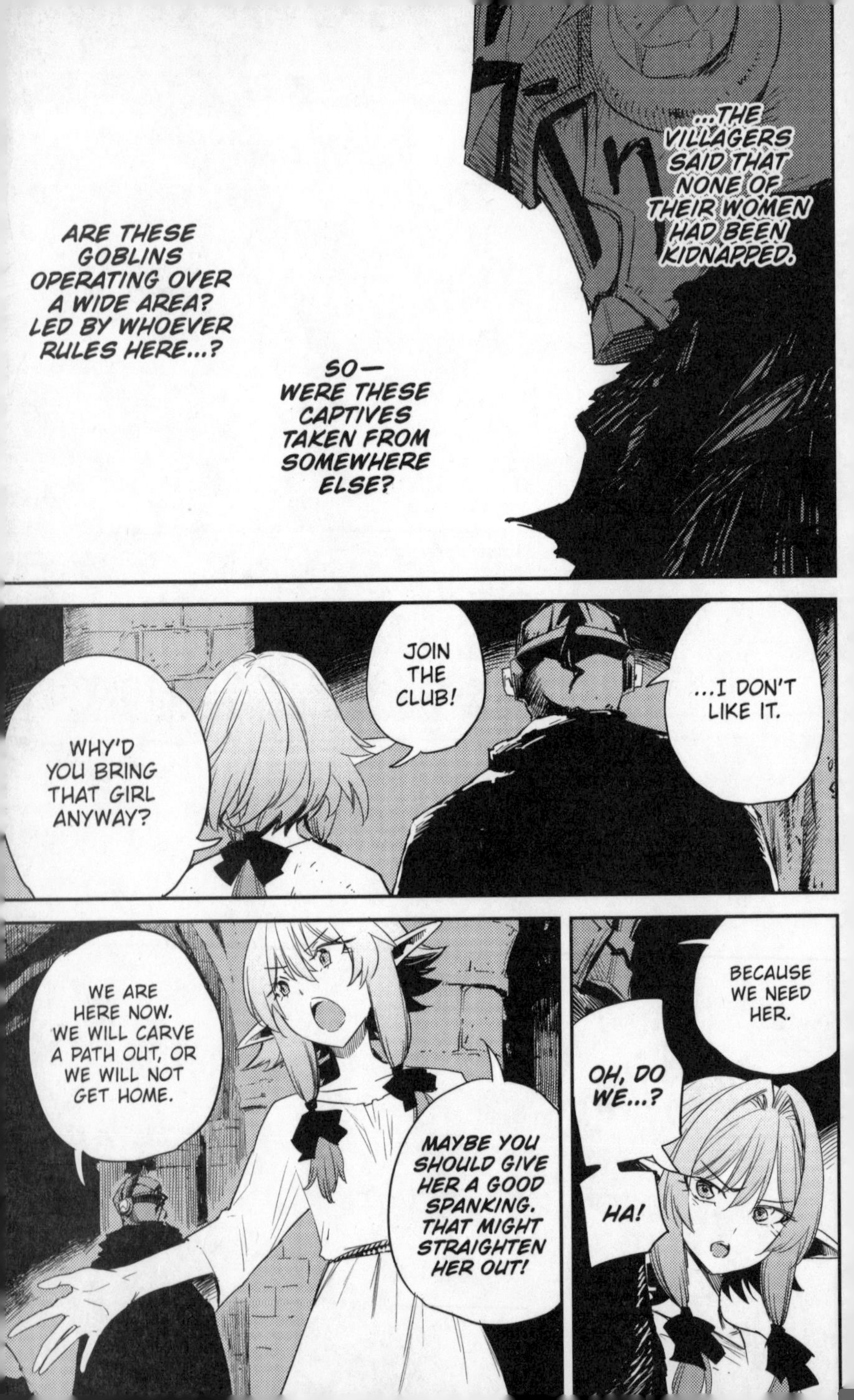
...THE VILLAGERS SAID THAT NONE OF THEIR WOMEN HAD BEEN KIDNAPPED.
SO— WERE THESE CAPTIVES TAKEN FROM SOMEWHERE ELSE?
ARE THESE GOBLINS OPERATING OVER A WIDE AREA? LED BY WHOEVER RULES HERE...?
...I DON'T LIKE IT.
JOIN THE CLUB!
WHY'D YOU BRING THAT GIRL ANYWAY?
BECAUSE WE NEED HER.
OH, DO WE...?
HA!
MAYBE YOU SHOULD GIVE HER A GOOD SPANKING. THAT MIGHT STRAIGHTEN HER OUT!
WE ARE HERE NOW. WE WILL CARVE A PATH OUT, OR WE WILL NOT GET HOME.

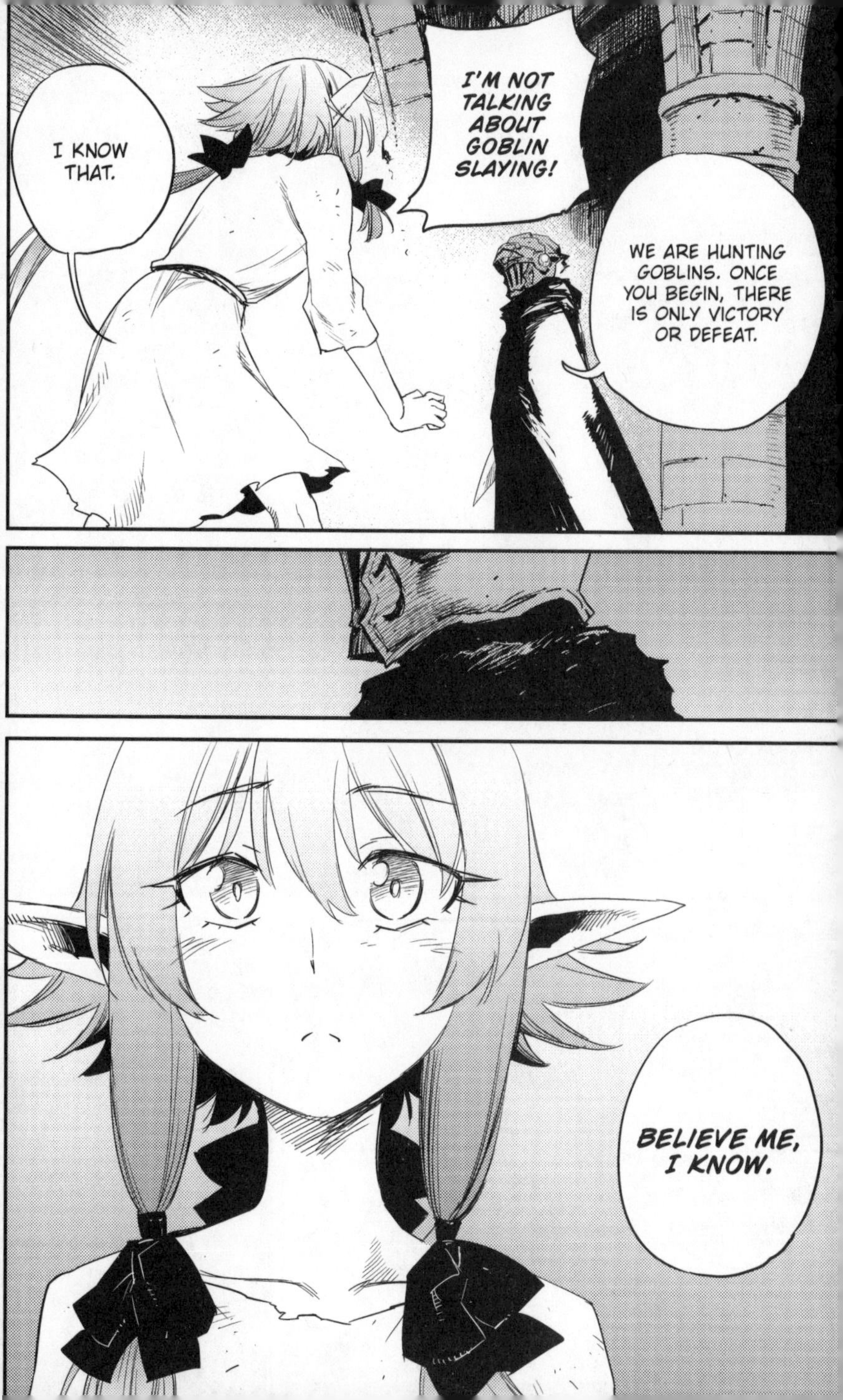
WE ARE HUNTING GOBLINS. ONCE YOU BEGIN, THERE IS ONLY VICTORY OR DEFEAT.
I'M NOT TALKING ABOUT GOBLIN SLAYING!
I KNOW THAT.
BELIEVE ME, I KNOW.

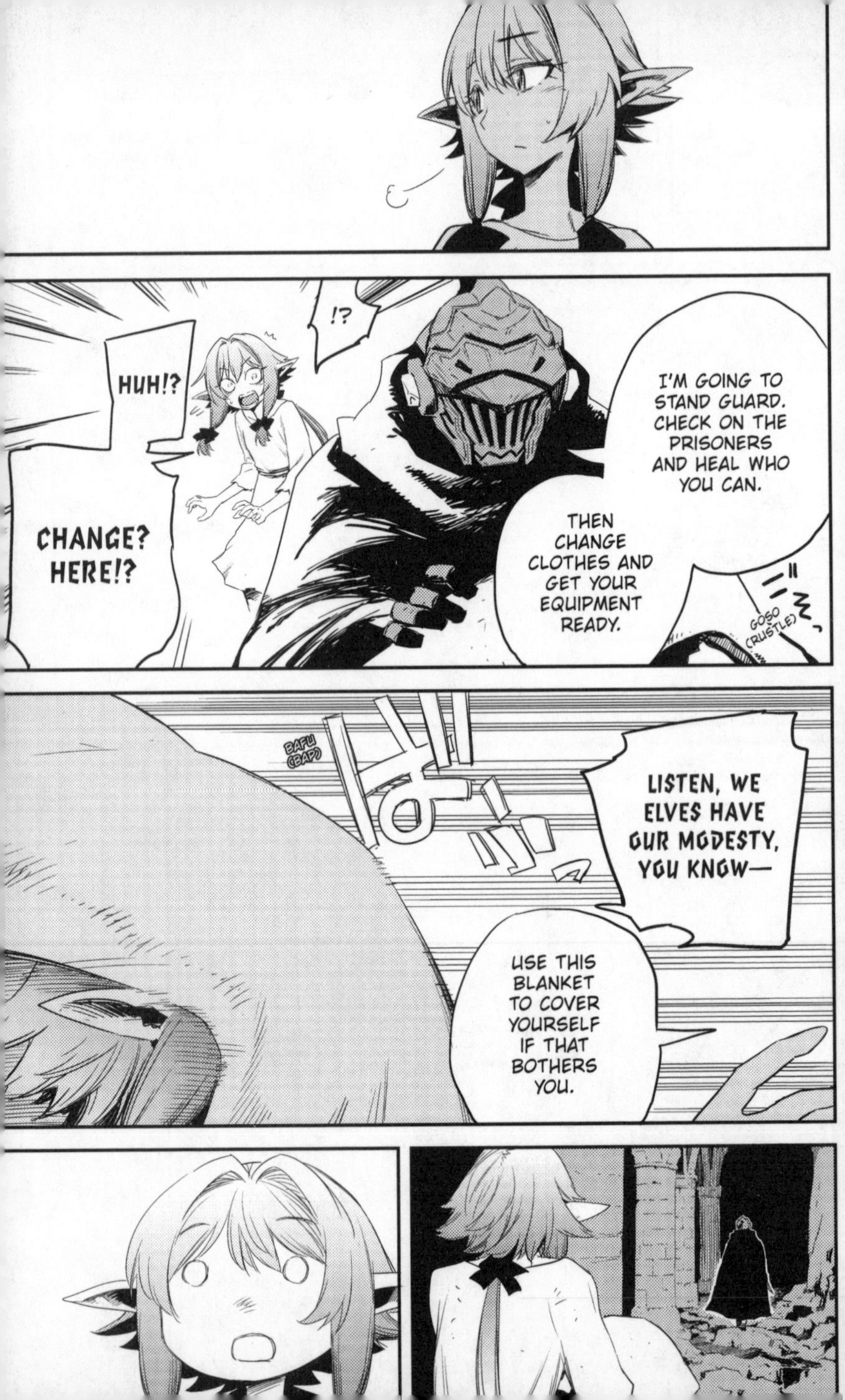
I'M GOING TO STAND GUARD. CHECK ON THE PRISONERS AND HEAL WHO YOU CAN.
THEN CHANGE CLOTHES AND GET YOUR EQUIPMENT READY.
GOSO (RUSTLE)
!?
HUH!?
CHANGE? HERE!?
LISTEN, WE ELVES HAVE OUR MODESTY, YOU KNOW—
USE THIS BLANKET TO COVER YOURSELF IF THAT BOTHERS YOU.
BAFU (BAP)

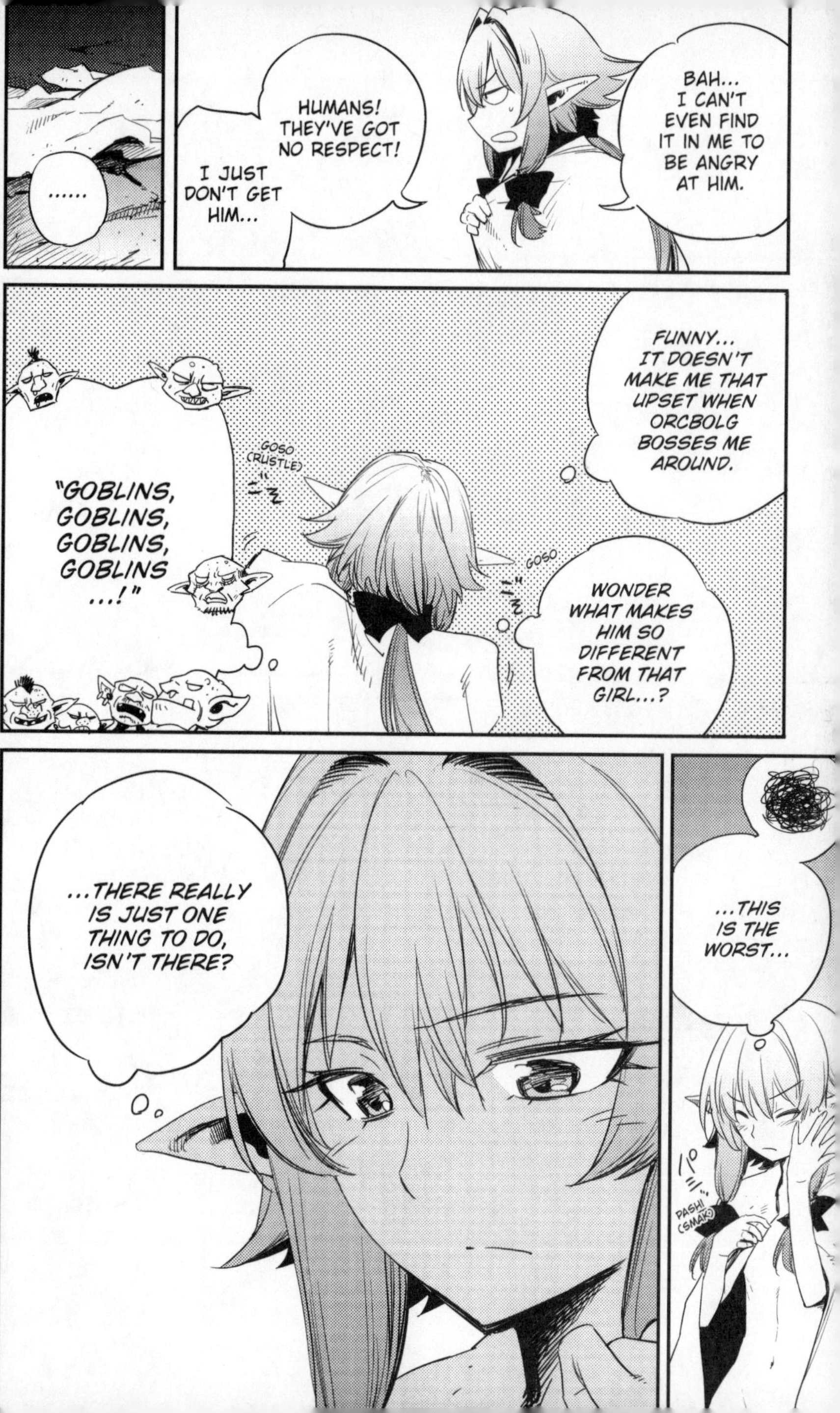
BAH... I CAN'T EVEN FIND IT IN ME TO BE ANGRY AT HIM.
HUMANS! THEY'VE GOT NO RESPECT!
I JUST DON'T GET HIM...
......
FUNNY... IT DOESN'T MAKE ME THAT UPSET WHEN ORCBOLG BOSSES ME AROUND.
GOSO
WONDER WHAT MAKES HIM SO DIFFERENT FROM THAT GIRL...?
GOSO (RUSTLE)
"GOBLINS, GOBLINS, GOBLINS, GOBLINS ...!"
...THIS IS THE WORST...
PASH! (SMAK)
...THERE REALLY IS JUST ONE THING TO DO, ISN'T THERE?

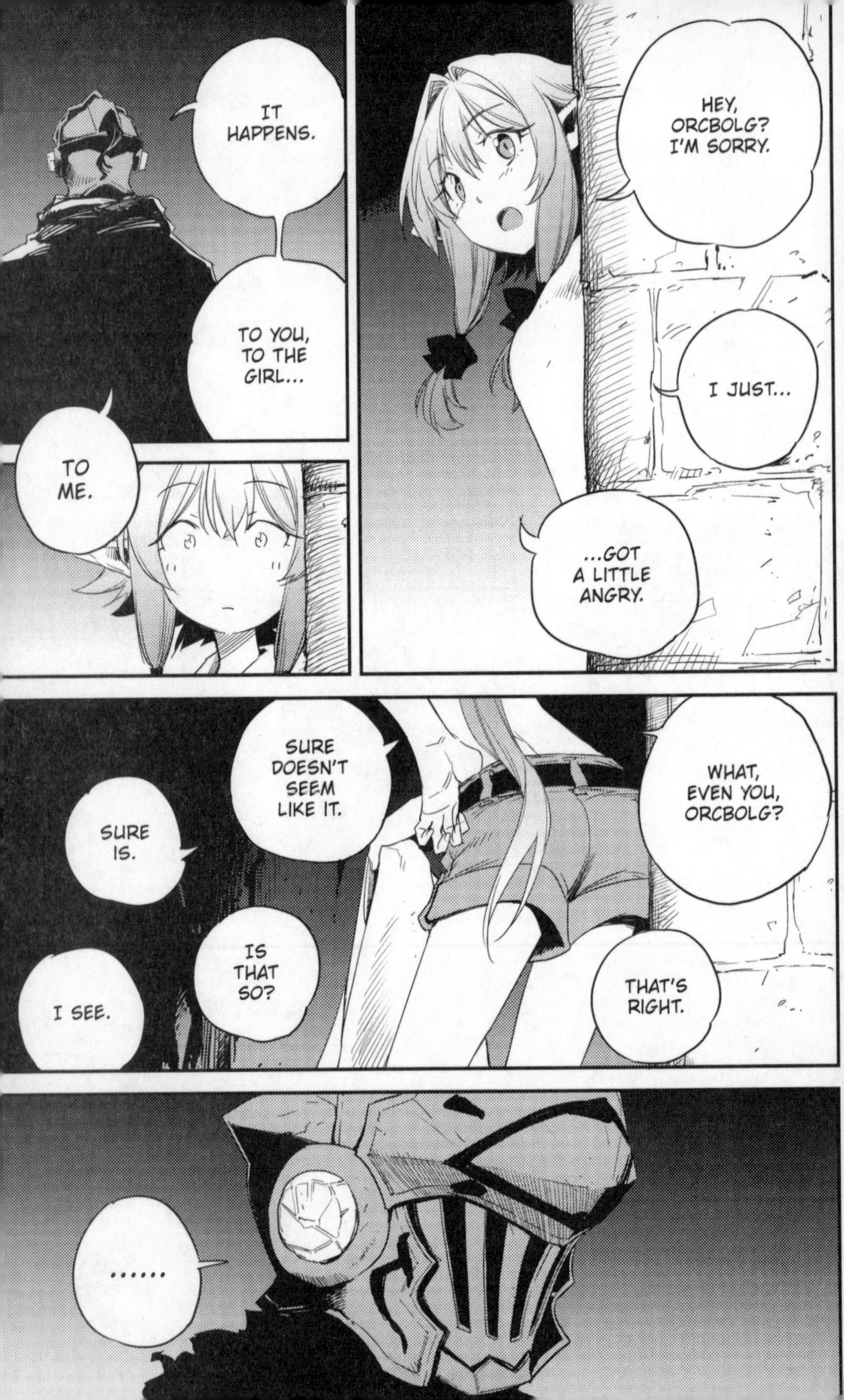
HEY, ORCBOLG? I'M SORRY.
I JUST...
...GOT A LITTLE ANGRY.
IT HAPPENS.
TO YOU, TO THE GIRL...
TO ME.
WHAT, EVEN YOU, ORCBOLG?
THAT'S RIGHT.
SURE DOESN'T SEEM LIKE IT.
SURE IS.
IS THAT SO?
I SEE.
......

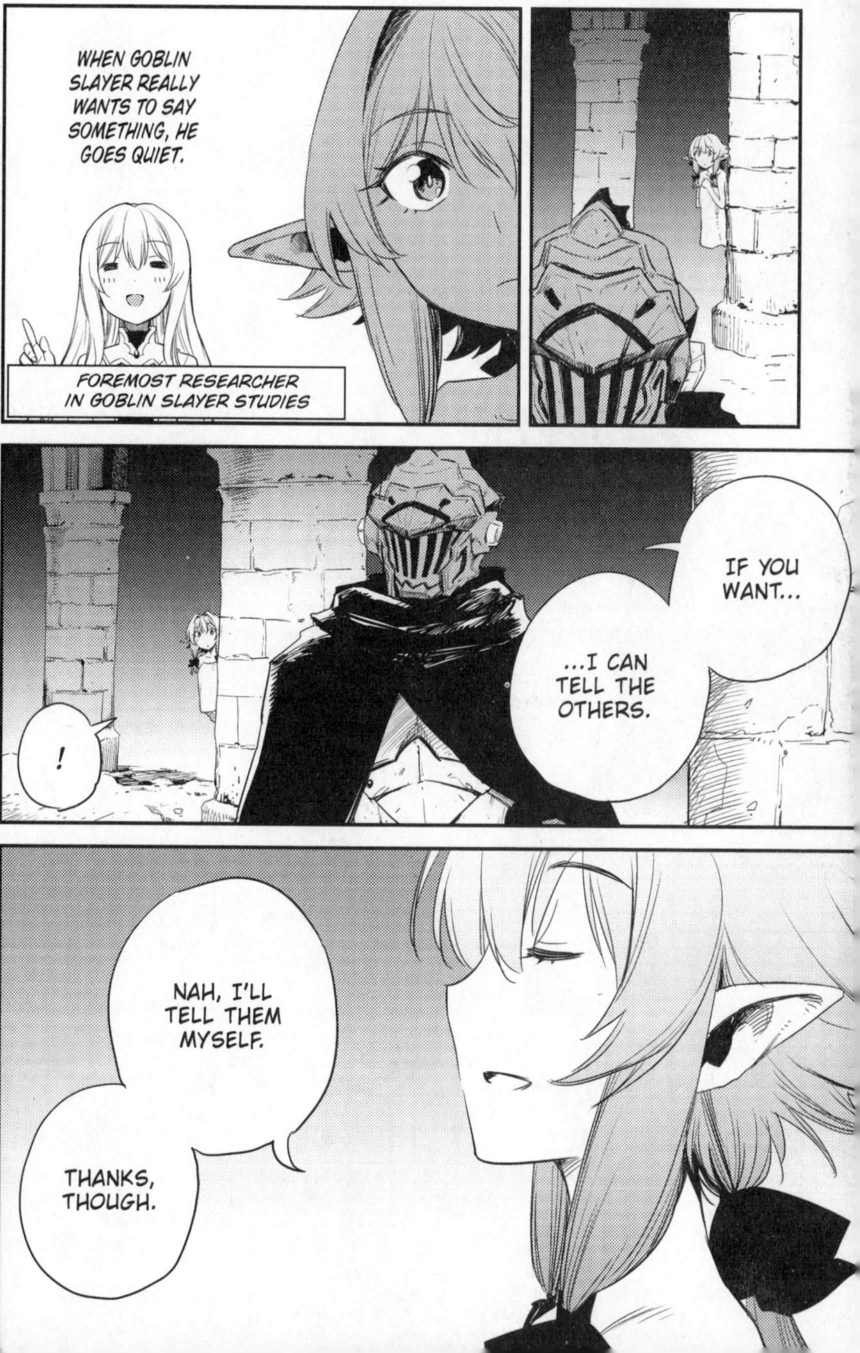
WHEN GOBLIN SLAYER REALLY WANTS TO SAY SOMETHING, HE GOES QUIET.
FOREMOST RESEARCHER IN GOBLIN SLAYER STUDIES
IF YOU WANT...
...I CAN TELL THE OTHERS.
!
NAH, I'LL TELL THEM MYSELF.
THANKS, THOUGH.

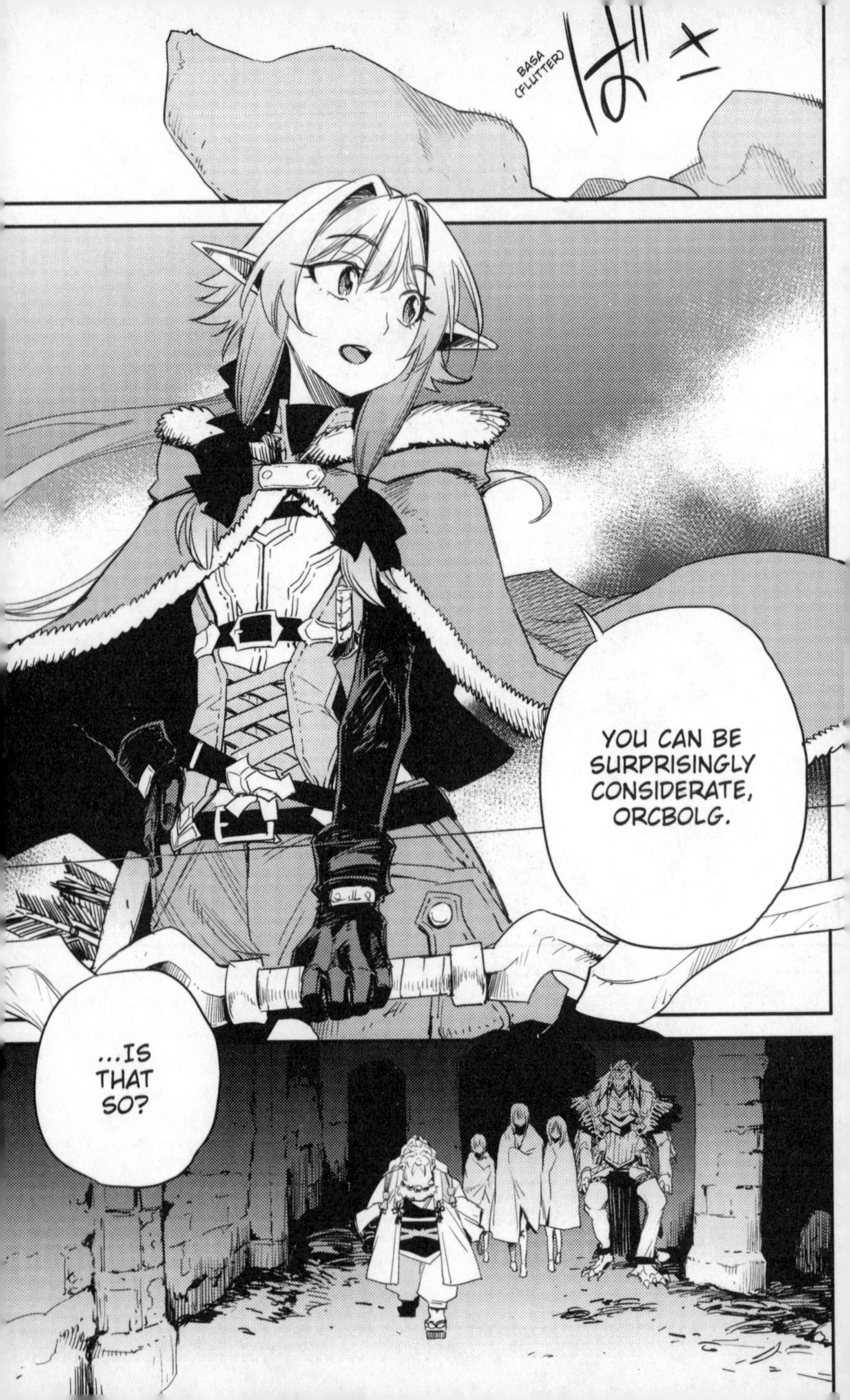
BASA (FLUTTER)
YOU CAN BE SURPRISINGLY CONSIDERATE, ORCBOLG.
...IS THAT SO?

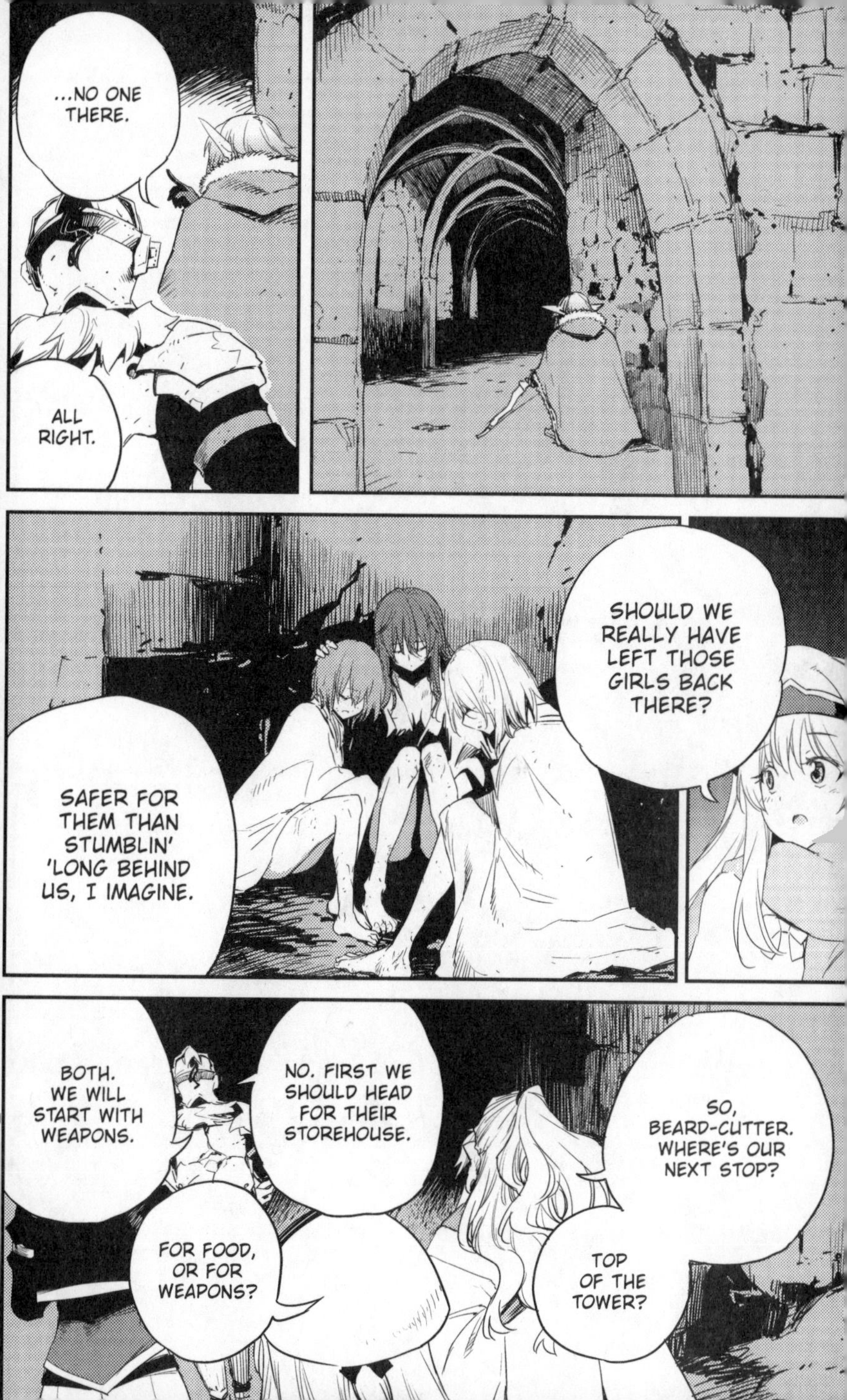
...NO ONE THERE.
ALL RIGHT.
SHOULD WE REALLY HAVE LEFT THOSE GIRLS BACK THERE?
SAFER FOR THEM THAN STUMBLIN' 'LONG BEHIND US, I IMAGINE.
SO, BEARD-CUTTER. WHERE'S OUR NEXT STOP?
TOP OF THE TOWER?
NO. FIRST WE SHOULD HEAD FOR THEIR STOREHOUSE.
FOR FOOD, OR FOR WEAPONS?
BOTH. WE WILL START WITH WEAPONS.

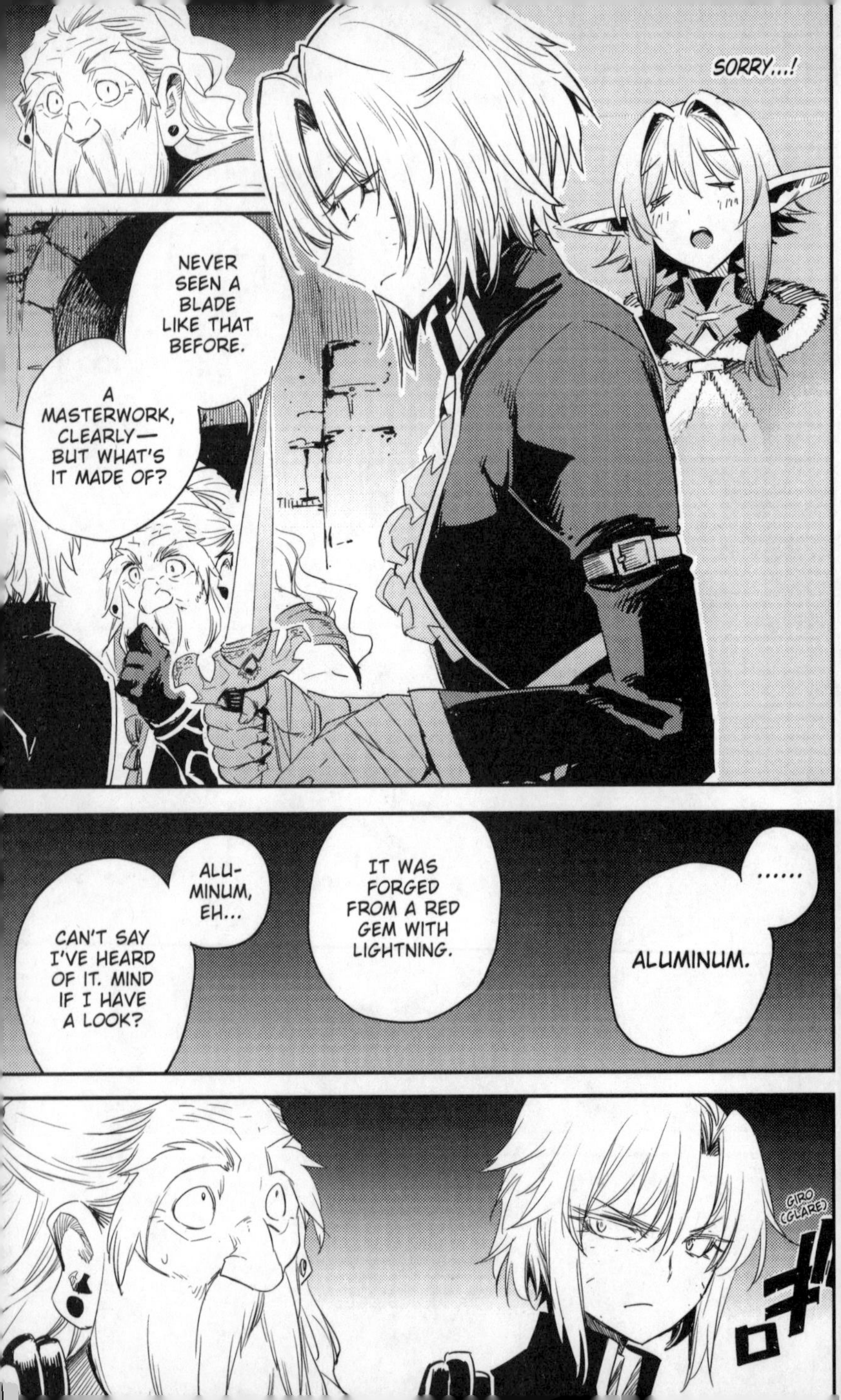
SORRY...!
NEVER SEEN A BLADE LIKE THAT BEFORE.
A MASTERWORK, CLEARLY—BUT WHAT'S IT MADE OF?
......
ALUMINUM.
IT WAS FORGED FROM A RED GEM WITH LIGHTNING.
ALU-MINUM, EH...
CAN'T SAY I'VE HEARD OF IT. MIND IF I HAVE A LOOK?
GIRO (GLARE)

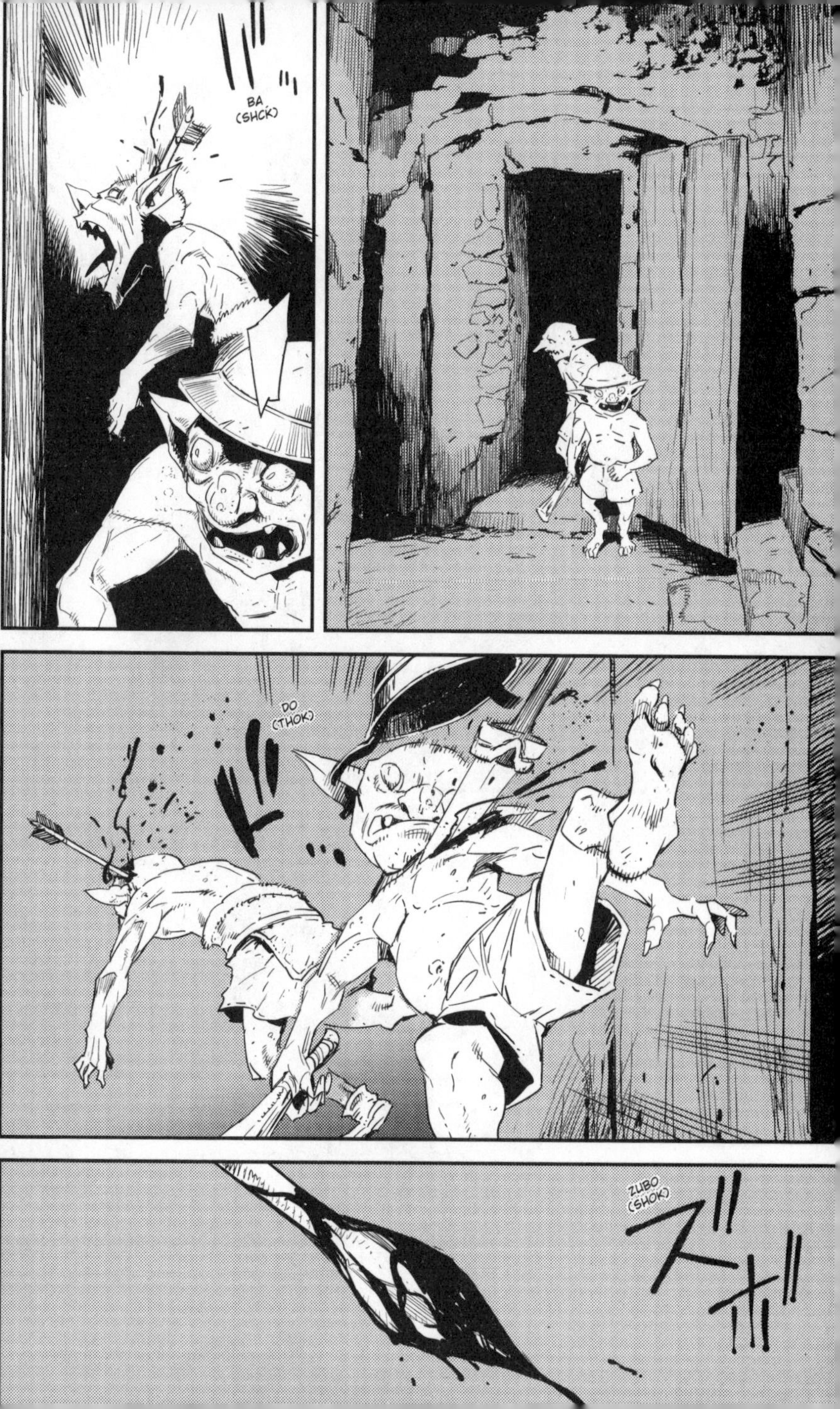
BA (SHCK)
DO (THOK)
ZUBO (SHOK)

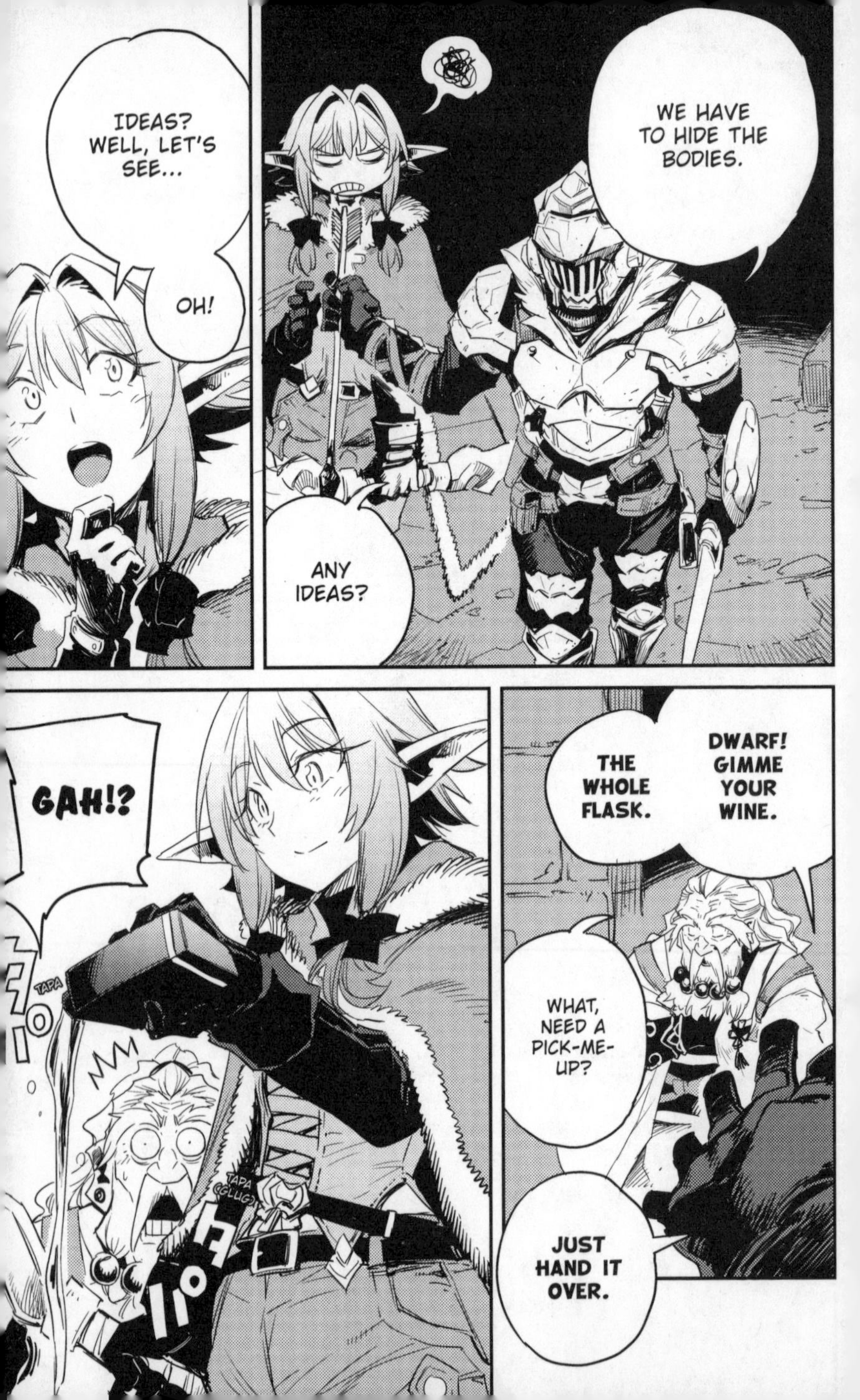
WE HAVE TO HIDE THE BODIES.
ANY IDEAS?
IDEAS? WELL, LET'S SEE...
OH!
DWARF! GIMME YOUR WINE.
THE WHOLE FLASK.
WHAT, NEED A PICK-ME-UP?
JUST HAND IT OVER.
GAH!?
TAPA
TAPA (GLUG)

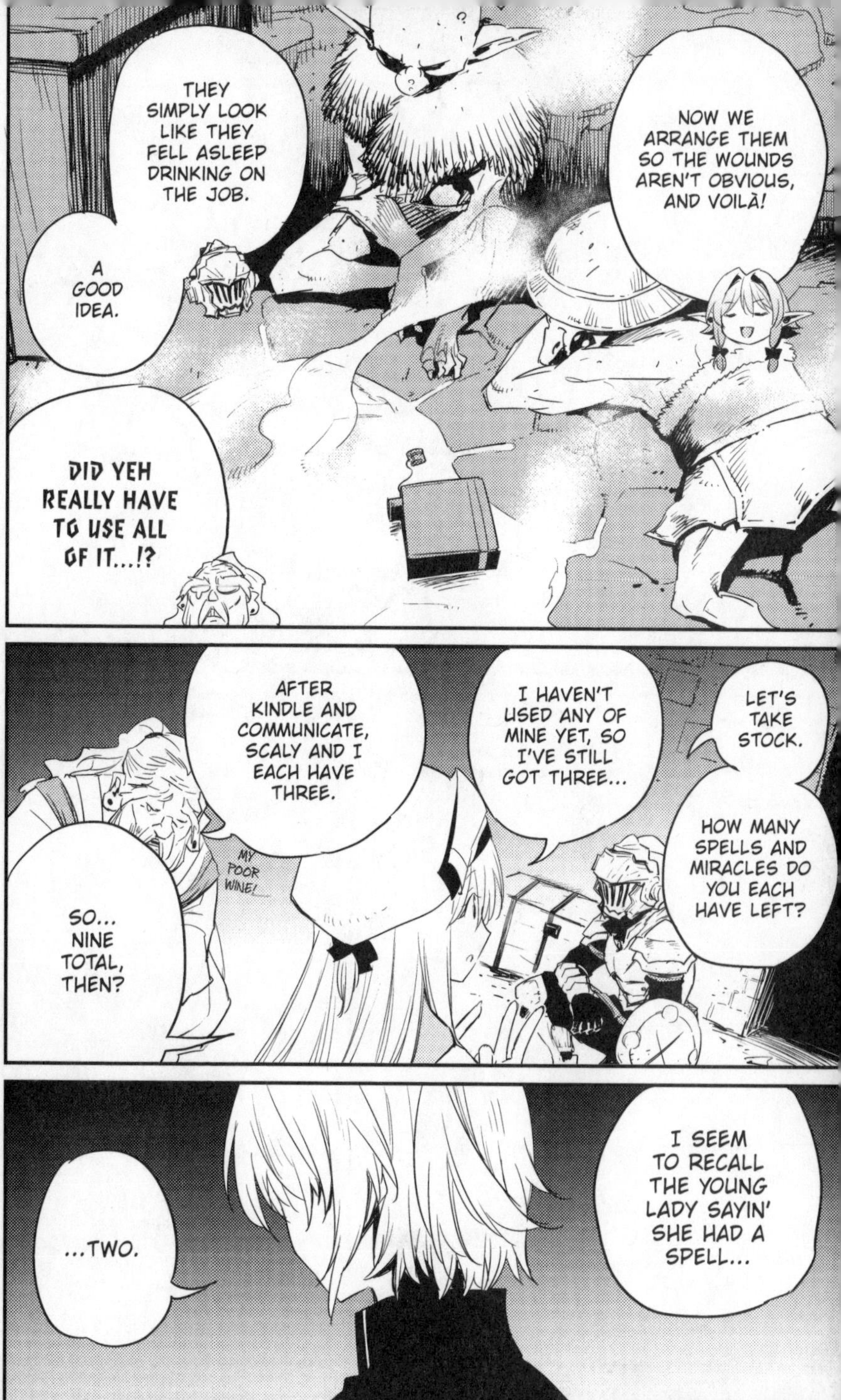
NOW WE ARRANGE THEM SO THE WOUNDS AREN'T OBVIOUS, AND VOILÀ!
THEY SIMPLY LOOK LIKE THEY FELL ASLEEP DRINKING ON THE JOB.
A GOOD IDEA.
DID YEH REALLY HAVE TO USE ALL OF IT...!?
LET'S TAKE STOCK.
HOW MANY SPELLS AND MIRACLES DO YOU EACH HAVE LEFT?
I HAVEN'T USED ANY OF MINE YET, SO I'VE STILL GOT THREE...
AFTER KINDLE AND COMMUNICATE, SCALY AND I EACH HAVE THREE.
MY POOR WINE!
SO... NINE TOTAL, THEN?
I SEEM TO RECALL THE YOUNG LADY SAYIN' SHE HAD A SPELL...
...TWO.

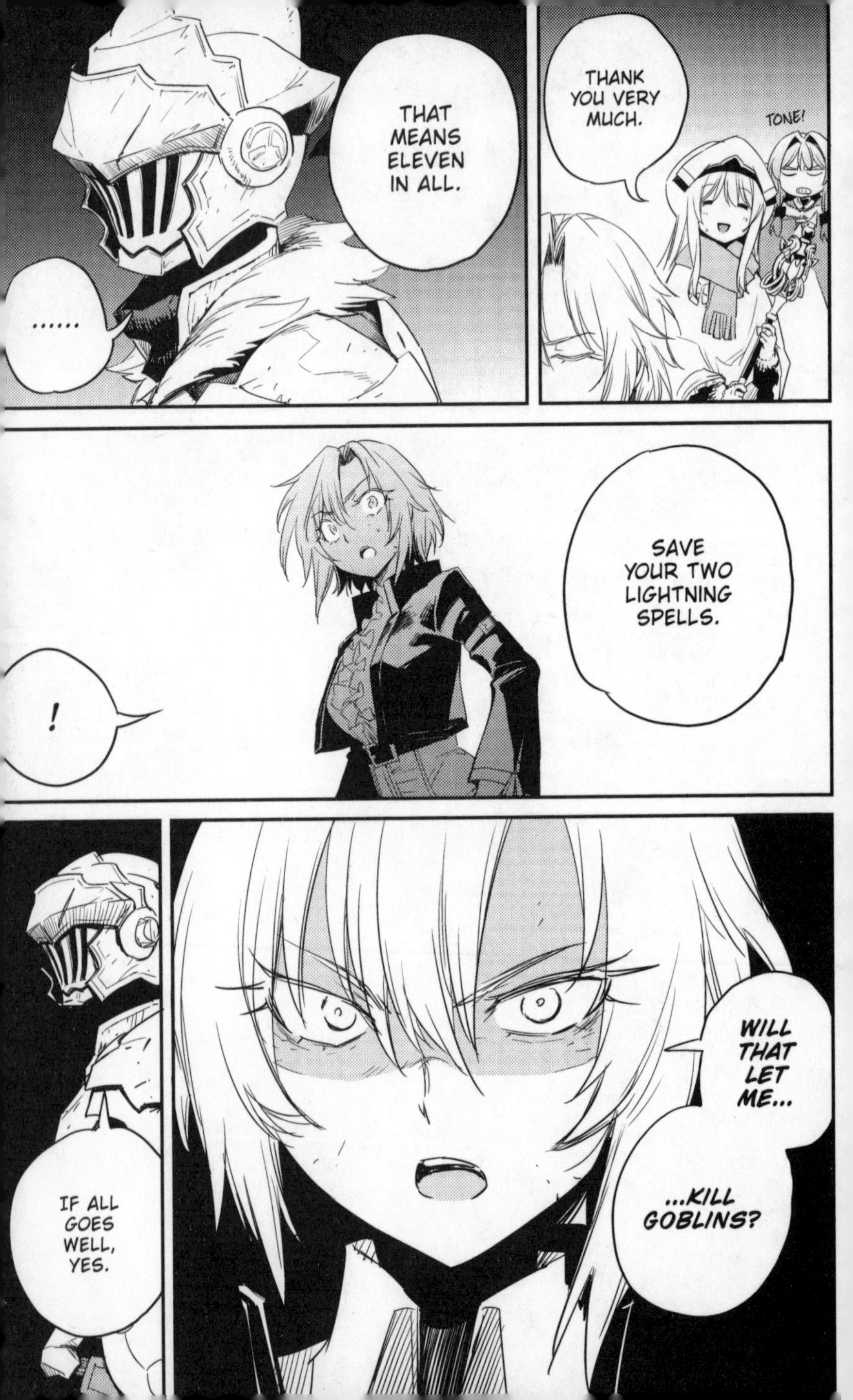
THANK YOU VERY MUCH.
TONE!
THAT MEANS ELEVEN IN ALL.
......
SAVE YOUR TWO LIGHTNING SPELLS.
!
WILL THAT LET ME...
...KILL GOBLINS?
IF ALL GOES WELL, YES.

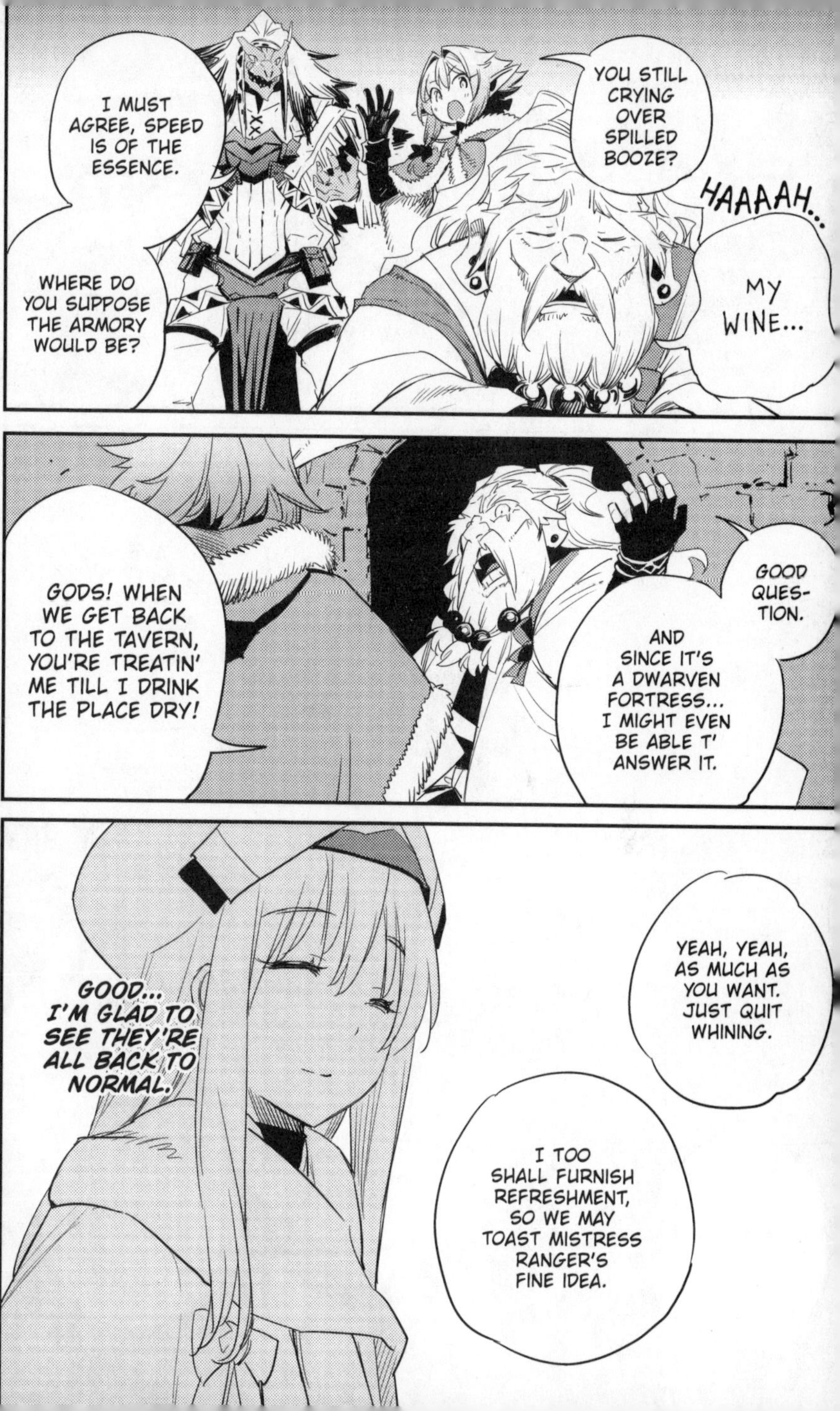
HAAAAH...
MY WINE...
YOU STILL CRYING OVER SPILLED BOOZE?
I MUST AGREE, SPEED IS OF THE ESSENCE.
WHERE DO YOU SUPPOSE THE ARMORY WOULD BE?
GOOD QUES-TION.
AND SINCE IT'S A DWARVEN FORTRESS... I MIGHT EVEN BE ABLE T' ANSWER IT.
GODS! WHEN WE GET BACK TO THE TAVERN, YOU'RE TREATIN' ME TILL I DRINK THE PLACE DRY!
YEAH, YEAH, AS MUCH AS YOU WANT. JUST QUIT WHINING.
I TOO SHALL FURNISH REFRESHMENT, SO WE MAY TOAST MISTRESS RANGER'S FINE IDEA.
GOOD... I'M GLAD TO SEE THEY'RE ALL BACK TO NORMAL.

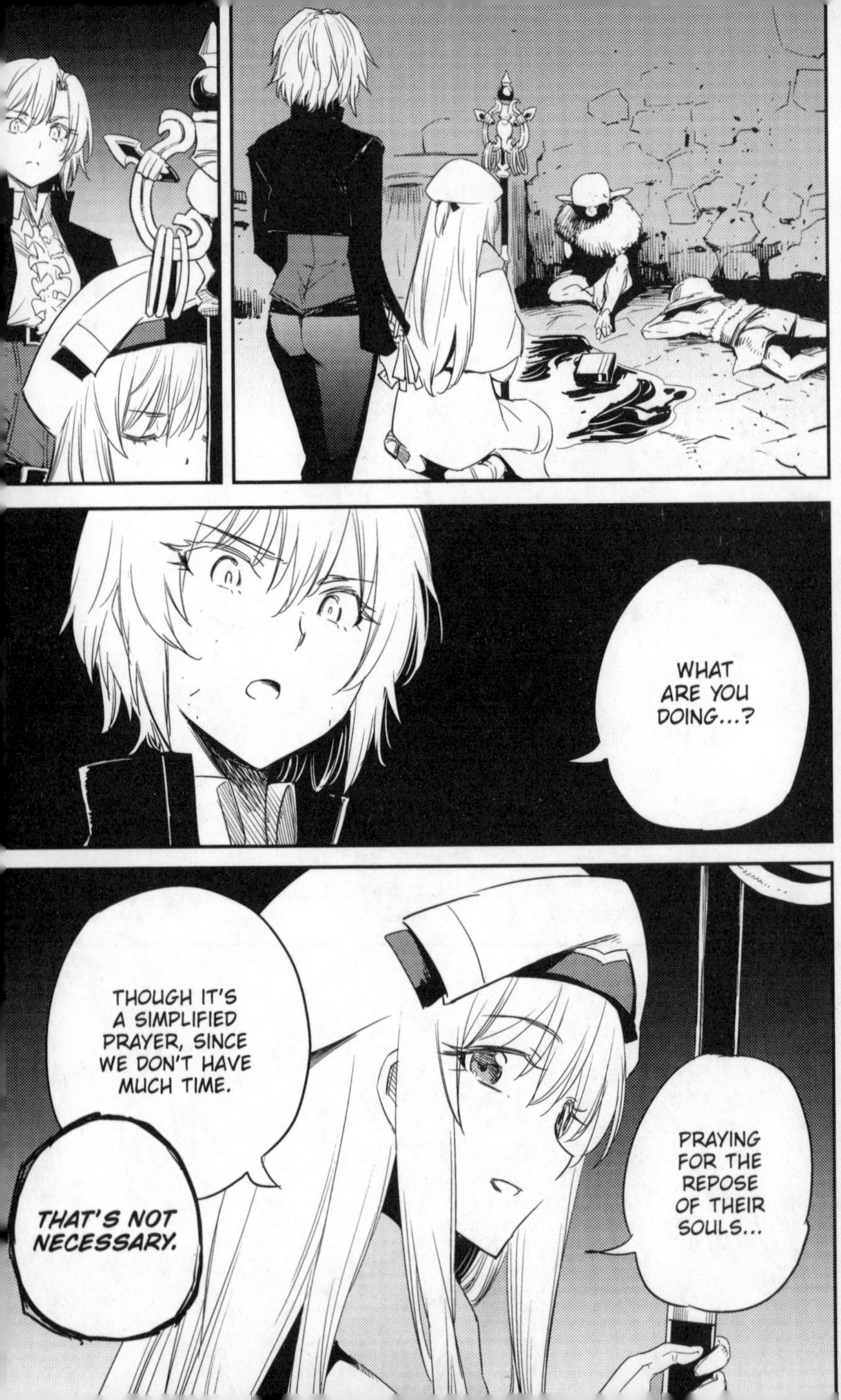
WHAT ARE YOU DOING...?
PRAYING FOR THE REPOSE OF THEIR SOULS...
THOUGH IT'S A SIMPLIFIED PRAYER, SINCE WE DON'T HAVE MUCH TIME.
THAT'S NOT NECESSARY.

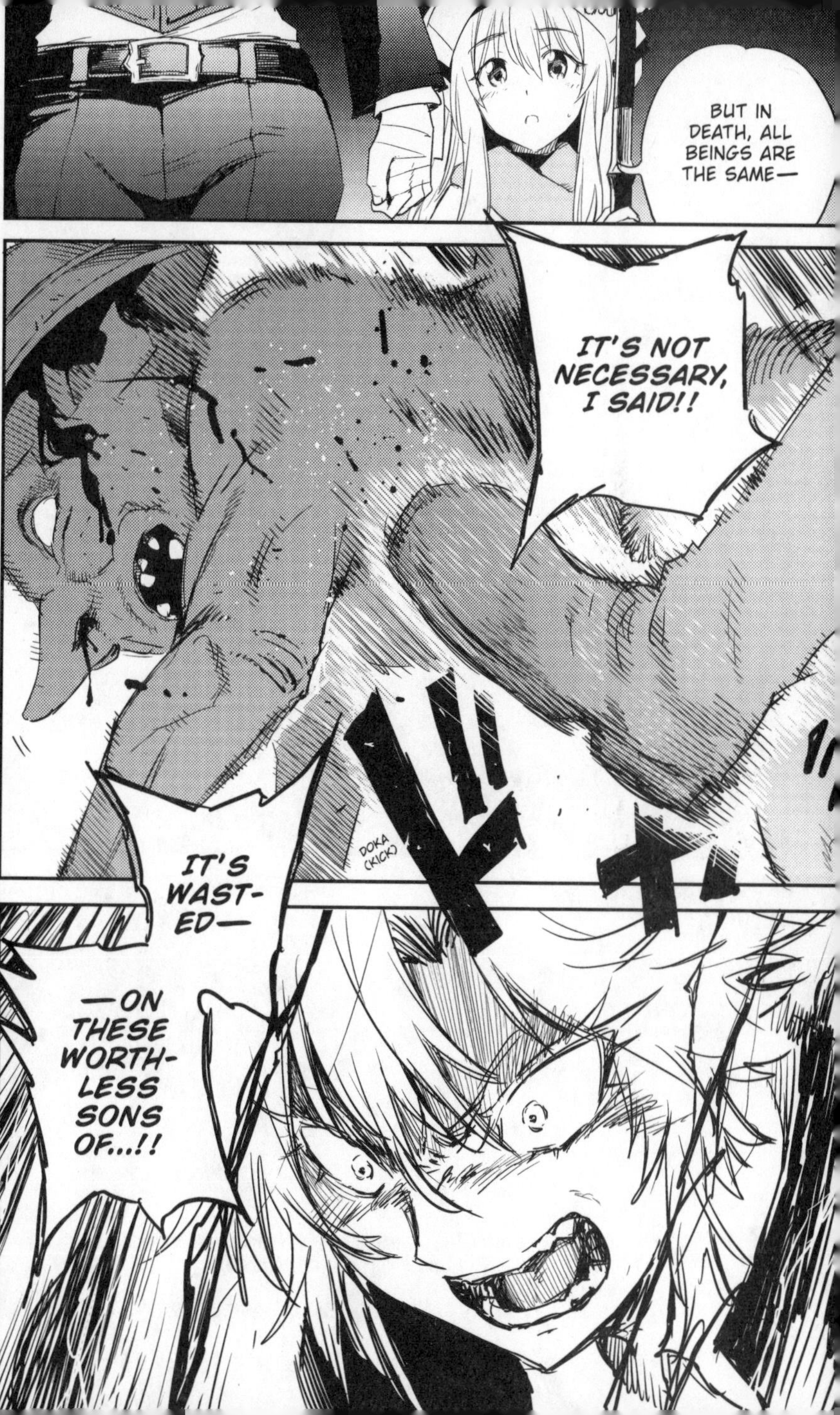
BUT IN DEATH, ALL BEINGS ARE THE SAME—
IT'S NOT NECESSARY, I SAID!!
DOKA (KICK)
IT'S WAST-ED—
—ON THESE WORTH-LESS SONS OF...!!

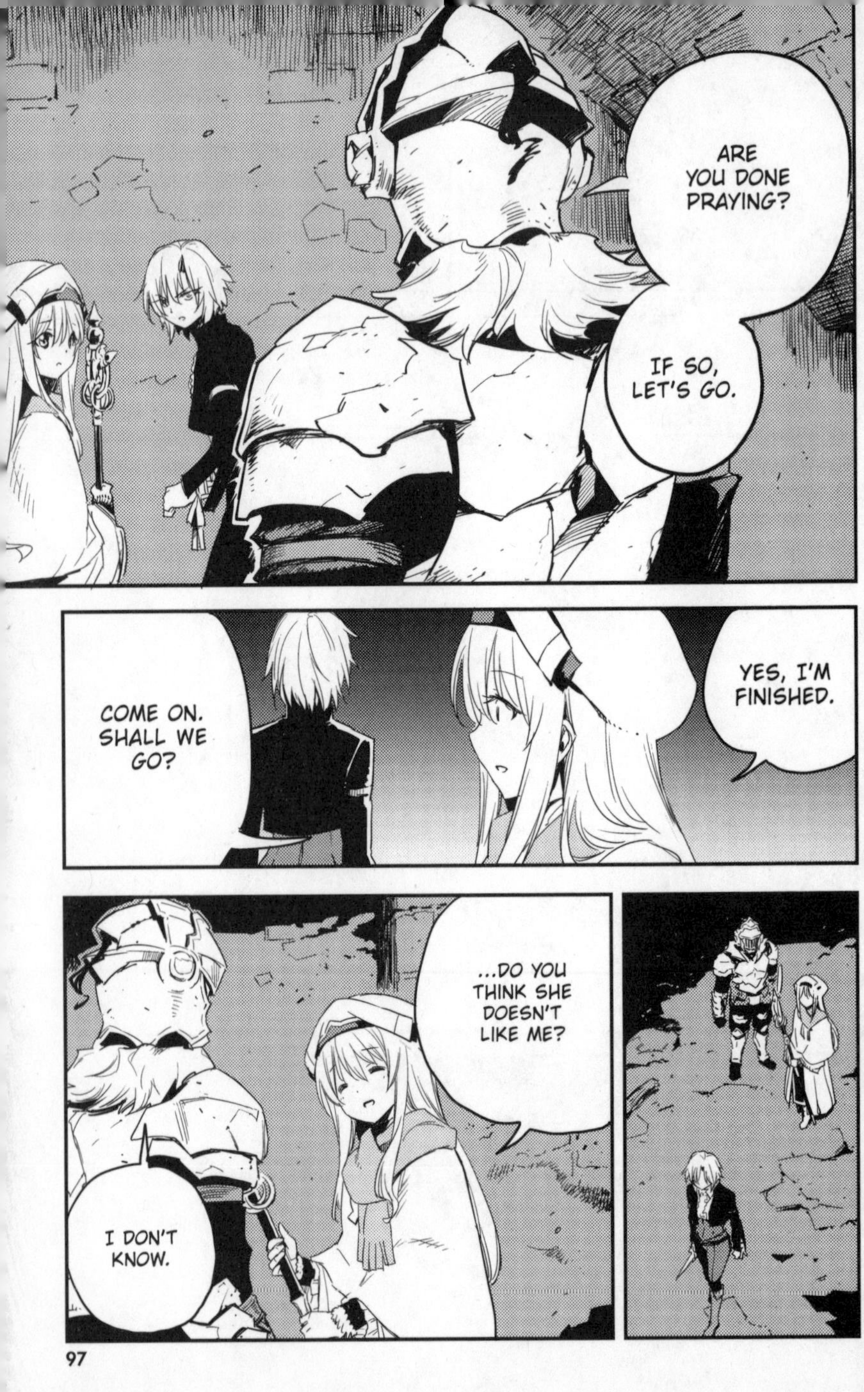
ARE YOU DONE PRAYING?
IF SO, LET'S GO.
YES, I'M FINISHED.
COME ON. SHALL WE GO?
...DO YOU THINK SHE DOESN'T LIKE ME?
I DON'T KNOW.

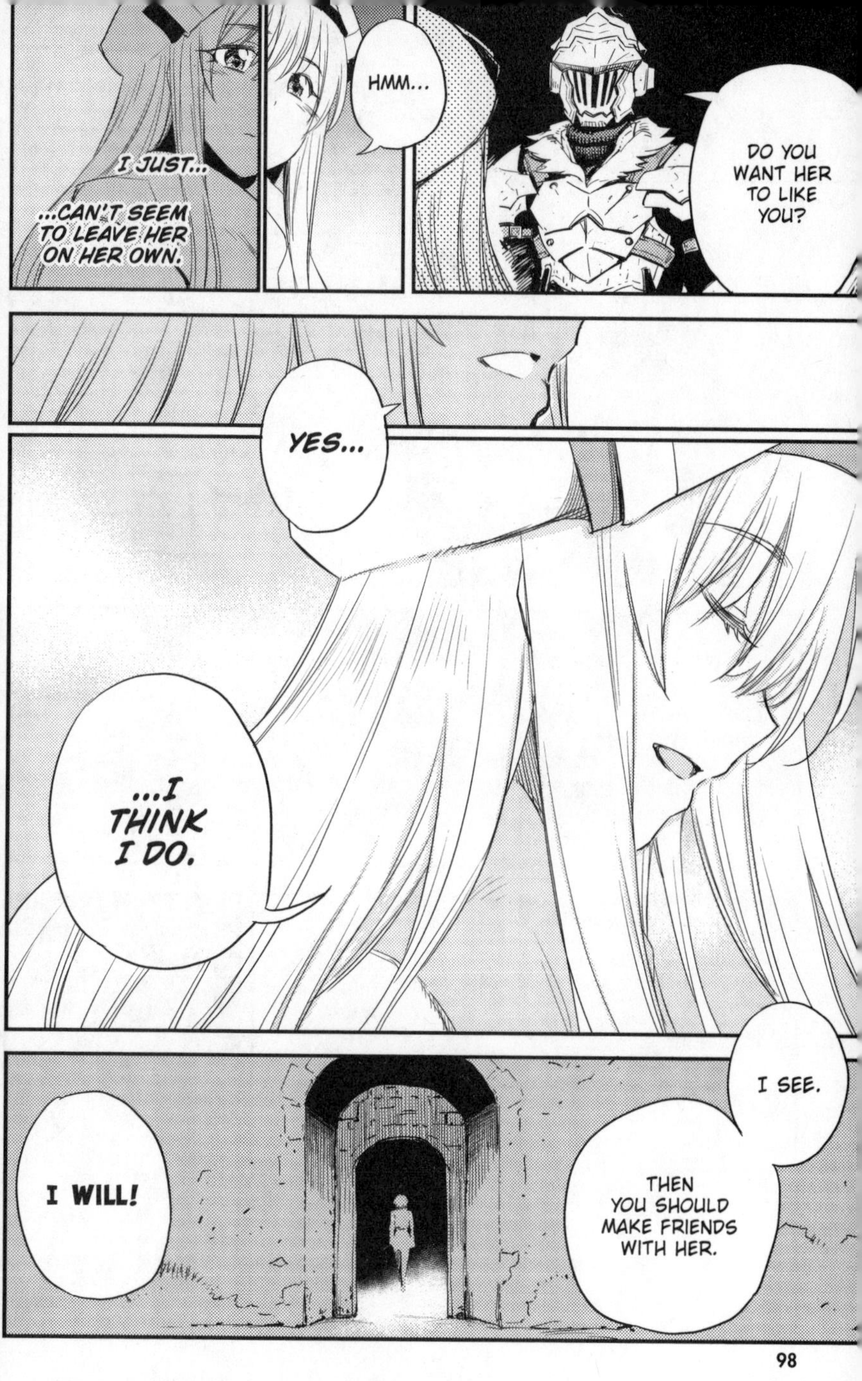
DO YOU WANT HER TO LIKE YOU?
HMM...
I JUST...
...CAN'T SEEM TO LEAVE HER ON HER OWN.
YES...
...I THINK I DO.
I SEE.
THEN YOU SHOULD MAKE FRIENDS WITH HER.
I WILL!

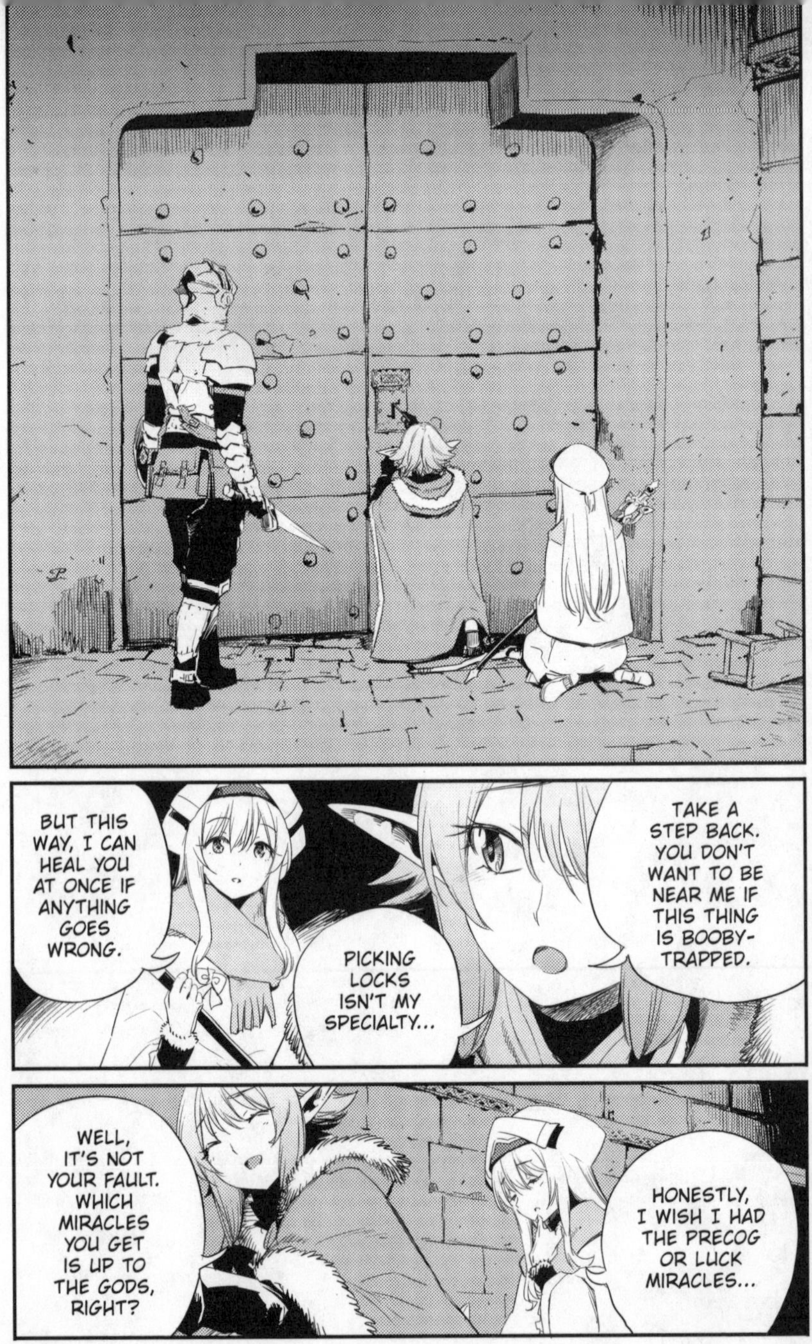

TAKE A STEP BACK. YOU DON'T WANT TO BE NEAR ME IF THIS THING IS BOOBY-TRAPPED.
BUT THIS WAY, I CAN HEAL YOU AT ONCE IF ANYTHING GOES WRONG.
PICKING LOCKS ISN'T MY SPECIALTY...
HONESTLY, I WISH I HAD THE PRECOG OR LUCK MIRACLES...
WELL, IT'S NOT YOUR FAULT. WHICH MIRACLES YOU GET IS UP TO THE GODS, RIGHT?

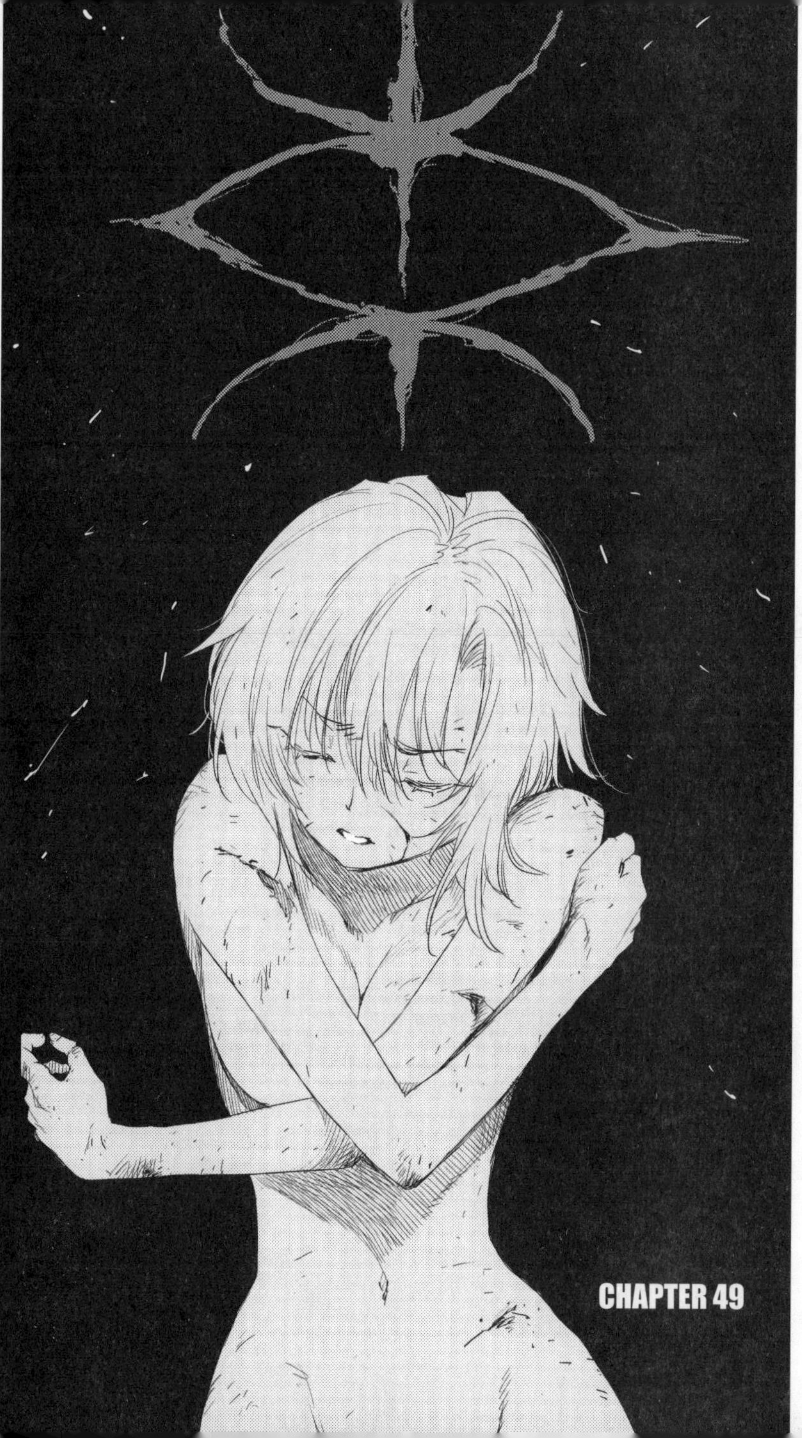
CHAPTER 49

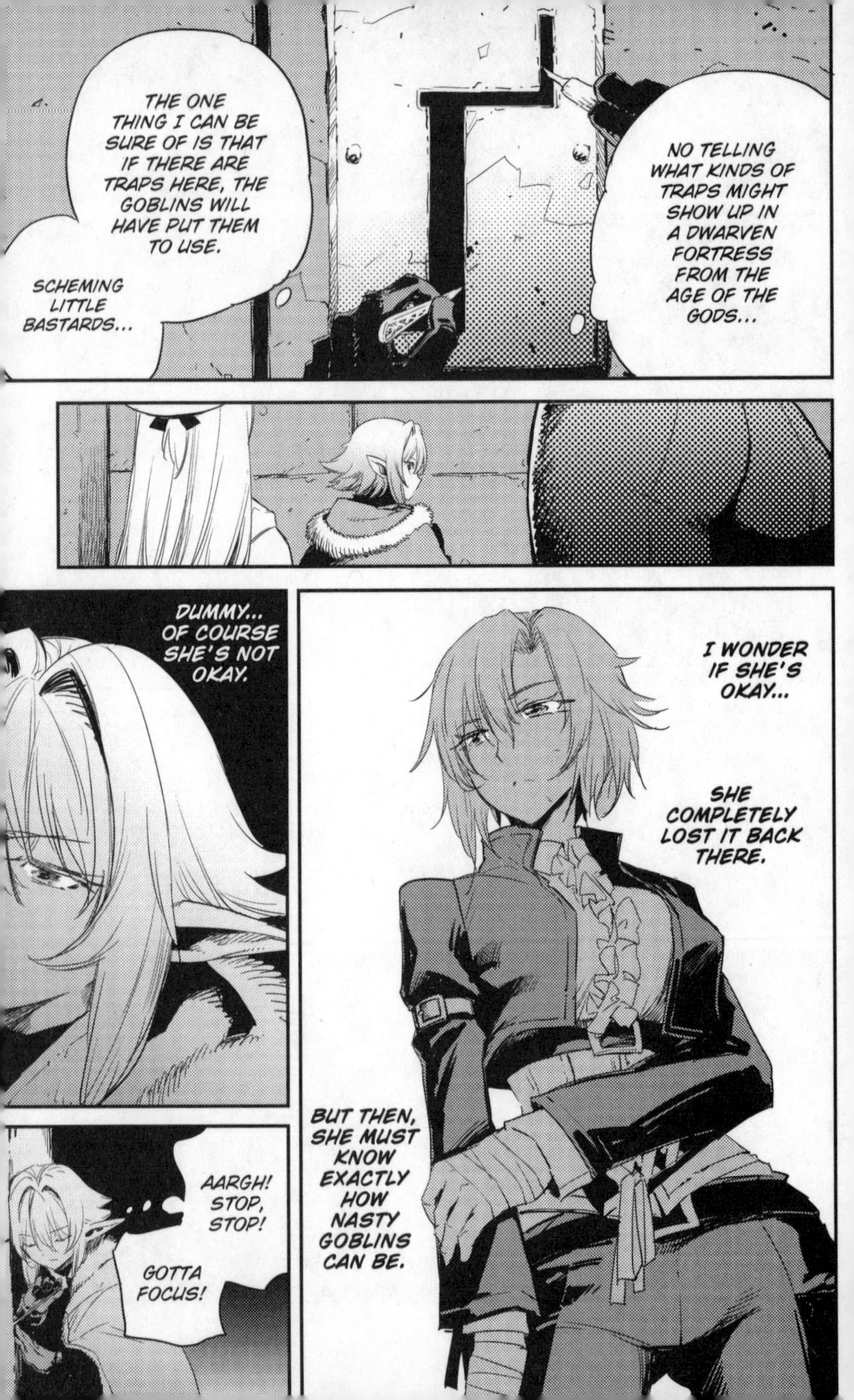
NO TELLING WHAT KINDS OF TRAPS MIGHT SHOW UP IN A DWARVEN FORTRESS FROM THE AGE OF THE GODS...
THE ONE THING I CAN BE SURE OF IS THAT IF THERE ARE TRAPS HERE, THE GOBLINS WILL HAVE PUT THEM TO USE.
SCHEMING LITTLE BASTARDS...
I WONDER IF SHE'S OKAY...
SHE COMPLETELY LOST IT BACK THERE.
BUT THEN, SHE MUST KNOW EXACTLY HOW NASTY GOBLINS CAN BE.
DUMMY... OF COURSE SHE'S NOT OKAY.
AARGH! STOP, STOP!
GOTTA FOCUS!

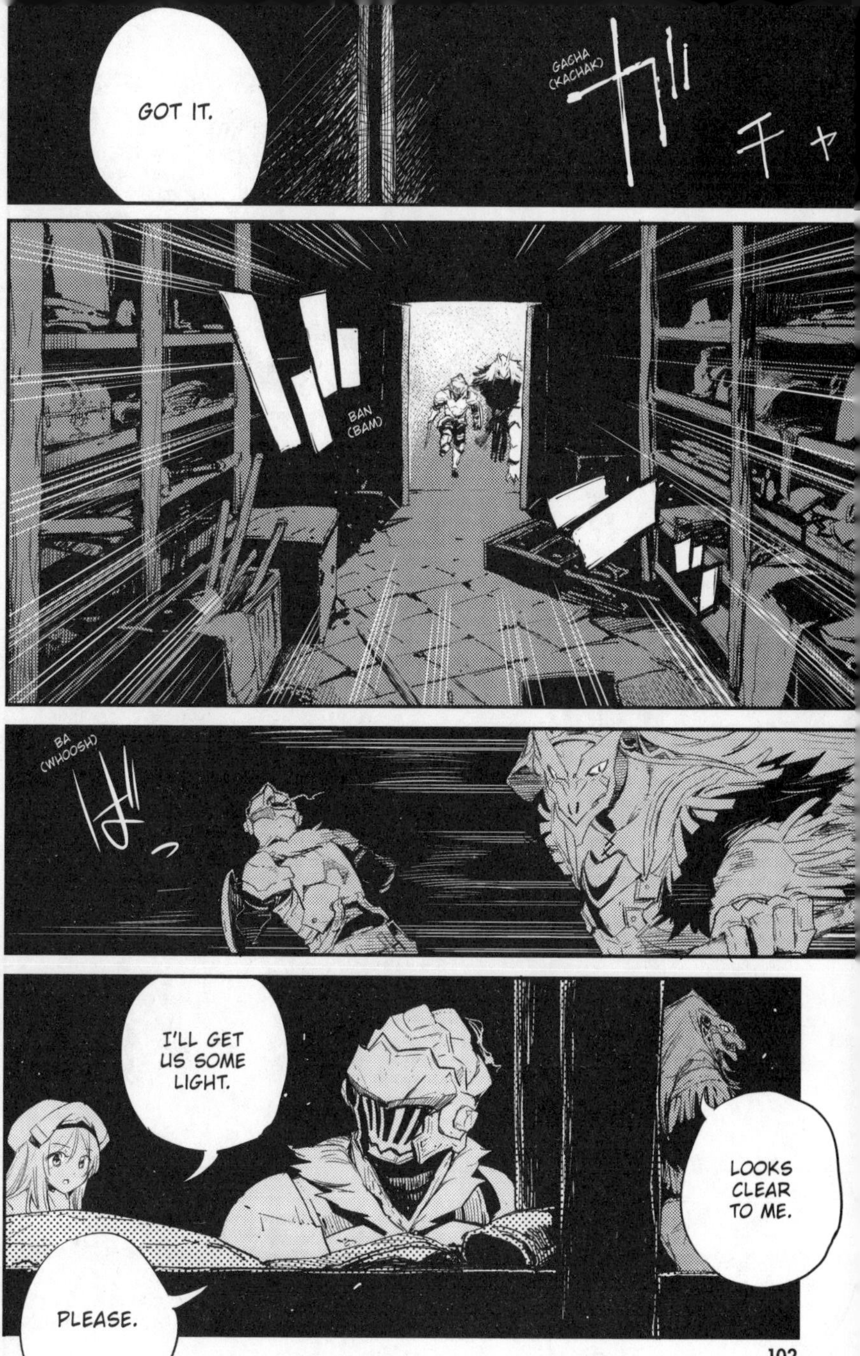
GAGHA (KACHAK)
ガチャ
GOT IT.
BAN (BAM)
BA (WHOOSH)
LOOKS CLEAR TO ME.
I'LL GET US SOME LIGHT.
PLEASE.

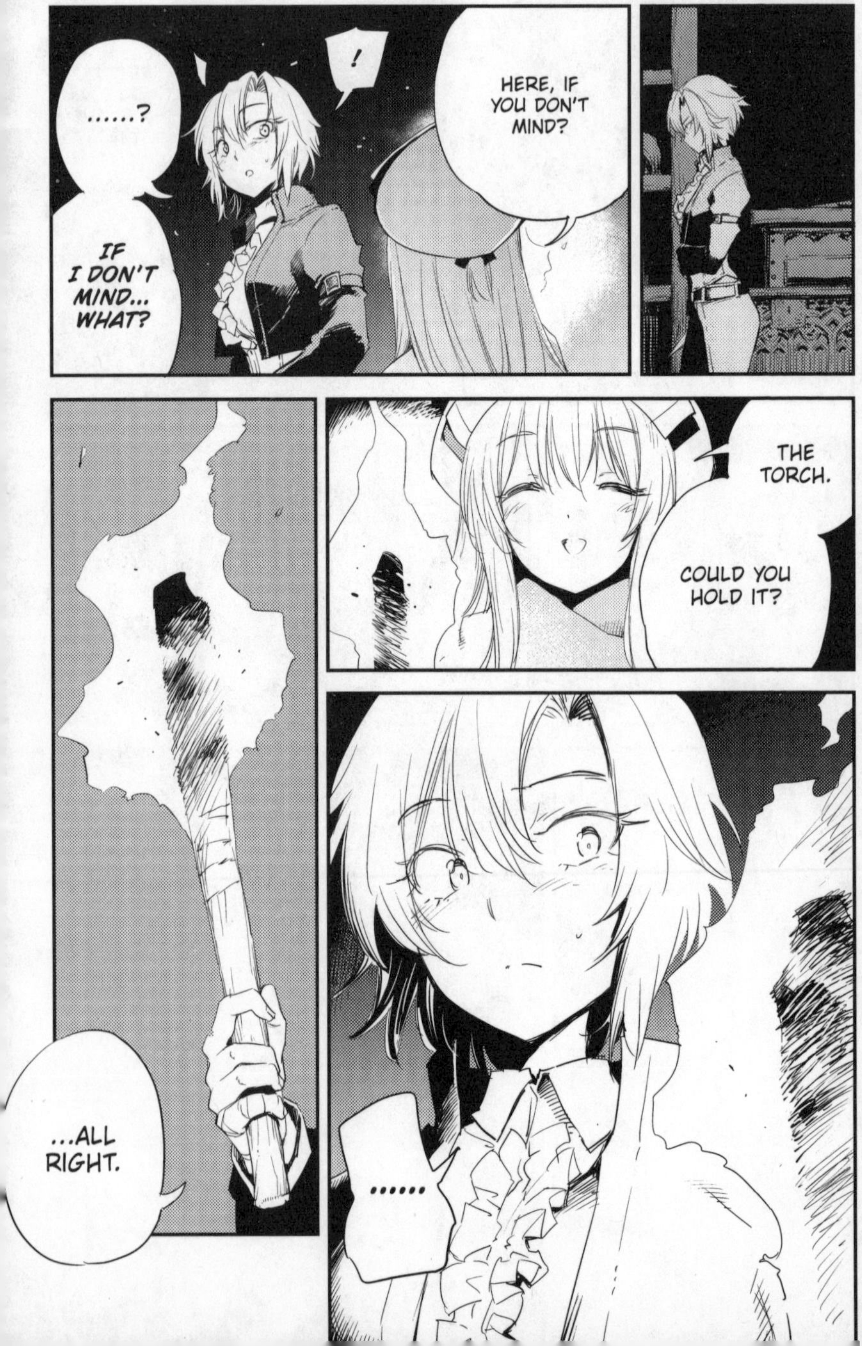
HERE, IF YOU DON'T MIND?
!
!
......?
IF I DON'T MIND... WHAT?
THE TORCH.
COULD YOU HOLD IT?
......
...ALL RIGHT.

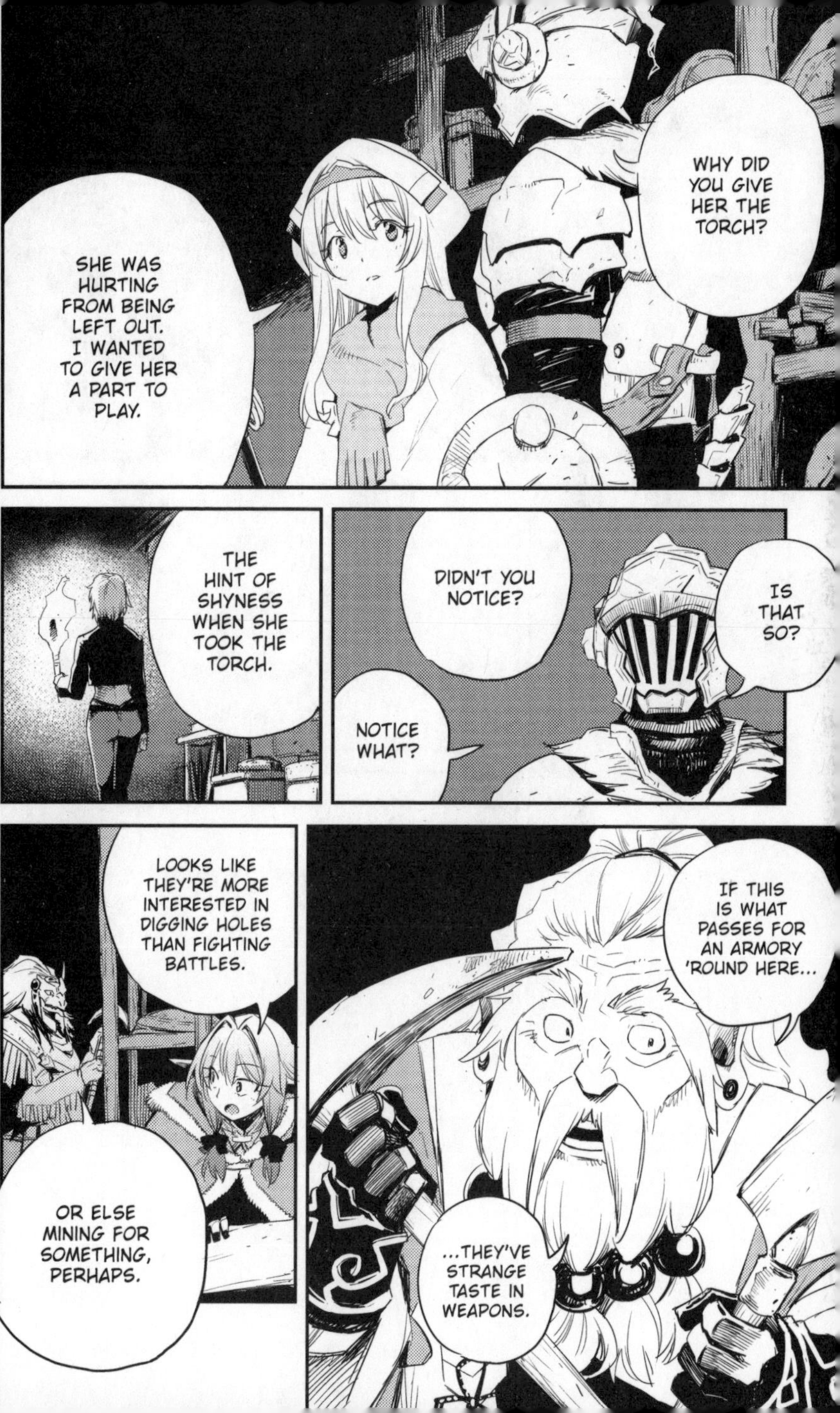
WHY DID YOU GIVE HER THE TORCH?
SHE WAS HURTING FROM BEING LEFT OUT. I WANTED TO GIVE HER A PART TO PLAY.
IS THAT SO?
DIDN'T YOU NOTICE?
NOTICE WHAT?
THE HINT OF SHYNESS WHEN SHE TOOK THE TORCH.
IF THIS IS WHAT PASSES FOR AN ARMORY 'ROUND HERE...
...THEY'VE STRANGE TASTE IN WEAPONS.
LOOKS LIKE THEY'RE MORE INTERESTED IN DIGGING HOLES THAN FIGHTING BATTLES.
OR ELSE MINING FOR SOMETHING, PERHAPS.

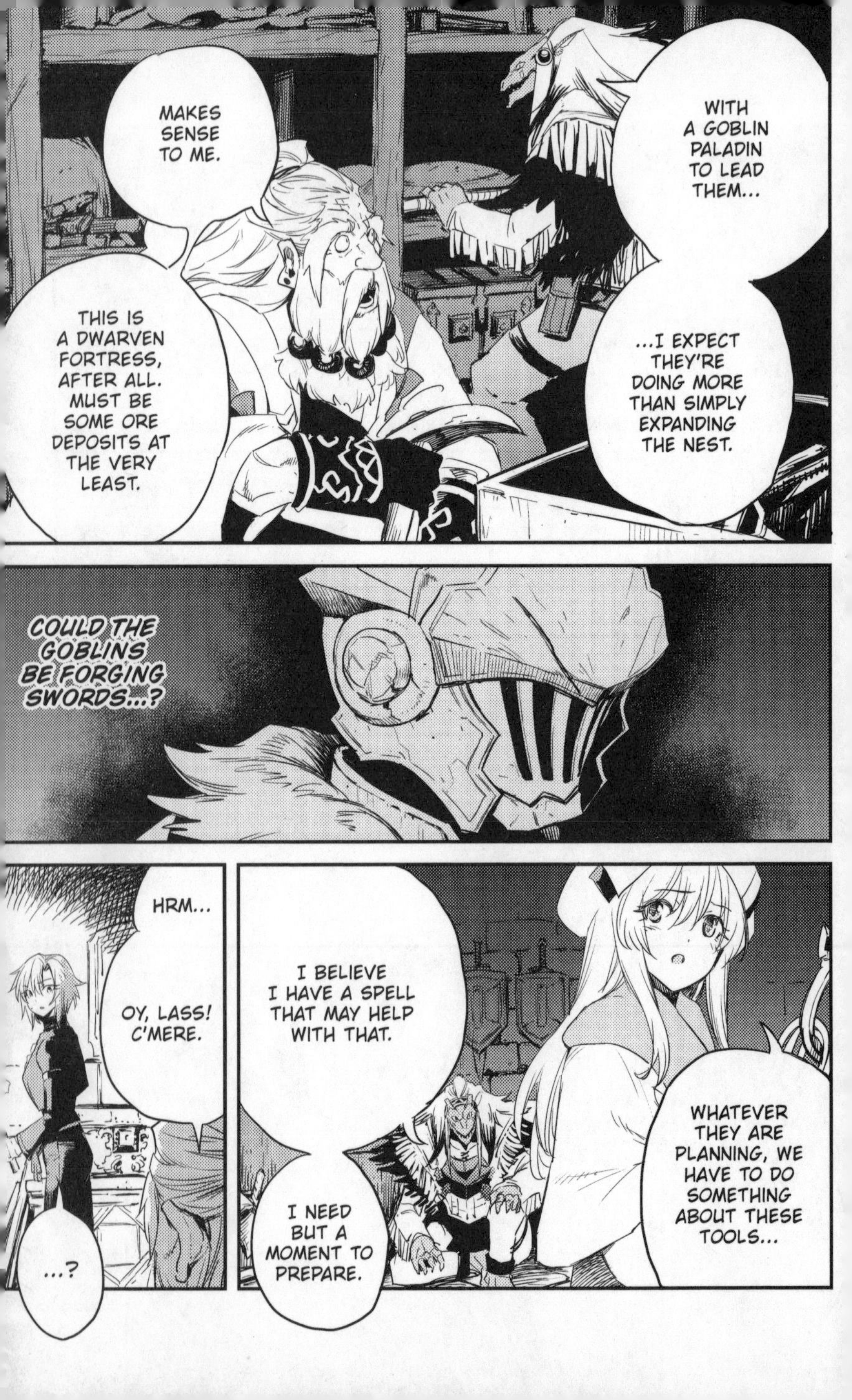
WITH A GOBLIN PALADIN TO LEAD THEM...
...I EXPECT THEY'RE DOING MORE THAN SIMPLY EXPANDING THE NEST.
MAKES SENSE TO ME.
THIS IS A DWARVEN FORTRESS, AFTER ALL. MUST BE SOME ORE DEPOSITS AT THE VERY LEAST.
COULD THE GOBLINS BE FORGING SWORDS...?
WHATEVER THEY ARE PLANNING, WE HAVE TO DO SOMETHING ABOUT THESE TOOLS...
I BELIEVE I HAVE A SPELL THAT MAY HELP WITH THAT.
I NEED BUT A MOMENT TO PREPARE.
HRM...
OY, LASS! C'MERE.
...?

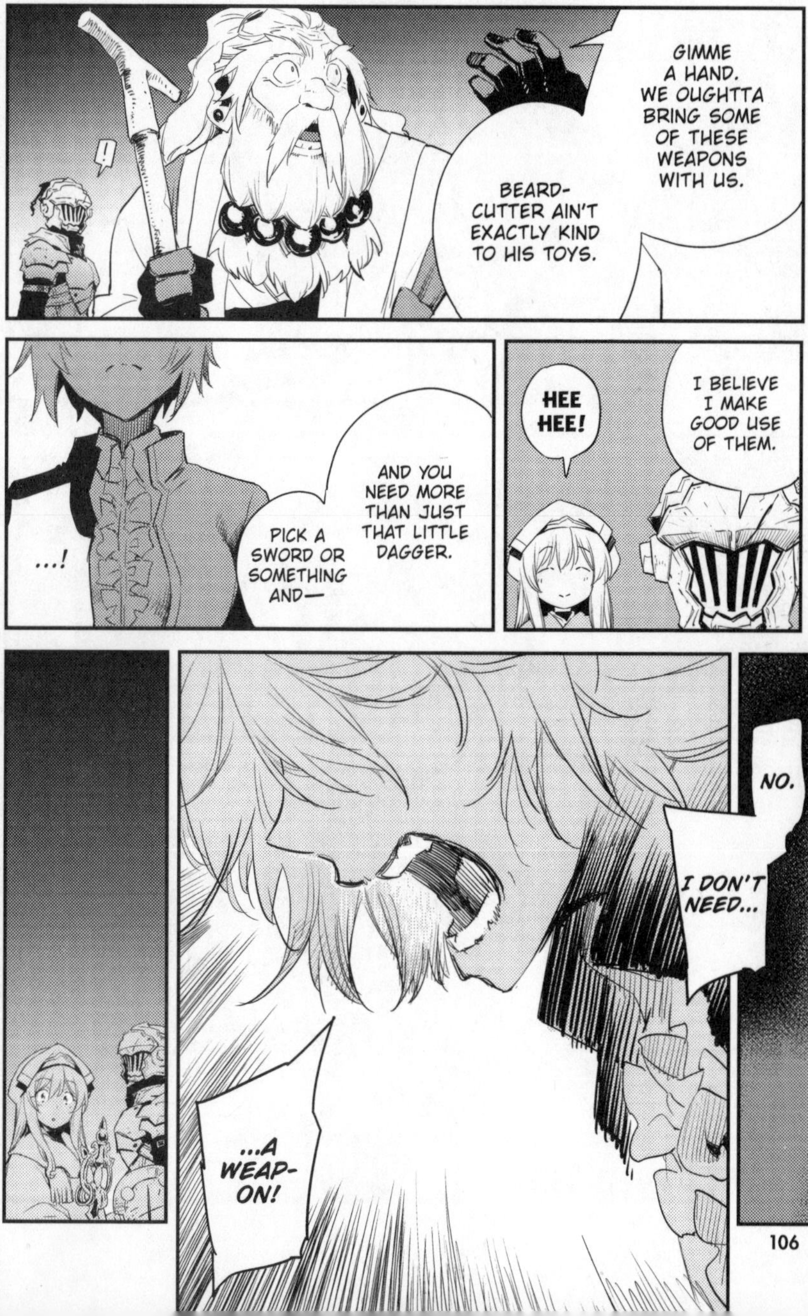
GIMME A HAND. WE OUGHTTA BRING SOME OF THESE WEAPONS WITH US.
BEARD-CUTTER AIN'T EXACTLY KIND TO HIS TOYS.
!
I BELIEVE I MAKE GOOD USE OF THEM.
HEE HEE!
AND YOU NEED MORE THAN JUST THAT LITTLE DAGGER.
PICK A SWORD OR SOMETHING AND—
...!
NO.
I DON'T NEED...
...A WEAP-ON!

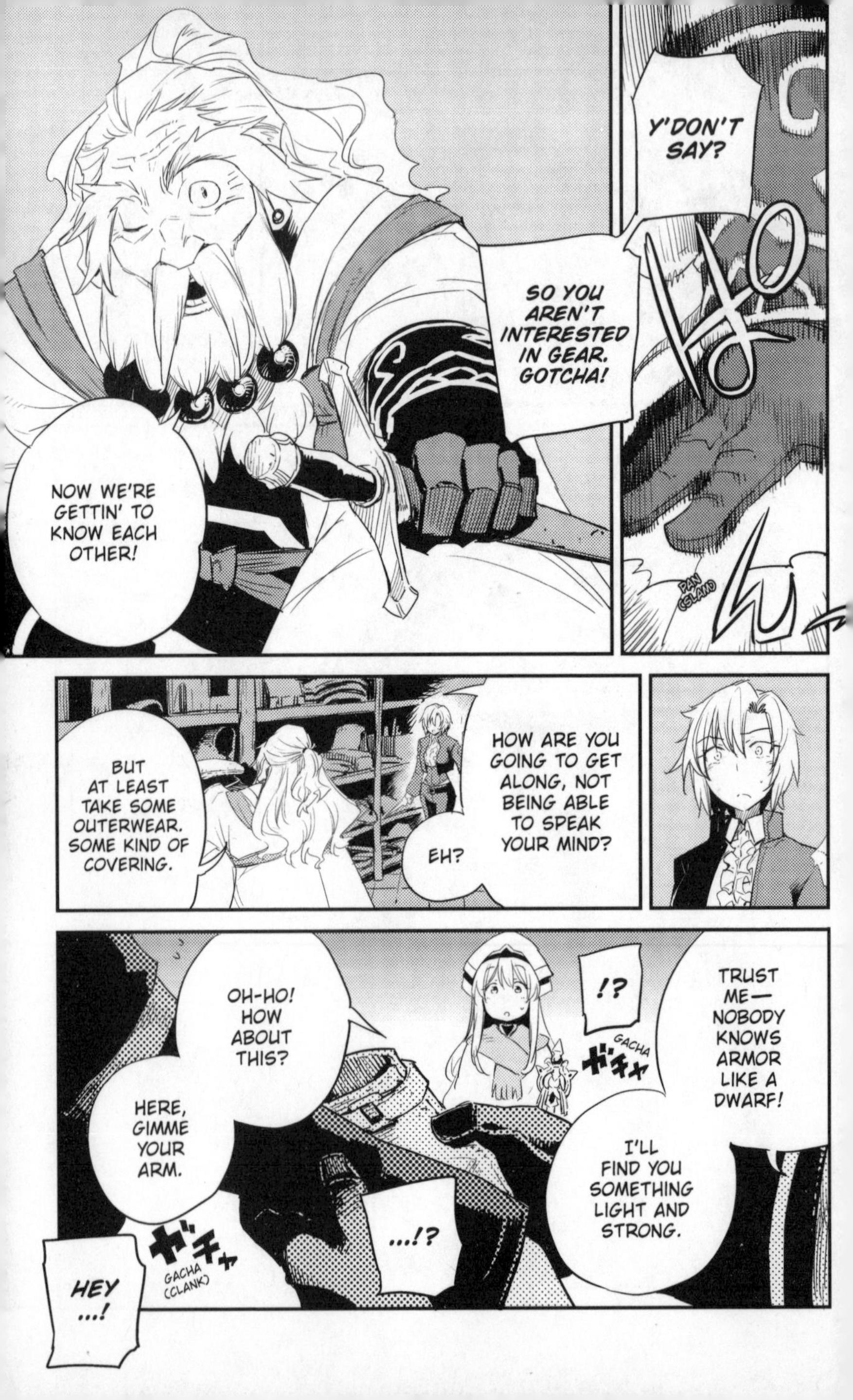
Y'DON'T SAY?
PAN (SLAM)
SO YOU AREN'T INTERESTED IN GEAR. GOTCHA!
NOW WE'RE GETTIN' TO KNOW EACH OTHER!
HOW ARE YOU GOING TO GET ALONG, NOT BEING ABLE TO SPEAK YOUR MIND?
EH?
BUT AT LEAST TAKE SOME OUTERWEAR. SOME KIND OF COVERING.
TRUST ME— NOBODY KNOWS ARMOR LIKE A DWARF!
!?
GACHA
OH-HO! HOW ABOUT THIS?
I'LL FIND YOU SOMETHING LIGHT AND STRONG.
HERE, GIMME YOUR ARM.
...!?
GACHA (CLANK)
HEY ...!

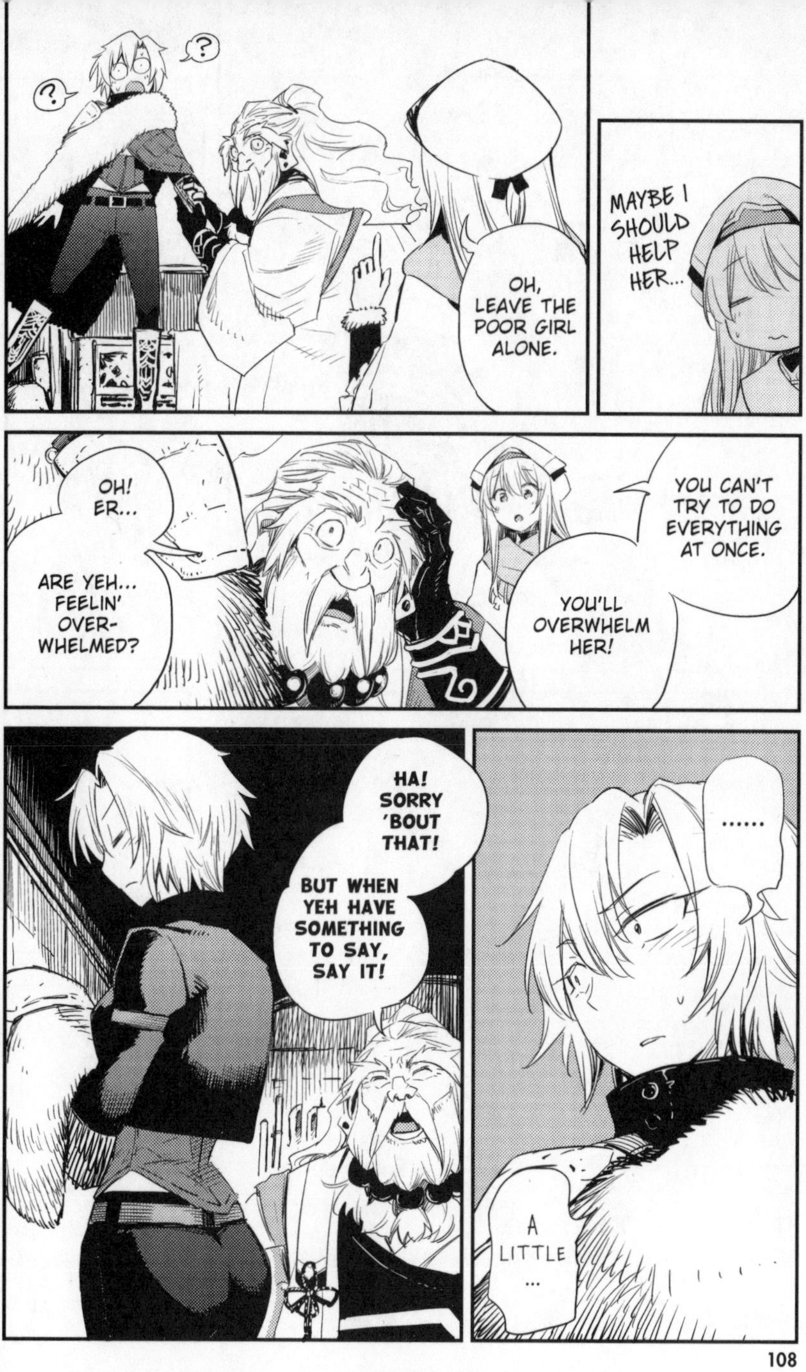
MAYBE I SHOULD HELP HER...
?
?
OH, LEAVE THE POOR GIRL ALONE.
YOU CAN'T TRY TO DO EVERYTHING AT ONCE.
YOU'LL OVERWHELM HER!
OH! ER...
ARE YEH... FEELIN' OVER-WHELMED?
......
A LITTLE ...
HA! SORRY 'BOUT THAT!
BUT WHEN YEH HAVE SOMETHING TO SAY, SAY IT!

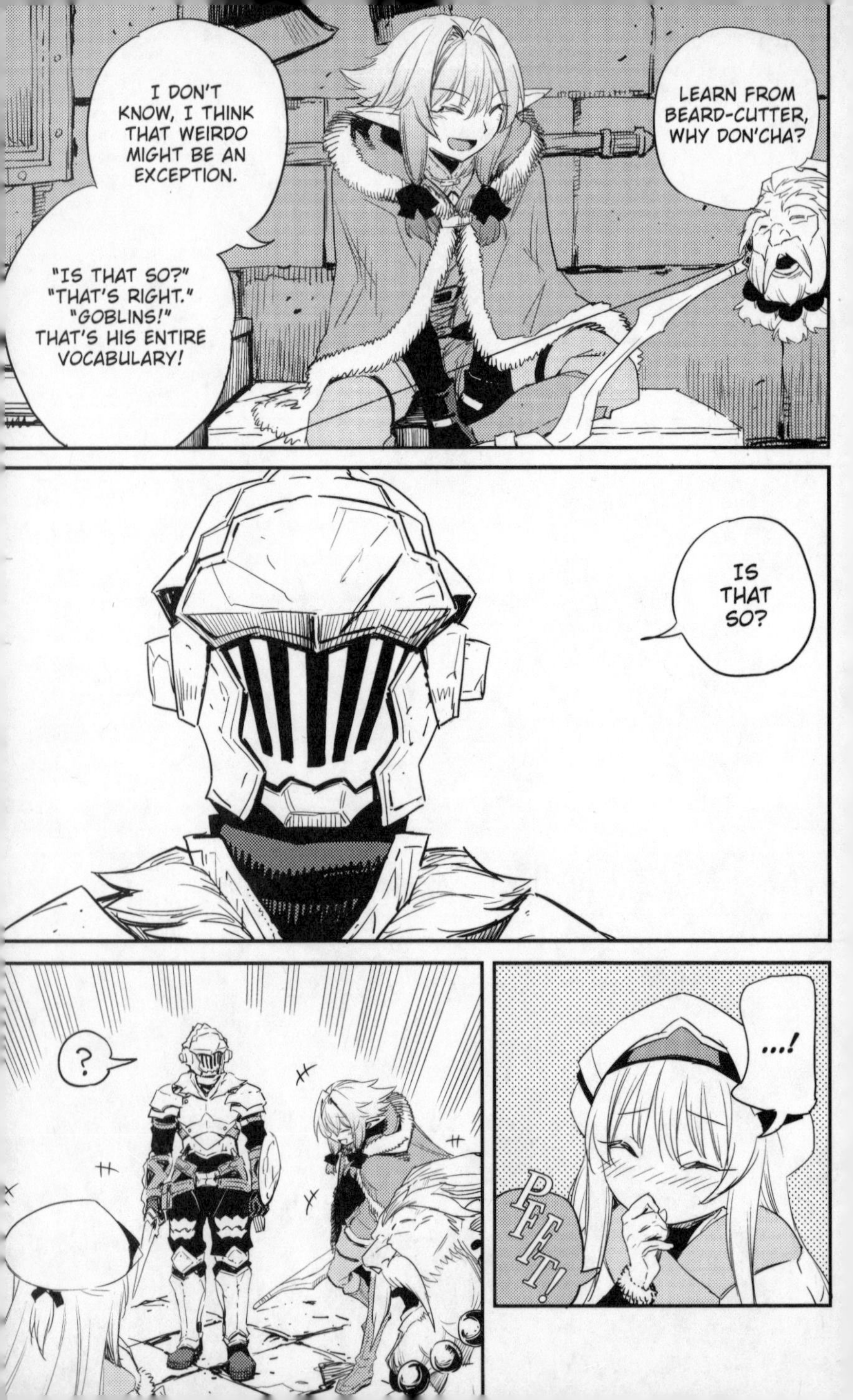
LEARN FROM BEARD-CUTTER, WHY DON'CHA?
I DON'T KNOW, I THINK THAT WEIRDO MIGHT BE AN EXCEPTION.
"IS THAT SO?" "THAT'S RIGHT." "GOBLINS!" THAT'S HIS ENTIRE VOCABULARY!
IS THAT SO?
...!
PFFT!
?

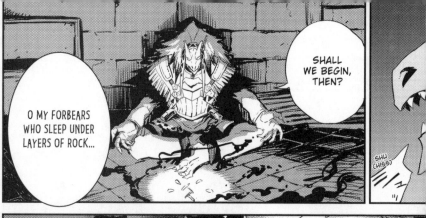

SHU (CHISS)
SHALL WE BEGIN, THEN?
O MY FORBEARS WHO SLEEP UNDER LAYERS OF ROCK...
...WITH ALL THE TIME THAT HAS PILED UPON YOU, GUIDE THESE OBJECTS.
ZUGU (SKRCH)
ZUGU
BORO (DROOP)

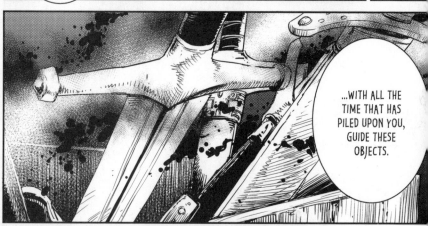

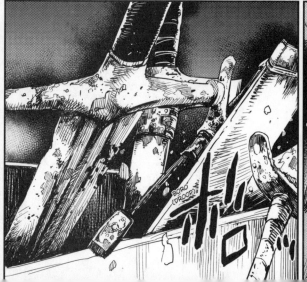

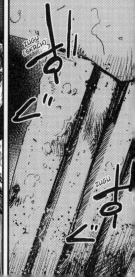

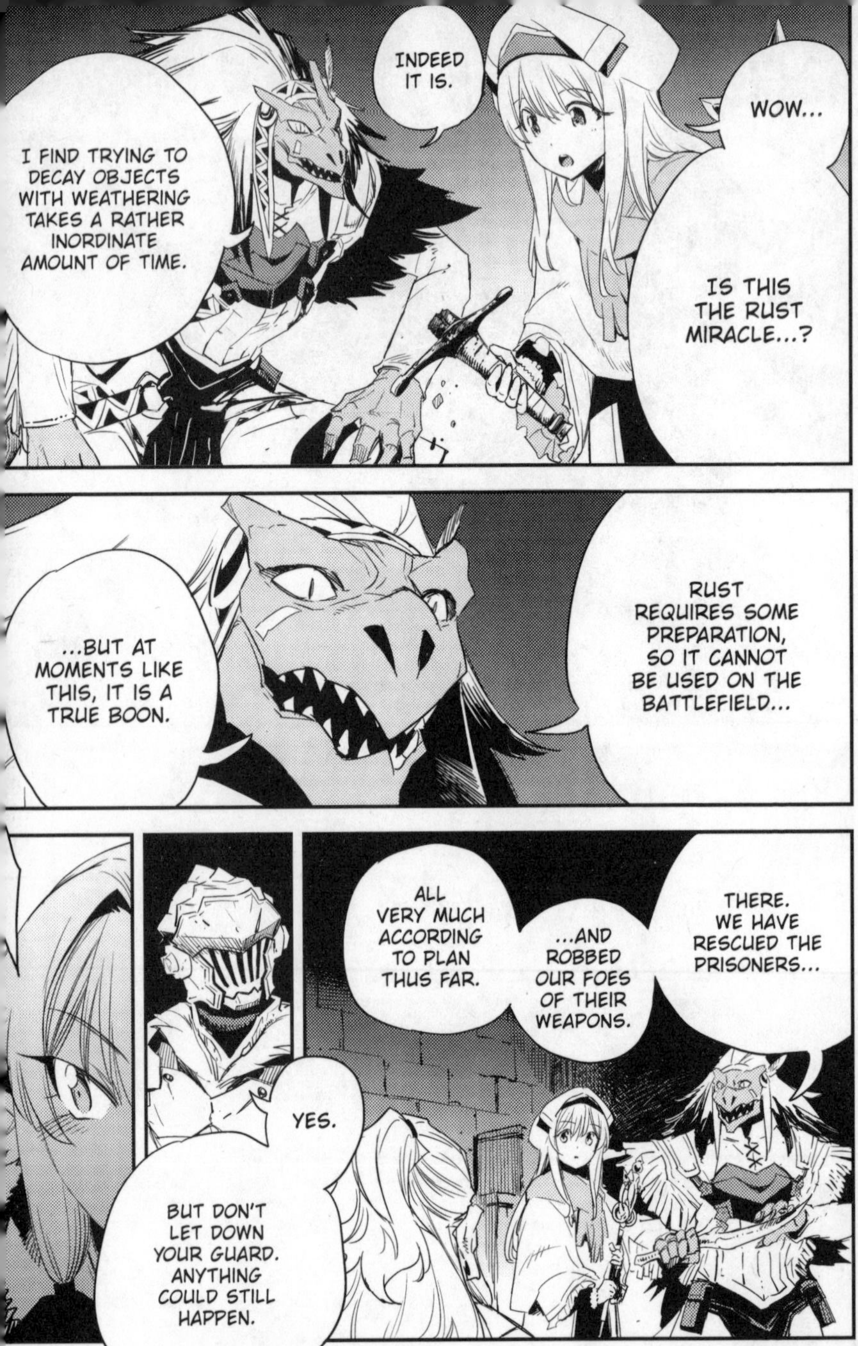
WOW...
IS THIS THE RUST MIRACLE...?
INDEED IT IS.
I FIND TRYING TO DECAY OBJECTS WITH WEATHERING TAKES A RATHER INORDINATE AMOUNT OF TIME.
RUST REQUIRES SOME PREPARATION, SO IT CANNOT BE USED ON THE BATTLEFIELD...
...BUT AT MOMENTS LIKE THIS, IT IS A TRUE BOON.
THERE. WE HAVE RESCUED THE PRISONERS...
...AND ROBBED OUR FOES OF THEIR WEAPONS.
ALL VERY MUCH ACCORDING TO PLAN THUS FAR.
YES.
BUT DON'T LET DOWN YOUR GUARD. ANYTHING COULD STILL HAPPEN.

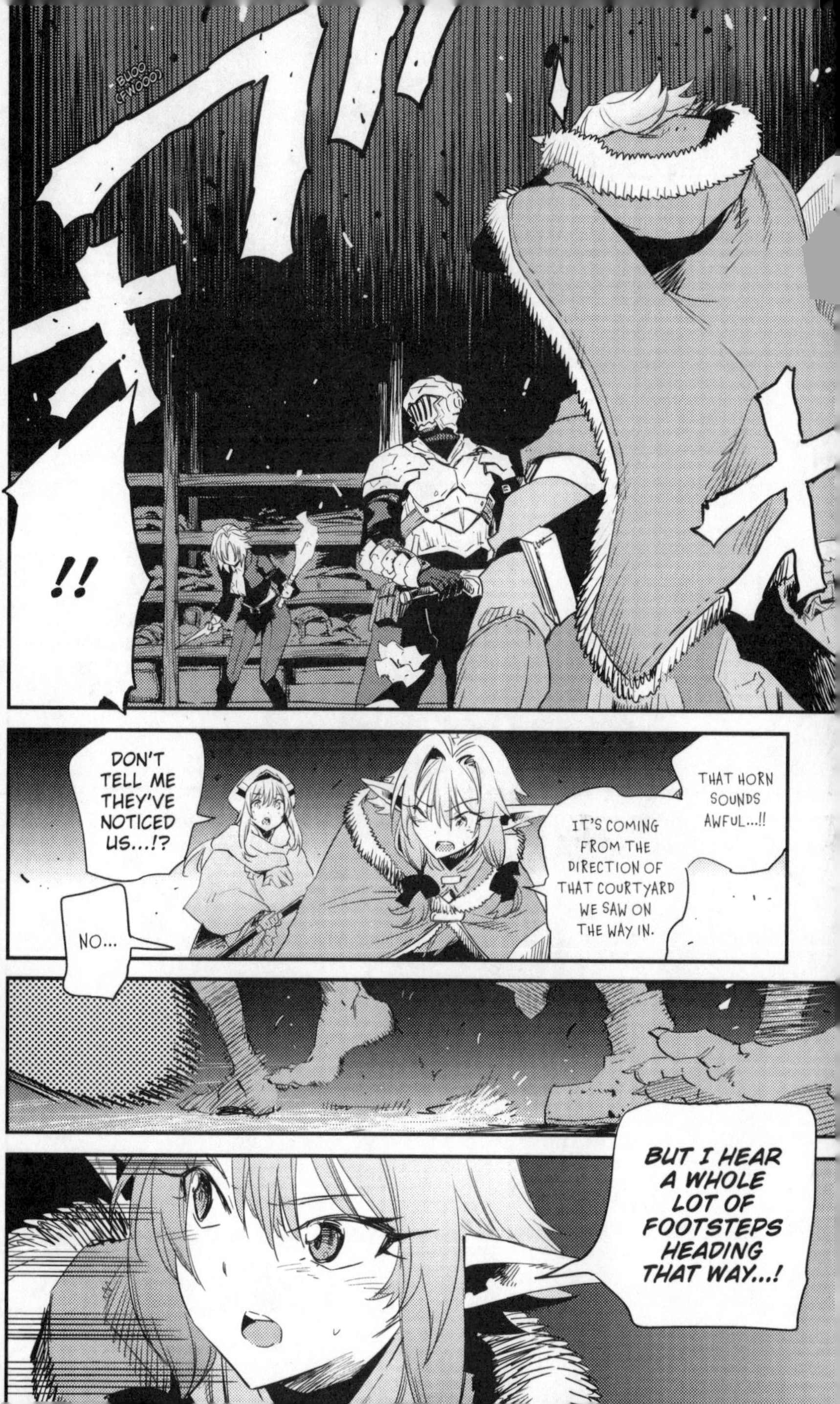
BLOO (FWOOO)
!!
THAT HORN SOUNDS AWFUL...!!
IT'S COMING FROM THE DIRECTION OF THAT COURTYARD WE SAW ON THE WAY IN.
DON'T TELL ME THEY'VE NOTICED US...!?
NO...
BUT I HEAR A WHOLE LOT OF FOOTSTEPS HEADING THAT WAY...!

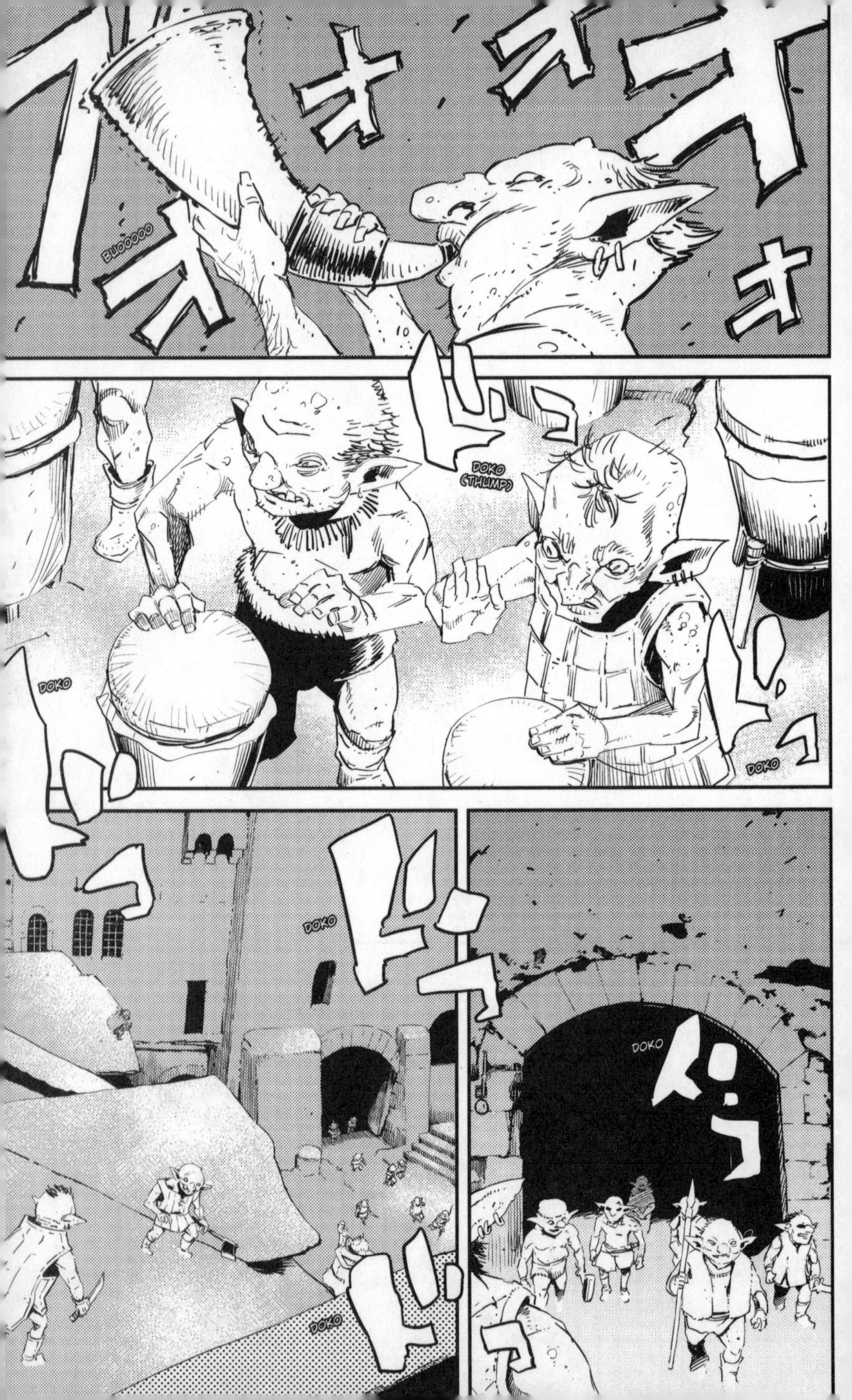
BUOOOOO
DOKO (THUMP)
DOKO
DOKO
DOKO
DOKO
DOKO

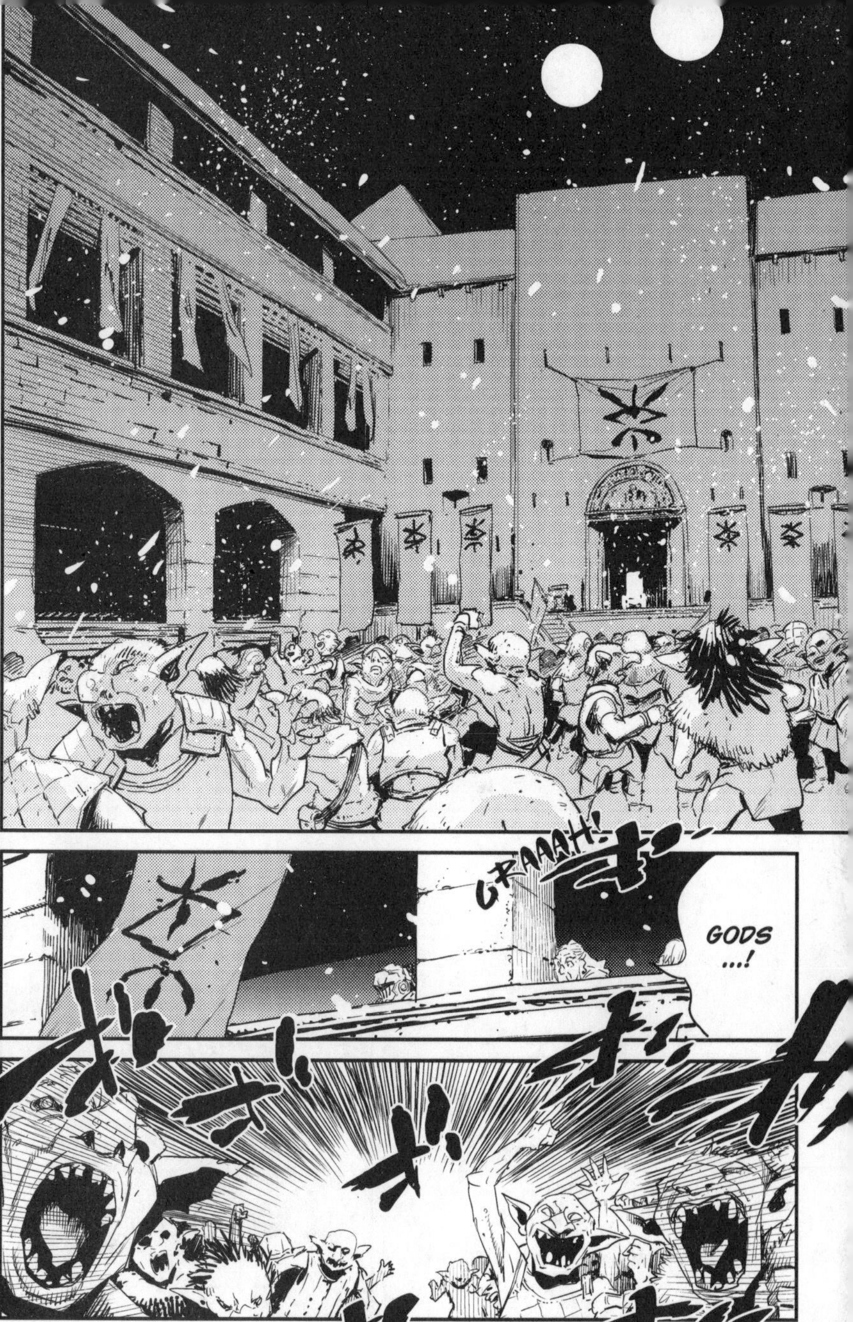
URAAAH!
GODS ...!

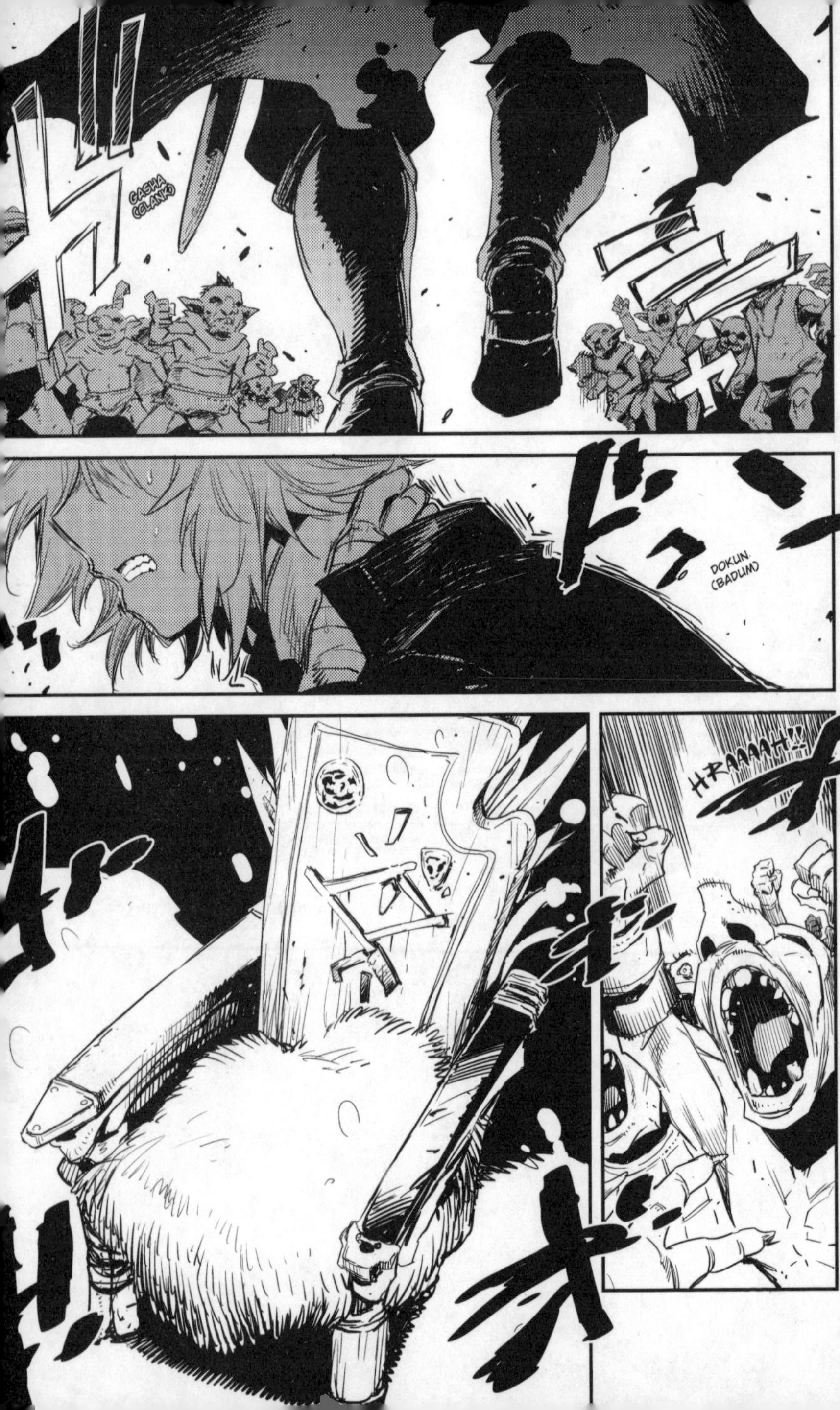
GASHA
(CLANK)
DOKUN.
(BADUM)
HRAAAAH!!

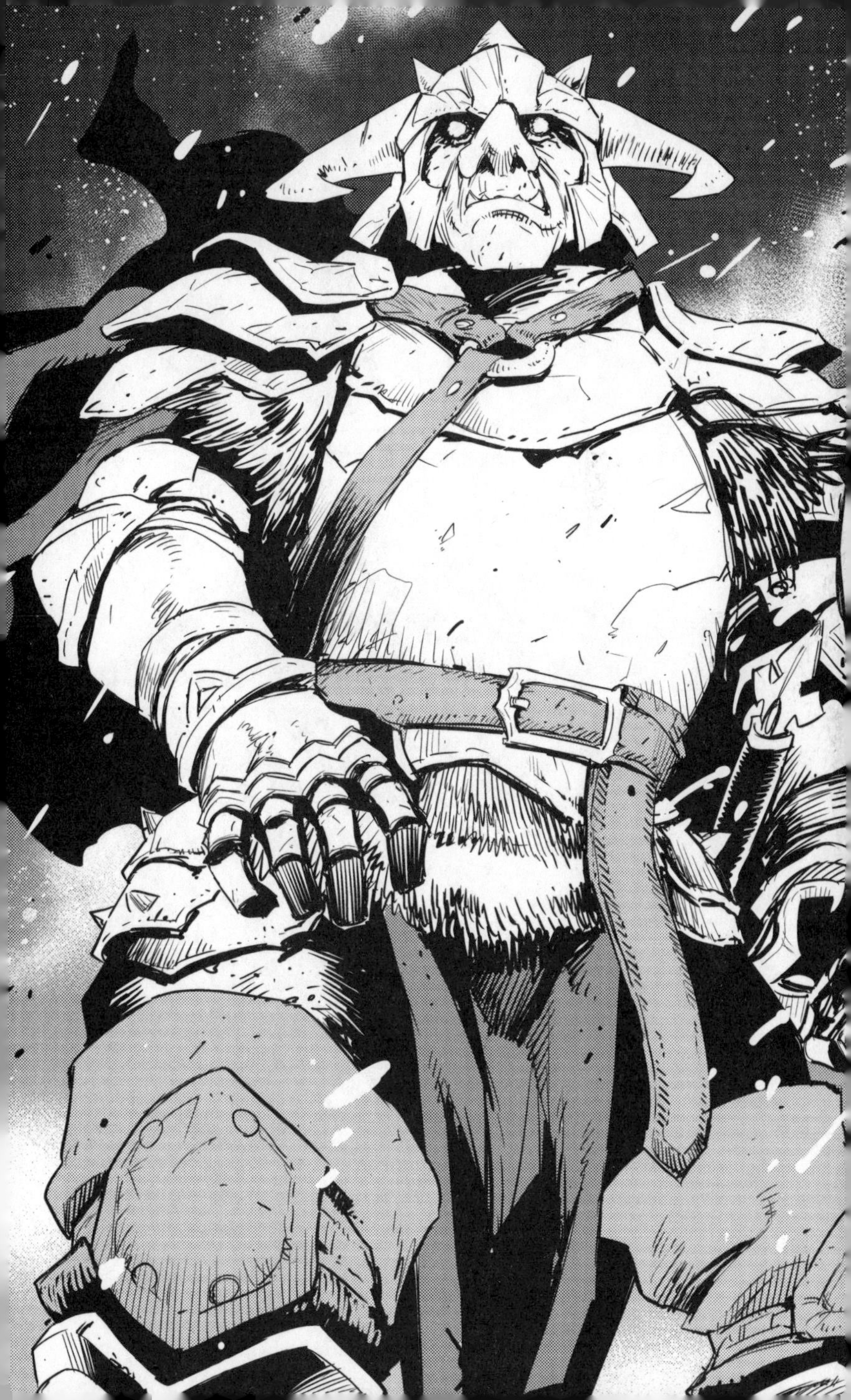

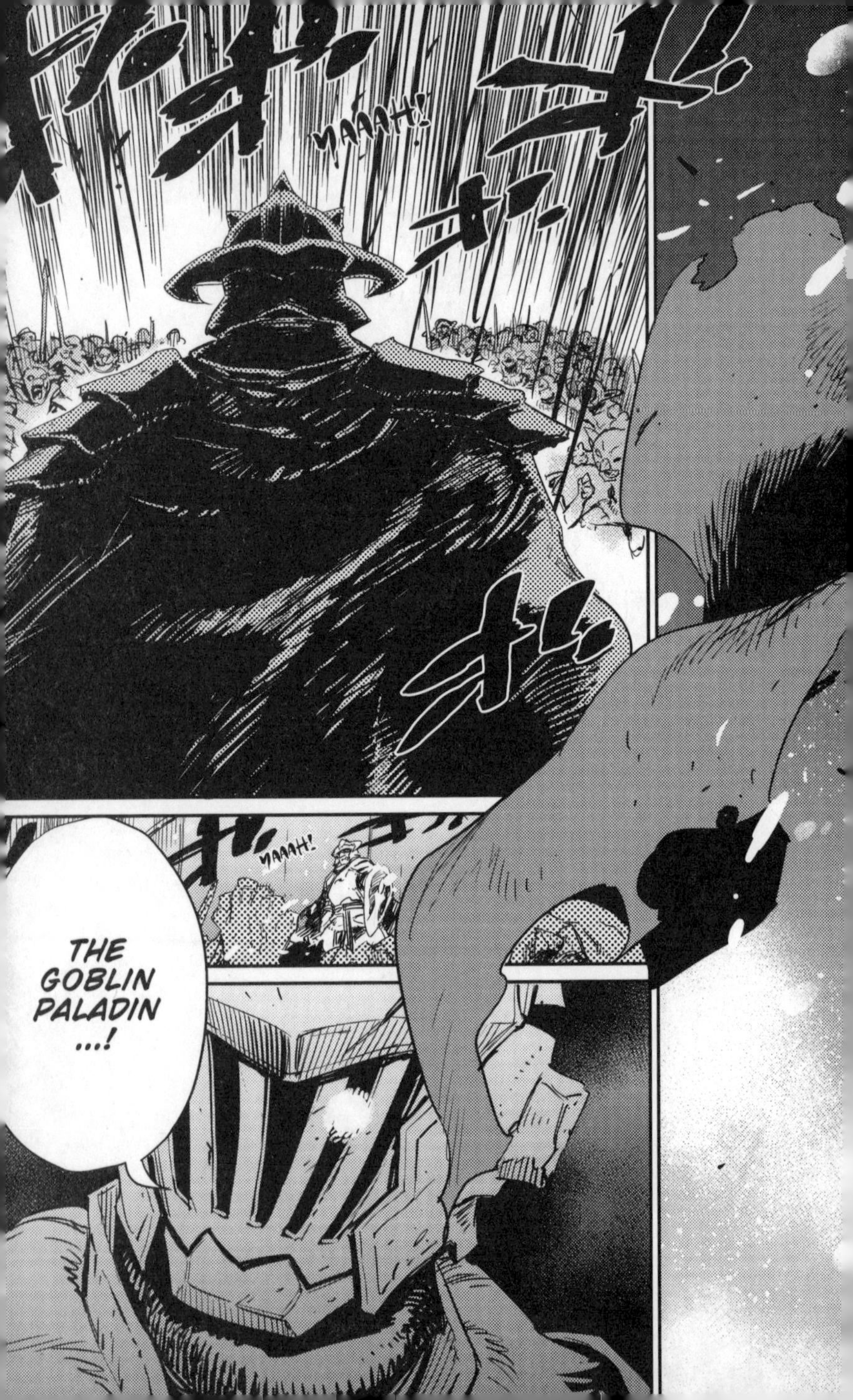
NYAAAH!
NYAAAH!
THE GOBLIN PALADIN ...!

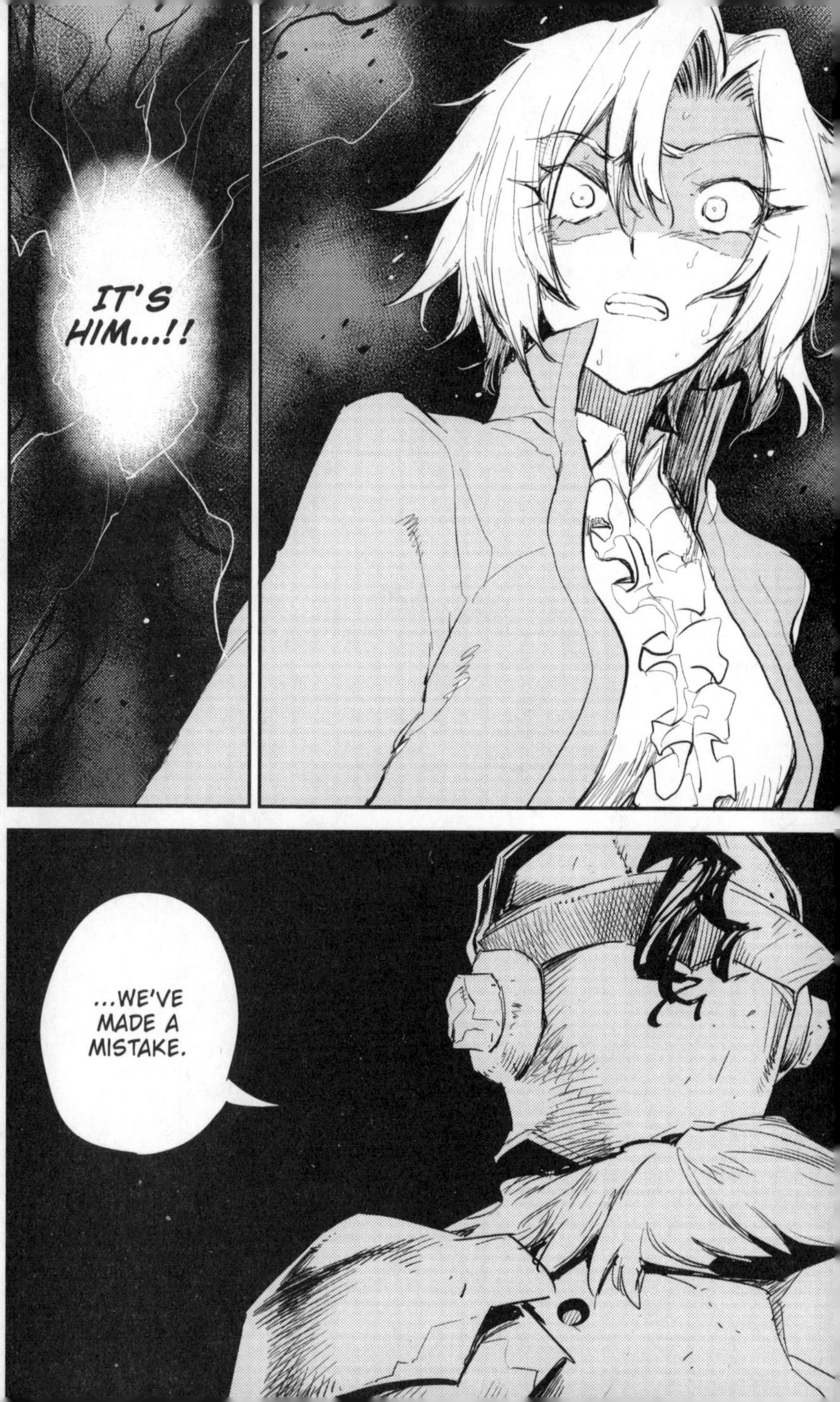
IT'S HIM...!!
...WE'VE MADE A MISTAKE.

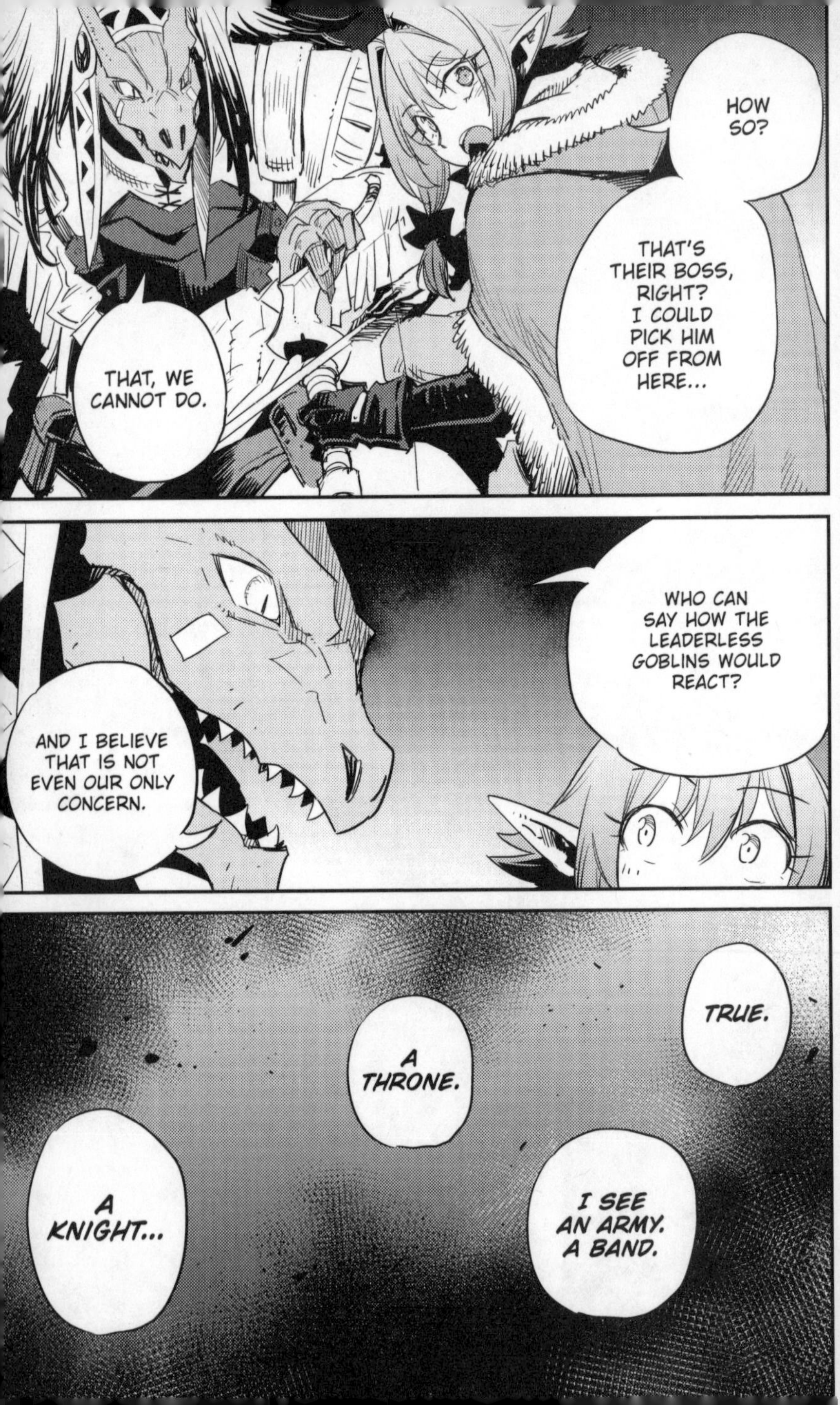
HOW SO?
THAT'S THEIR BOSS, RIGHT? I COULD PICK HIM OFF FROM HERE...
THAT, WE CANNOT DO.
WHO CAN SAY HOW THE LEADERLESS GOBLINS WOULD REACT?
AND I BELIEVE THAT IS NOT EVEN OUR ONLY CONCERN.
TRUE.
A THRONE.
I SEE AN ARMY. A BAND.
A KNIGHT...

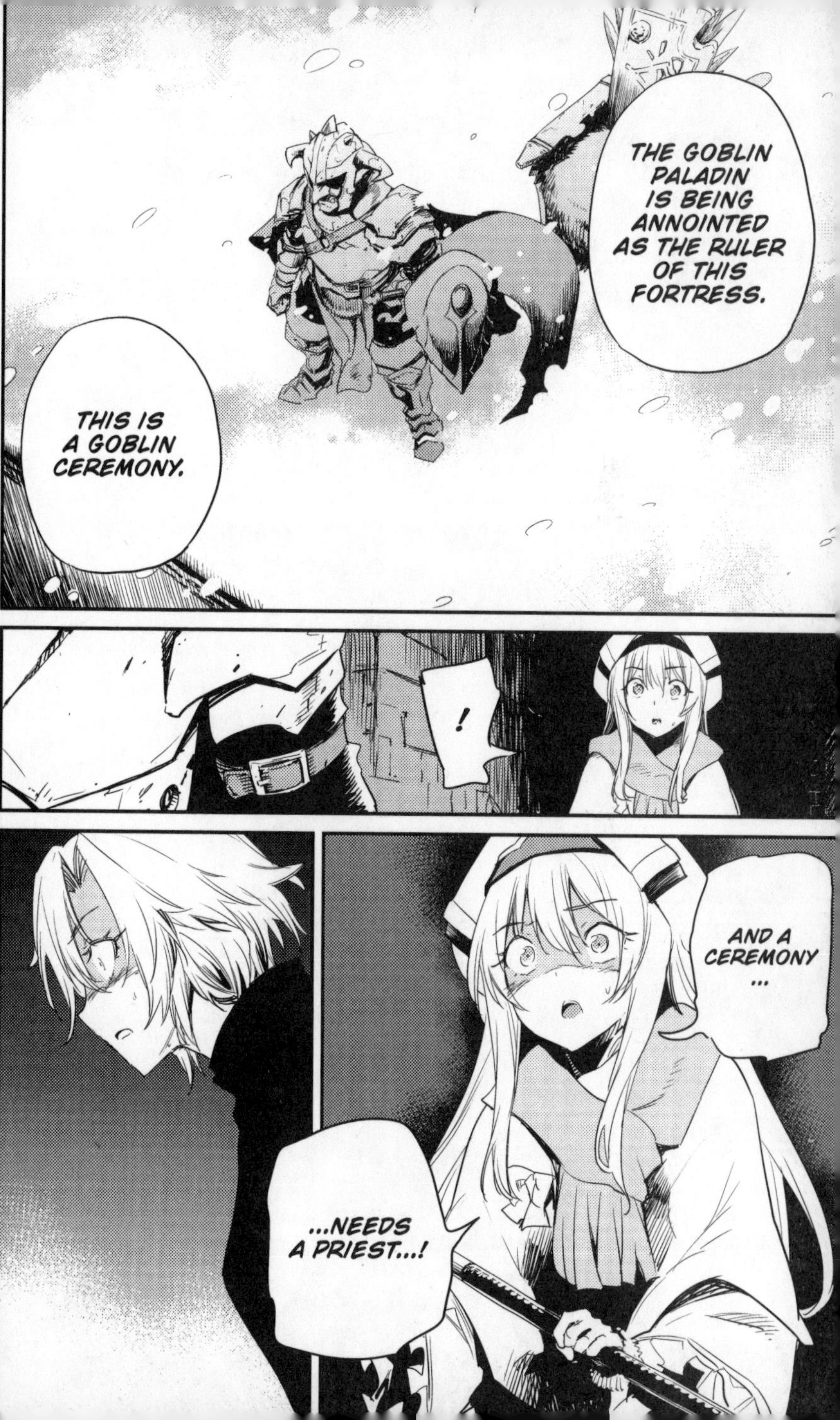
THE GOBLIN PALADIN IS BEING ANNOINTED AS THE RULER OF THIS FORTRESS.
THIS IS A GOBLIN CEREMONY.
!
AND A CEREMONY ...
...NEEDS A PRIEST...!

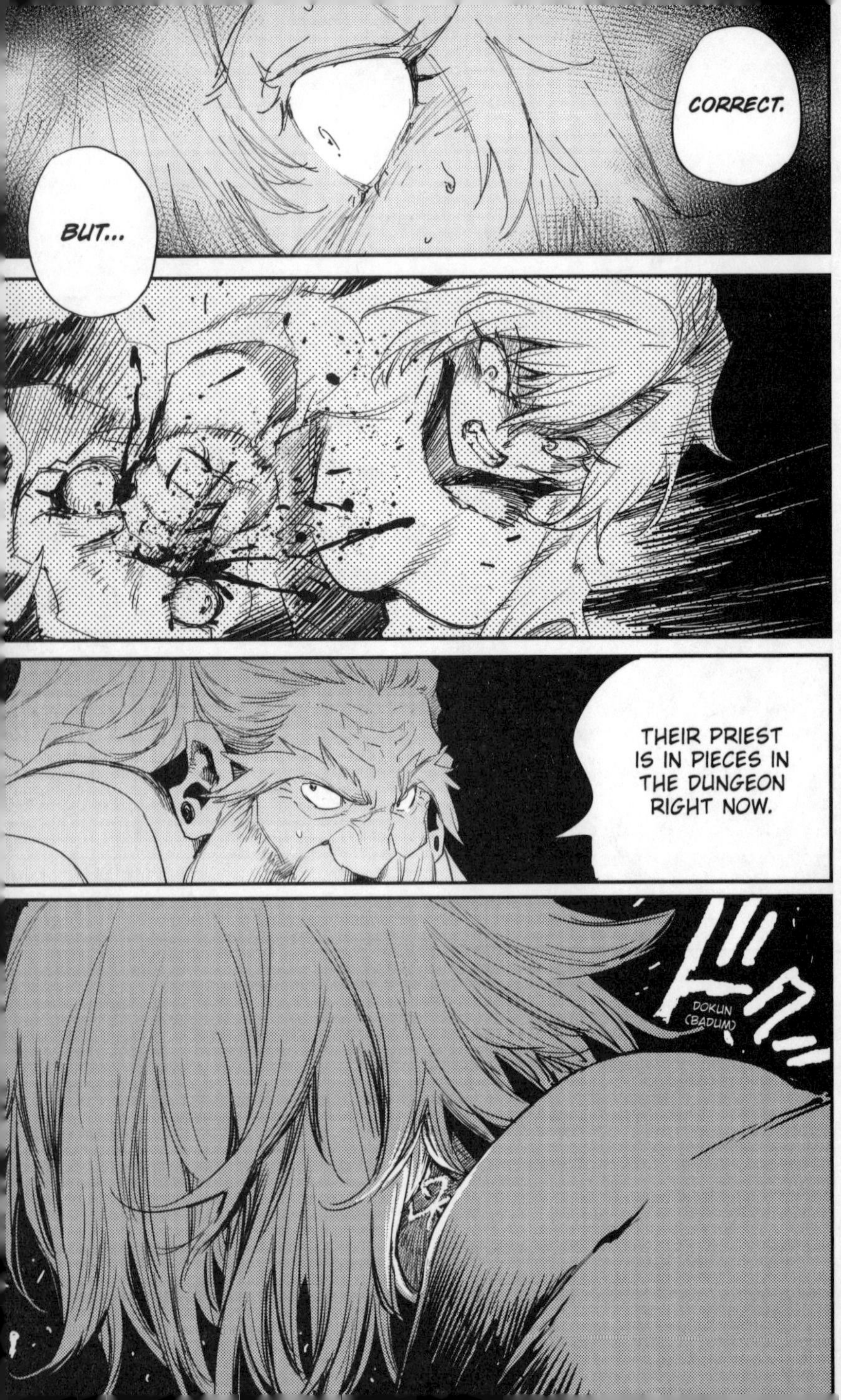
CORRECT.
BUT...
THEIR PRIEST IS IN PIECES IN THE DUNGEON RIGHT NOW.
DOKUN (BADUM)

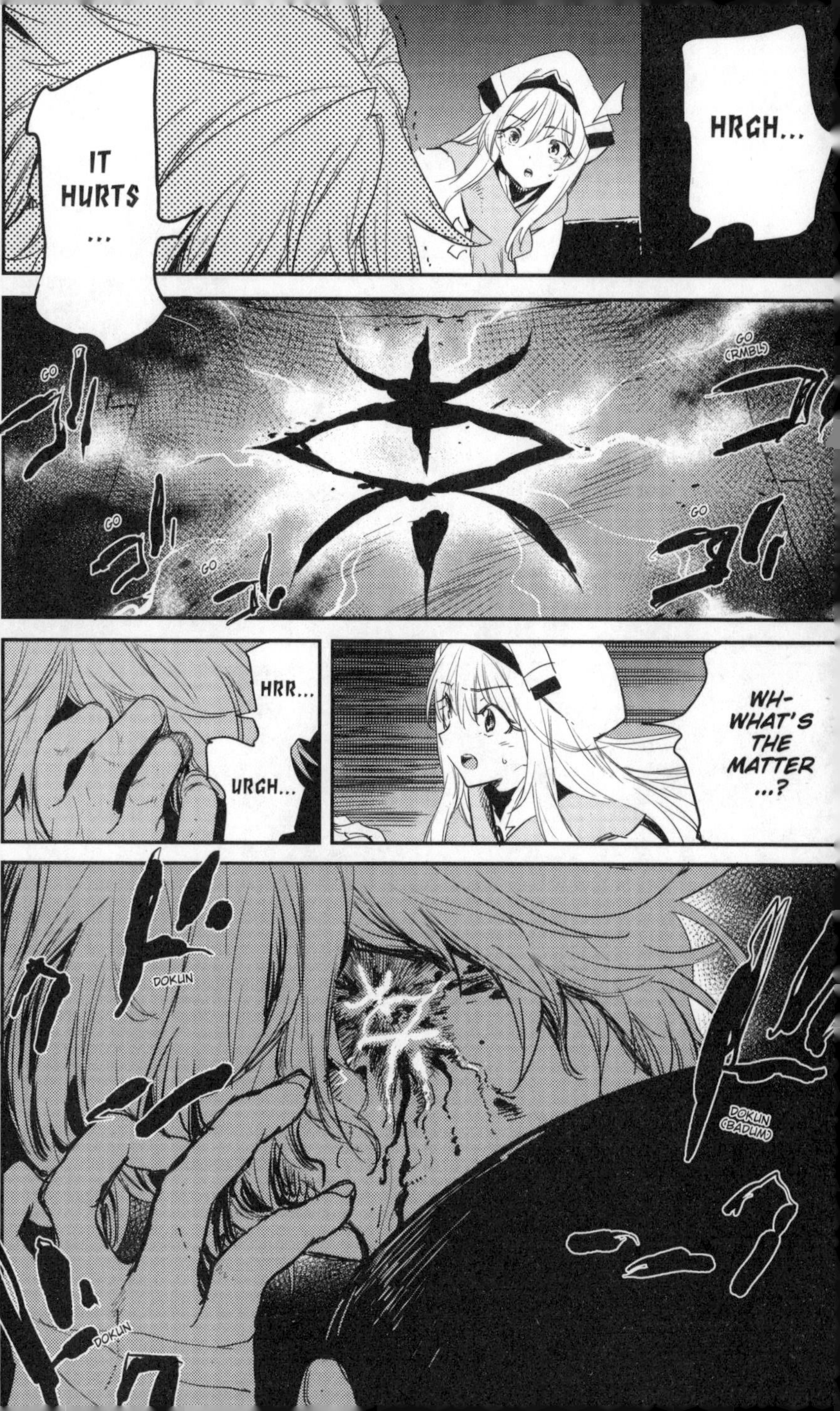
HRGH...
IT HURTS ...
GO (RMBL)
GO
GO
GO
GO
WH-WHAT'S THE MATTER ...?
HRR...
URGH...
DOKUN (BADUM)
DOKUN
DOKUN

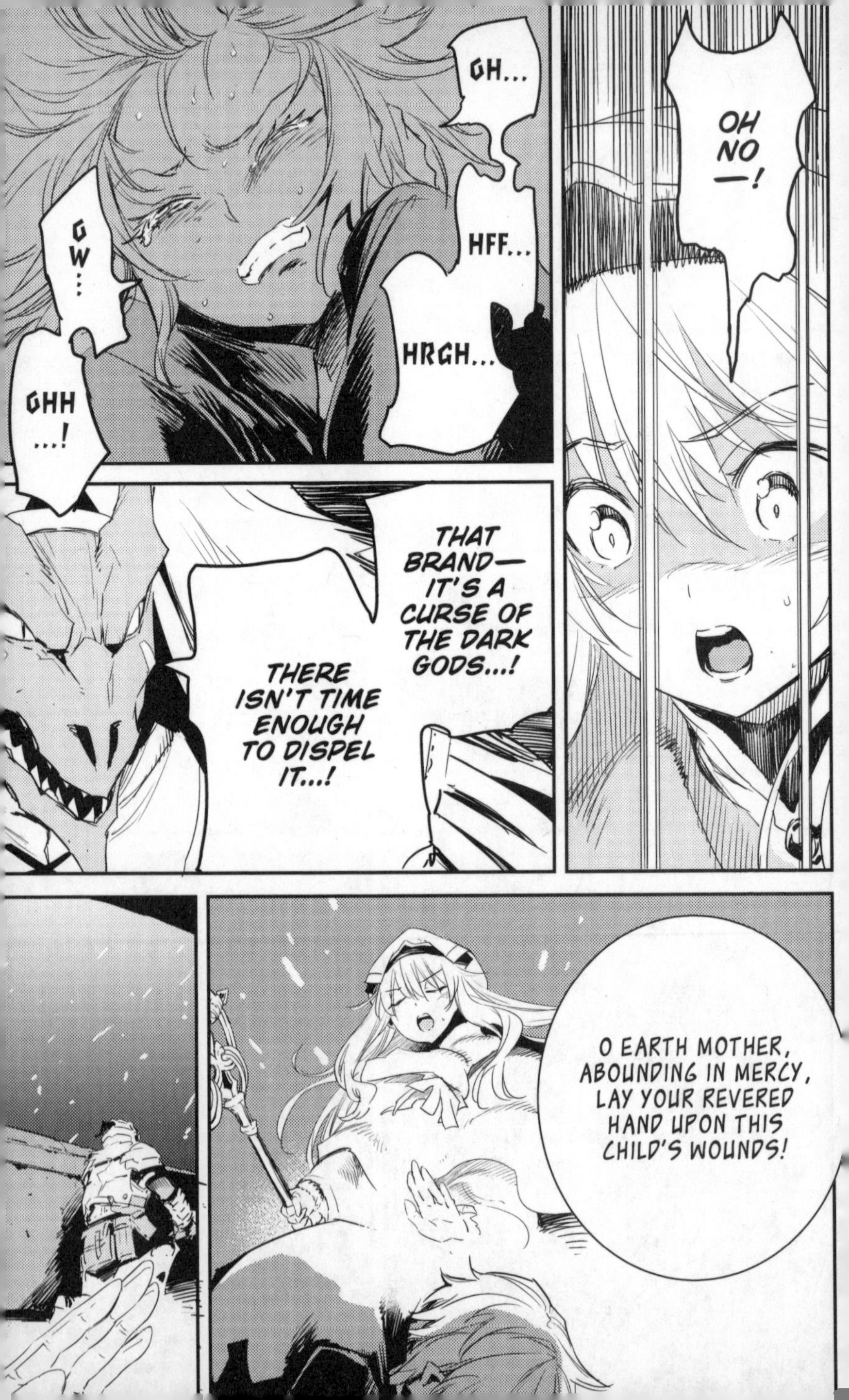
OH NO—!
GH...
HFF...
HRGH...
GW...
GHH...!
THAT BRAND—IT'S A CURSE OF THE DARK GODS...!
THERE ISN'T TIME ENOUGH TO DISPEL IT...!
O EARTH MOTHER, ABOUNDING IN MERCY, LAY YOUR REVERED HAND UPON THIS CHILD'S WOUNDS!

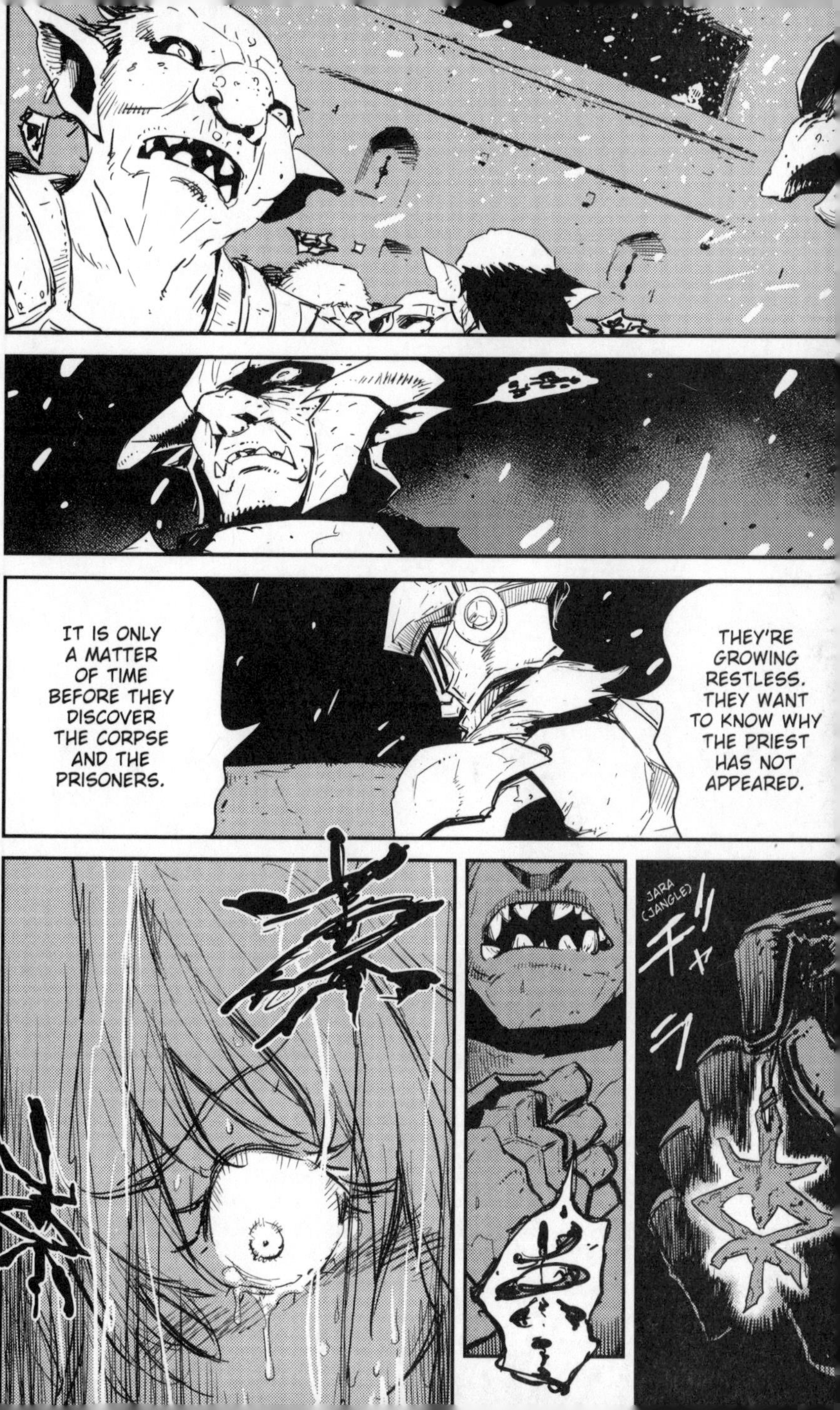
THEY'RE GROWING RESTLESS. THEY WANT TO KNOW WHY THE PRIEST HAS NOT APPEARED.
IT IS ONLY A MATTER OF TIME BEFORE THEY DISCOVER THE CORPSE AND THE PRISONERS.
JARA (JANGLE)

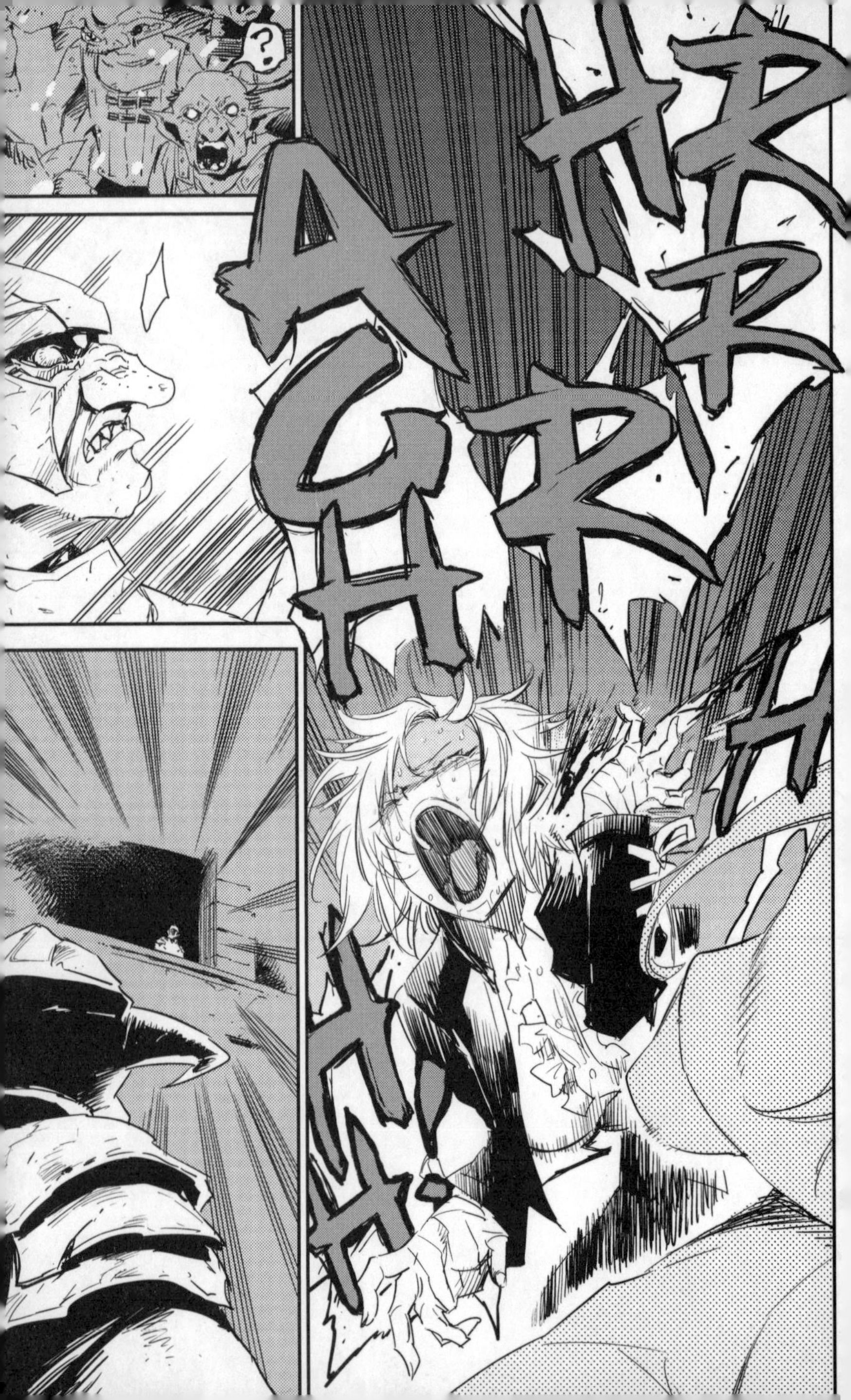
?
HRRR
AGH

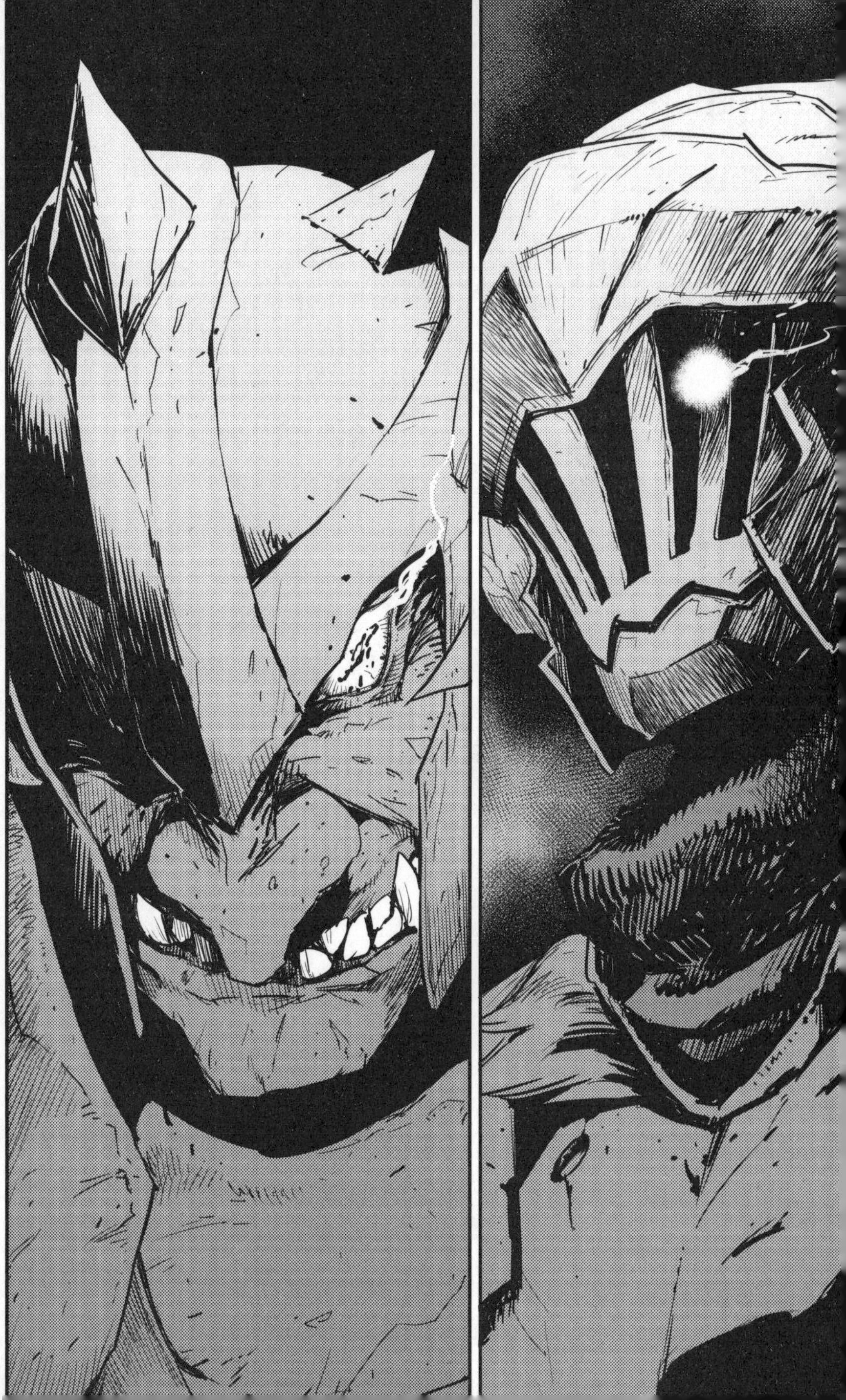

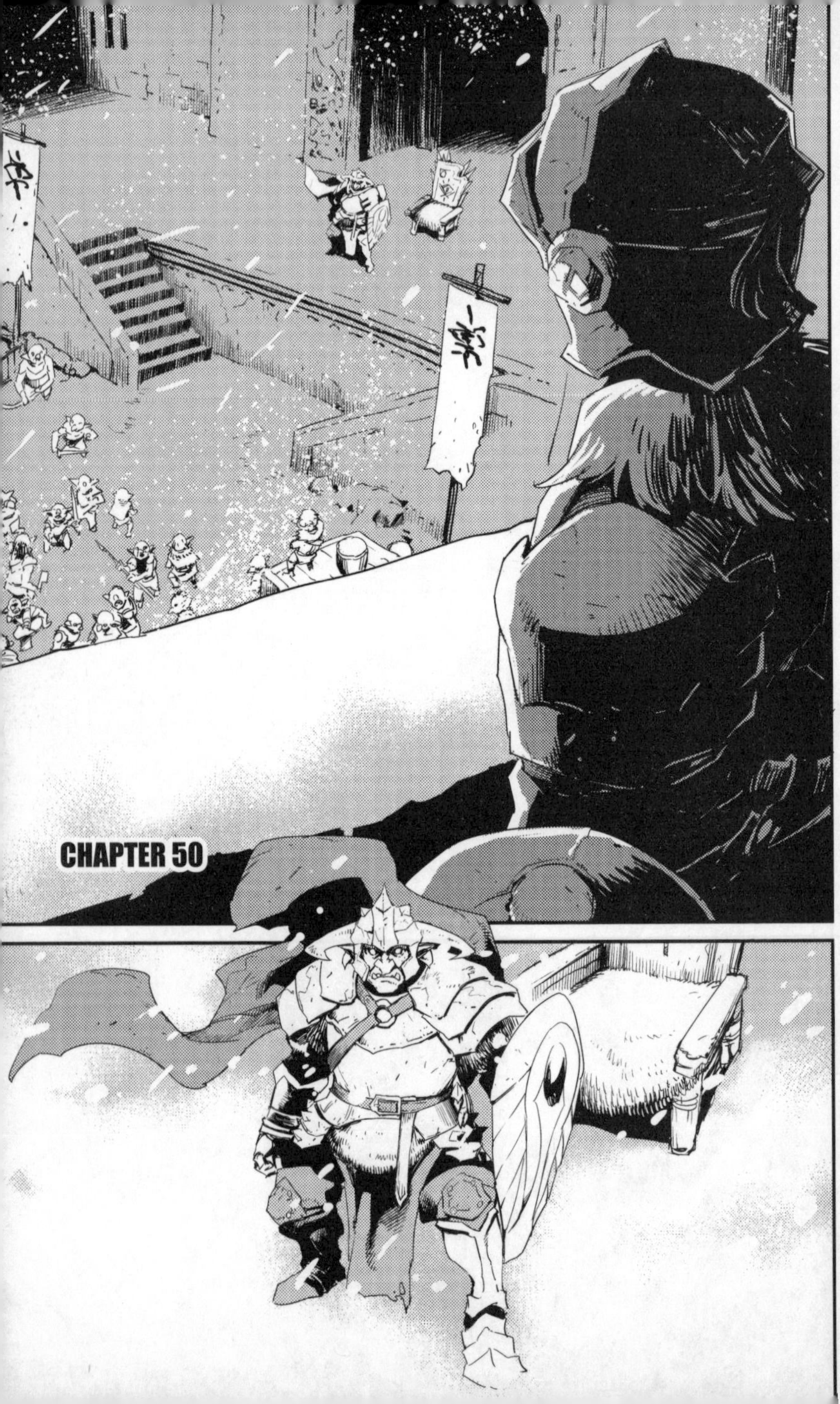
CHAPTER 50

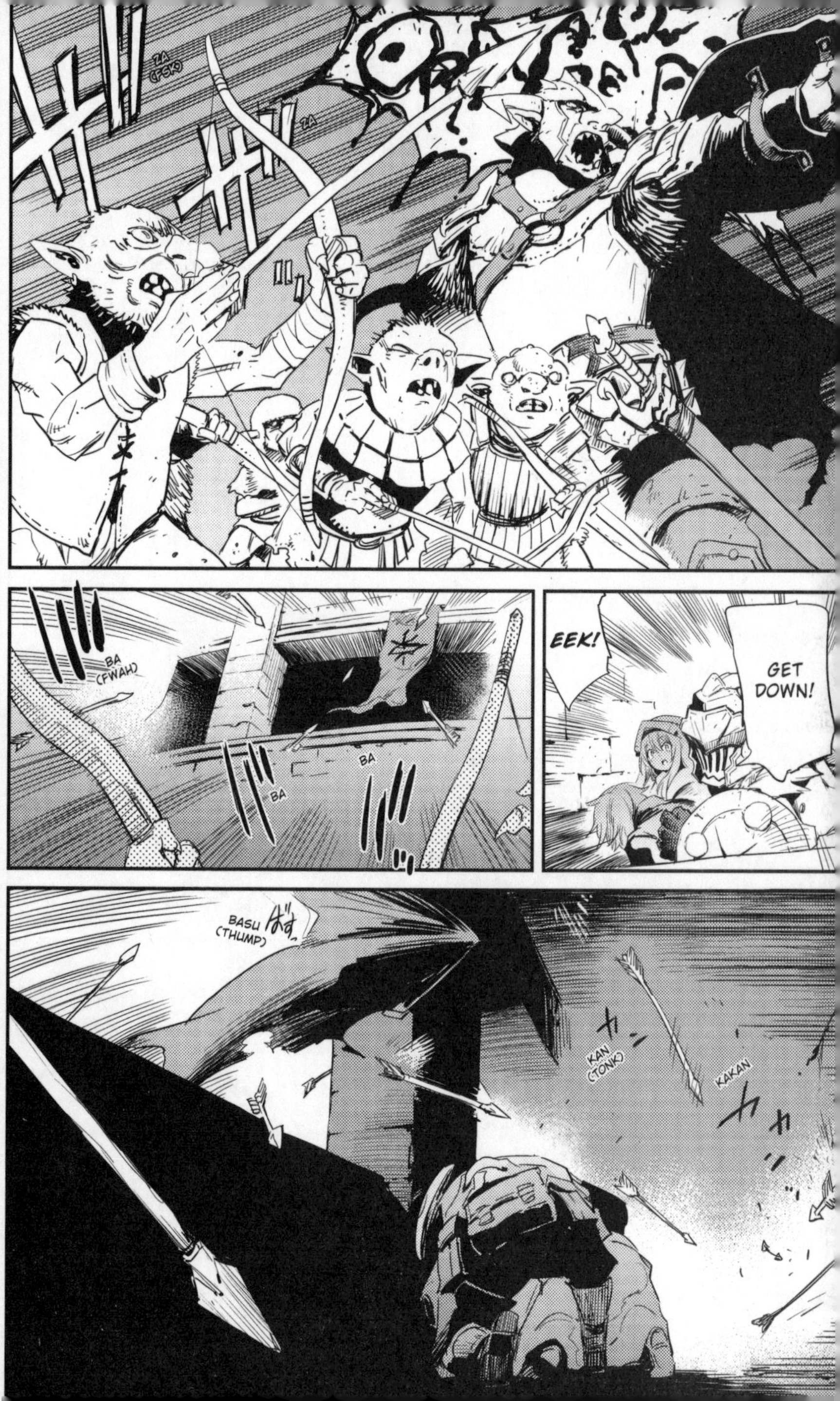
ZA (FSK)
ZA
GET DOWN!
EEK!
BA (FWAH)
BA
BA
BASU (THUMP)
KAKAN
KAN (TONK)

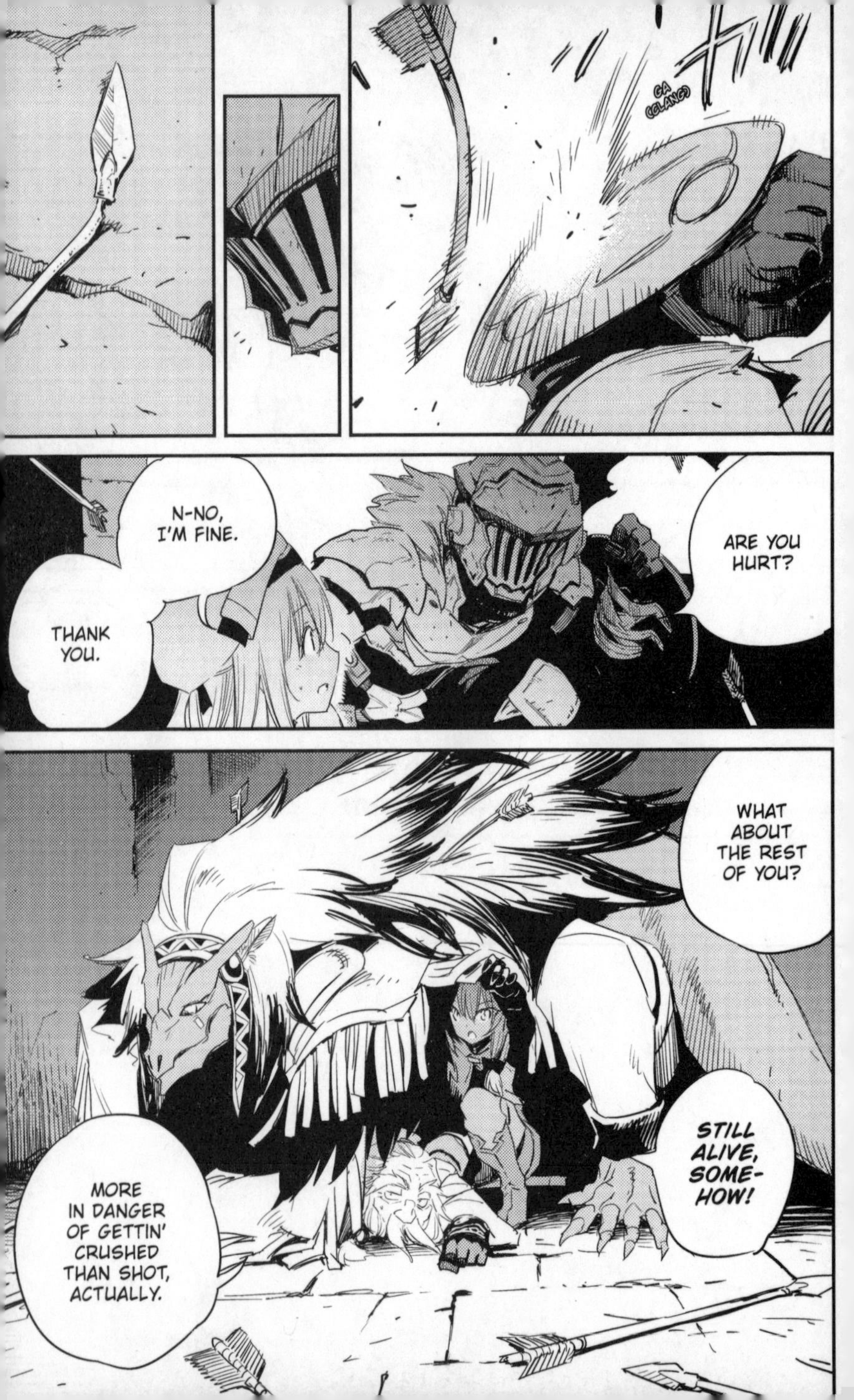
GA (CLANG)
ARE YOU HURT?
N-NO, I'M FINE.
THANK YOU.
WHAT ABOUT THE REST OF YOU?
STILL ALIVE, SOME-HOW!
MORE IN DANGER OF GETTIN' CRUSHED THAN SHOT, ACTUALLY.

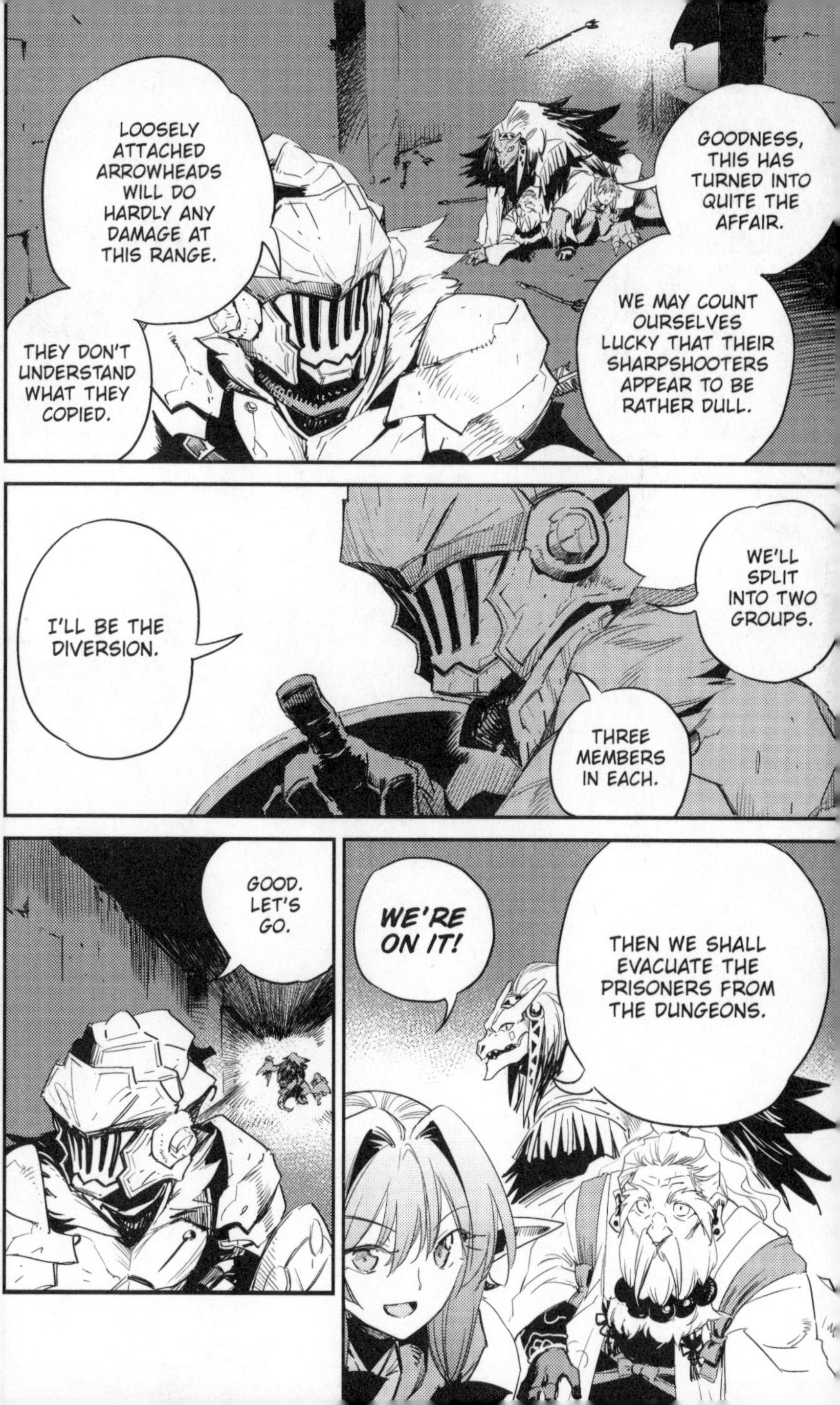
GOODNESS, THIS HAS TURNED INTO QUITE THE AFFAIR.
WE MAY COUNT OURSELVES LUCKY THAT THEIR SHARPSHOOTERS APPEAR TO BE RATHER DULL.
LOOSELY ATTACHED ARROWHEADS WILL DO HARDLY ANY DAMAGE AT THIS RANGE.
THEY DON'T UNDERSTAND WHAT THEY COPIED.
WE'LL SPLIT INTO TWO GROUPS.
THREE MEMBERS IN EACH.
I'LL BE THE DIVERSION.
THEN WE SHALL EVACUATE THE PRISONERS FROM THE DUNGEONS.
WE'RE ON IT!
GOOD. LET'S GO.

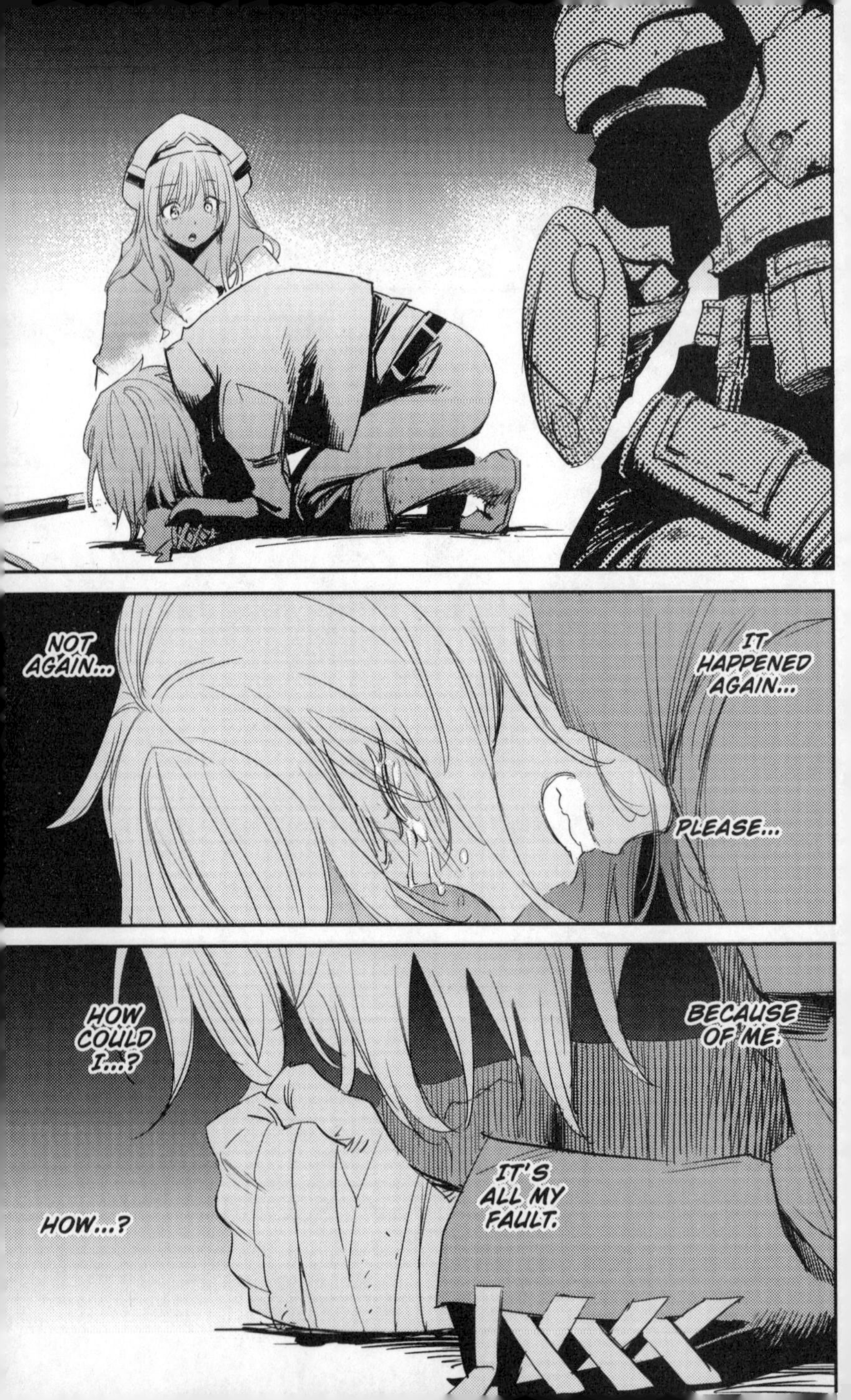
IT HAPPENED AGAIN...
NOT AGAIN...
PLEASE...
BECAUSE OF ME.
HOW COULD I...?
IT'S ALL MY FAULT.
HOW...?

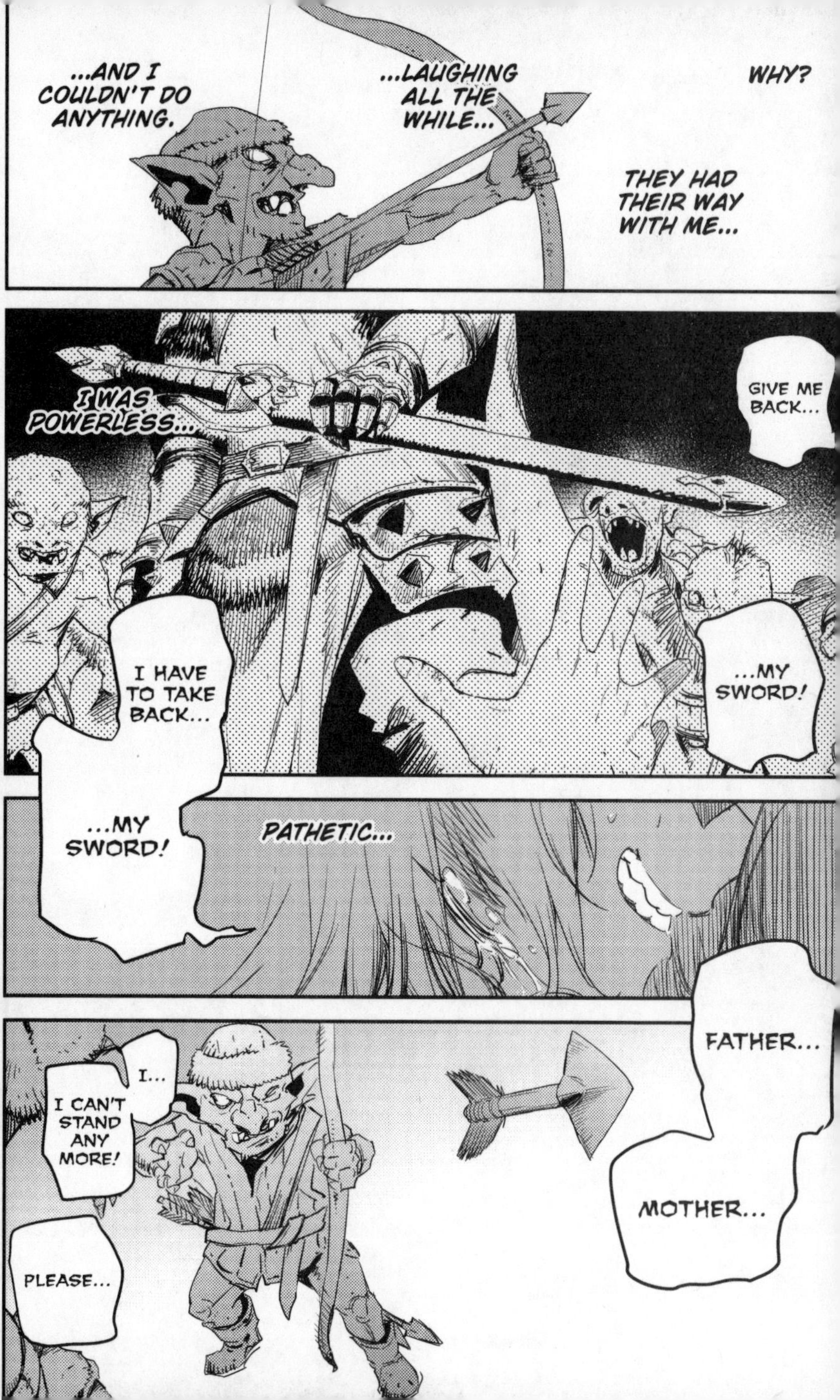
WHY?
THEY HAD THEIR WAY WITH ME...
...LAUGHING ALL THE WHILE...
...AND I COULDN'T DO ANYTHING.
GIVE ME BACK...
...MY SWORD!
I WAS POWERLESS...
I HAVE TO TAKE BACK...
...MY SWORD!
PATHETIC...
FATHER...
MOTHER...
I...
I CAN'T STAND ANY MORE!
PLEASE...

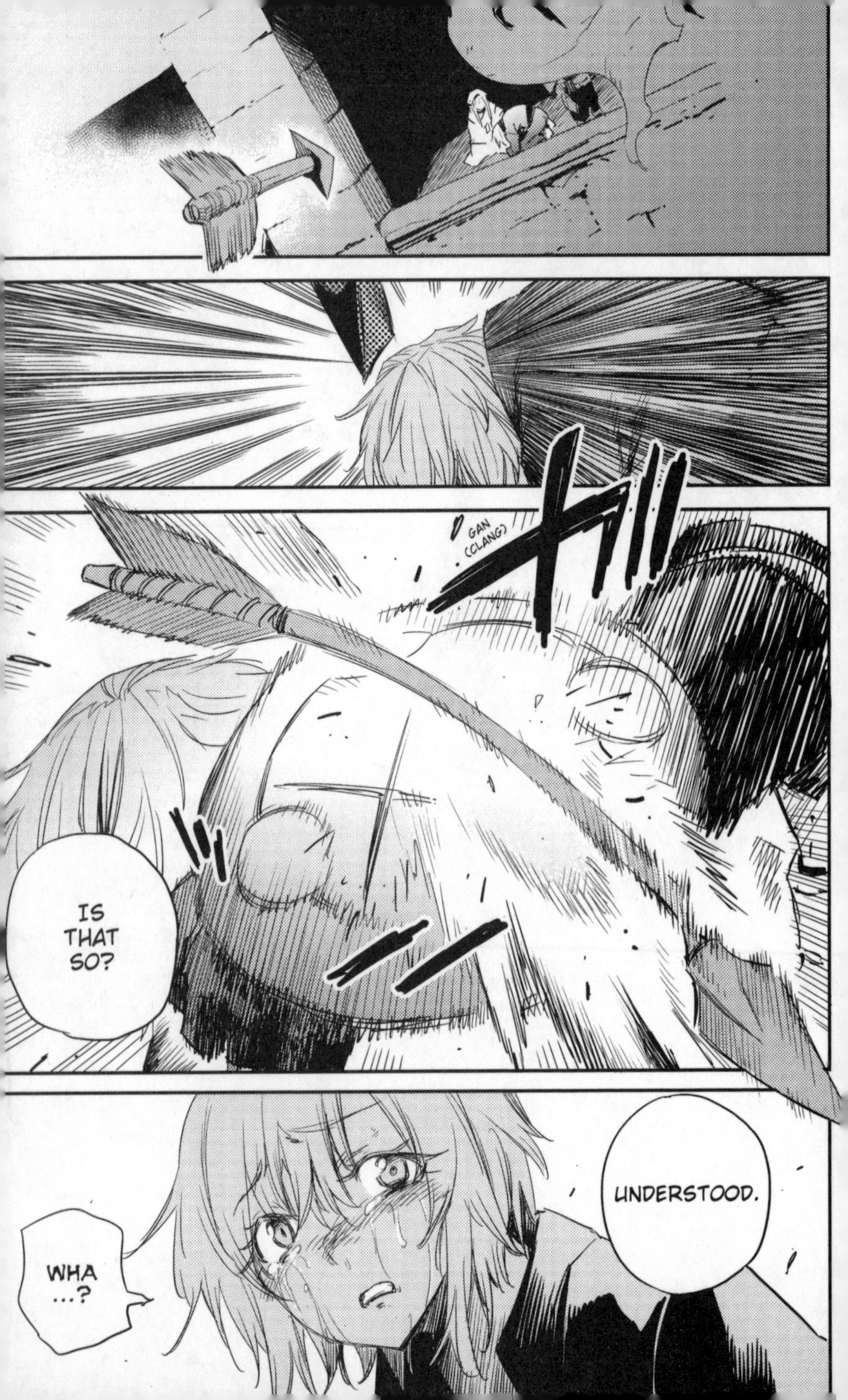
GAN (CLANG)
IS THAT SO?
UNDERSTOOD.
WHA ...?

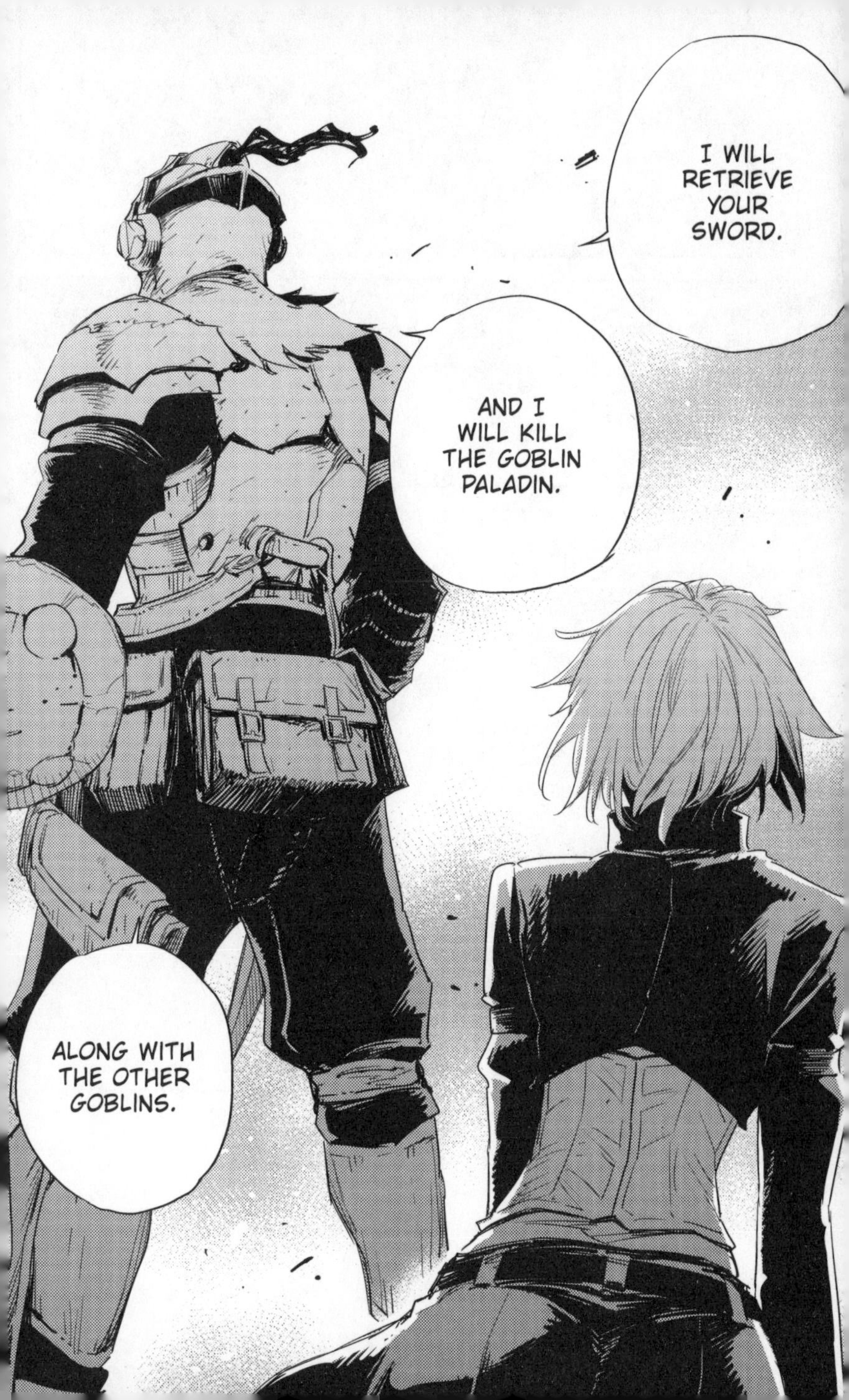
I WILL RETRIEVE YOUR SWORD.
AND I WILL KILL THE GOBLIN PALADIN.
ALONG WITH THE OTHER GOBLINS.

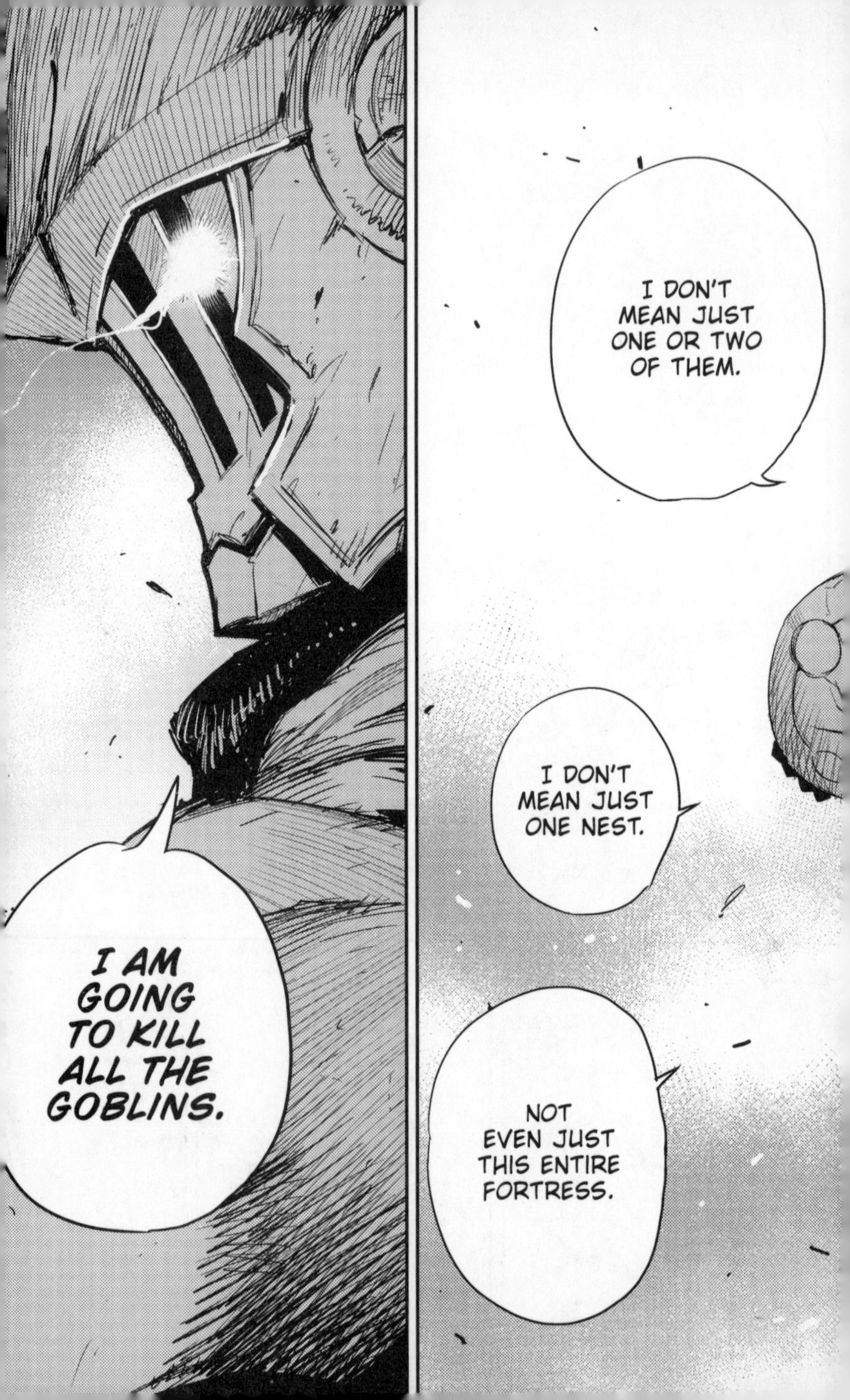
I DON'T MEAN JUST ONE OR TWO OF THEM.
I DON'T MEAN JUST ONE NEST.
NOT EVEN JUST THIS ENTIRE FORTRESS.
I AM GOING TO KILL ALL THE GOBLINS.

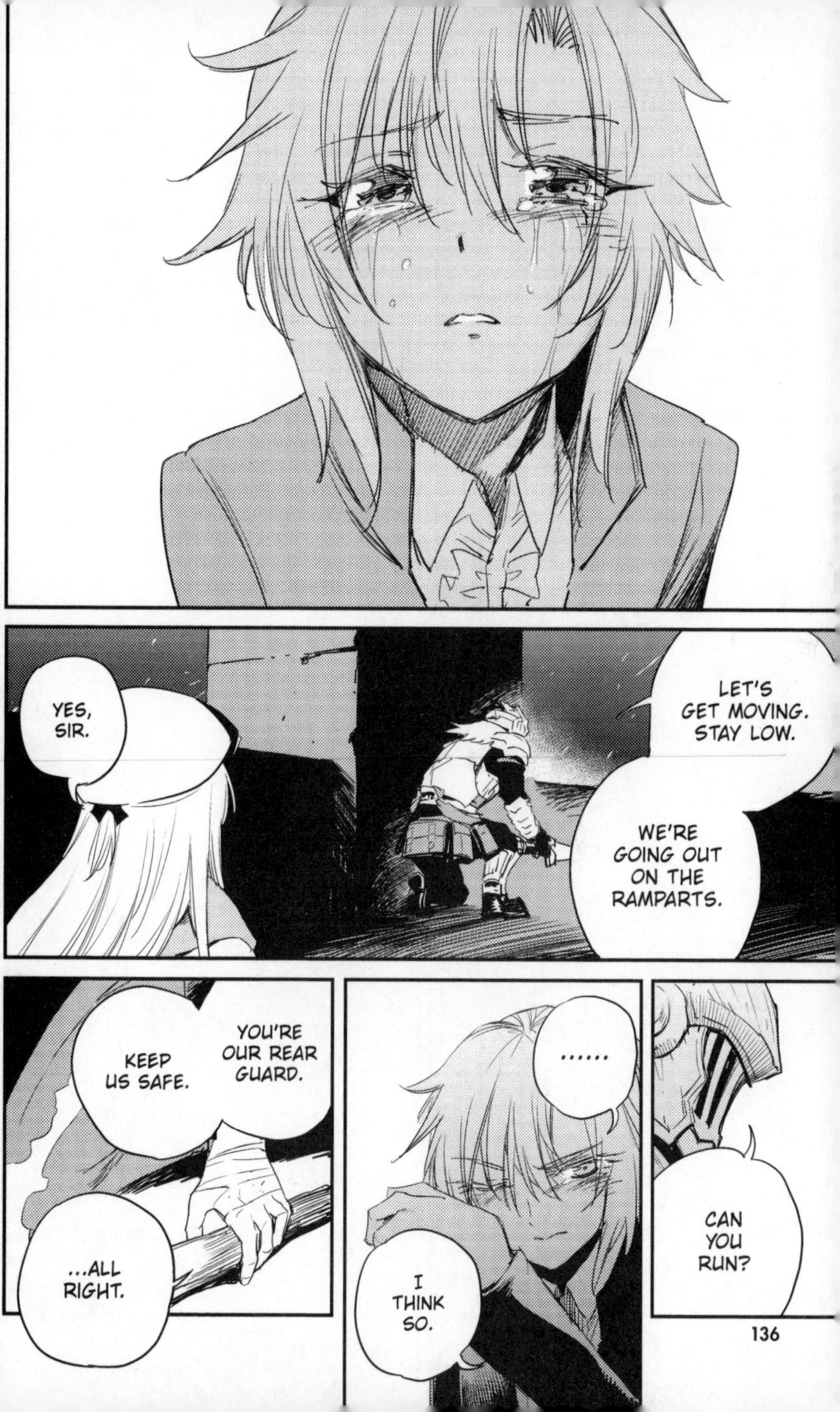
LET'S GET MOVING. STAY LOW.
WE'RE GOING OUT ON THE RAMPARTS.
YES, SIR.
CAN YOU RUN?
......
I THINK SO.
YOU'RE OUR REAR GUARD.
KEEP US SAFE.
...ALL RIGHT.

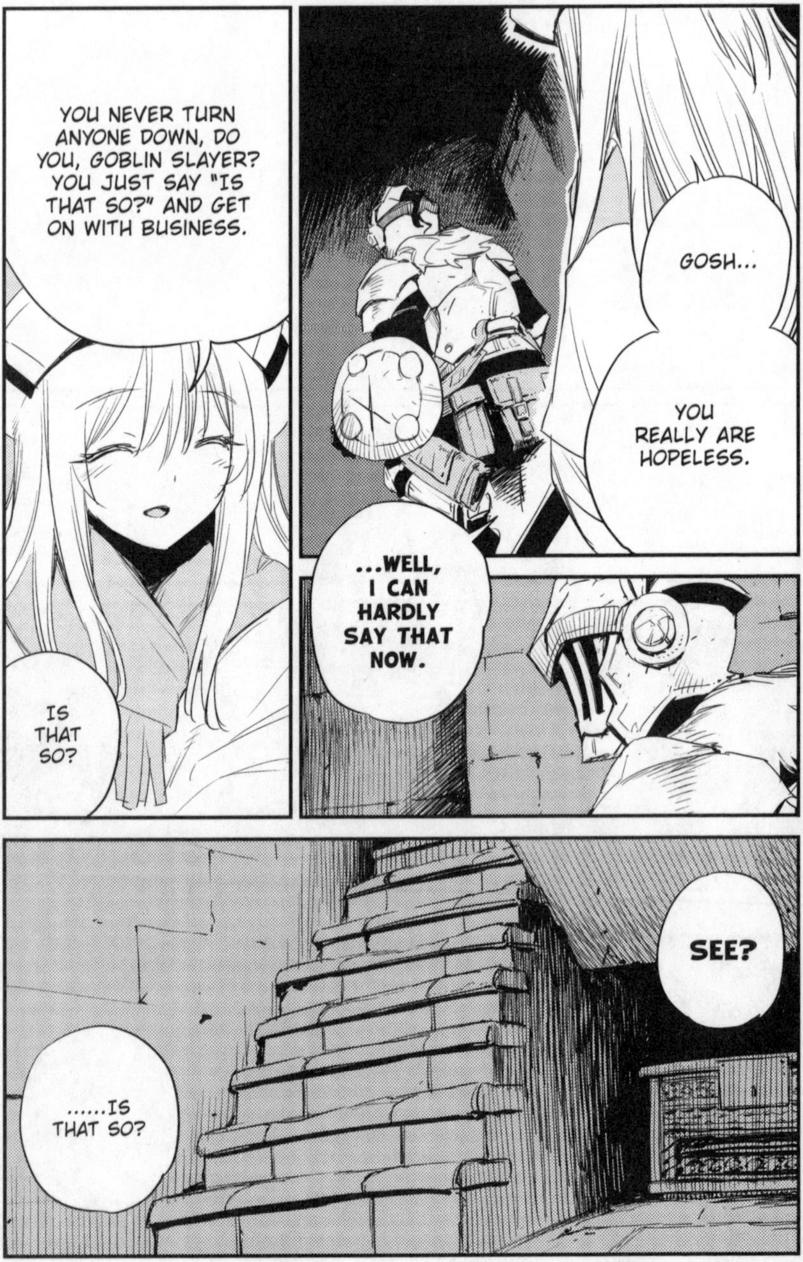
GOSH...
YOU REALLY ARE HOPELESS.
...WELL, I CAN HARDLY SAY THAT NOW.
YOU NEVER TURN ANYONE DOWN, DO YOU, GOBLIN SLAYER? YOU JUST SAY "IS THAT SO?" AND GET ON WITH BUSINESS.
IS THAT SO?
SEE?
......IS THAT SO?

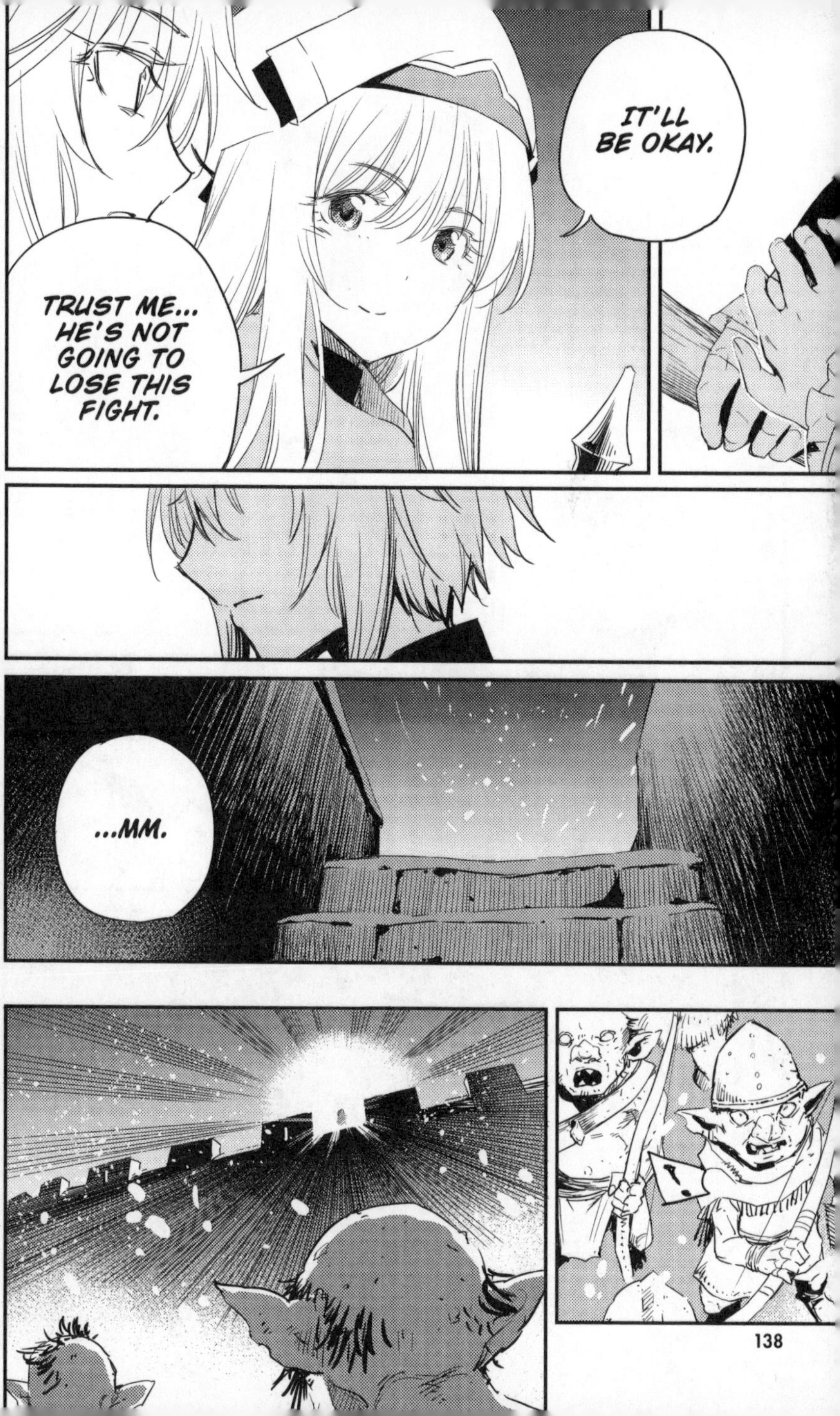
IT'LL BE OKAY.
TRUST ME... HE'S NOT GOING TO LOSE THIS FIGHT.
...MM.

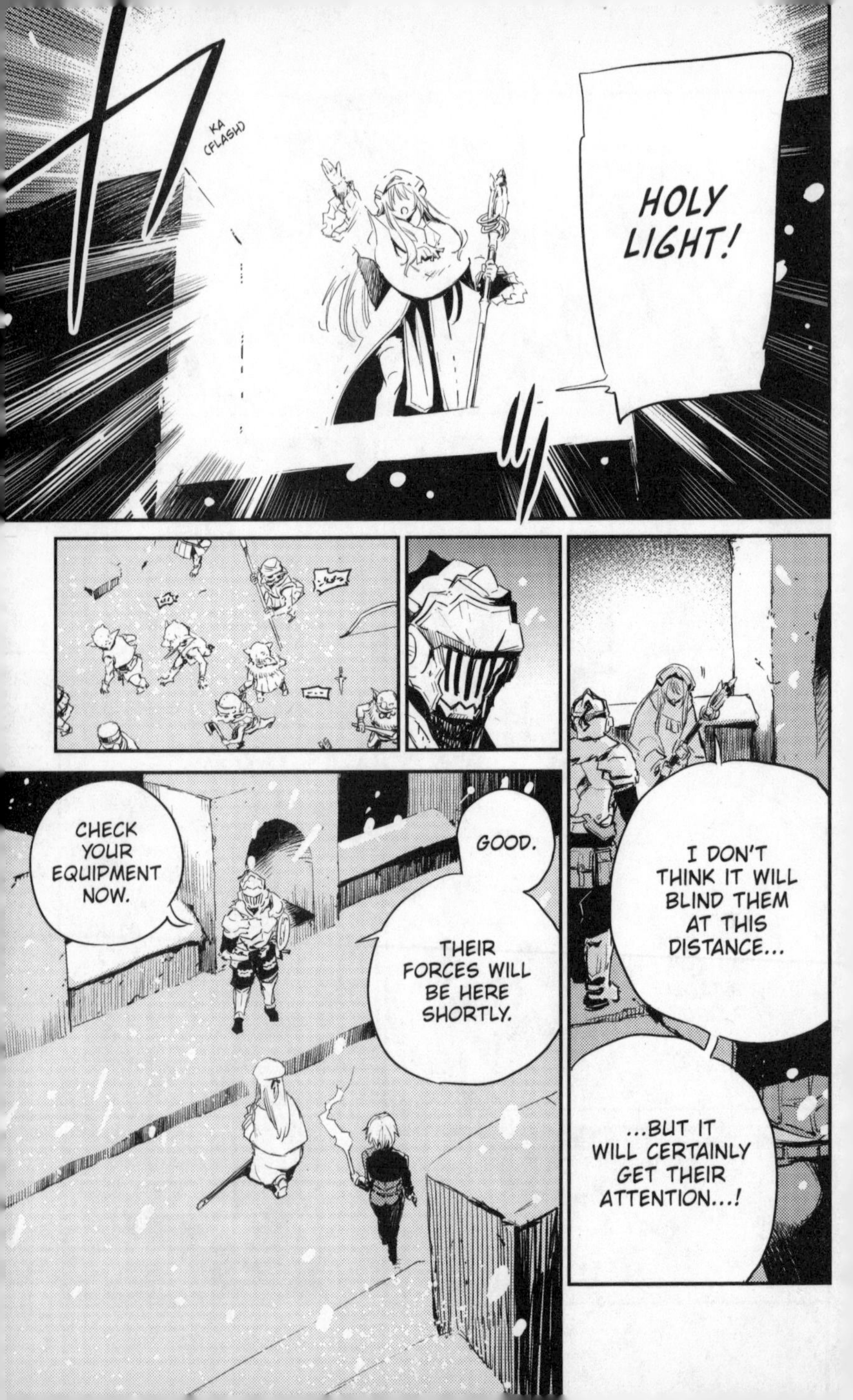
HOLY LIGHT!
KA (FLASH)
I DON'T THINK IT WILL BLIND THEM AT THIS DISTANCE...
...BUT IT WILL CERTAINLY GET THEIR ATTENTION...!
GOOD.
THEIR FORCES WILL BE HERE SHORTLY.
CHECK YOUR EQUIPMENT NOW.

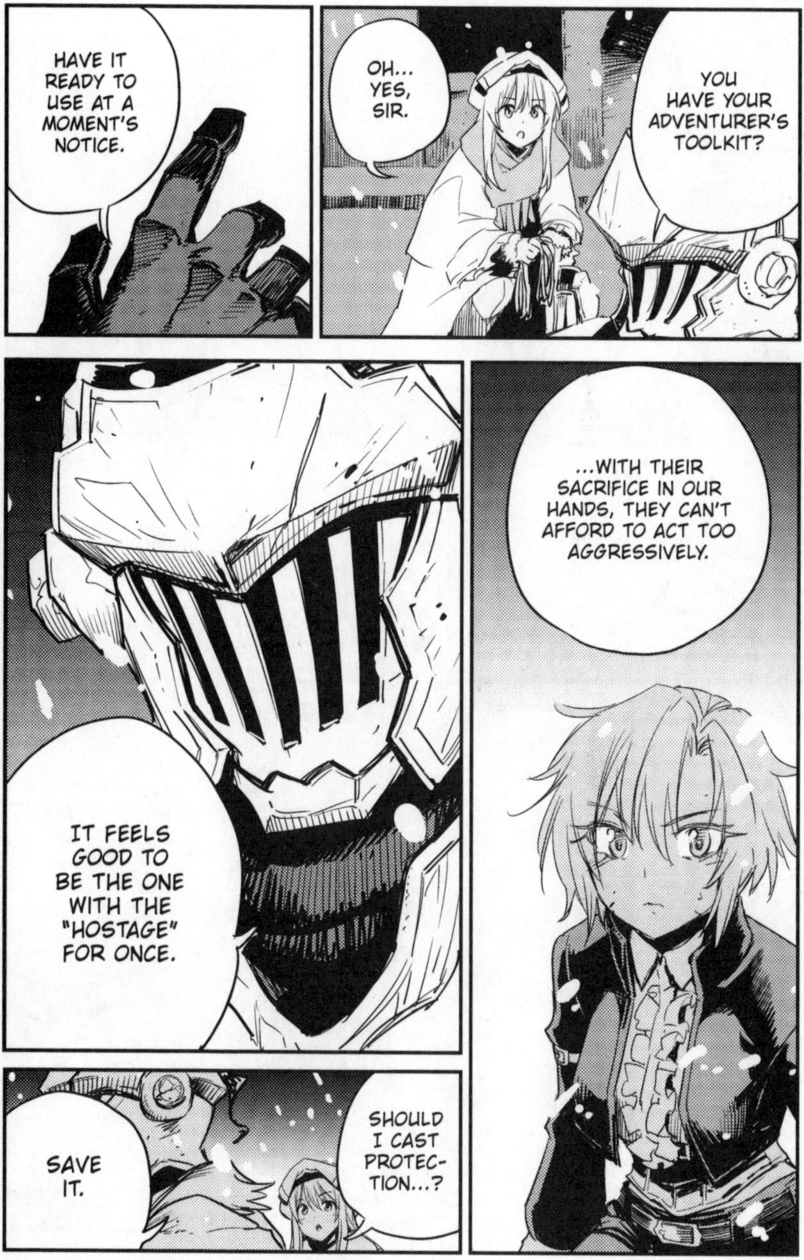
YOU HAVE YOUR ADVENTURER'S TOOLKIT?
OH... YES, SIR.
HAVE IT READY TO USE AT A MOMENT'S NOTICE.
...WITH THEIR SACRIFICE IN OUR HANDS, THEY CAN'T AFFORD TO ACT TOO AGGRESSIVELY.
IT FEELS GOOD TO BE THE ONE WITH THE "HOSTAGE" FOR ONCE.
SHOULD I CAST PROTECTION...?
SAVE IT.

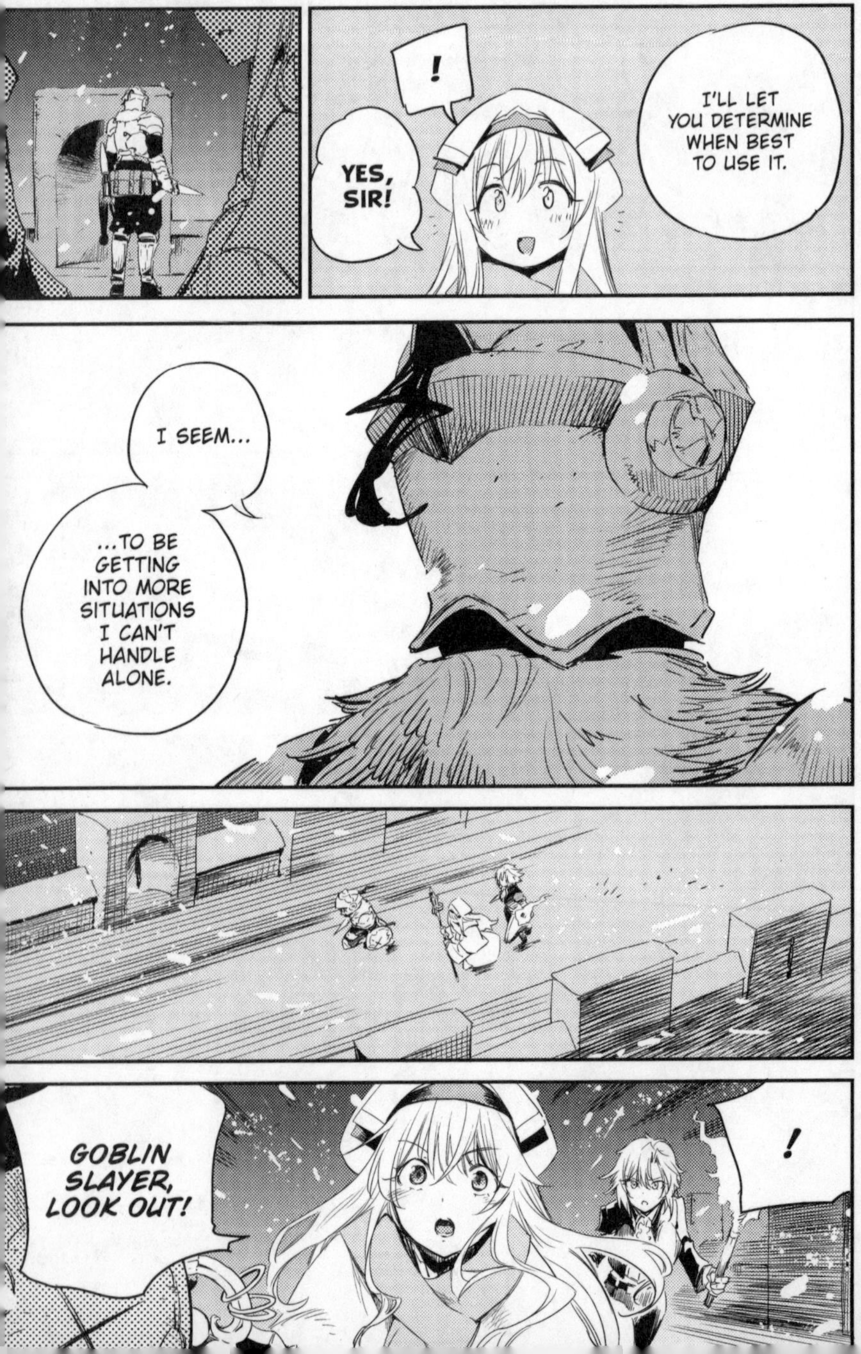
I'LL LET YOU DETERMINE WHEN BEST TO USE IT.
!
YES, SIR!
I SEEM...
...TO BE GETTING INTO MORE SITUATIONS I CAN'T HANDLE ALONE.
!
GOBLIN SLAYER, LOOK OUT!

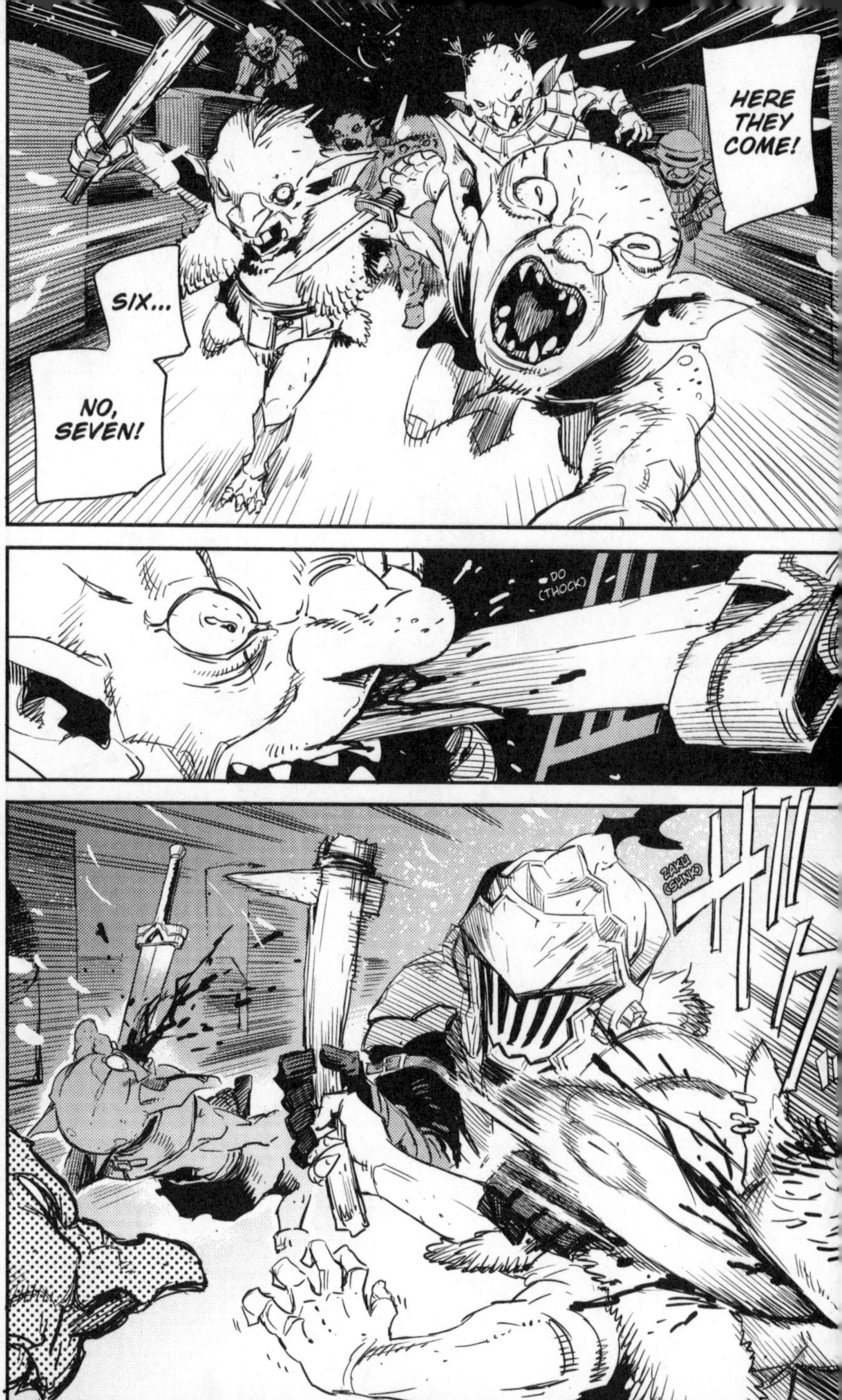
HERE THEY COME!
SIX...
NO, SEVEN!
DO (THOCK)
ZAKU (SHNK)

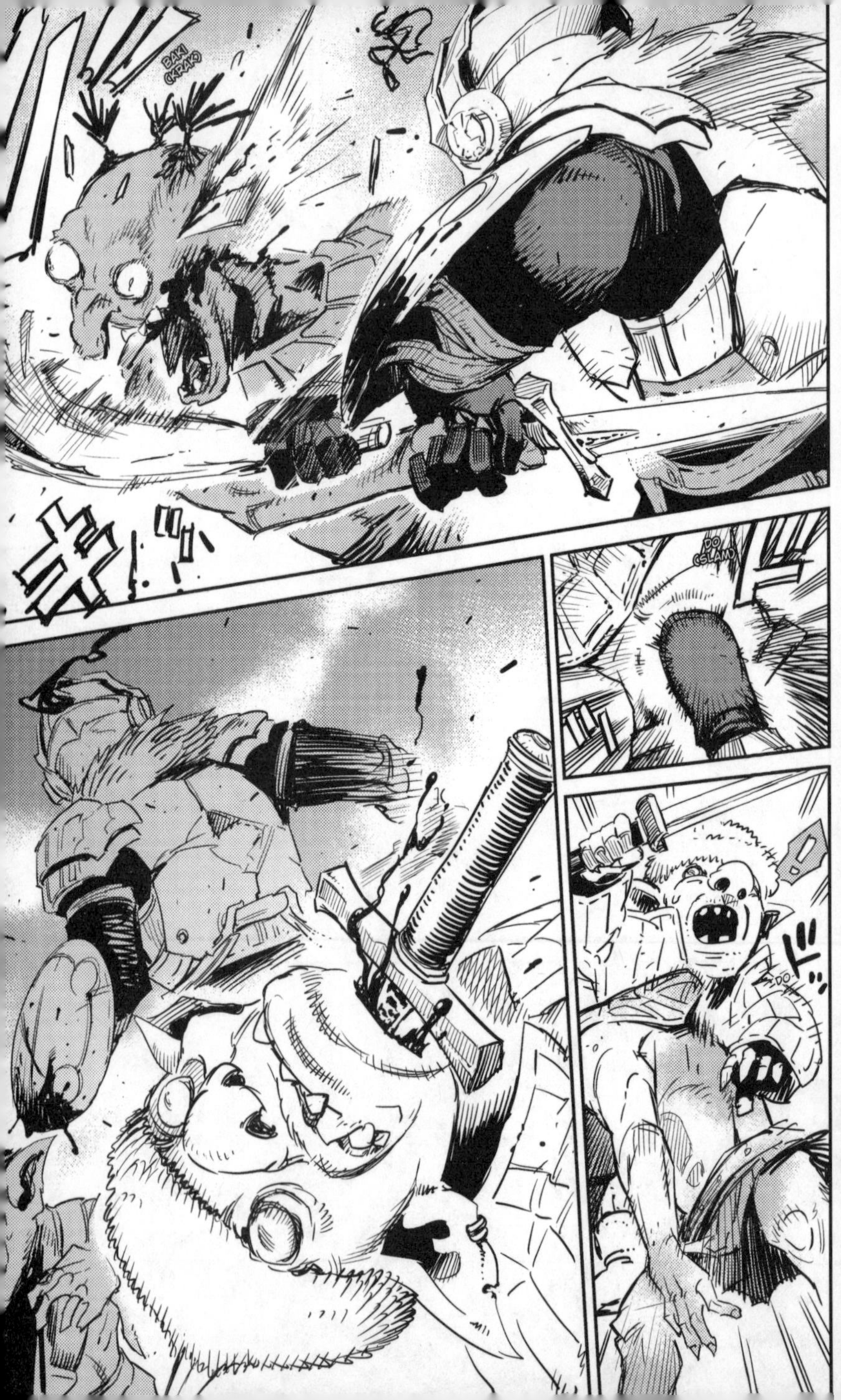
BAKI (KRAK)
DO (SLAM)
DO

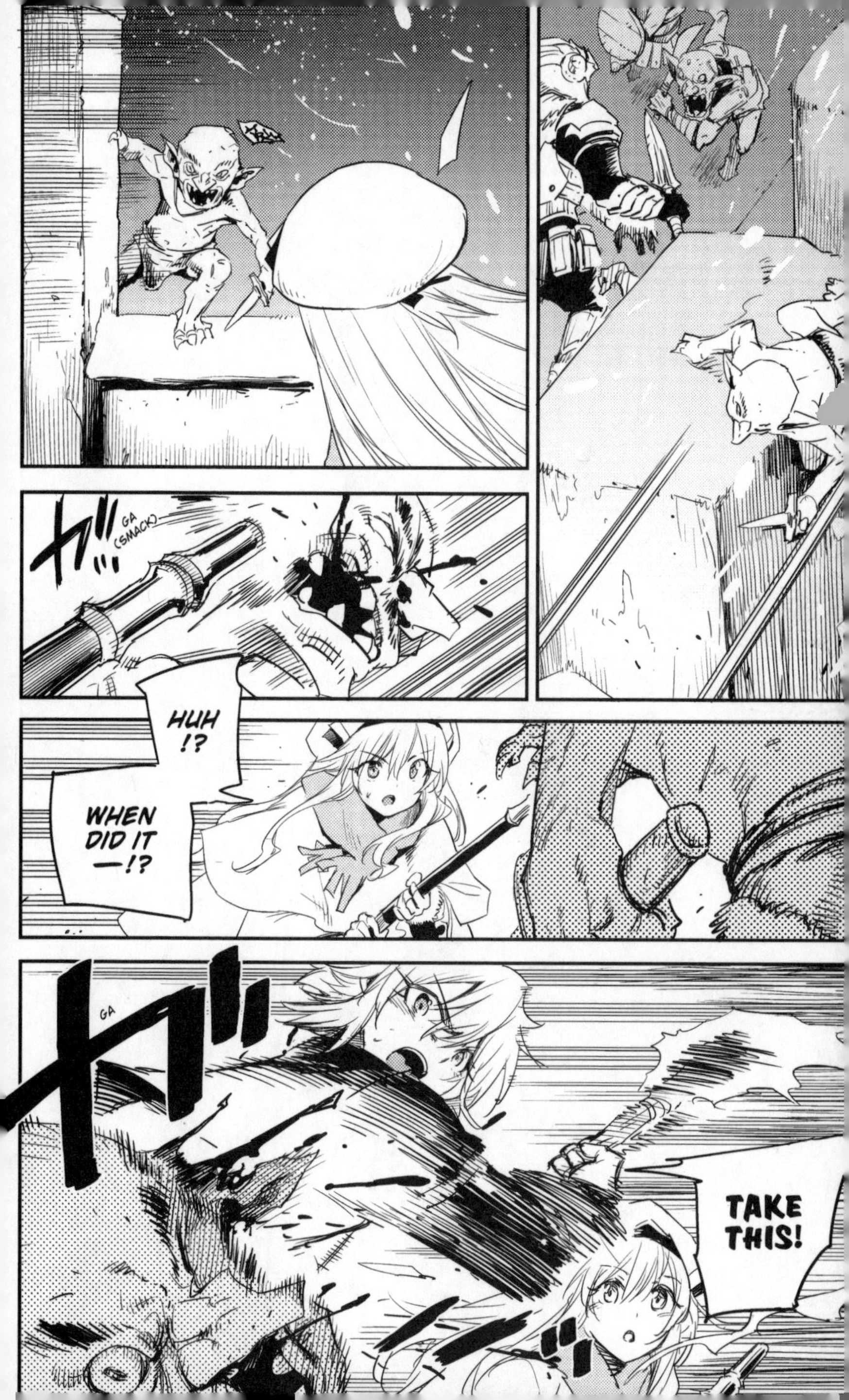
GA (SMACK)
HUH !?
WHEN DID IT —!?
TAKE THIS!
GA

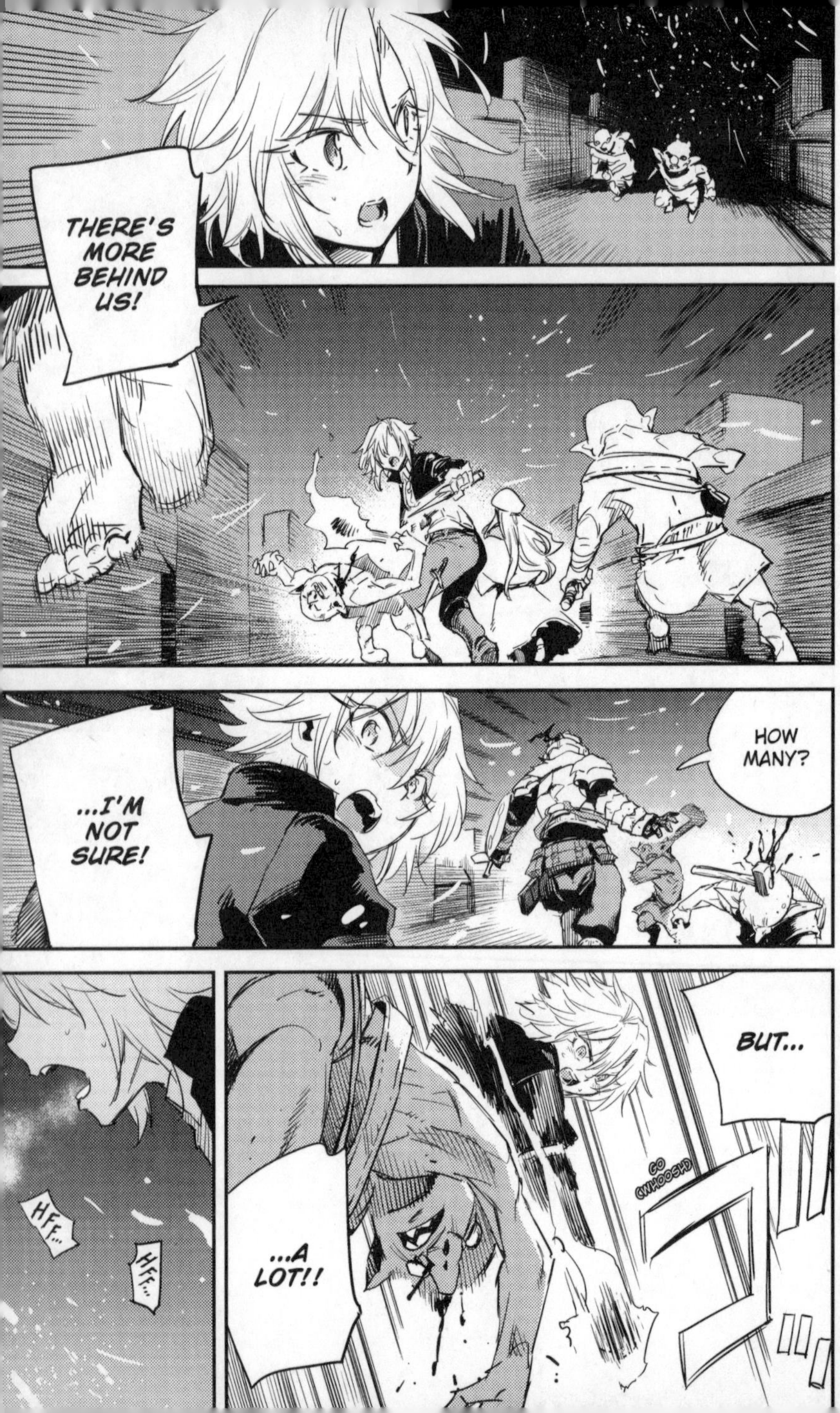
THERE'S MORE BEHIND US!
HOW MANY?
...I'M NOT SURE!
BUT...
GO (WHOOSH)
...A LOT!!
HFF...
HFF...

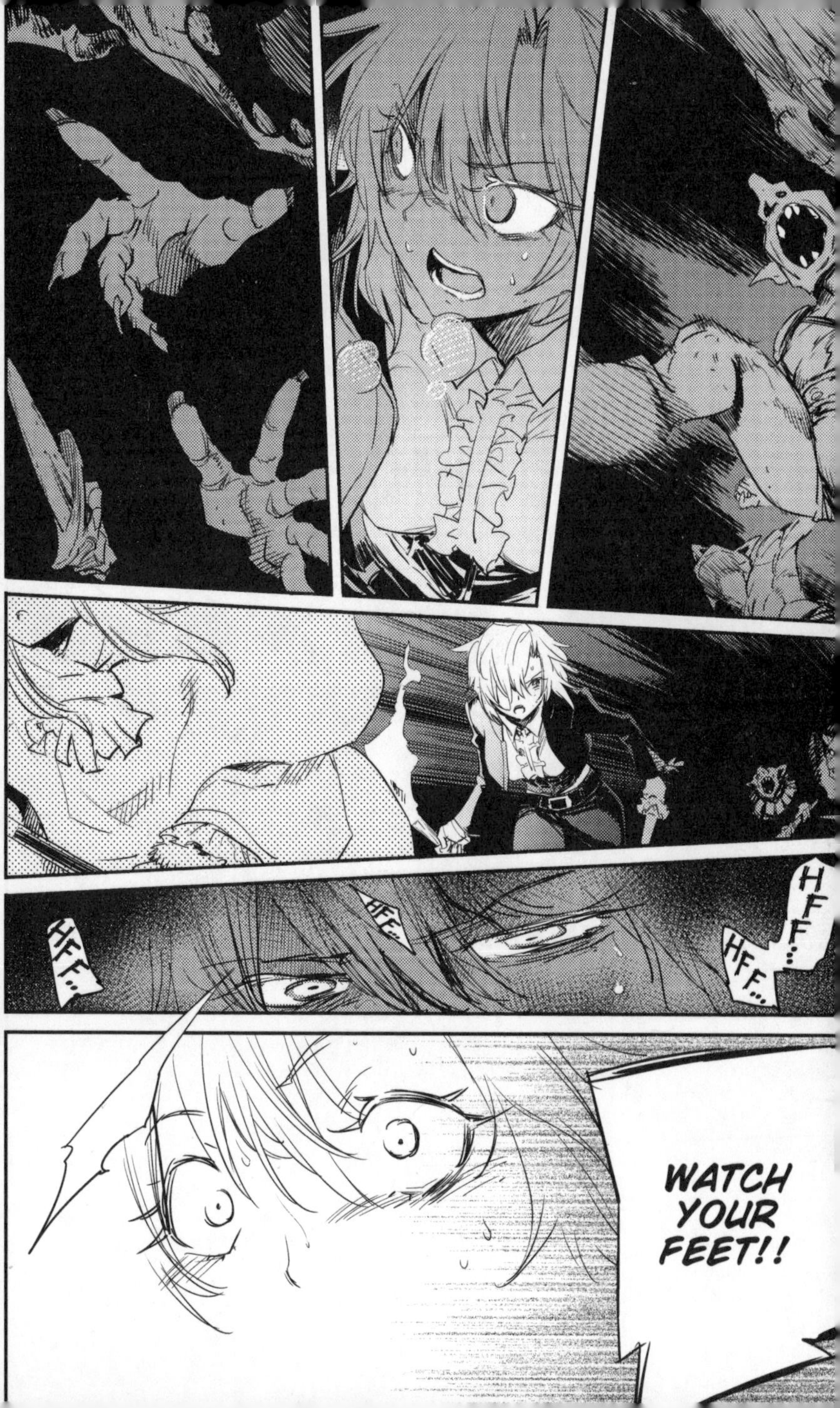
HFF...
HFF...
HFF...
HFF...
WATCH YOUR FEET!!

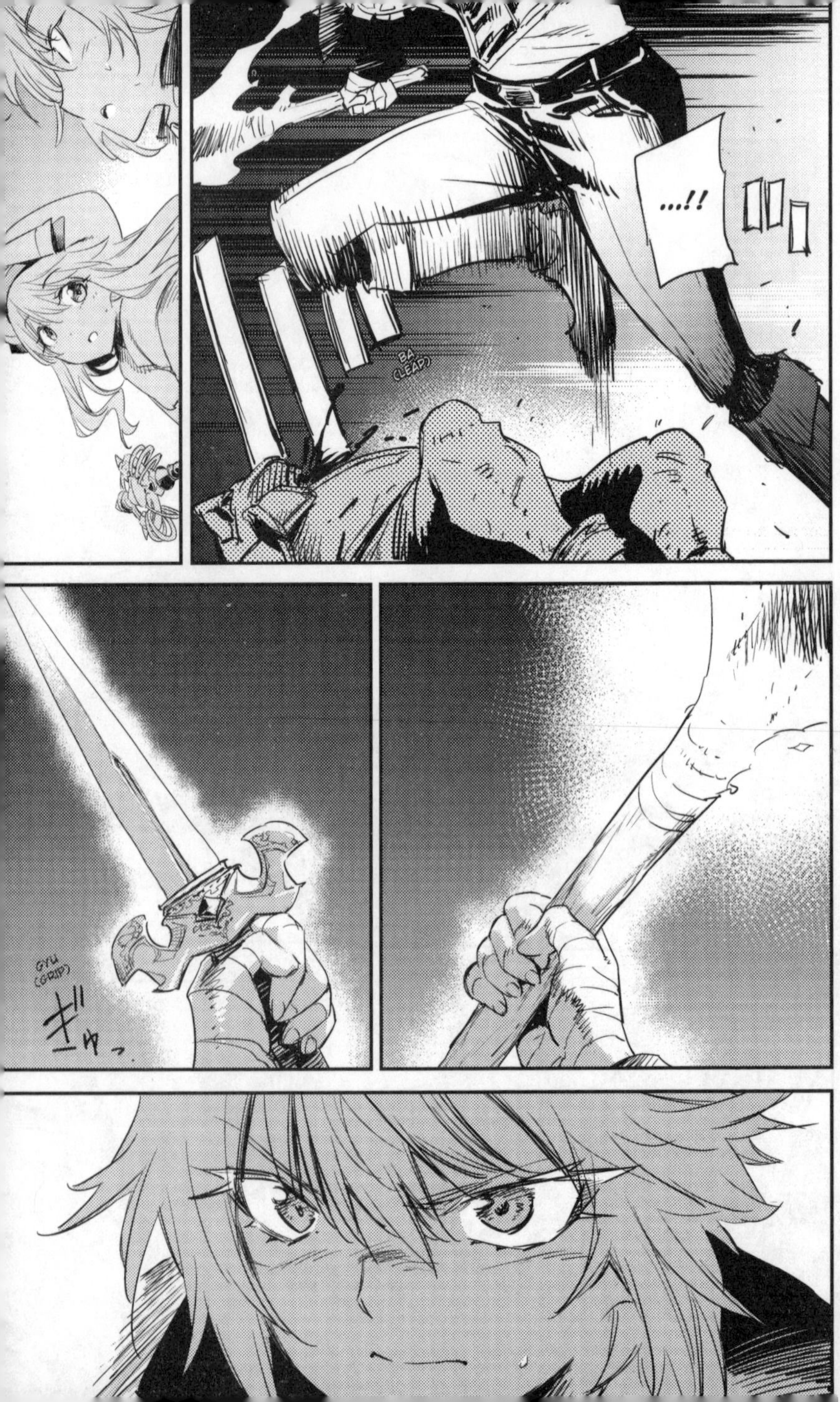
...!!
BA (LEAP)
GYU (GRIP)
ぎゅっ

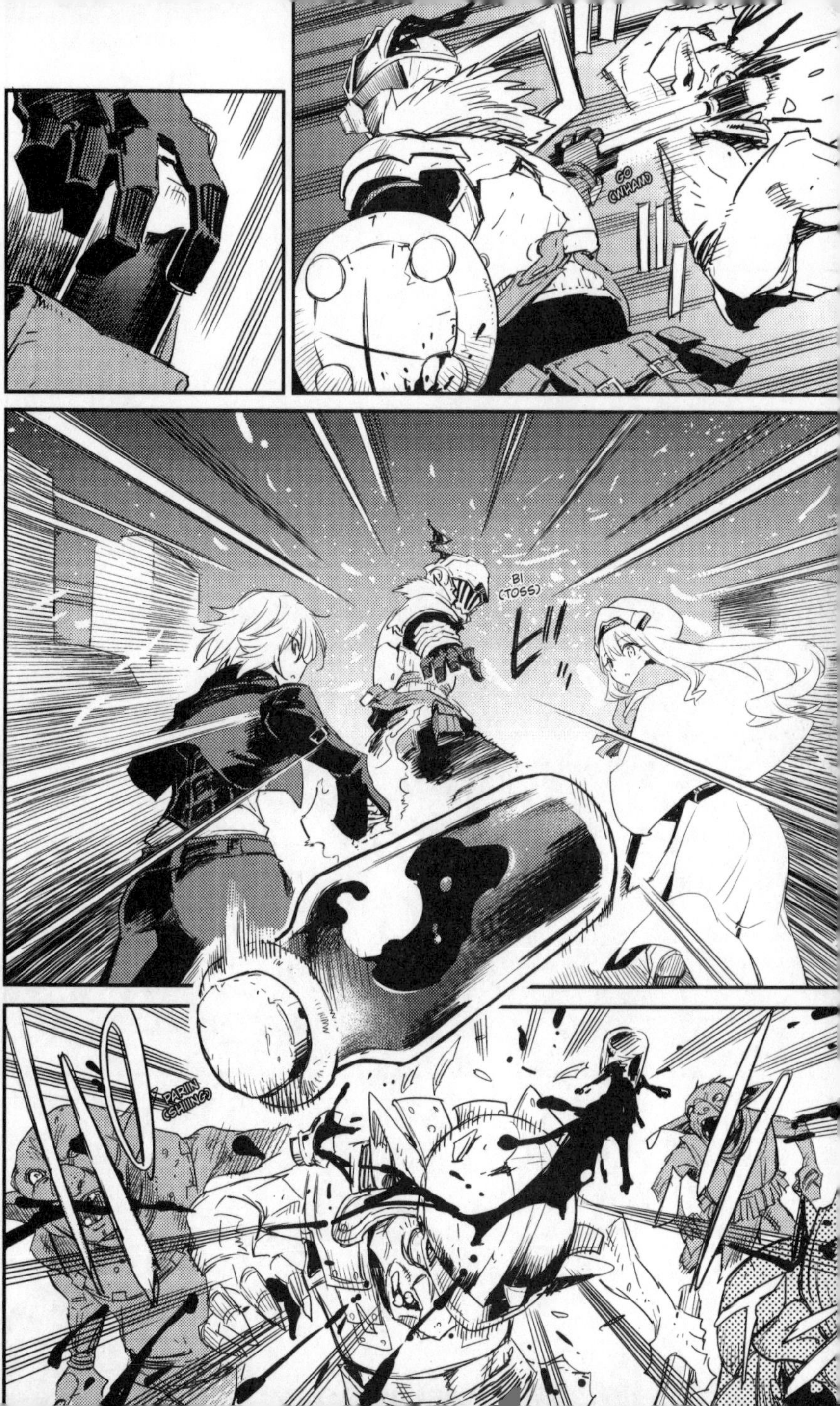
GO (WHAM)
BI (TOSS)
PARIIN (SHIIING)

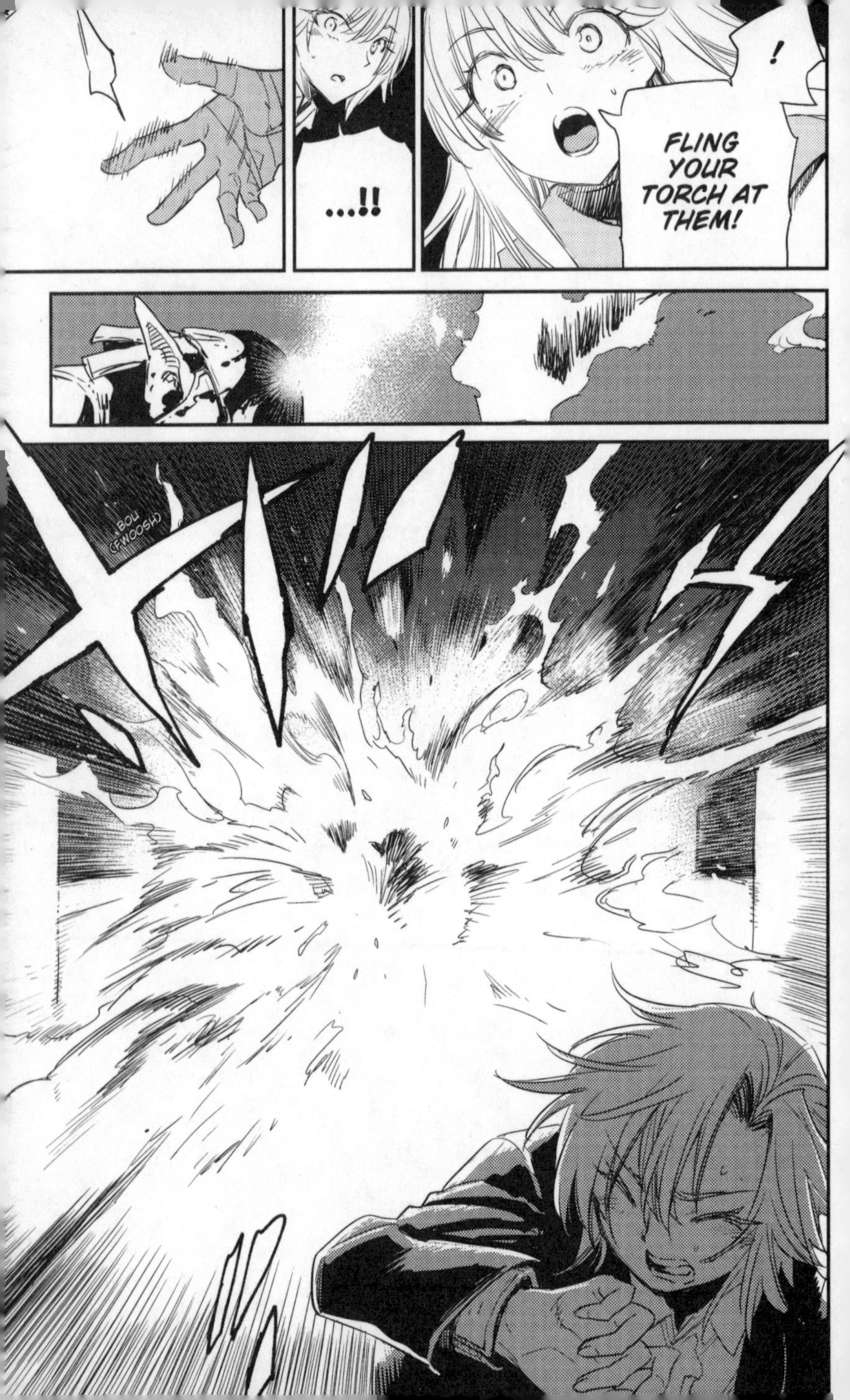
!
FLING YOUR TORCH AT THEM!
...!!
BOU (FWOOSH)

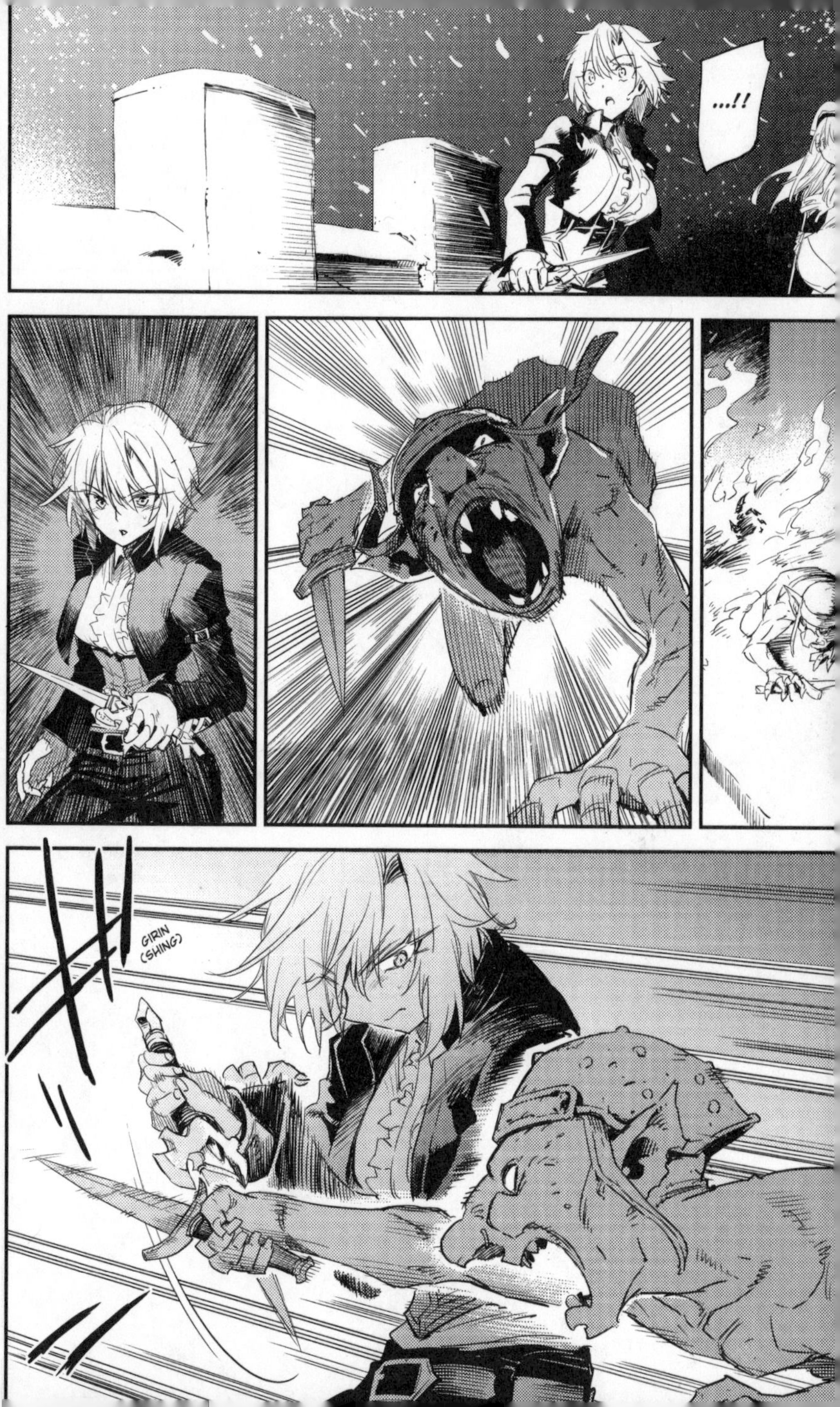
...!!
GIRIN (SHING)

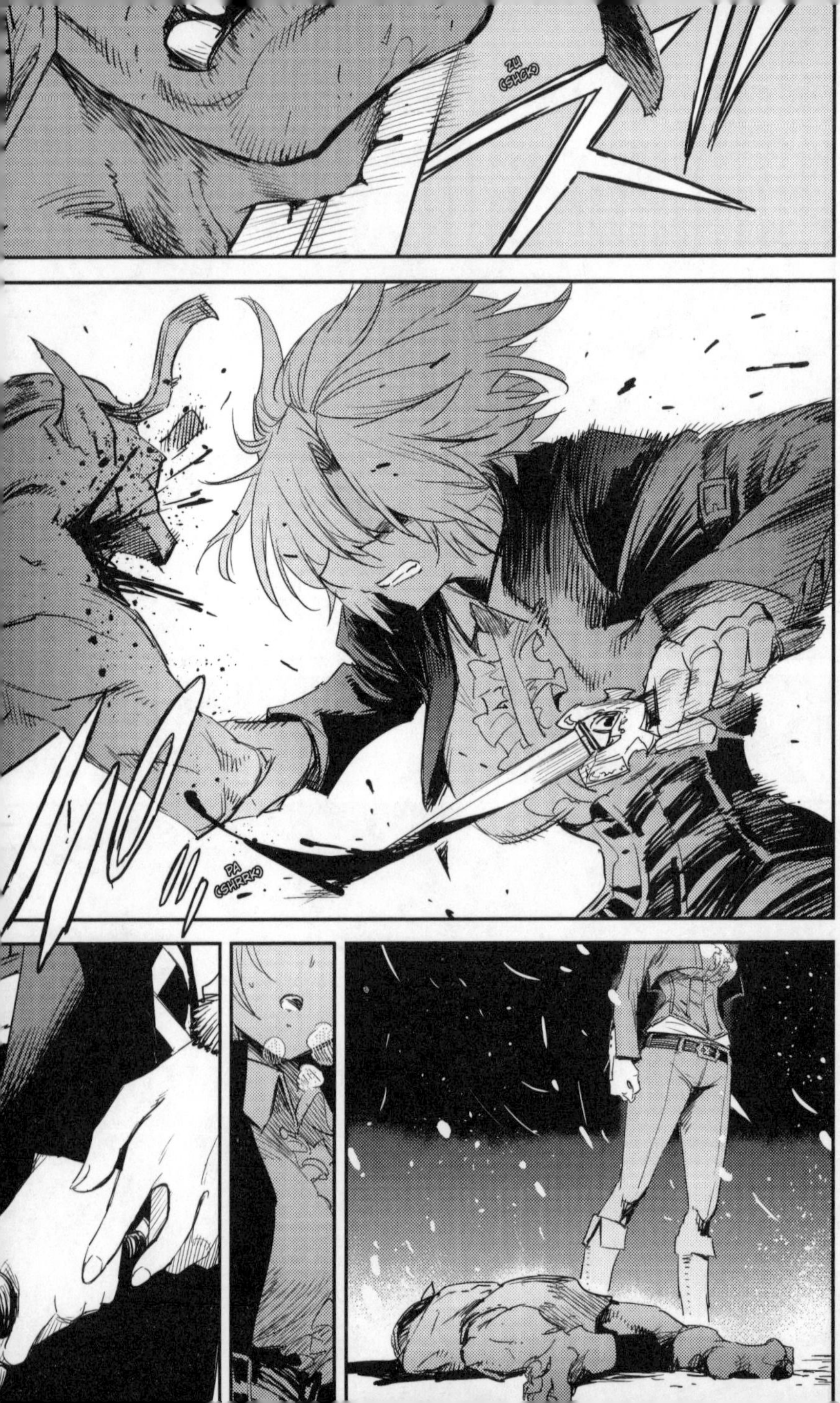
ZU (SHCK)
PA (SHRRK)

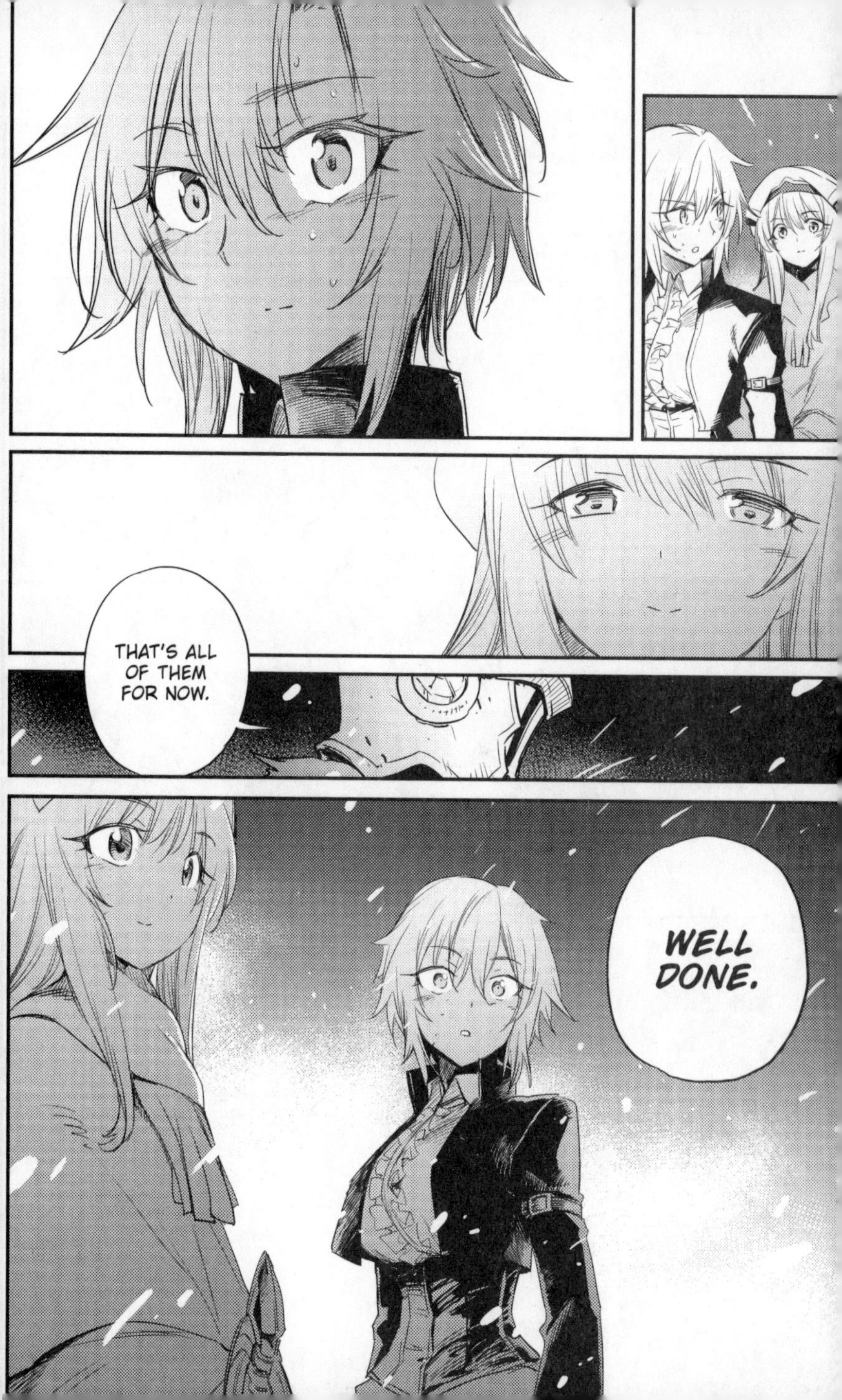
THAT'S ALL OF THEM FOR NOW.
WELL DONE.

CHAPTER 51

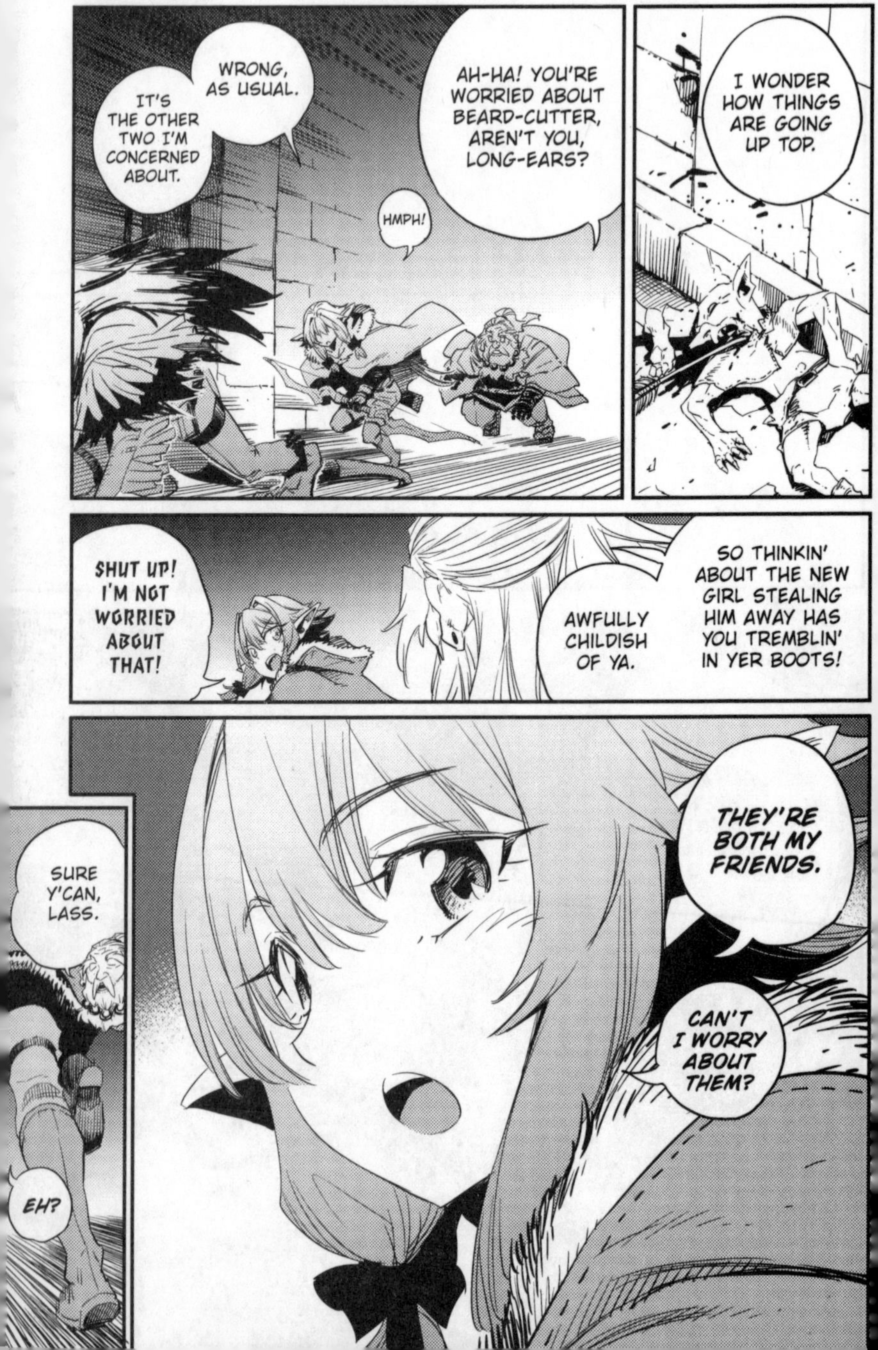
I WONDER HOW THINGS ARE GOING UP TOP.
AH-HA! YOU'RE WORRIED ABOUT BEARD-CUTTER, AREN'T YOU, LONG-EARS?
HMPH!
WRONG, AS USUAL.
IT'S THE OTHER TWO I'M CONCERNED ABOUT.
SO THINKIN' ABOUT THE NEW GIRL STEALING HIM AWAY HAS YOU TREMBLIN' IN YER BOOTS!
AWFULLY CHILDISH OF YA.
SHUT UP! I'M NOT WORRIED ABOUT THAT!
THEY'RE BOTH MY FRIENDS.
CAN'T I WORRY ABOUT THEM?
SURE Y'CAN, LASS.
EH?

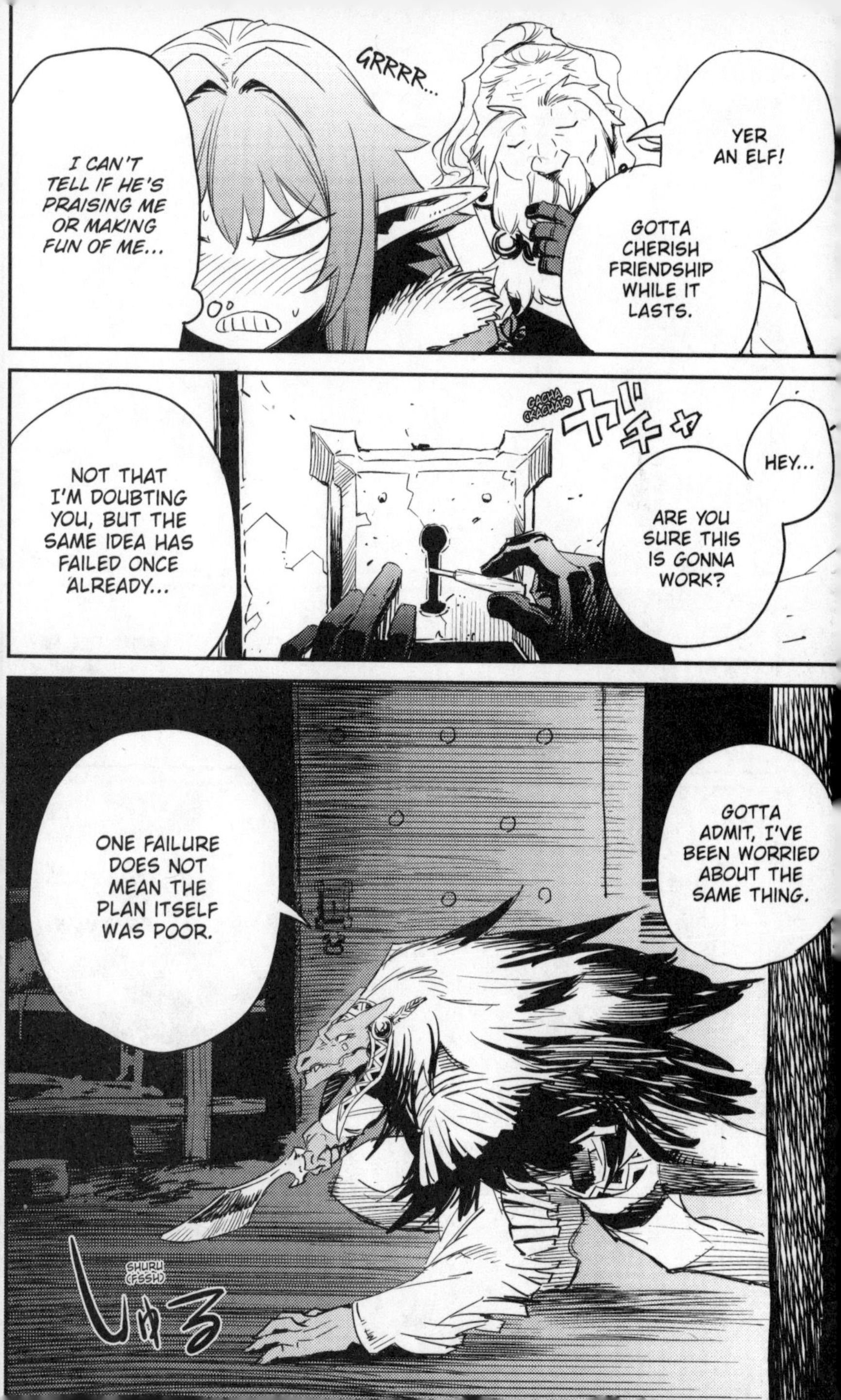
YER AN ELF!
GOTTA CHERISH FRIENDSHIP WHILE IT LASTS.
GRRRR...
I CAN'T TELL IF HE'S PRAISING ME OR MAKING FUN OF ME...
HEY...
ARE YOU SURE THIS IS GONNA WORK?
GACHA (KACHAK)
NOT THAT I'M DOUBTING YOU, BUT THE SAME IDEA HAS FAILED ONCE ALREADY...
GOTTA ADMIT, I'VE BEEN WORRIED ABOUT THE SAME THING.
ONE FAILURE DOES NOT MEAN THE PLAN ITSELF WAS POOR.
SHURU (FSSH)

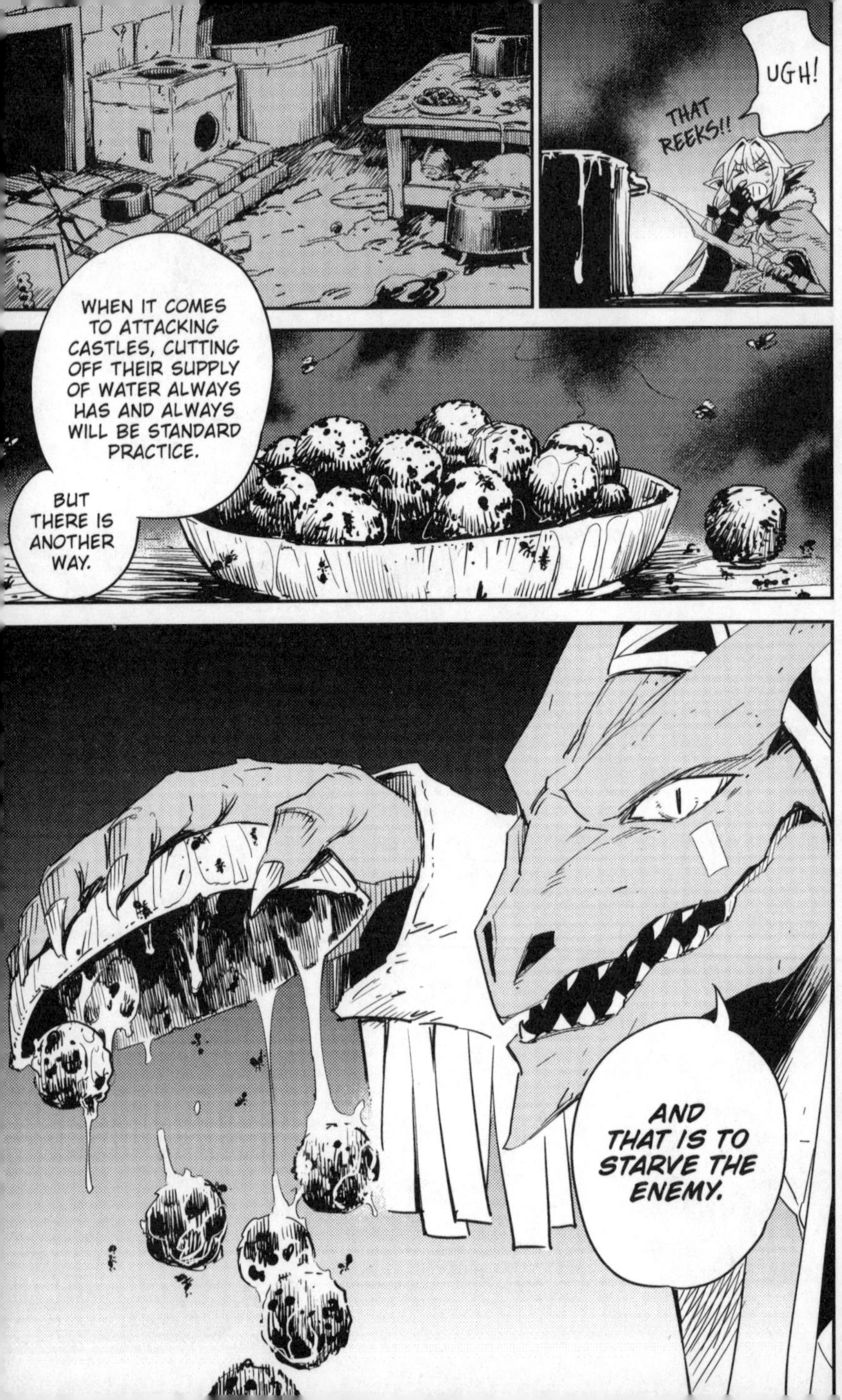
UGH!
THAT REEKS!!
WHEN IT COMES TO ATTACKING CASTLES, CUTTING OFF THEIR SUPPLY OF WATER ALWAYS HAS AND ALWAYS WILL BE STANDARD PRACTICE.
BUT THERE IS ANOTHER WAY.
AND THAT IS TO STARVE THE ENEMY.

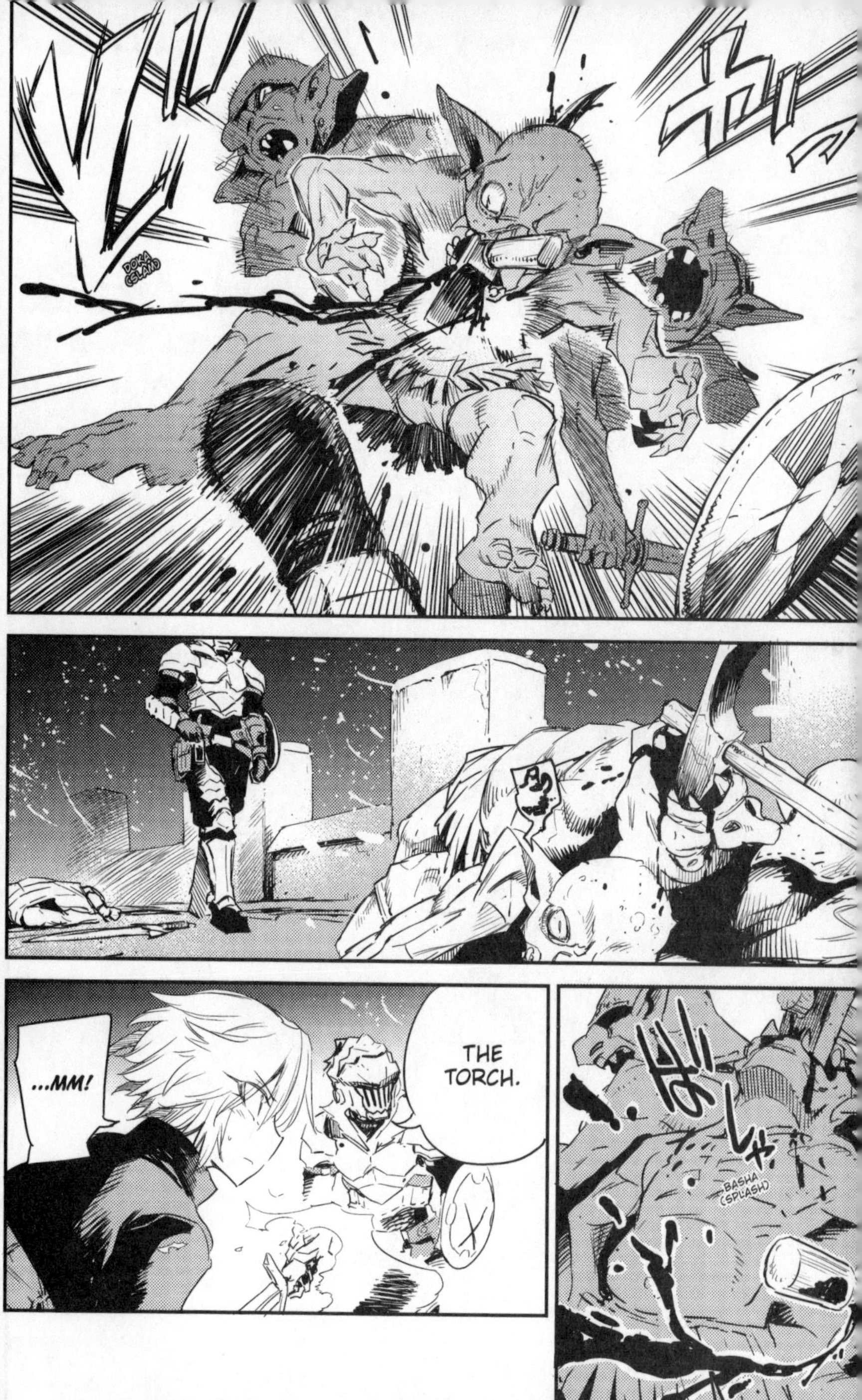
DOKA (SLAM)
BASHA (SPLASH)
THE TORCH.
...MM!

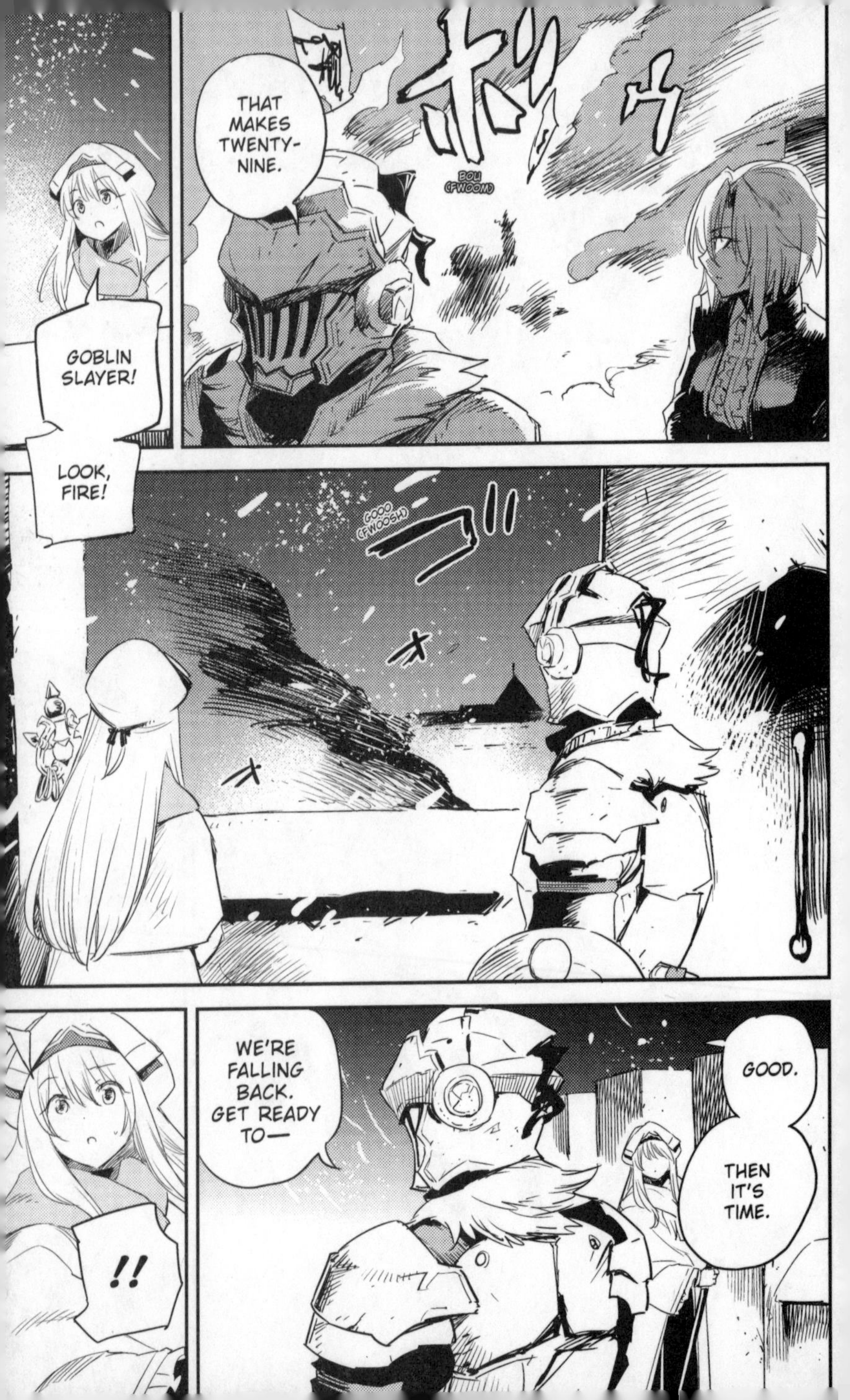
BOU (FWOOM)
THAT MAKES TWENTY-NINE.
GOBLIN SLAYER!
LOOK, FIRE!
GOOO (FWOOSH)
GOOD.
THEN IT'S TIME.
WE'RE FALLING BACK. GET READY TO—
!!

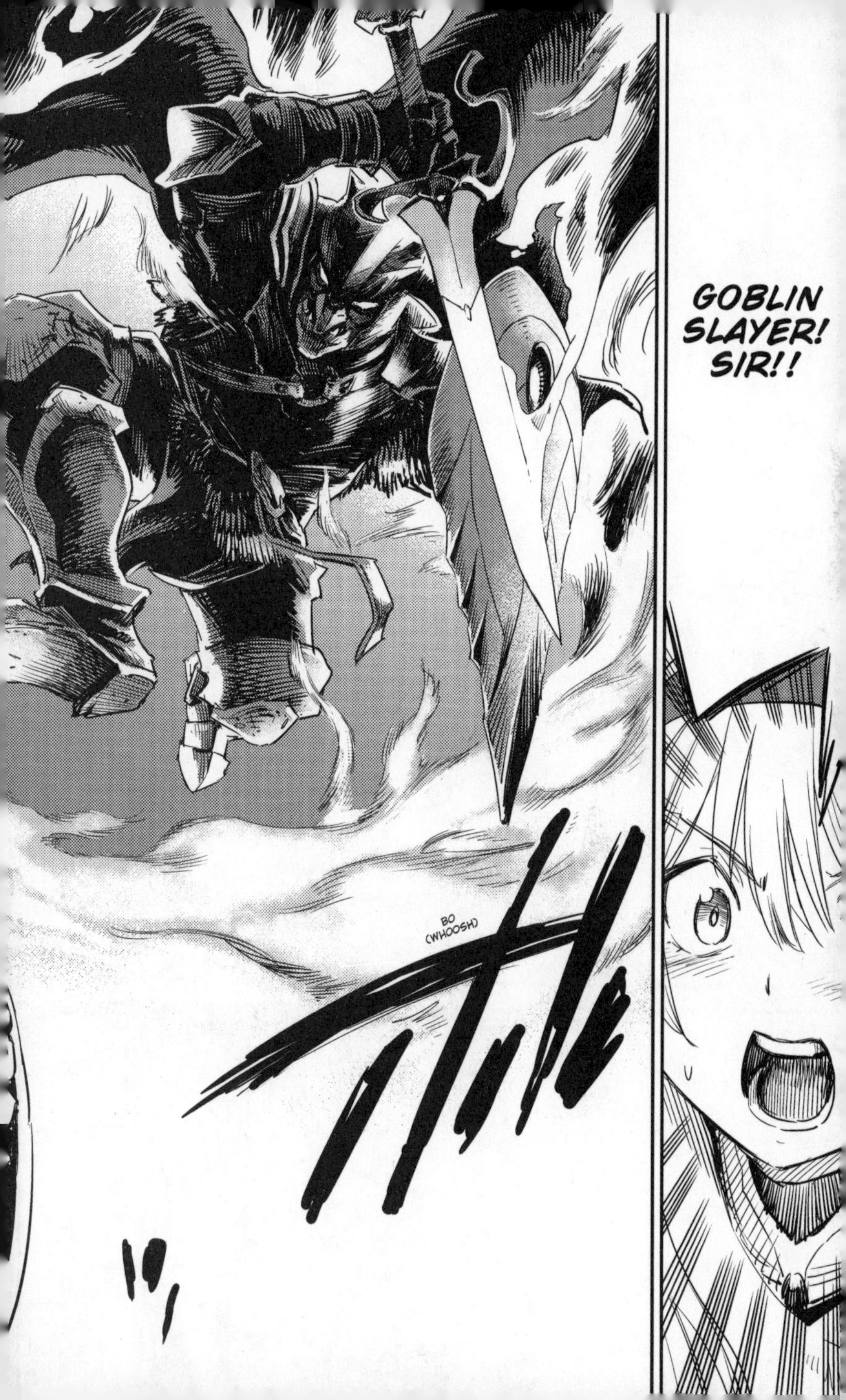
GOBLIN SLAYER! SIR!!
BO (WHOOSH)

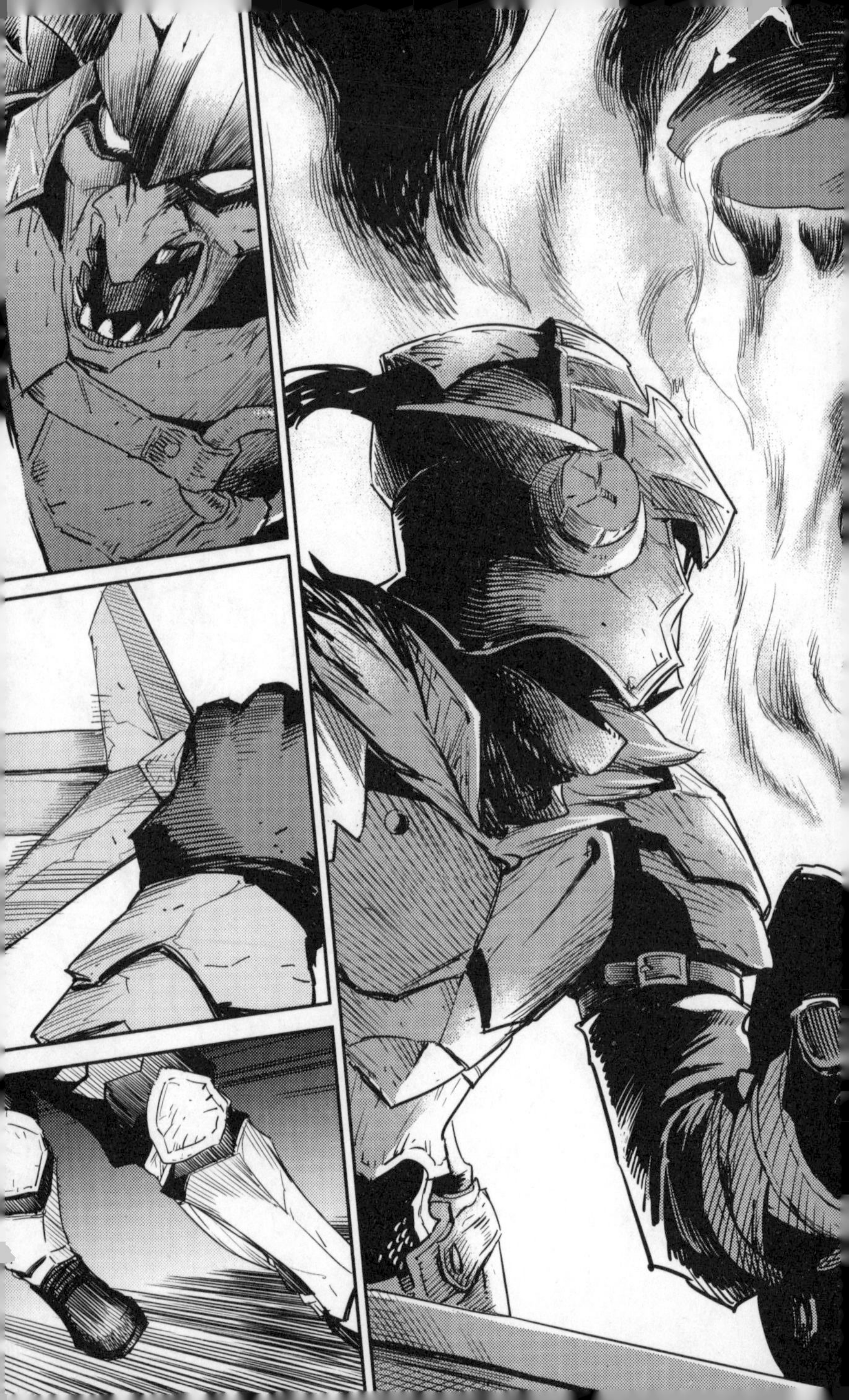

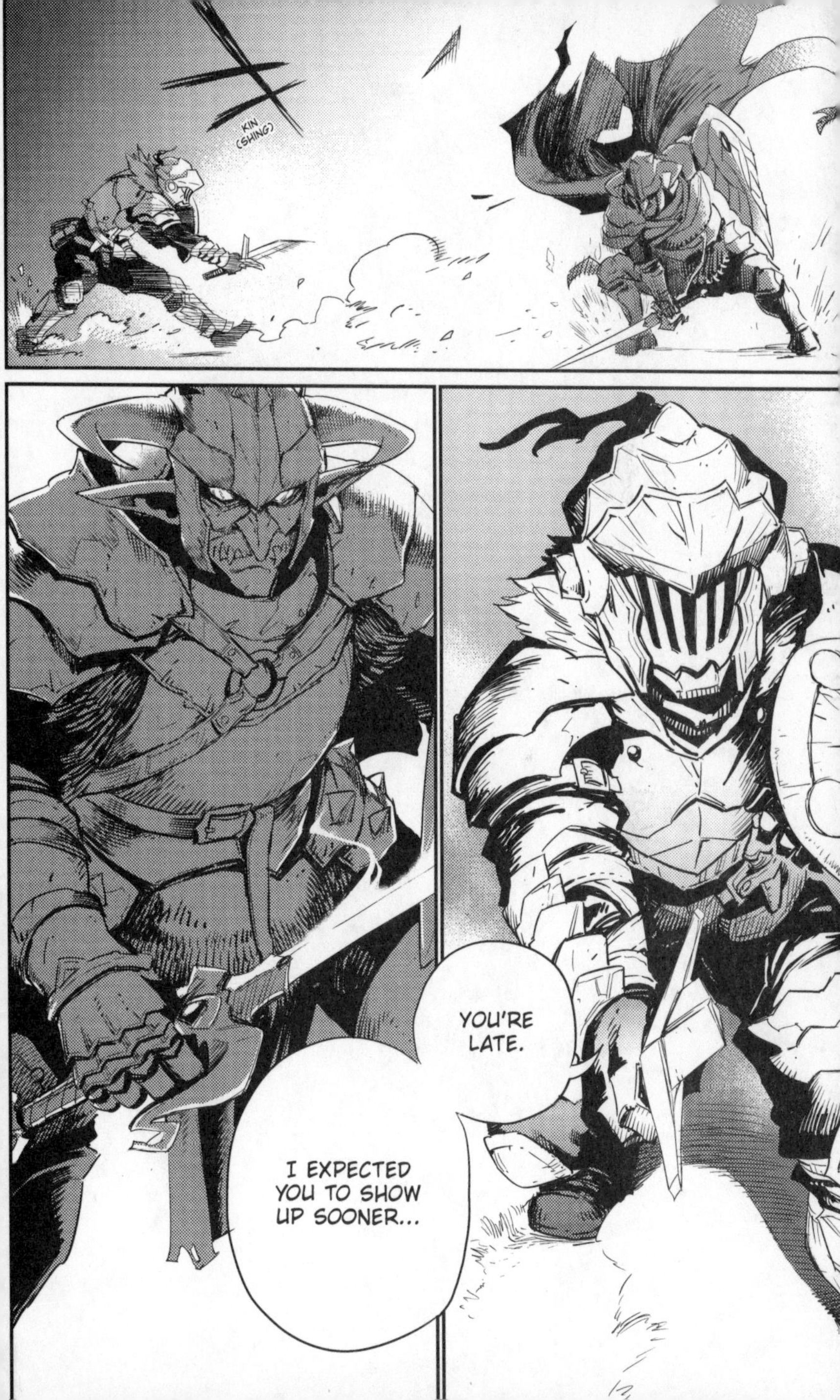
KIN (SHING)
YOU'RE LATE.
I EXPECTED YOU TO SHOW UP SOONER...

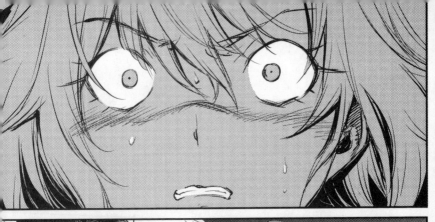

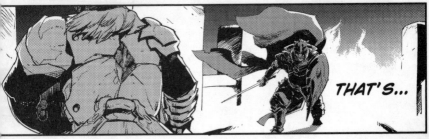

THAT'S...

...MY...

MY SWORD...

THE ONE HE...

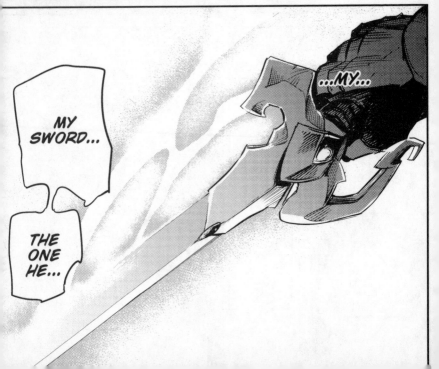

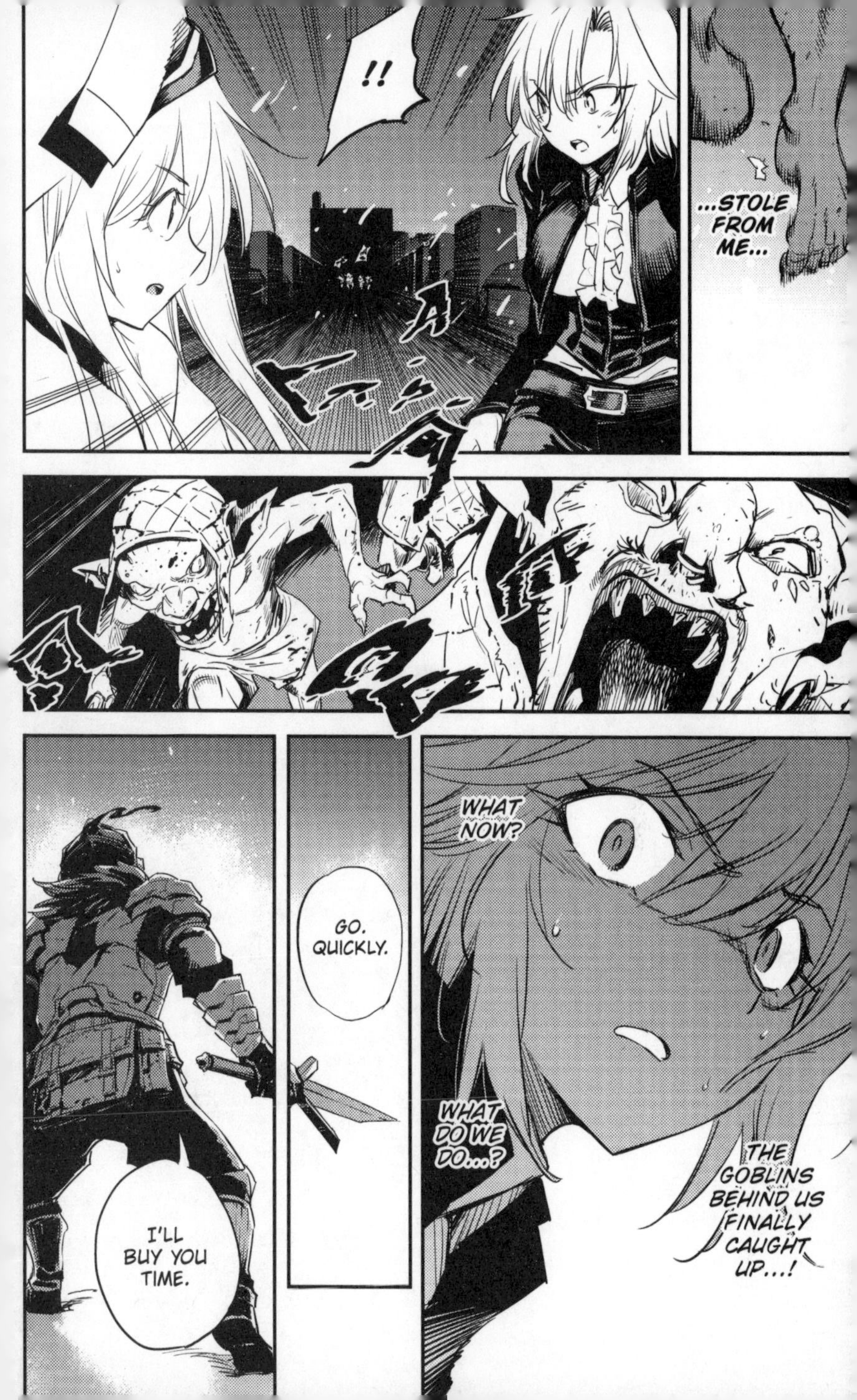
...STOLE FROM ME...
!!
WHAT NOW?
WHAT DO WE DO...?
THE GOBLINS BEHIND US FINALLY CAUGHT UP...!
GO. QUICKLY.
I'LL BUY YOU TIME.

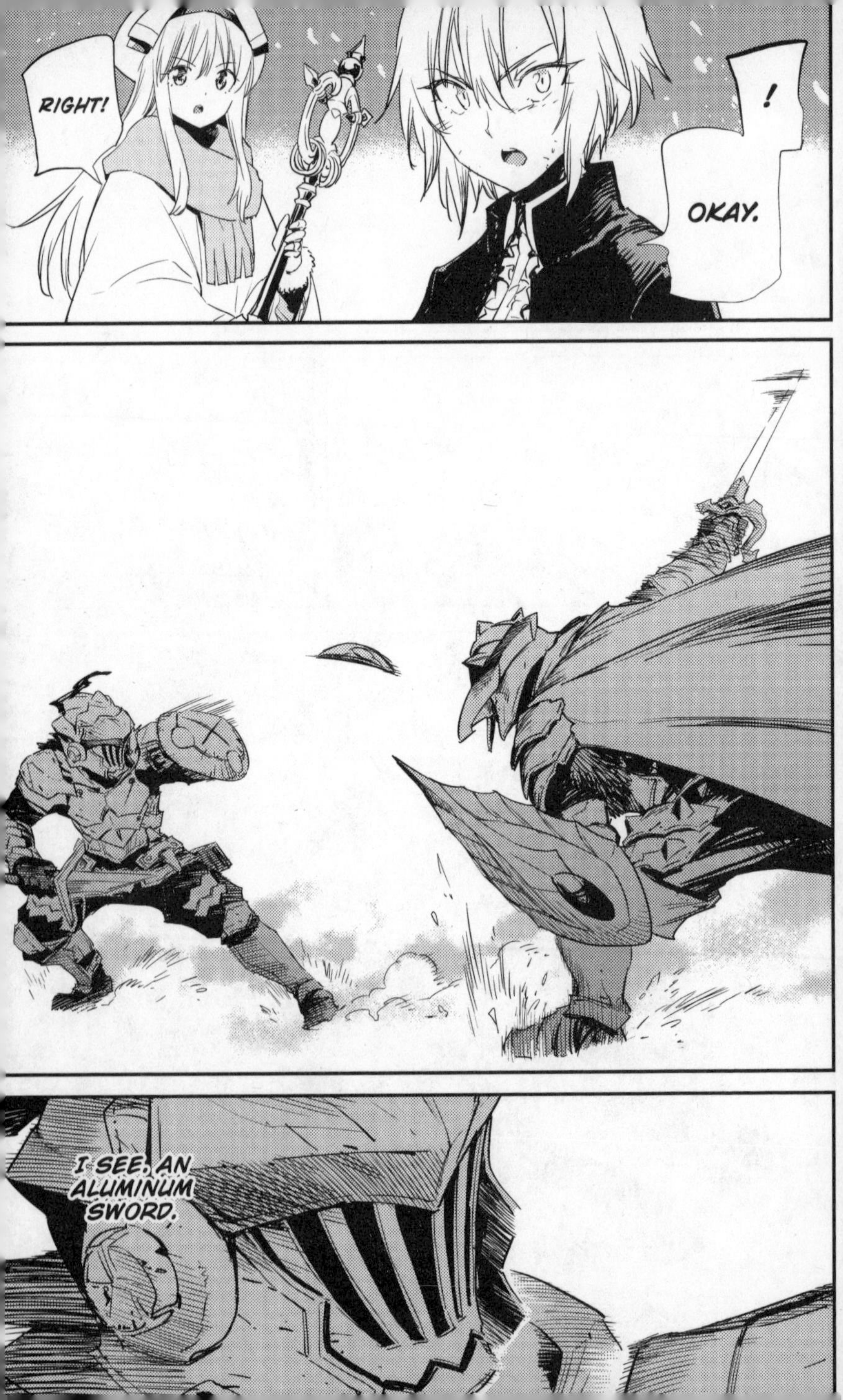
!
OKAY.
RIGHT!
I SEE. AN ALUMINUM SWORD.

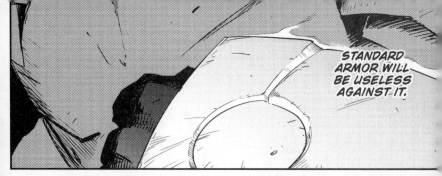

STANDARD ARMOR WILL BE USELESS AGAINST IT.

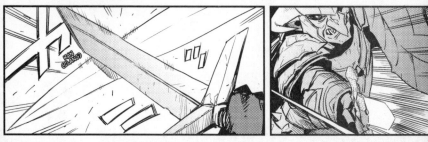

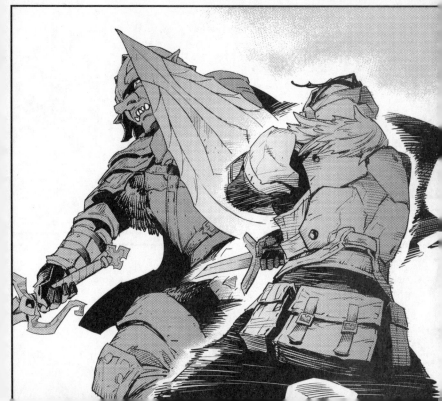

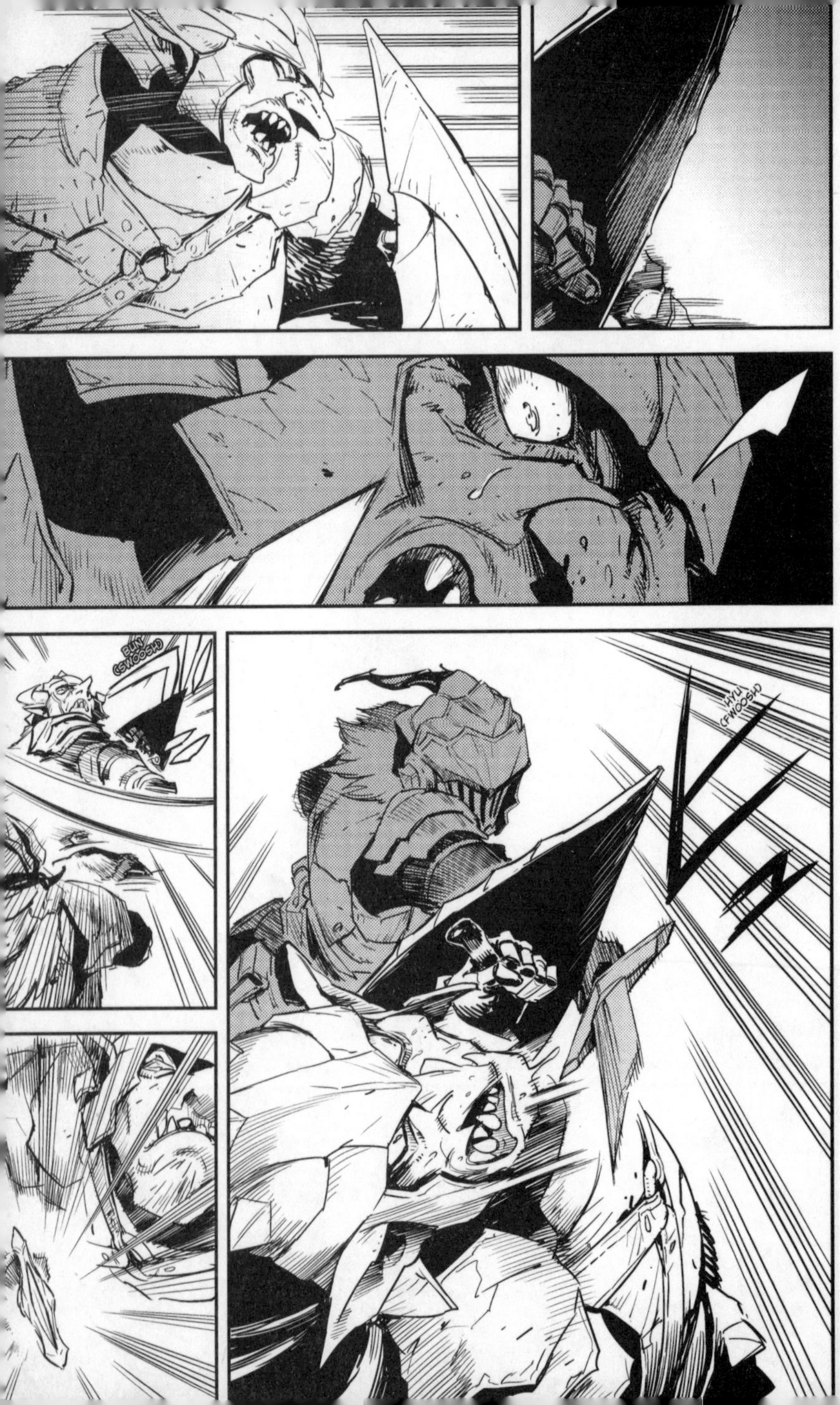
HYU
(FWOOSH)
BUN
(SWOOSH)

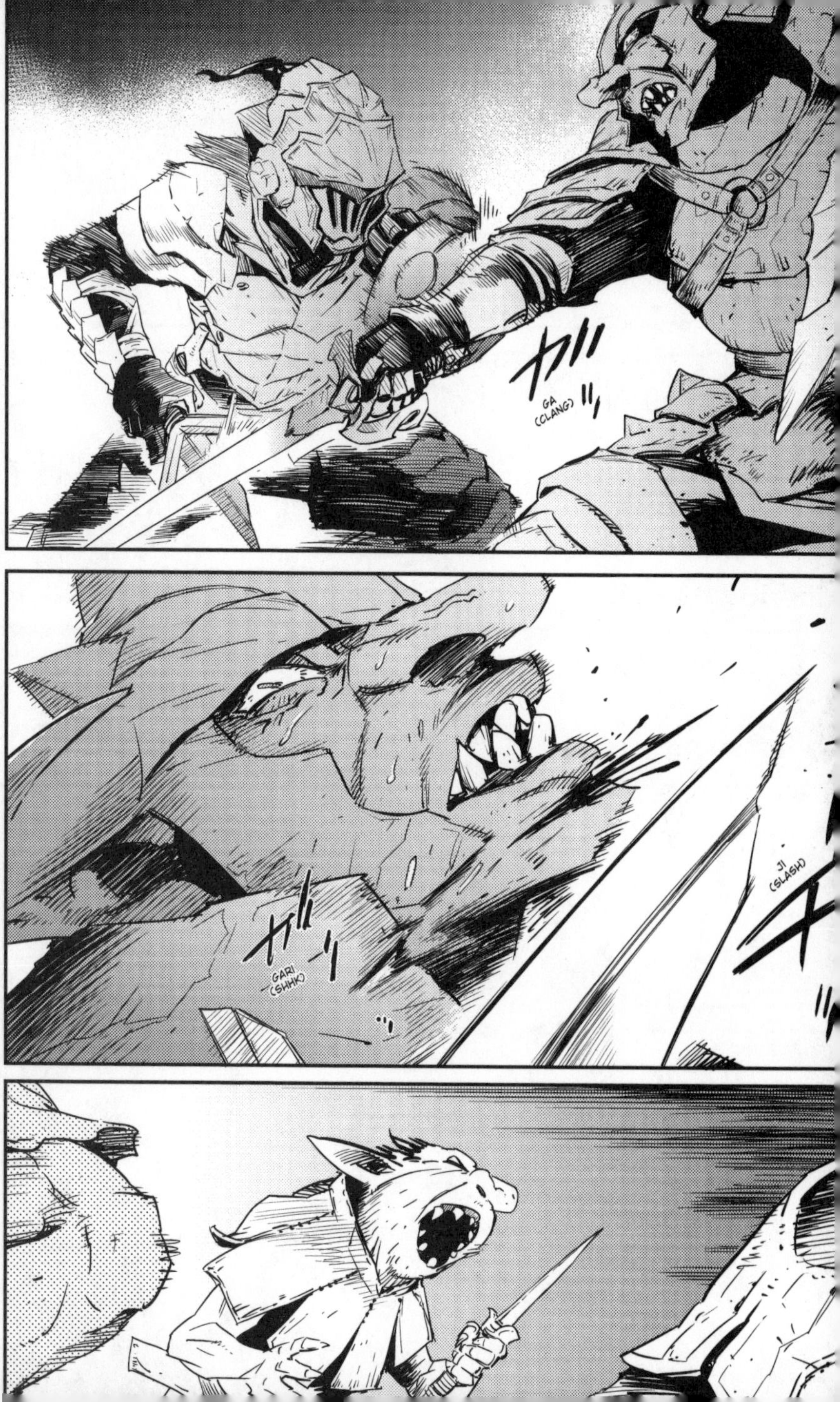
GA
(CLANG)
JI
(SLASH)
GARI
(SHHK)

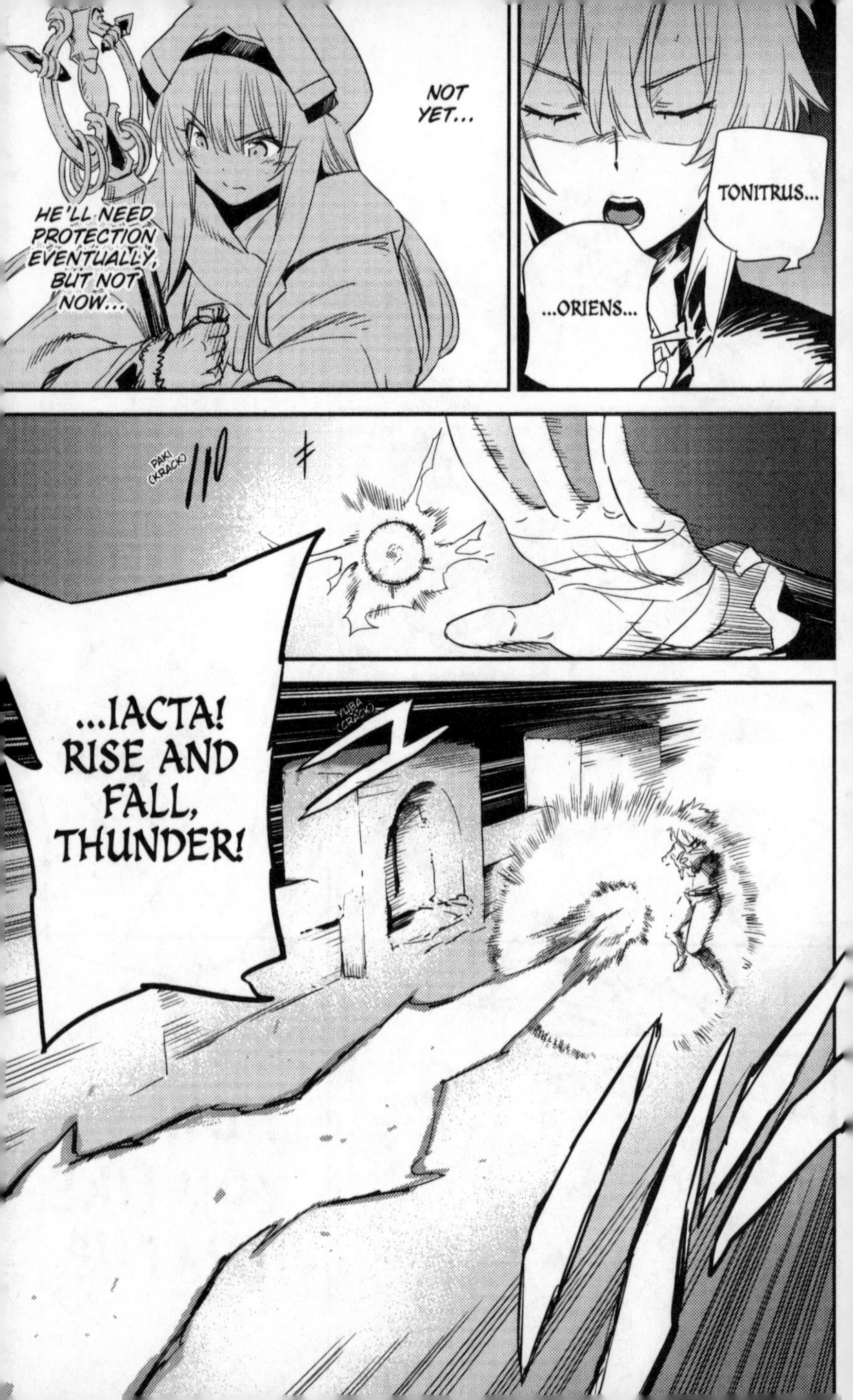
TONITRUS...
...ORIENS...
NOT YET...
HE'LL NEED PROTECTION EVENTUALLY, BUT NOT NOW...
PAKI (KRACK)
...IACTA! RISE AND FALL, THUNDER!
YUBA (CRACK)

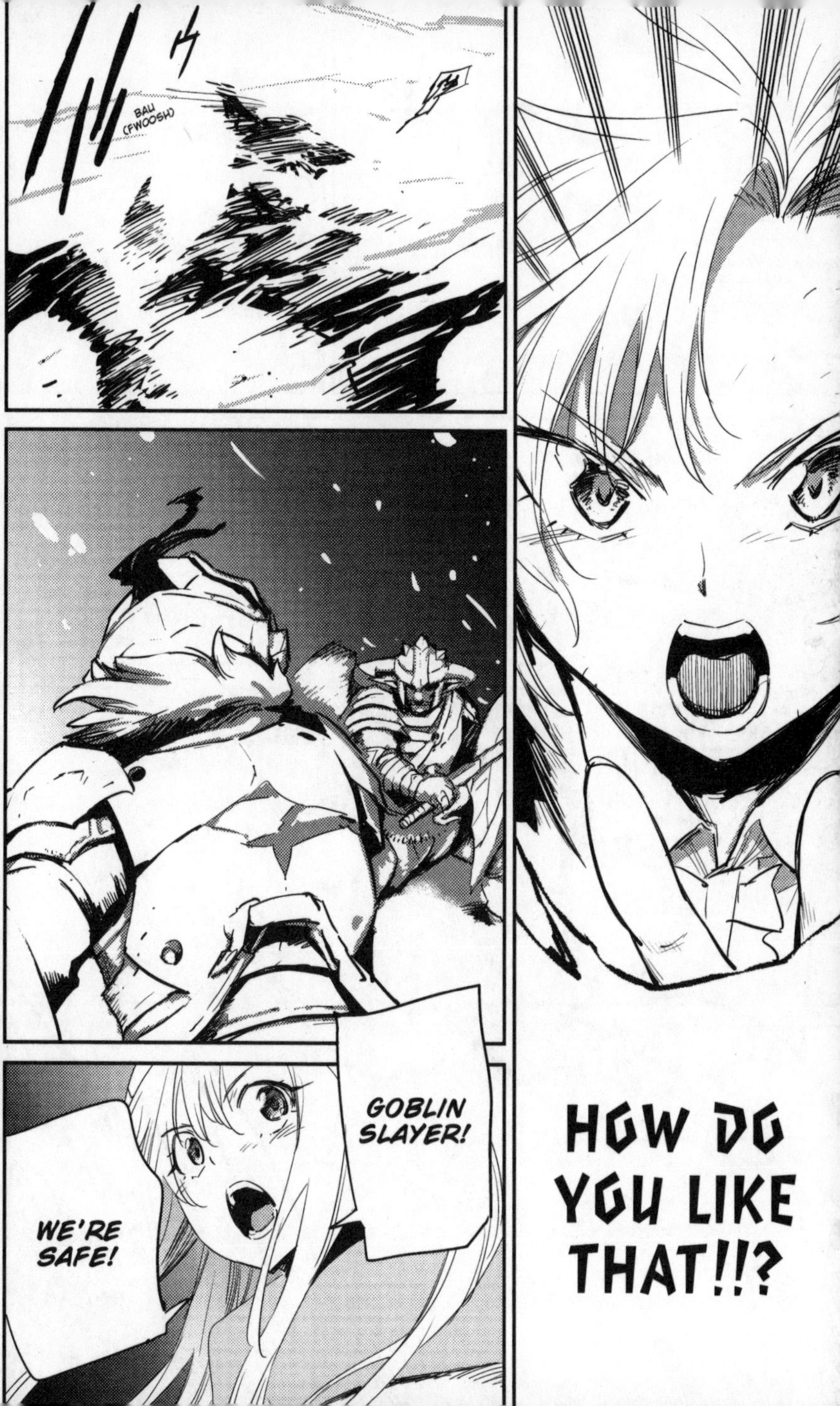
HOW DO YOU LIKE THAT!!?
BAU (FWOOSH)
GOBLIN SLAYER!
WE'RE SAFE!

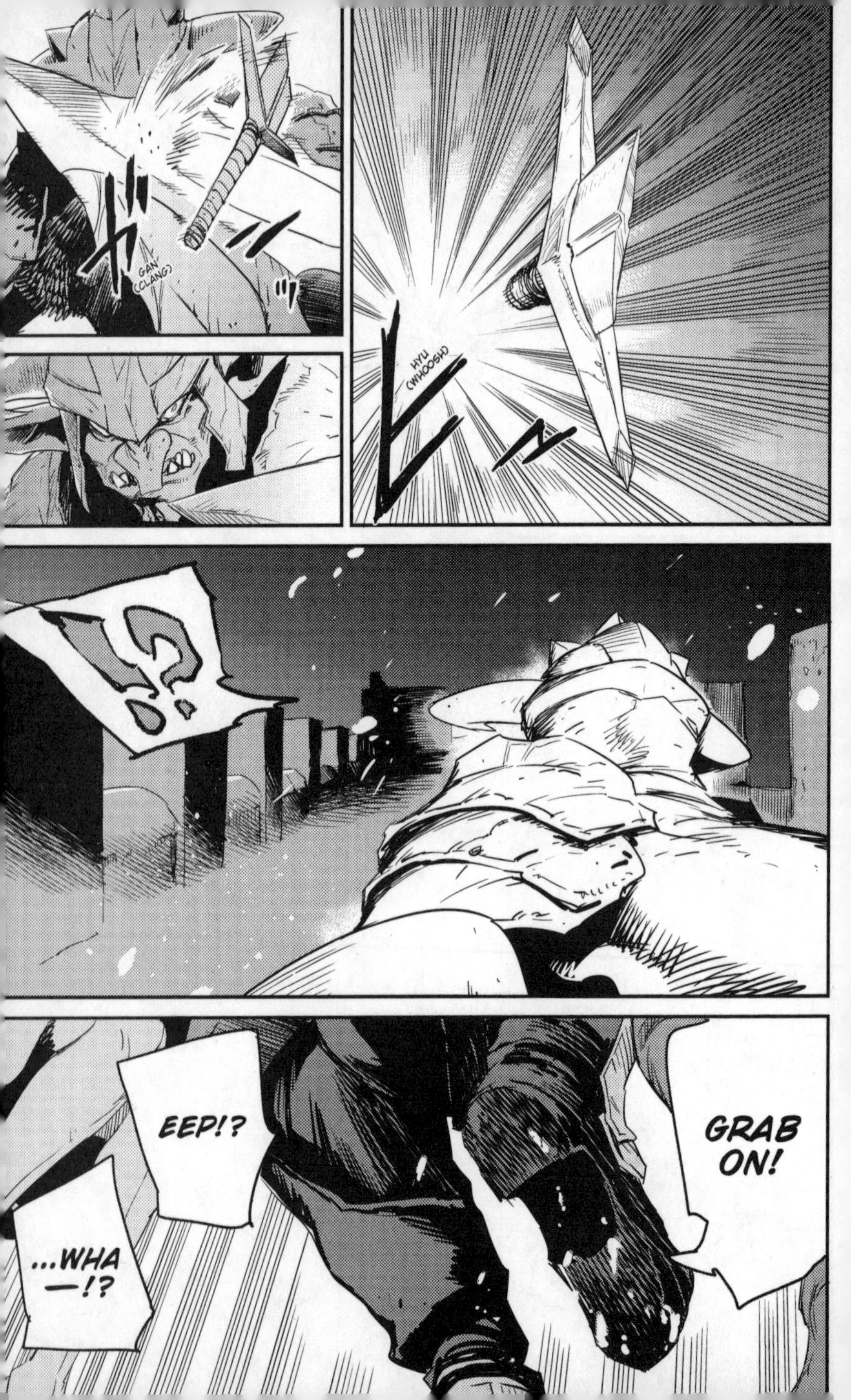
HYU (WHOOSH)
GAN (CLANG)
!?
GRAB ON!
EEP!?
...WHA—!?

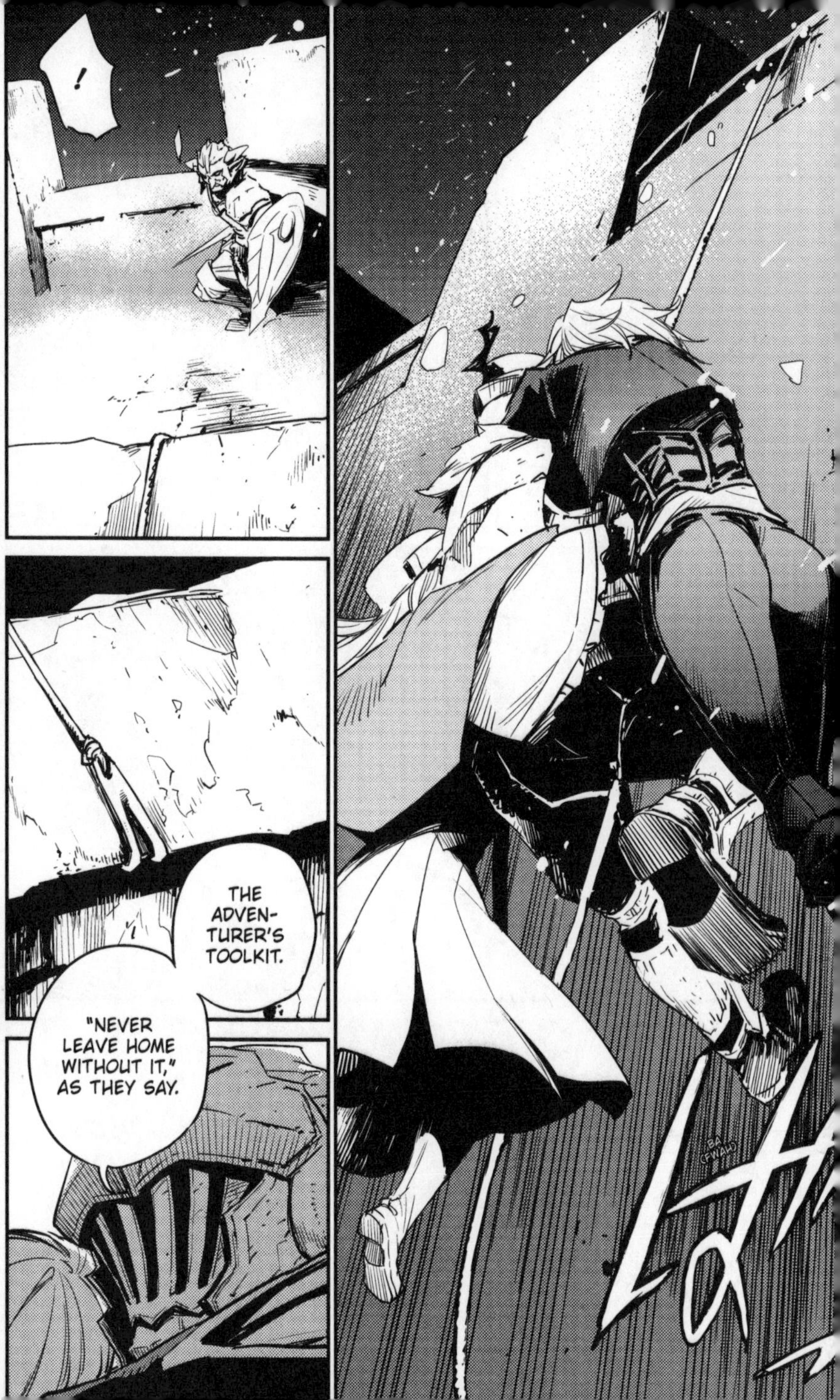
BA (FWAH)
!
THE ADVENTURER'S TOOLKIT.
"NEVER LEAVE HOME WITHOUT IT," AS THEY SAY.

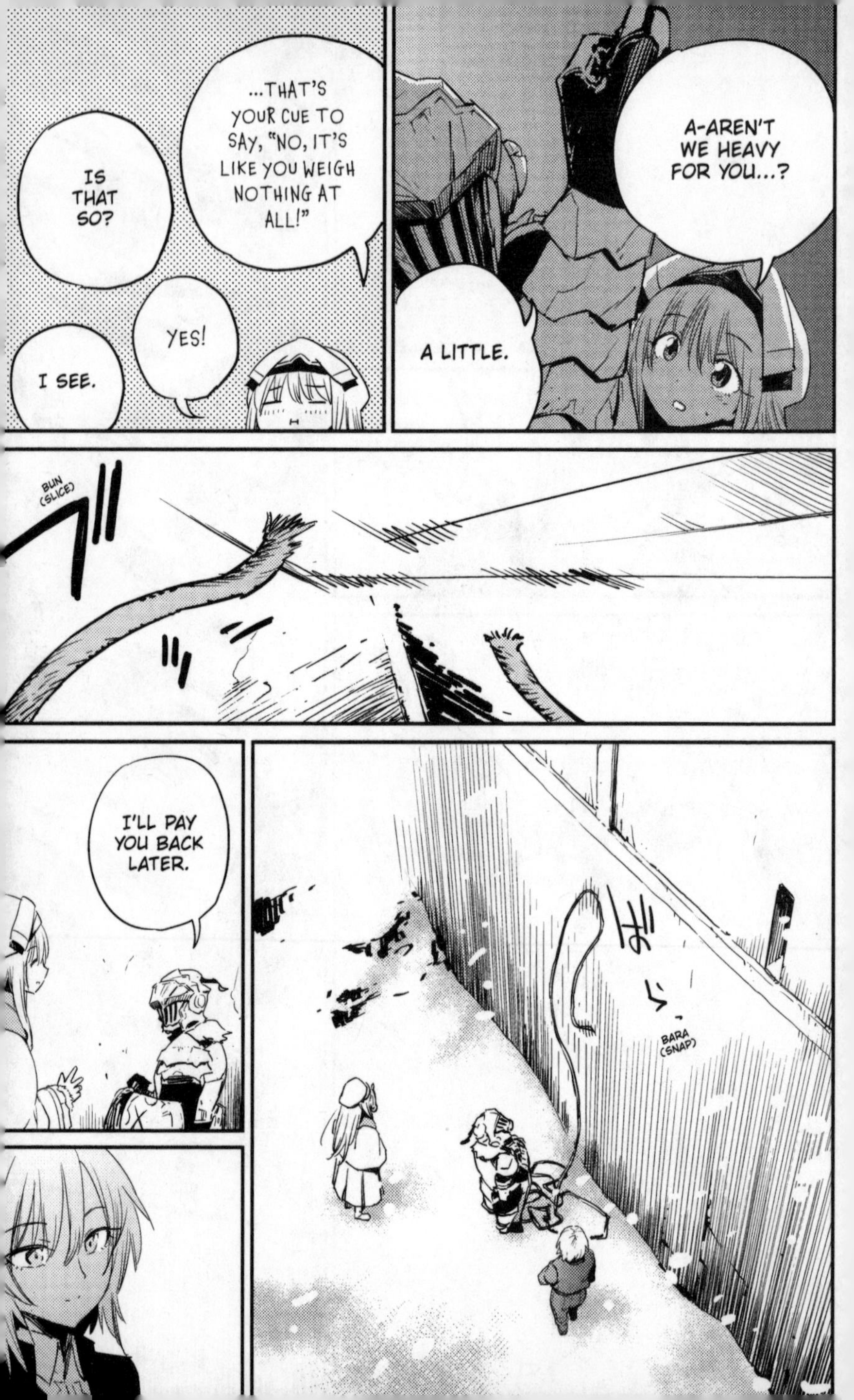
A-AREN'T WE HEAVY FOR YOU...?
A LITTLE.
...THAT'S YOUR CUE TO SAY, "NO, IT'S LIKE YOU WEIGH NOTHING AT ALL!"
IS THAT SO?
YES!
I SEE.
BUN (SLICE)
BARA (SNAP)
I'LL PAY YOU BACK LATER.

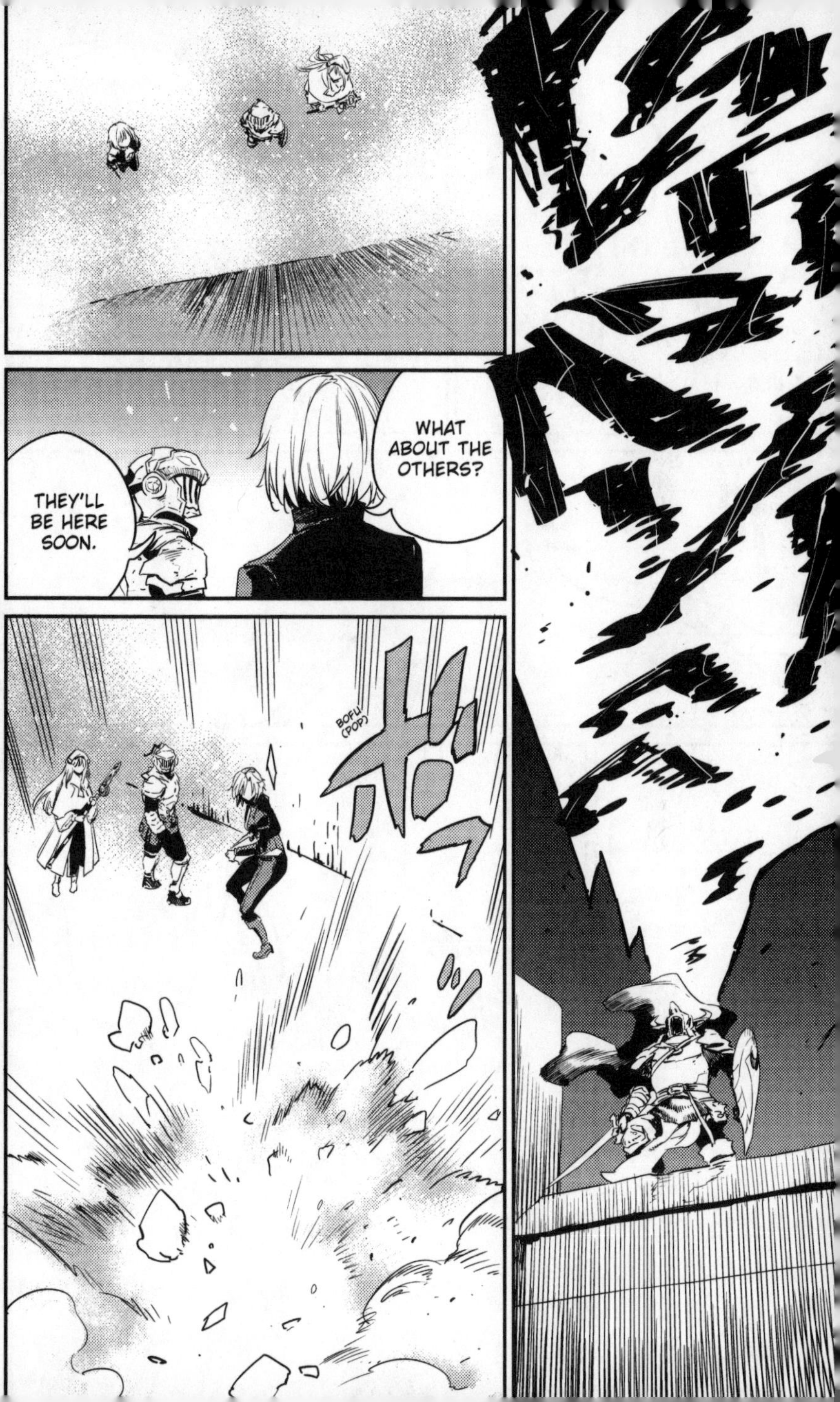
WHAT ABOUT THE OTHERS?
THEY'LL BE HERE SOON.
BOFU (POP)

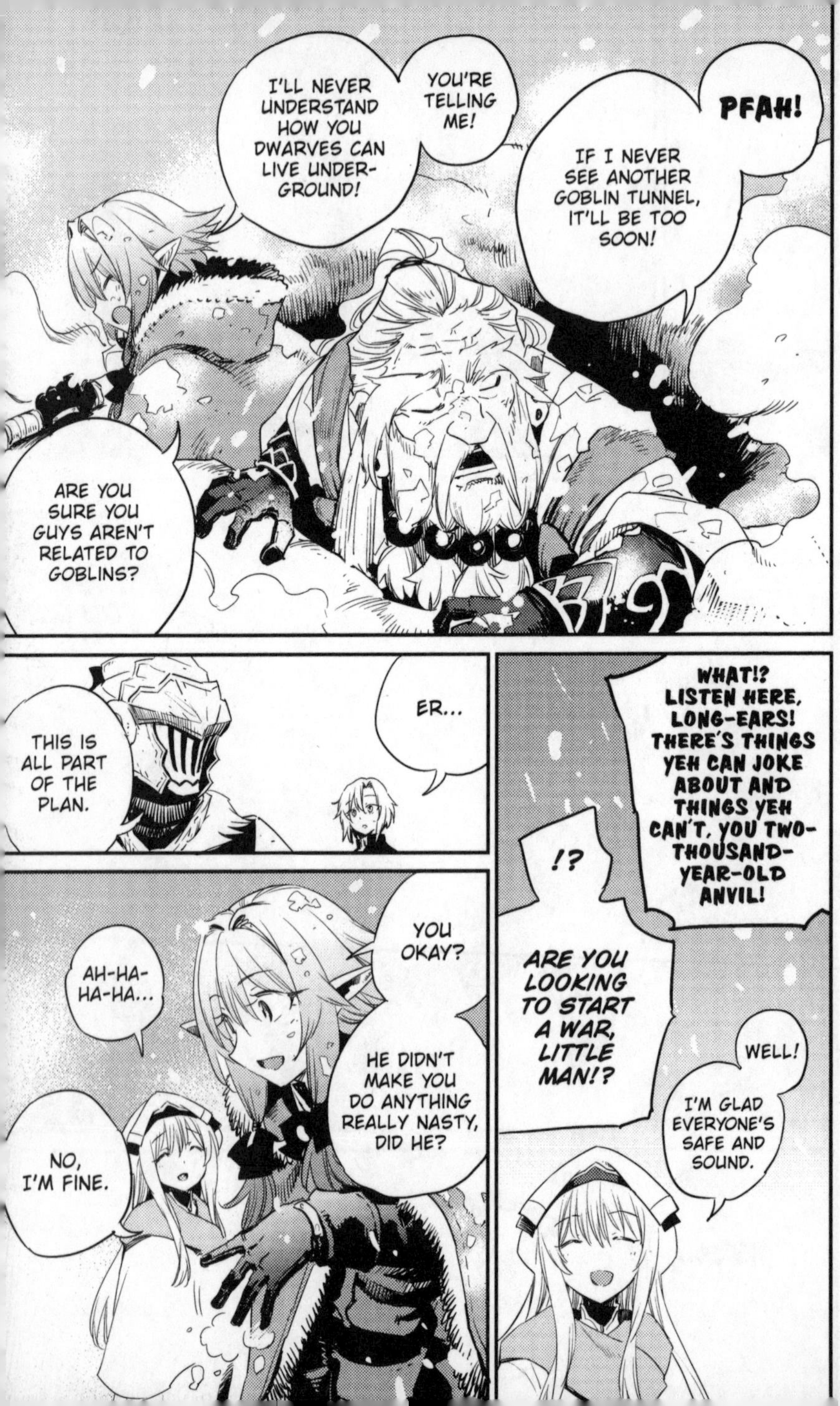
PFAH!
IF I NEVER SEE ANOTHER GOBLIN TUNNEL, IT'LL BE TOO SOON!
YOU'RE TELLING ME!
I'LL NEVER UNDERSTAND HOW YOU DWARVES CAN LIVE UNDER-GROUND!
ARE YOU SURE YOU GUYS AREN'T RELATED TO GOBLINS?
WHAT!? LISTEN HERE, LONG-EARS! THERE'S THINGS YEH CAN JOKE ABOUT AND THINGS YEH CAN'T, YOU TWO-THOUSAND-YEAR-OLD ANVIL!
!?
ARE YOU LOOKING TO START A WAR, LITTLE MAN!?
WELL!
I'M GLAD EVERYONE'S SAFE AND SOUND.
ER...
THIS IS ALL PART OF THE PLAN.
YOU OKAY?
AH-HA-HA-HA...
HE DIDN'T MAKE YOU DO ANYTHING REALLY NASTY, DID HE?
NO, I'M FINE.

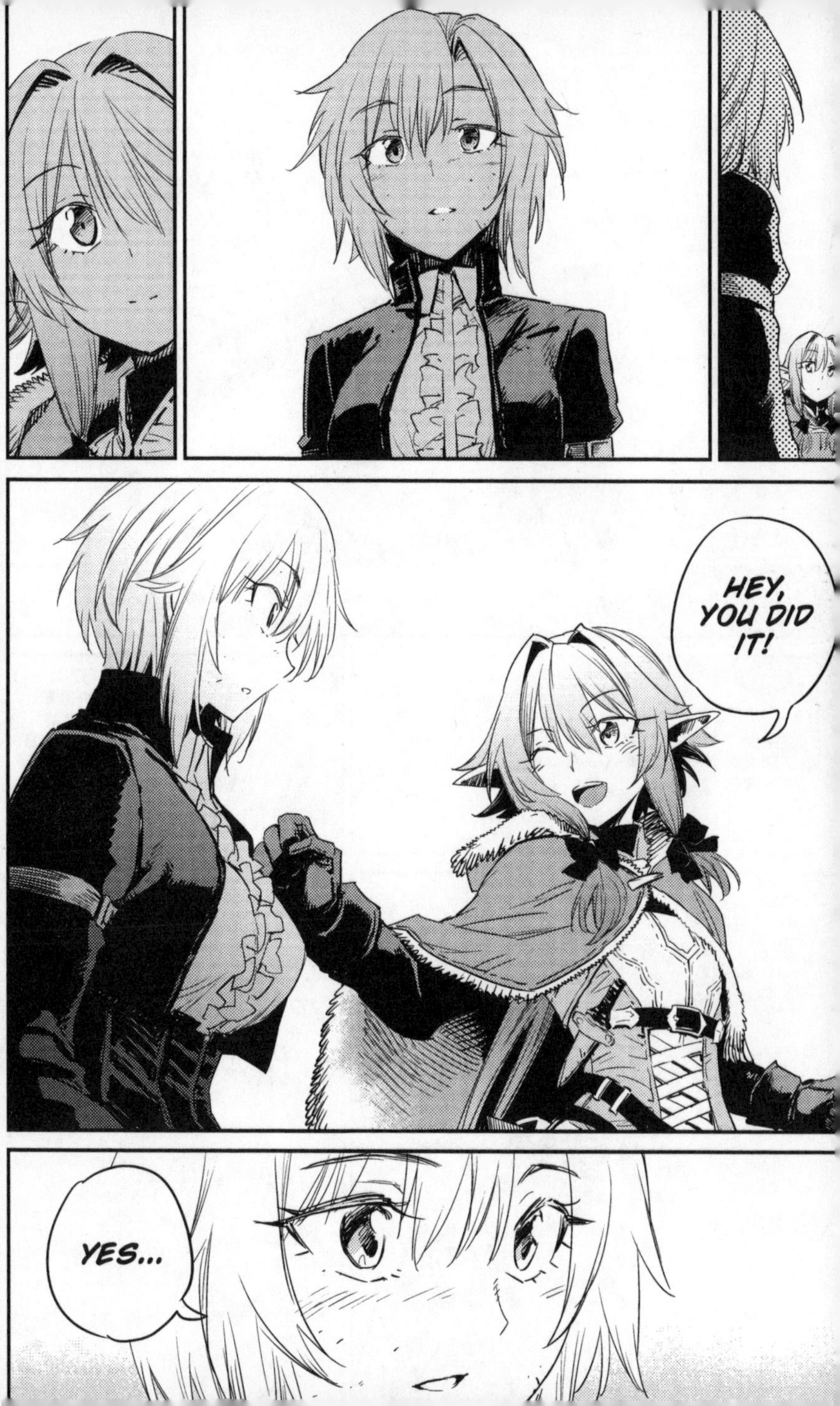
HEY, YOU DID IT!
YES...

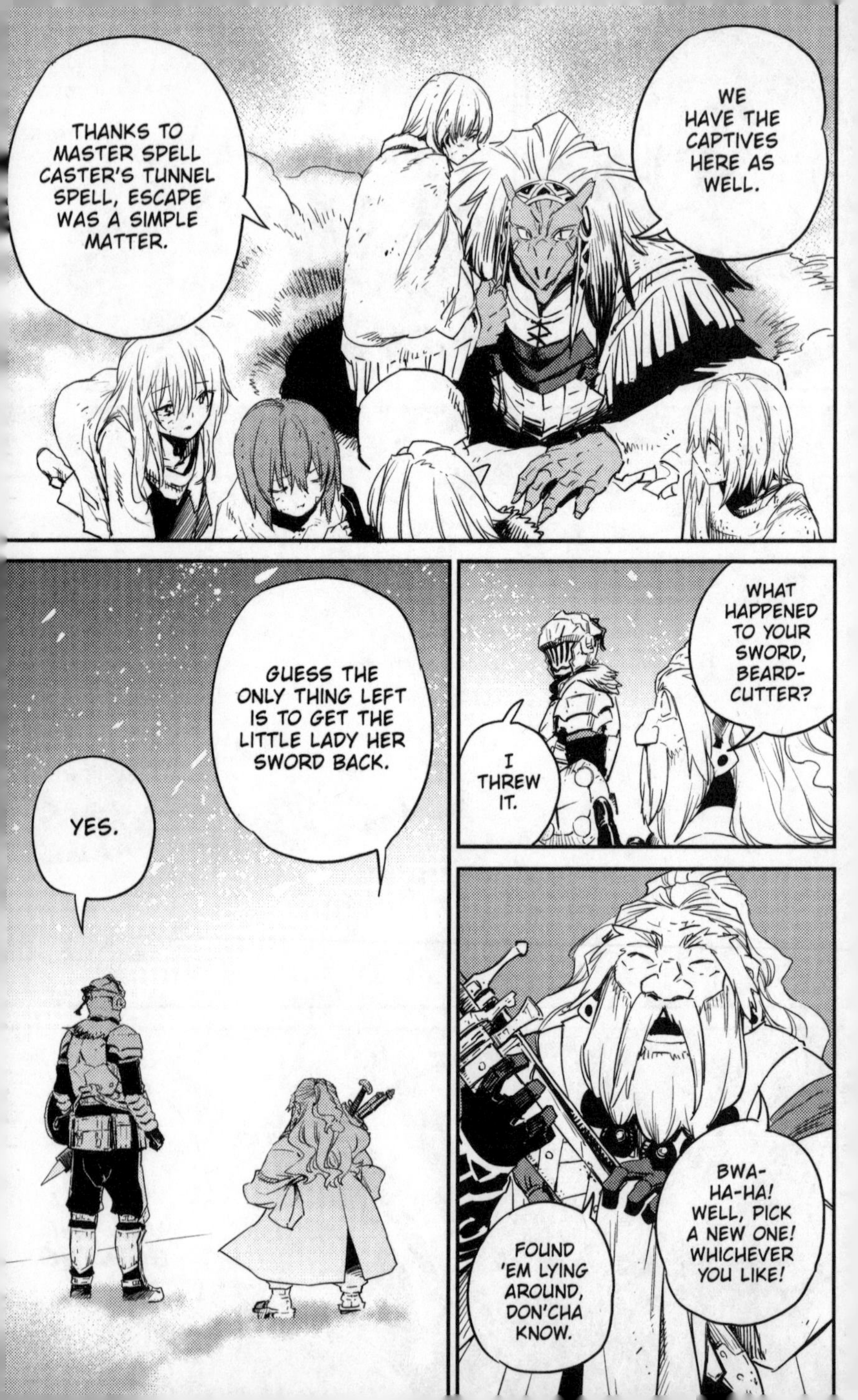
WE HAVE THE CAPTIVES HERE AS WELL.
THANKS TO MASTER SPELL CASTER'S TUNNEL SPELL, ESCAPE WAS A SIMPLE MATTER.
WHAT HAPPENED TO YOUR SWORD, BEARD-CUTTER?
I THREW IT.
BWA-HA-HA! WELL, PICK A NEW ONE! WHICHEVER YOU LIKE!
FOUND 'EM LYING AROUND, DON'CHA KNOW.
GUESS THE ONLY THING LEFT IS TO GET THE LITTLE LADY HER SWORD BACK.
YES.

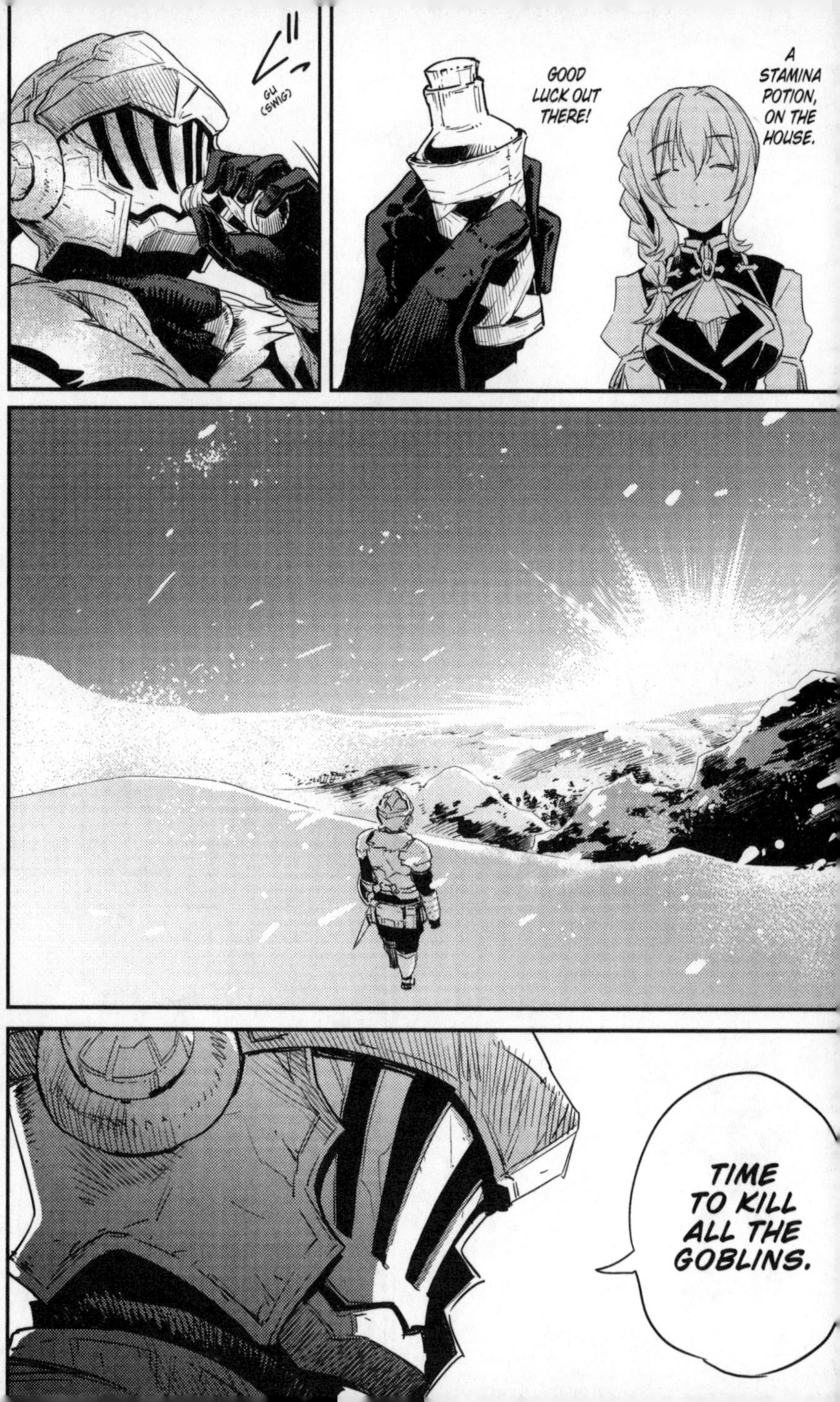
A STAMINA POTION, ON THE HOUSE.
GOOD LUCK OUT THERE!
GU (SWIG)
TIME TO KILL ALL THE GOBLINS.

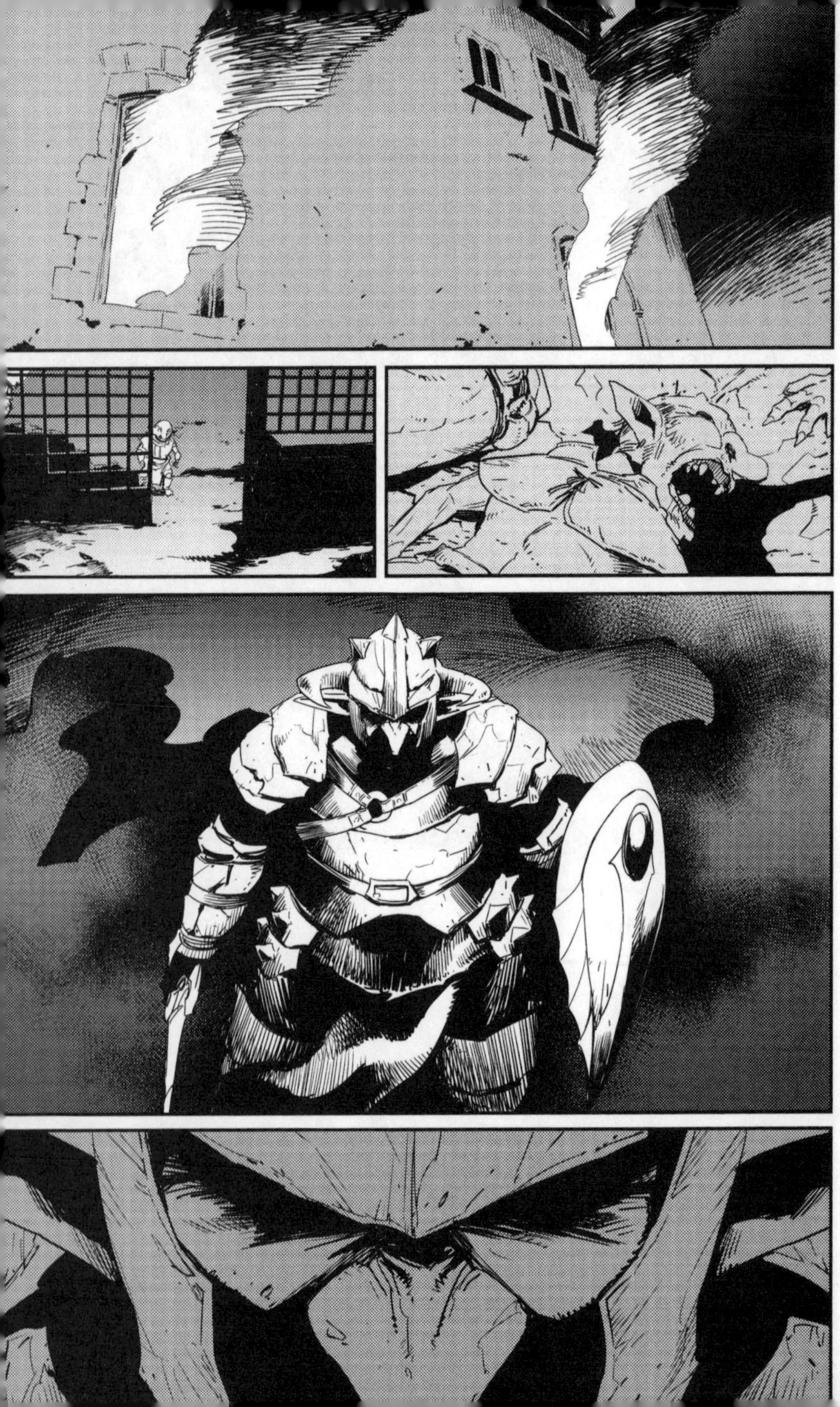

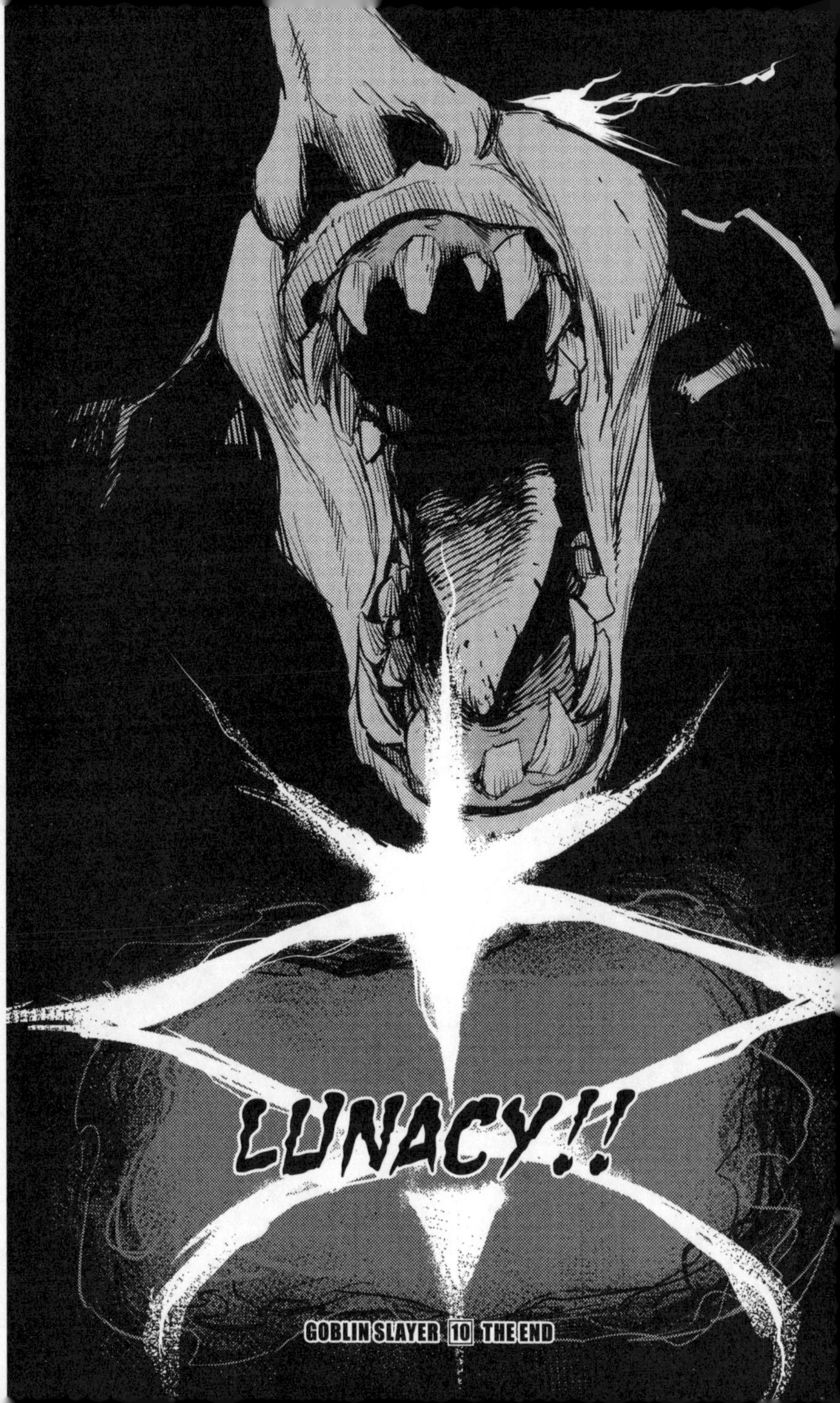
LUNACY!!
GOBLIN SLAYER 10 THE END

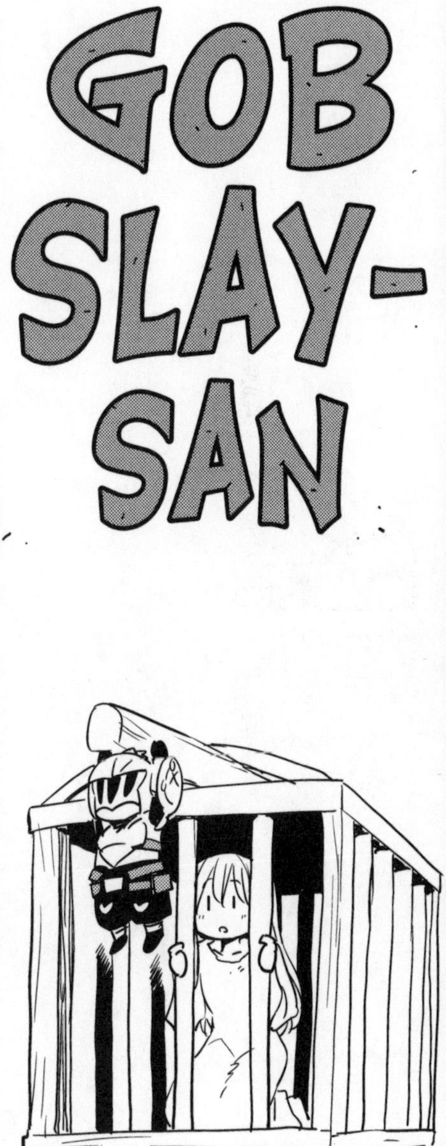
GOB SLAY-SAN

THERE'S NO MISTAKE

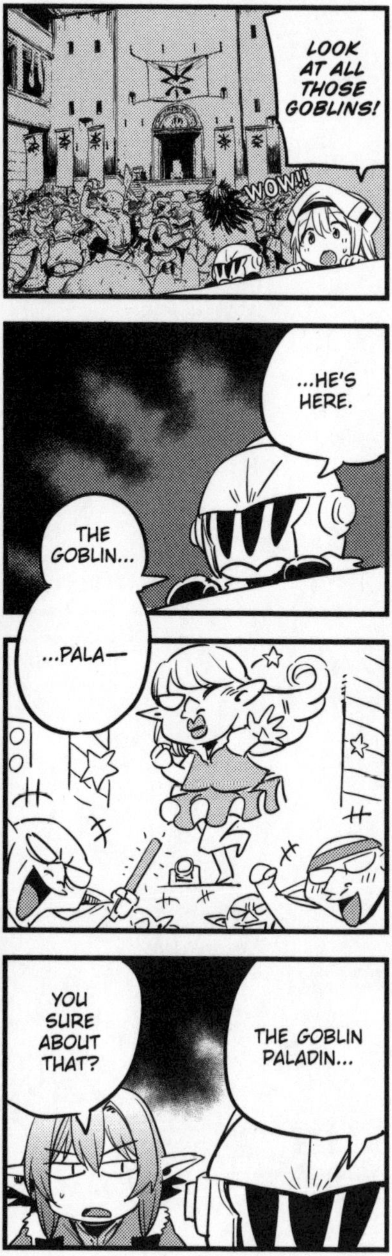
LOOK AT ALL THOSE GOBLINS!
WOW!!
...HE'S HERE.
THE GOBLIN...
...PALA—
THE GOBLIN PALADIN...
YOU SURE ABOUT THAT?

TOUGH QUESTION

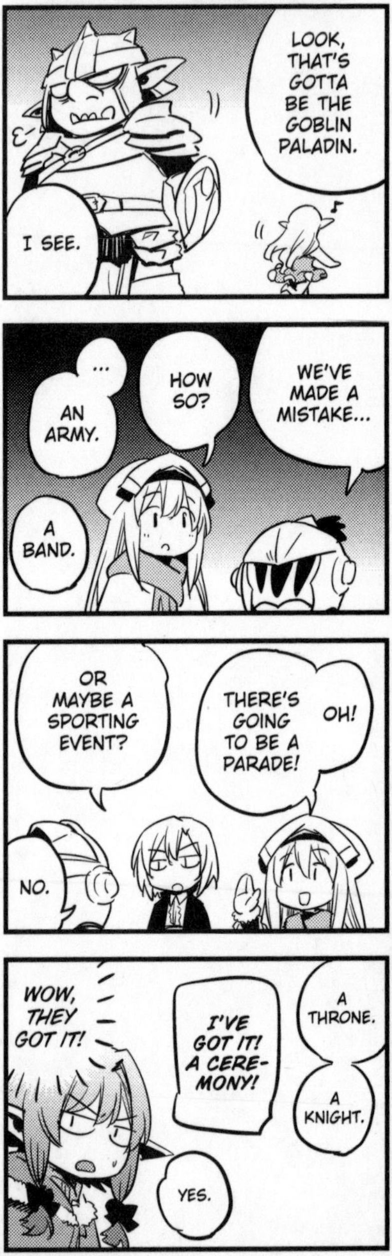
LOOK, THAT'S GOTTA BE THE GOBLIN PALADIN.
I SEE.
WE'VE MADE A MISTAKE...
HOW SO?
...
AN ARMY.
A BAND.
OH!
THERE'S GOING TO BE A PARADE!
OR MAYBE A SPORTING EVENT?
NO.
A THRONE.
A KNIGHT.
I'VE GOT IT! A CEREMONY!
YES.
WOW, THEY GOT IT!

TRUST

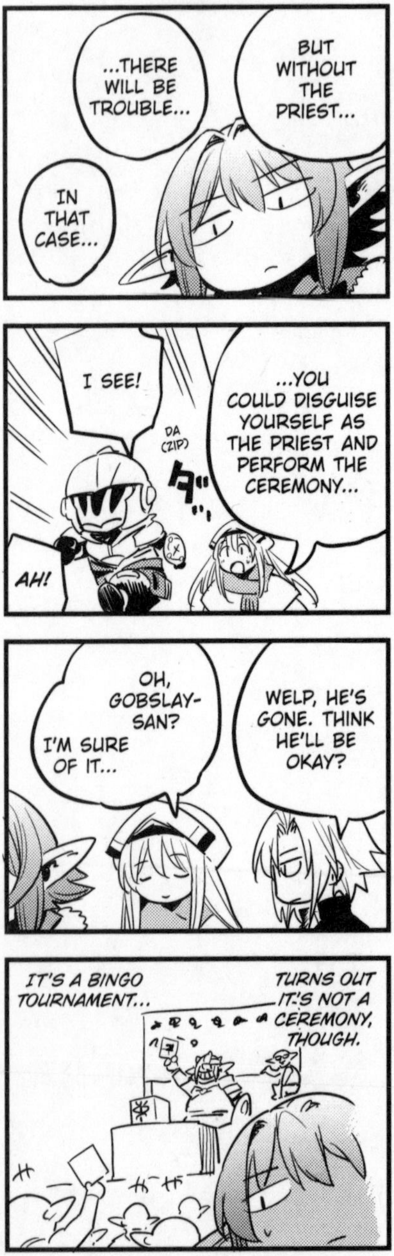
BUT WITHOUT THE PRIEST...
...THERE WILL BE TROUBLE...
IN THAT CASE...
...YOU COULD DISGUISE YOURSELF AS THE PRIEST AND PERFORM THE CEREMONY...
I SEE!
DA (ZIP)
AH!
WELP, HE'S GONE. THINK HE'LL BE OKAY?
OH, GOBSLAY-SAN? I'M SURE OF IT...
TURNS OUT IT'S NOT A CEREMONY, THOUGH.
IT'S A BINGO TOURNAMENT...

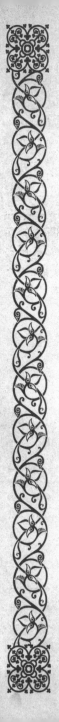

Turn to the back of the
book for a short story by
Kumo Kagyu!

GOBLIN
SLAYER

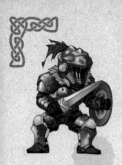
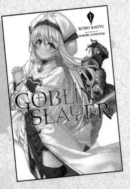
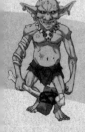
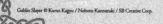

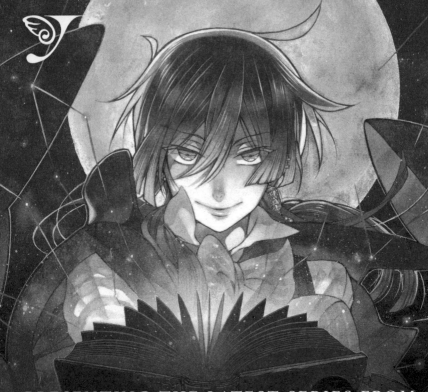
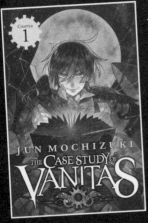

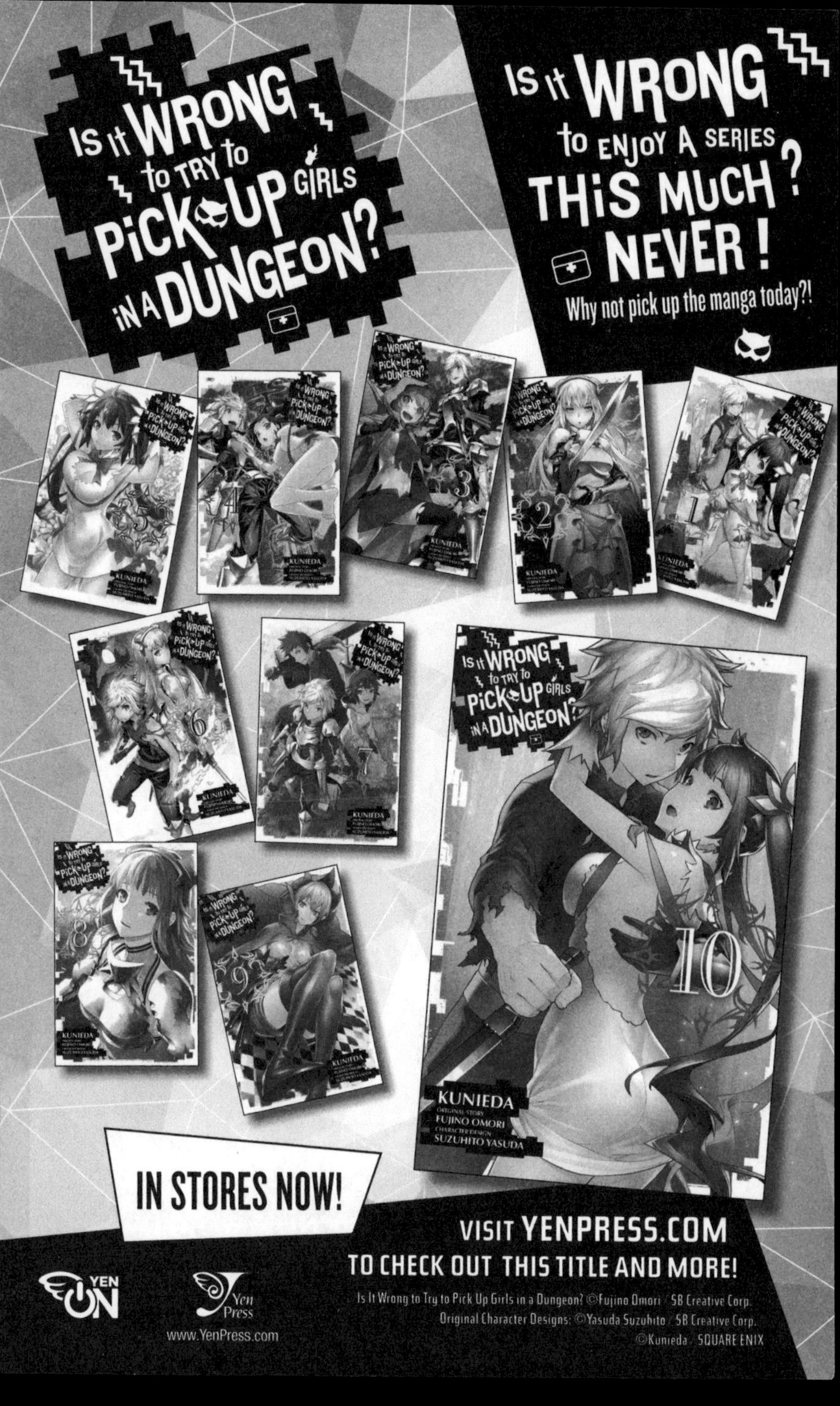
IS IT WRONG TO TRY TO PICK UP GIRLS IN A DUNGEON?
IS IT WRONG TO ENJOY A SERIES THIS MUCH?
NEVER!
Why not pick up the manga today?!
KUNIEDA
ORIGINAL STORY
FUJINO OMORI
CHARACTER DESIGN
SUZUHITO YASUDA
IN STORES NOW!
VISIT YENPRESS.COM
TO CHECK OUT THIS TITLE AND MORE!
YEN ON
Yen Press
www.YenPress.com
Is It Wrong to Try to Pick Up Girls in a Dungeon? ©Fujino Omori / SB Creative Corp.
Original Character Designs: ©Yasuda Suzuhito / SB Creative Corp.
©Kunieda / SQUARE ENIX

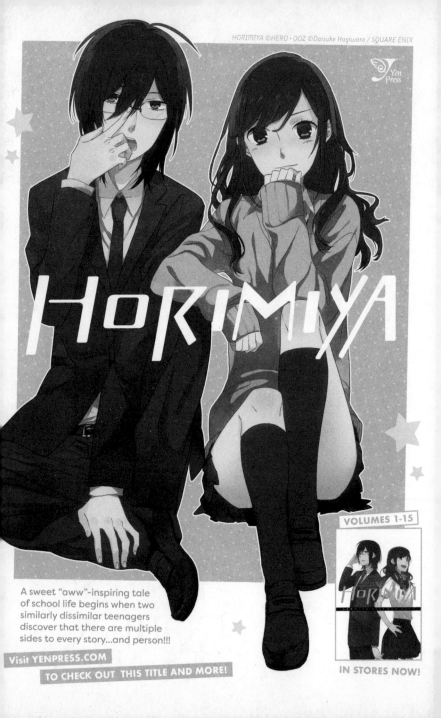

GOBLIN
SLAYER

Well, or maybe...

With a look on her face like she had come up with an especially mischievous idea, Guild Girl said, "Want to try braiding it? So it looks...as pretty as mine?"

"I'd love th—wait, what?" Priestess said, and her pose collapsed.

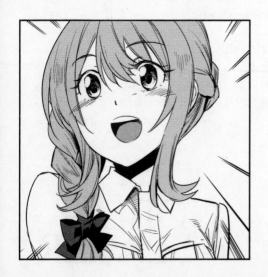

"Scared...? I wouldn't say... Well, maybe I was," Guild Girl said, giggling.

This colleague had not been the type to speak sharply or raise her voice, but Guild Girl would feel tense just from being in the same room with her, like her back was a little straighter than usual.

Am I finally...

...as good at this as her colleague had been? Maybe not quite? Guild Girl didn't know. She couldn't know, by herself. All she knew was that Priestess was watching her, desperately trying to imitate her, and straining to maintain the posture, to follow along. Maybe Guild Girl had looked the same way to her colleague, back then.

I sort of hope so. That would be...nice.

"Huh? What's nice?" Priestess asked, perplexed by the word that had suddenly slipped out of Guild Girl's mouth.

"Oh, it's nothing..."

The girl's long hair glistened gold as it caught the evening sun that shone through the window. It was beautiful hair. When she was little, Guild Girl had thought all her problems would be solved if only she had hair like that.

"It's just—your hair," she said.

"Yes? What about it?"

"I just thought maybe you should tie it up."

"Oh, you're... You're right. Maybe...when we're done with this pose..."

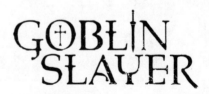

back. Then she reached the other hand around overhead, taking the fingers of the hand wrapped around her leg so as to anchor herself in that position.

"Mm... Ahhh." Guild Girl breathed in, then out, still in the same stance with her chest gracefully thrust forward. "This is...what they call...the pigeon pose."

"P-pigeon...?" Priestess asked, struggling to contort herself in such an unusual way. But despite the difficulty, her body had an adventurer's training, and soon grew more flexible and accustomed to the motions. Her bare skin, of which plenty was visible beneath her single layer of undergarments, displayed well-toned muscles and a healthy color besides. Though she had to let out a few soft grunts, she managed to maintain the posture, suggesting that her trunk was quite trained as well.

No doubt thanks to his *training.*

And her own effort. Guild Girl smiled slightly as she realized that.

"This pose is something...a more experienced colleague of mine taught me...back in the capital."

"Someone...more...experienced...?" Priestess, as she did her best to continue breathing, managed to shoot a disbelieving glance her way. It was like she couldn't imagine anyone being senior to Guild Girl. (Though perhaps Guild Girl's own efforts played some role in that impression.) "What...kind of person...was she?"

"Pretty strict, I guess..."

"Were you...scared of her?"

one with the power to bind the sun and moon together." Having just remembered her own initiation to this secret, Guild Girl made sure to imbue the words with magic by puffing out her gorgeous chest the same way the person who'd taught her had. Priestess blinked at that, though whether from confusion or fascination, Guild Girl couldn't tell.

"It's an exercise that will steady your breathing, calm your heart, and bring the two of them together."

"An...exercise?"

"Or a kind of meditation, if you prefer—not that I can use magic or miracles." Guild Girl winked, then began curling her legs, which had been gracefully stretched out on the carpet, into a pose. She started breathing slowling and steadily—now, what could this be?

I like that it's simple, but you still have the feeling that you're doing something. She realized the same thought had gone through her head the first time she did this, which she found a little funny.

"First, bend one leg like this and stretch the other one out behind you."

"Um, like...this?"

"That's right. Very good. Don't hold your breath—keep breathing slowly and deeply." After making sure Priestess, who was sitting across from her, could easily see her and copy what she was doing, Guild Girl twisted her body further. She bent the leg that was behind her, catching it with her elbow as she bent her upper body

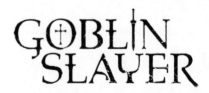

generally didn't feel compelled to be too fastidious, but...

Thank goodness I just gave this place a quick tidying up...!
She tried not to let her pride in her last-weekend self be too evident.

"All right, let's get ready." Guild Girl started taking off her outer layers, which Priestess flinched back at the sight of. Trying to look as nonchalant as possible, Guild Girl slipped out of her uniform with a rustle of cloth. "Come on, now—you too."

"Er, ah, right...!" At this urging, Priestess quickly sloughed off her vestments. It would have been possible to do this with their clothes still on, of course, but it would have wrinkled them. So this was better to do in their underclothes, though Guild Girl did feel a little ticklish as the other woman's gaze shifted over her shoulders, hips, chest, and butt.

"Are you that interested?" she asked.

"No! I mean—no, but..."

Guild Girl had only been teasing Priestess for her roving eyes, but the way she shrank back was so pitiful as to be almost comical. Priestess blushed and averted her gaze but still couldn't help herself from stealing glances in Guild Girl's direction now and then, clothes or no clothes.

I can't really blame her.

When Guild Girl had first learned about this, she'd been the same way, now that she thought about it.

"So, what I'm about to show you is a secret technique—

Besides, just think about those trendy whitening powders and lipsticks that turned out to be poisonous. As a daughter of nobility who once ran in high social circles herself, those discoveries had hit close to home. Not to mention the stories of people who had drunk a sparkling blue potion on the premise that it was good for your health, only to die from having their bodies rot away. Guild Girl didn't think that such a devout follower of the Earth Mother would get mixed up with sketchy cosmetics and downright snake oil, but...

All right—only one thing to do.

"Ugh, I can't believe it. You saw right through me. No use trying to hide it anymore."

"Wha...?" Priestess blinked, and Guild Girl placed a slim finger against the girl's lips.

"Do you have a few minutes right now?"

I'll tell you my biggest secret of all.

And then she did her best impression of Witch's portentous laugh.

§

"Good, right this way—come on in. Don't be shy."

"Th-thank you. Pardon me." Priestess made a stiff, doll-like bow of her head as Guild Girl ushered her into her personal room. The gesture had an awkward quality to it, like her body was being controlled by strings dangling above her. Guild Girl rarely had visitors, so she

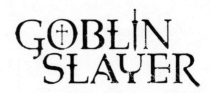

the human body, so if you make an effort to do them, everything else follows naturally."

"But..." Guild Girl had tried to explain as clearly as she could, but Priestess didn't seem convinced. "I'm not, um, doing anything special either. But when I compare myself with other people, I don't think I'm very..."

Judging by Priestess's dejected whispering, she must have been fretting deeply about this, as was her wont. In Guild Girl's eyes, Priestess was just on the cusp of transforming from a child into an adult woman, like a blossom ready to open. Her slender body, toned from long days of adventuring, was starting to take on a certain supple roundness. And above all, she had that beautiful golden hair. She had nothing to worry about or envy.

Then again, it doesn't feel too bad to be included among the "other people" she's comparing herself to.

Take that witch, for example: even as her friend and a member of the same sex, Guild Girl couldn't keep her heart from fluttering at the woman's good looks. Then there was the waitress at the restaurant, who had the enviably luscious body of a padfoot. There was Female Knight, of course. There was even the high elf in Priestess's own party, who was so lithe you would swear she was a faerie.

Considering all that, Guild Girl didn't think it was at all silly for Priestess to imagine there must be some secret, and she certainly wouldn't laugh at her for it.

to blame for the red glow now covering the cheeks of this cleric of the Earth Mother.

"I don't think I do anything special..."

"That's what everyone says." Priestess sullenly puffed out her cheeks but then looked at the ground as she realized how childish she must seem.

Another "Hmm..." escaped Guild Girl's mouth as she put a finger to her cheek and tilted her head thoughtfully.

It's not like I eat anything that unusual or use any special products...

She didn't even, say, powder her hair and skin each morning and evening to make them pale and glossy, which was just the tip of the iceberg when it came to beauty regimens. In the capital, it had become popular for women to undergo phlebotomies to whiten their skin and have their back teeth pulled to make their faces appear daintier. Guild Girl had been slightly intrigued by these methods, but she didn't have the courage to undertake them herself. Less still did she want to ask a dark elf to remove a bone or two just so she could squeeze into an even tighter corset.

"It's true. And you don't need to do anything out of the ordinary—in fact, that can be bad for your body."

"Really?"

"Make sure to eat a healthy meal morning, noon, and night; get plenty of exercise; and sleep well too." Guild Girl counted off on her fingers as she offered each piece of advice. "Those three things have the most effect on

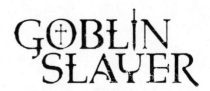

Interlude:

Of How a Healthy Body Is the Product of a Healthy Mind
– by Kumo Kagyu

"Uh, u-um, how... How can I become as pretty as you...?"

"I'm sorry?"

Guild Girl had just finished her work for the day and was about to head home, but she twisted back around in response to this unexpected question. The extra tension on her uniform pushed up and accentuated certain graceful curves, ones in which she would admit to taking some small amount of pride.

Although, when someone actually compliments me on my looks...

Well, it was embarrassing, and all the more so when the one flattering her was a certain young woman she knew quite well by now. She was far better equipped to deal with teasing comments from her colleagues or crude jokes from adventurers.

"Hmm..."

Guild Girl's voice just sort of slipped out as Priestess stared straight at her with a dead serious look in her eyes. Priestess had probably screwed up her courage in order to blurt out that question, but she soon returned to her usual shyness and began to look uncomfortable. Guild Girl knew perfectly well that the setting sun wasn't

GOBLIN SLAYER 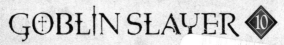 10

Original Story: Kumo Kagyu
Art: Kousuke Kurose
Character Design: Noboru Kannatuki

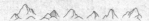

Translation: Kevin Steinbach ✦ Lettering: Bianca Pistillo

This book is a work of fiction. Names, characters, places, and incidents are
the product of the author's imagination or are used fictitiously. Any resemblance
to actual events, locales, or persons, living or dead, is coincidental.

GOBLIN SLAYER Volume 10
©Kumo Kagyu/SB Creative Corp.
Original Character Designs:©Noboru Kannatuki/SB Creative Corp.
©2020 Kousuke Kurose/SQUARE ENIX CO., LTD. First published in Japan in 2020 by
SQUARE ENIX CO., LTD. English translation rights arranged with SQUARE ENIX CO.,
LTD. and YEN PRESS, LLC through Tuttle-Mori Agency, Inc., Tokyo.

English translation ©2021 by SQUARE ENIX CO., LTD.

Yen Press
150 West 30th Street, 19th Floor
New York, NY 10001

Visit us at yenpress.com
facebook.com/yenpress
twitter.com/yenpress
yenpress.tumblr.com
instagram.com/yenpress

First Yen Press Edition: August 2021
The chapters in this volume were originally published as ebooks by Yen Press.

Yen Press is an imprint of Yen Press, LLC.
The Yen Press name and logo are trademarks of Yen Press, LLC.

The publisher is not responsible for websites (or their content) that are
not owned by the publisher.

Library of Congress Control Number: 2017954163

ISBNs: 978-1-9753-2483-4 (paperback)
      978-1-9753-2484-1 (ebook)

10 9 8 7 6 5 4 3 2 1

WOR

Printed in the United States of America